INTERNATIONAL COMPETITIVENESS IN FINANCIAL SERVICES

A Special Issue of the Journal of Financial Services Research

edited by

Marvin H. Kosters
Allan H. Meltzer

Reprinted from the Journal of Financial Services Research

Vol. 4, No. 4 (1990)

KLUWER ACADEMIC PUBLISHERS
BOSTON/DORDRECHT/LONDON

Distributors for North America:
Kluwer Academic Publishers
101 Philip Drive
Assinippi Park
Norwell, Massachusetts 02061 USA

Distributors for all other countries:
Kluwer Academic Publishers Group
Distribution Centre
Post Office Box 322
3300 AH Dordrecht, THE NETHERLANDS

Library of Congress Cataloging-in-Publication Data

International competitiveness in financial services/ edited by Marvin
   H. Kosters and Allan H. Meltzer.
      p. cm.
   "A special issue of the Journal of financial services research.
  Vol. 4, no. 4 (1990)."
   ISBN 0–7923–9148–9
   1. Financial services industry—United States.   2. Competition,
International.   3. International finance.
  HG181.I56   1991
  332.1 '5 '0973—dc20   90-27343
                                           CIP

Printed on acid-free paper.

Printed in The Netherlands

JOURNAL OF FINANCIAL SERVICES RESEARCH
Vol. 4, No. 4 December 1990

INTERNATIONAL COMPETITIVENESS IN FINANCIAL SERVICES
A Special Issue of the Journal of Financial Services Research

Journal of Financial Services Research, 4:259–261 (1990)
© 1990 Kluwer Academic Publishers

Introduction

MARVIN H. KOSTERS
Resident Scholar and Director of Economic Policy Studies
American Enterprise Institute for Public Policy Research
1150 17th St., NW
Washington, DC 20036

ALLAN H. MELTZER
John M. Olin Professor of Political Economy and Public Policy
Carnegie-Mellon University
Pittsburgh, PA 15213
and Visiting Scholar
American Enterprise Institute for Public Policy Research
1150 17th St., NW
Washington, DC 20036

Markets for financial services continue to change under the stimulus provided by new technologies and means of communication, new trading opportunities and strategies, and more vigorous competition. Many financial firms now compete in markets around the world.

For a long time, regulatory changes have lagged behind. Major regulatory changes in Western European countries as they prepare for 1992 and the gradual deregulation of Japanese financial markets have moved these countries toward more flexible arrangements. In the United States, regulatory changes continue to lag behind. Much of the current U.S. regulatory structure is still based on policies shaped by experience in the depression of the 1930s. Its emphasis is on prohibition of particular activities instead of on incentives to develop new services, increase efficiency, and reduce risk. The result has been that risks have often been shifted and competition discouraged.

Serious consideration is now being given to the most significant changes in the federal regulatory structure for banking and other financial services since the 1930s. Congressional committees have held hearings on the issues, and the executive branch is examining deposit insurance, issues of safety and soundness, and international competition. Careful research on the role of financial markets, on the influence of regulation on their performance, and on changes in regulatory structures that would foster efficiency and stability can provide a valuable frame of reference for evaluation of policy proposals and informed debate.

Increased attention to financial services policies has been forced upon the national policy leadership not only by international competition but by a wide range of current problems and concerns. The problem area most visible to the public involves depository institutions—banks and thrifts. By the late 1980s, insolvency of firms in the thrift industry had grown far beyond the capacity of government insurance agencies to resolve their problems routinely, with the result that major losses were shifted explicitly to taxpayers.

The banking industry showed similar, though much milder, symptoms. These developments demonstrated the failure of existing policy arrangements, such as deposit insurance, that were intended to protect individual depositors against losses and to prevent financial firm failures from creating macroeconomic disturbances. Countries with alternative structures and systems of regulation have avoided many of these problems.

Several aspects of the performance of securities markets also gave rise to public concern. The sharp drop in the stock market in October 1989 revived many of the concerns that were discussed after the 1987 crash. The widespread use of high-yield bonds in corporate takeovers that led to restructuring of firms and their managements raised concerns about both these financial instruments and the strategies in which they were employed—concerns that were underscored by the collapse of the "junk" bond market and of a major firm identified with this financial innovation. These developments seemed to raise questions about the risks to investors, the efficacy of modern securities markets in allocating capital, and the performance of the regulatory structures under which they are operated.

The international competitiveness of U.S. financial institutions and markets has been an issue of less immediate concern to the general public. But just as the large trade deficit led many observers to question the competitiveness of U.S. industry, trends in the financial sector—such as the decline in the relative size of U.S. banks compared to banks based in other countries (particularly Japan), the declining share of world financial activity accounted for by U.S. firms, the growth of financial markets abroad, and the emergence of around-the-clock financial market trading—led to similar questions about the international competitiveness of the U.S. financial sector. Continuing limitations on the services that banks can provide and where they can provide them raised questions about whether current legal and regulatory structures impede the efficiency of the financial service industry and reduce the competitive strength of U.S. financial firms. Proposals that would impose new taxes on short-term financial trading or raise margin requirements for futures markets highlight the policy relevance of concerns about international competitiveness in view of the ease with which financial activities can be shifted abroad.

Several recent developments have in combination contributed to closer linkages between different components of domestic markets and financial markets around the world. Financial innovations—such as the new instruments and trading strategies made possible by modern computers and communications technology—have strengthened interrelationships between cash and futures markets. The development of sophisticated risk management and hedging strategies has brought new opportunities for handling financial aspects of commercial transactions and making investment commitments. The speed with which markets respond to events has increased with increased speed of information transmission. Increased competition and deregulation have lowered transaction costs. The growing importance of investment and trading by large institutions has also contributed to closer linkages between markets at home and abroad. In analyzing the consequences of regulation for a particular financial sector such as banking or securities, it is therefore essential to consider their influence on financial services as a whole.

Economies of scope and scale induce financial institutions to expand their product range and broaden the market for their services. The growing interdependence of world financial markets suggests that factors such as differences in capital requirements, limitations on size or on the range of financial activities in which firms can engage, government guarantee arrangements for deposits or payments, and reporting or disclosure requirements can have important effects on the efficiency of industrial and commercial firms and thus on the international competitive positions of major sectors of the U.S. economy. Regulatory and tax policies must therefore take into account effects on international competitive positions in addition to domestic concerns. The articles in this issue analyze differences in market organization and regulation across countries and examine how efficiency in producing financial services is influenced by these differences.

These articles were presented and discussed at a conference sponsored by the American Enterprise Institute in Washington, D.C., on May 31 and June 1, 1990. This conference on International Competitiveness in Financial Services brought to the attention of Washington policy officials these analyses by leading scholars in finance. Publication of these studies and critiques in the *Journal of Financial Services Research* is intended to stimulate further interest in research on these important issues.

Journal of Financial Services Research 263–300 (1990)
© 1990 Kluwer Academic Publishers

The Financial System and Economic Performance

ROBERT C. MERTON
George Fisher Baker Professor of Business Administration
Graduate School of Business Administration
Harvard University
Dillon 32, Soldiers Fields
Boston, MA 02163

The core function of the financial system is to facilitate the allocation and deployment of economic resources, both spatially and across time, in an uncertain environment. This system includes the basic payment system through which virtually all transactions clear and the capital markets which include the money, fixed-income, equity, futures, and options markets and financial intermediaries. The capital markets are the medium that makes possible the basic cash-flow cycle of household savings flowing to capital investments by firms, followed by a return to households (via profits and interest payments) for consumption and recycling as new savings. Through often-elaborate financial securities and intermediaries, the capital markets provide risk-pooling and risk-sharing opportunities for both households and business firms. Well-developed capital markets allow for separation of the responsibility for the capital-flow requirements of investments from the risk-bearing responsibility for those investments. In both an international and domestic context, this facility permits efficient specialization in production activities, according to the principle of comparative advantage. In addition to these manifest functions, the capital market serves an important, perhaps more latent, function as a key source of information that helps coordinate decentralized decision-making in various sectors of the international economy. Interest rates and security prices are used by households or their agents in making their consumption-saving decisions and in choosing the portfolio allocations of their wealth. These same prices provide critical signals to managers of firms in their selection of investment projects and financings.

The basic functions of a financial system are essentially the same in all economies—past and present, East and West. However, for reasons involving differences in size, complexity, and available technology, as well as differences in political, cultural, and historical backgrounds, the institutional mechanisms by which these functions are performed vary considerably among economies. Therefore, a functional approach to analyzing the financial system and its economic performance may provide a more useful organizing perspective than an institutional approach, especially in an environment of rapid technological changes and movement toward increasingly global connections among financial markets.

Parts of the section on financial innovation are extracted from Merton (1989, section 6; 1990, chapter 14). I thank Zvi Bodie for many helpful discussions. Thanks also to George Benston and Allan Meltzer for comments on an earlier draft.

As the term is used here, improvement in economic performance with respect to activities within the financial system means increases in the social value or efficiency (in the sense of Pareto optimality) with which the system performs its economic function. Thus, activities that provide private gains to individual sectors of the system but overall reduce its efficiency are not improvements in economic performance.

Promoting competition, ensuring market integrity including macro credit risk protections, and managing "public-good" type externalities cover the broad potential roles for regulation and other government activities in improving economic performance of the financial system. The potential costs of such activities fall into four categories: direct costs to participants, such as fees for using the markets or costs of filings; distortions of market prices and resource allocations; transfers of wealth among private party participants in the financial markets; and transfers of wealth from taxpayers to participants in the financial markets. There are five categories to classify the paths by which government affects the financial markets: as a market participant following the same rules for action as other private-sector transactors, such as with open-market operations; as an industry competitor or benefactor of innovation, by supporting development or directly creating new financial products or markets such as index-linked bonds or all-savers accounts; as a legislator and enforcer, by setting and enforcing rules and restrictions on market participants, financial products and markets such as up-tick rules, margin requirements, circuit breakers, patents on products; as a negotiator, by representing its domestic constituents in dealings with other sovereigns that involve financial markets; as an unwitting intervenor, by changing general corporate regulations, taxes and other laws or policies that frequently have significant unanticipated and unintended consequences for the financial-services industry.

In this article, the general topic of the financial system and economic performance is addressed by analyzing three specific ones: financial innovation, below-investment grade debt, and loan guarantees. These topics, of course, have substantive importance of their own. Indeed, each is touched upon in other articles in this issue. However, their prime use here is as "strategic research sites," concrete settings from which to establish propositions, raise general questions, and expose some common fallacies about financial markets and institutions, including the functional and dysfunctional roles of government in the economic performance of the system.[1]

1. Financial innovation[2]

I need hardly do more than mention round-the-clock-trading Tokyo-London-New York, financial futures, swaps, mortgage-backed bonds, exchange-traded options, "junk" bonds, shelf registration, electronic funds transfer and security trading, automated teller machines, NOW accounts, asset-based financing, LBO, MBO, and all the other acronymic approaches to corporate restructuring, to make the case that cumulative financial innovation over the past 20 years has led to revolutionary changes in the international financial system. And these are but a small sampling.[3] Of course, financial innovation has been going on for a considerable time (cf. Dewing, 1934); indeed, many of the innovations of the last two decades, although heralded as novel, were not entirely new. Consider, for example, exchange-traded stock options and futures contracts. As Miller (1986) notes, options on commodity futures were traded on the Chicago Board of Trade in the 1920s. In the seventeenth century, options and contracts resembling futures accounted for the bulk of transactions on the Amsterdam stock exchange, which at the time was the financial center of the Western world. Moreover, from the accounts given by Joseph de la Vega (1688), it appears that the concerns raised about those contracts in Amsterdam at that time (for instance, insider trading, manipulation, excessive speculation and price volatility, and default risks) are much the same as those expressed about options and futures trading today. I suppose some things never change.

While options and futures may not be entirely new, the proliferation of organized trading markets in both equity and fixed-income derivative securities during the past 15 years is unprecedented. Development of these markets in turn made possible the creation of a wide range of financial products, many custom-designed to meet selected needs of investors and corporate issuers. Concurrently, mainstream financial institutions and pension-fund-plan sponsors increasingly adopted quantitative techniques, including computerized trading strategies, to help manage their portfolios. The composition of both their equity and fixed-income portfolios has become more global. These changes have been accompanied by an explosion of trading volume in just about every sector of the financial markets. All this everyone knows. The question is what has this wave of innovation done for economic performance, in the past and prospectively in the future.

There are some in the academic, financial, and regulatory communities who see all this alleged innovation as nothing more than a giant fad, driven by institutional investors and corporate issuers with wholly unrealistic expectations of greater expected returns with less risk, and fueled by financial-services firms and organized exchanges that see huge profits from this vast activity. From this viewpoint, pure rent-seekers develop innovations that have no function other than to differentiate their products superficially. As the story goes, beyond the direct waste of resources in this activity, the feeding of unrealistic expectations among investors and issuers can impose additional, potentially much larger, social costs in the form of ex ante distortions of investment capital allocations and ex post excessive volatility in capital market prices, as faulty expectations are not realized. Perhaps. Any virtue can readily become a vice if taken to excess, and just so with innovations (cf. Van Horne, 1985). There have surely been instances of financial products and trading strategies that have not delivered ex post the performance promised ex ante. But, notwithstanding such examples, there are other, significant examples that run counter to this negative view of the relation between innovations in the recent past and economic performance. Prime among these is the creation of a national mortgage market along with a wide array of mortgage-backed securities to promote broad distribution and liquidity. It is difficult to assess quantitatively the social wealth gain from the transformation of residential housing finance from fragmented, local-based sources to a free-flowing, international base of capital. But, given the sheer size of the market, even a modest per dollar unit improvement in efficiency would aggregate to enormous benefit. Money-market, fixed-income, international, real-estate, and equity-indexed mutual funds and a variety of pension, life insurance, and annuity products are among the important innovations developed during the past two decades that directly benefit households. Collectively, these innovations have

7

greatly improved the opportunities for households to receive efficient risk-return trade-offs and more effective tailoring to individual needs over the entire life-cycle, including accumulation during the work years and distribution in retirement.

We could continue with a listing of past innovations and their benefits as part of an inductive process of refutation. It will perhaps instead be more interesting and instructive to examine in greater detail a single innovation that has not yet been introduced, but could be, using current technology. In keeping with the global focus of this issue, the problem that this product addresses is international diversification under capital controls.

Numerous empirical studies of stock market returns have documented the gains in diversification from investing internationally.[4] By diversifying across the world stock markets, there is significant improvement in the efficient frontier of risk versus expected return. As we know, the last decade has seen widespread implementation of such international diversification among investors in the large developed countries with the major stock markets (e.g., the United States, United Kingdom, Germany, and Japan). However, international diversification has not yet evolved in many smaller, developed countries where indeed it may be more important.

A major barrier to foreign stock market investment by citizens of some of these countries is capital controls, imposed by their governments to prevent flight of domestic capital. A common rationale for such restrictions is that they reduce the risk that the local economy will have inadequate domestic investment to promote growth.[5] Another important barrier is that the transaction cost paid by large foreign investors when they buy shares directly in these domestic stock markets can be so large that it offsets any diversification benefits that would otherwise accrue. The cost in lost welfare from less-efficient diversification affects both large-country and small-country citizens. However, the per capita magnitude of the cost is much larger for the latter, since the potential gains from international diversification are greatest for the smallest countries with domestic economies that are by necessity less well diversified. Alternatively, part of the cost may be that domestic physical investment is driven to become more diversified than would otherwise be efficient according to the principle of comparative advantage.

Of course, one (and perhaps the best) solution is to simply eliminate capital flow restrictions and open capital markets. However, taking the capital controls as a given, the constrained solution involves separating the capital-flow effects of investment from its risk-sharing aspects. Suppose that small-country domestic investors (perhaps through domestic mutual funds or financial intermediaries) who already own the domestic equity were to enter into "swap" agreements[6] with large foreign investors. In the swap, the total return per dollar on the small-country's domestic stock market is exchanged annually for the total return per dollar on a market-value weighted-average of the world stock markets. This exchange of returns could be in a common currency, dollars, as described or adjusted to different currencies along similar lines to currency-swap agreements. The magnitudes of the dollar exchanges are determined by the "notional" or principal amount of the swap to which per dollar return differences apply. As is the usual case with swaps, there is no initial payment by either party to the other for entering the agreement.

Without pursuing too many details of implementation, we see that the swap agreement effectively transfers the risk of the small-country stock market to foreign investors and provides the domestic investors with the risk-return pattern of a well-diversified world portfolio.[7] Since there are no initial payments between parties, there are no initial capital flows in or out of the country. Subsequent payments which may be either inflows or outflows involve only the *difference* between the *returns* on the two stock market indices, and no "principal" amounts flow. For example, on a notional or principal amount of $1 billion, if, ex post, the world stock market earns 10 percent and the small-country market earns 12 percent, there is only a flow of $(.12 - .10) \times \$1$ billion or $20 million out of the country. Note further that the small-country investors make net payments out precisely when they can "best" afford it: namely, when their local market has outperformed the world markets. In those years in which the domestic market underperforms the world stock markets, the swap generates net cash flows into the country to its domestic investors. Hence, in our example, if the small-country market earns 8 percent and the world stock market earns 11 percent, then domestic investors receive $(.11 - .08) \times \$1$ billion $= \$30$ million, a net cash inflow for the small country. Moreover, with this swap arrangement, trading and ownership of actual shares remain with domestic investors.[8]

Foreign investors also benefit from the swap by avoiding the costs of trading in individual securities in the local markets and by not having the problems of corporate control issues that arise when foreigners acquire large ownership positions in domestic companies. Unlike standard cash investments in equities or debt, the default or expropriation exposure of foreign investors is limited to the difference in returns instead of the total gross return plus principal (in our example, $20 million versus $1.12 billion).

The potential exposure of foreign investors to manipulation by local investors is probably less for the swap than for direct transactions in individual stocks. It is more difficult to manipulate a broad market index than the price of a single stock. Even if settlement intervals for swaps are standardized at six months or one year, the calendar settlement dates will differ for each swap, depending upon the date of its initiation. Hence, with some swaps being settled every day, manipulators would have to keep the prices of shares permanently low to succeed. Furthermore, with the settlement terms of swaps based on the per period rate of return, an artificially low price (and low rate of return) for settlement this year will induce an artificially high rate of return for settlement next year. Thus, gains from manipulation in the first period are given back in the second, unless the price can be kept low over the entire life of the swap. Since typical swap contract maturities might range from two to ten years (with semi-annual or annual settlements), this would be difficult to achieve.

Note that this swap innovation is *not* designed to circumvent the stated objective of the capital-control regulation, to prevent domestic capital flight. Instead, it is designed to eliminate (or at least reduce) the unintended and undesirable "side effects" of this policy on efficient risk bearing and diversification. Whether or not this "real-time" proposed solution of using a swap turns out to be an effective real-world solution is not the central point of the exercise here. Rather, it is to demonstrate how a simple but "finely-tuned" financial innovation of trivial intrinsic cost could help reduce the social cost of "blunt" policy tools that affect a number of countries around the world.

This swap example can also serve to clarify another issue surrounding the relation between financial innovation and economic performance over the last two decades. A widely accepted theory is that cost reduction or otherwise lessening the constraints of regulation including taxes and accounting conventions is a driving force behind financial innovations. Indeed, Miller (1986) claims that frequent and unanticipated changes in regulatory and tax codes have been the prime motivators for financial innovation during the past 25 years. Silber's (1983) view that financial innovation arises from attempts to reduce the cost of various constraints on corporations is consistent with this view as is Kane's (1977, 1984, 1988) theory of dynamic regulation.[9] It is a common belief among many economists that activities whose purpose is to circumvent regulations or avoid taxes are zero or negative-sum games of wealth transfers that can only increase the total cost of achieving the intended objectives of the regulations. From this perspective, financial innovation, as the instrument for implementing such activities, has a zero or negative social value.[10] However, as our swap example illustrates, it is possible to have an innovation entirely motivated by regulation that nevertheless reduces the social cost of achieving the intended objectives of the regulation. And this is the case, whether or not those intended objectives of the regulation are socially optimal.

Having touched on issues surrounding financial innovation and economic performance in the past, I turn now to a prospective view on future economic performance as it relates to innovation. Following the work of Black and Scholes (1974), Benston and Smith (1976), Van Horne (1985), Allen and Gale (1988), Ross (1989b), and Merton (1989, 1990), I assume that the systematic driving forces behind financial innovation fall into three categories: (1) demand for "completing the markets" by providing opportunities for risk-sharing, risk-pooling, hedging, and intertemporal or spatial transfers of resources that are not currently available; (2) the lowering of transactions costs or increasing of liquidity; (3) reductions in "agency" costs caused by either asymmetric information between trading parties or principals' incomplete monitoring of their agents' performance. All three of these forces are consistent with financial innovation working in the direction of improving economic efficiency and increasing social wealth.

The influence of regulation on innovation is not considered in this "simulation" of the future. As Miller (1986) notes, it is *unanticipated* regulatory changes that have the major impact. Moreover, regulation both shapes and is shaped by the time path of financial innovation. Exogenous changes in regulation are surely possible in the short run. However, such changes induce responses in financial innovation which in turn feed back into the dynamics of regulation. As a result, the long-run role of regulatory change as an exogenous force for financial innovation is limited.

From the perspective of the three included forces for innovation, the broad facts about the dramatic changes of the past two decades are seen as consistent with a real-world dynamic path evolving toward an idealized target of an efficient financial market and intermediation system. On this premise, these changes can be interpreted as part of a "financial innovation spiral." That is, the proliferation of new trading markets in standardized securities such as futures makes feasible the creation of new custom-designed financial products that improve "market completeness"; to hedge their exposures on these products, producers (typically, financial intermediaries) trade in these new markets and volume expands; increased volume reduces marginal transaction costs and thereby makes possible further implementation of new products and trading strategies, which in turn leads to still more volume. Success of these trading markets encourages investment in creating additional markets, and so on it goes, spiraling toward the theoretically limiting case of zero marginal transactions costs and dynamically complete markets.

Consider now a small sampling of the implications for the future evolution of the system from this view of the process. In this scenario, aggregate trading volume expands secularly, and trading is increasingly dominated by institutions. As more financial institutions employ dynamic strategies to hedge their product liabilities, incentives rise for further expansion in round-the-clock trading that permits more effective implementation of these strategies. Supported by powerful trading technologies for creating financial products,[11] financial-services firms will increasingly focus on providing individually tailored solutions to their clients' investment and financing problems.

Retail customers ("households") will continue to move away from direct, individual financial market participation such as trading in individual stocks or bonds where they have the greatest and growing comparative disadvantage. Better diversification, lower trading costs, and less informational disadvantage will continue to move their trading and investing activities toward aggregate bundles of securities, such as mutual funds, basket-type and index securities, and custom-designed products issued by intermediaries. This secular shift, together with informational effects as described in Gammill and Perold (1989), will cause liquidity to deepen in the basket/index securities while individual stocks become relatively less liquid. With ever greater institutional ownership of individual securities, there is less need for the traditional regulatory protections and other subsidies of the costs of retail investors trading in stocks and bonds. The emphasis on disclosure and regulations to protect those investors will tend to shift up the "security-aggregation chain" to the interface between investors and investment companies, asset allocators, and insurance and pension products.

Whether the financial-services industry becomes more concentrated or more diffuse in this scenario is ambiguous. The central functions of information and transactions processing would seem to favor economies of scale. Similarly, the greater opportunities for netting and diversifying risk exposures by an intermediary with a diverse set of products suggests both fewer required hedging transactions and less risk-capital per dollar of product liability as size increases. Increased demand for custom products and private contracting services would seem to forecast that more of the financial service business will be conducted as principal instead of agent, which again favors size. On the other hand, expansion in the types of organized trading markets, reductions in transactions costs, and continued improvements in information-processing and telecommunications technologies will all make it easier for a greater variety of firms to serve the financial service functions. These same factors also improve the prospects for expanding asset-based financing, and such expanded opportunities for "securitization" permit smaller, agent-type firms to compete with larger firms in traditionally principal-type activities. Continuing the scenario, locational and regulatory advantages currently available to some financial institutions will be reduced because more firms will be capable of offering a broader range of financial products and servicing a wider geographic area. Traditional institutional identifications with specific types of products are likely to become increasingly blurred.

As we know, many but not all of these changes have been underway and furthermore this represents one scenario, growing out of our model of the innovation process. Nonetheless, it serves as a means to speculate about the future course of financial market regulation and more specifically, public policy toward financial innovation.

The overriding theme of our scenario has financial innovation as the engine driving the financial system on its prospective journey to economic efficiency. With its focus on product innovation, this theme largely abstracts from the concurrent changes in financial infrastructure (institutional and regulatory practices, organization of trading facilities, and the communication and information processing systems for transactions) required to support realization of this journey. But, as I have pointed out elsewhere,[12] perhaps the single most important implication for public policy on innovation is the explicit recognition of the interdependence between product and infrastructure innovations and of the inevitable conflicts that arise between the two.

As an analogy of supreme simplicity, consider the creation of a high-speed passenger train, surely a beneficial product innovation. Suppose however, that the tracks of the current rail system are inadequate to handle such high speeds. In the absence of policy rules, the innovator, either through ignorance or a willingness to take risk, could choose to fully implement his product and run the train at high speed. If the train subsequently crashes, it is, of course, true that the innovator and his passenger-clients will pay a dear price. But, if in the process the track is also destroyed, then those, such as freight operators, who use the system for a different purpose will also be greatly damaged. Hence the need for policy to safeguard the system. A simple policy that fulfills that objective is to permanently fix a safe, but low speed limit. But, of course, this narrowly focused policy has a rather unfortunate consequence that the benefits of innovation will never be realized. An obviously better, if more complex, policy solution is to facilitate the needed upgrading of the track and, at the same time, to set transient limits on speed, while there is a technological imbalance between the product and its infrastructure.

As in this hypothetical rail system, the financial system is used by many for a variety of purposes. When treated atomistically, financial innovations in products and services can be implemented unilaterally and rather quickly. Hence, these innovations take place in an entrepreneurial and opportunistic manner. In contrast, innovations in financial infrastructure must be more coordinated and, therefore, take longer to implement. It is thus wholly unrealistic to expect financial innovation to proceed along a balanced path of development for all elements in the system. It is indeed possible that at times, the imbalance between product innovation and infrastructure could become large enough to jeopardize the functioning of the system. Hence the need for policy to protect against such breakdown. But, as we have seen, a single-minded policy focused exclusively on this concern could derail the engine of innovation and bring to a halt the financial system's trip to greater efficiency.

A related policy issue is whether government should itself be a financial innovator. If so, should policy hold that innovative financial instruments be issued if and only if they reduce the direct cost of government financing? Are there other social benefits? Would, for example, the national mortgage market have evolved without government-guaranteed mortgages? For another example, not centered around credit enhancement, it has been suggested that there are certain types of index-linked bonds for which the government may have a comparative advantage over private-sector issuers.[13]

The dramatic increases over the last decade in the size and complexity of transactions together with the global linking of financial markets have raised concerns about macro credit risk and the possibility of broad financial market "breakdown." The 1987 crash in world stock markets still casts a shadow that heightens those concerns. The changes in practice projected by our scenario of innovation imply, ipso facto, further increases in the interdependence among institutions and markets in the international financial system.[14] This greater interdependence, in turn, promises renewed intensity of the policy debate on ensuring market integrity and where to draw the line on government guarantees, both explicit obligations set by contract and implicit ones set by public expectations. Our scenario on macro credit risk may thus seem to suggest an increasing role for regulation. On the other hand, continuing improvements in telecommunications, information processing, and electronic transactions technologies will make monitoring security prices and transferring securities for collateral considerably less costly. Such technologies may eventually make practical the creation of "narrow" depository banks, perhaps run along the lines of money market funds, but with additional marked-to-market collateral and a federal deposit-insurance "wraparound." This less comprehensive deposit insurance, lower cost monitoring, and lower cost collateralization work in the direction of reducing the need for regulation.

Whatever may be the change in the quantity of regulation in the future, a major change in the format of regulation from "institutional" to "functional" seems inevitable. As already noted, increasingly more sophisticated trading technologies, together with low-transaction-cost markets to implement them, tend to blur the lines among financial products and services. The existence of these technologies and markets also implies easier entry into the financial services. As a result, the lines between financial institutions become less distinct. Indeed, insurance companies now offer U.S. Treasury money-market funds with check writing, while banks use option and futures markets transactions to provide stock-and-bond-value insurance that guarantees a minimum return on customer portfolios. Credit subsidiaries of major manufacturing firms have moved from the single, specialized function of providing financing for customers of their parents to multiple-function financial institutions, with services ranging from merchant banking for takeovers and restructurings to equity-indexed mutual funds sold to retail investors. In contrast, a financial product's function from the perspective of the user is relatively well defined. Electronics has also rendered as problematic the meaning of "the location of the vendor" of these products. Most financial regulation involves products and services for household customers, and hence the user's location is often better defined than the vendor's. Over time, functional uses of products are typically more stable than the institutional forms of their vendors. In keeping with the trend toward greater user access to international financial markets, I note further that product and service functions appear to be more uniform across national borders than are the institutions that provide them. Functional regulation also reduces the opportunities for institutions to engage in "regulatory arbitrage," which wastes real resources and can undermine the intent of the regulation. Functional regulation thus promises a more level "playing field" for all providers of the product or service and thereby, reduces the opportunities for rent-seeking and regulatory capture.[15]

The perceived benefits from a move to functional regulation might seem to support a broader case for widespread coordination, and even standardization, of financial regulations, both domestically and across national borders. However, such extrapolation is valid *only if* the coordinated regulatory policies chosen are socially optimal. The reduction in "regulatory diversification," which by necessity occurs with more effective coordination, will cause larger social losses if the selected common policies are suboptimal. Understanding something of the cost of repetitive, but not competitive, actions, we say no more on this matter here with the confidence that the issue of the tradeoff between the benefits of regulatory cooperation and the benefits of regulatory competition will be addressed in earnest in the other articles in this issue.[16] Instead, we turn now to the broad issue of credit risk, which is explored by analyzing low-grade bonds and loan guarantees.

2. Below-investment-grade debt: a functional analysis

2.1. Introduction

The widespread issuing of below-investment-grade bonds to restructure firms and finance management buyouts and hostile takeovers surely ranks as a major innovation in terms of impact on the financial markets during the 1980s. As Taggart and Perry (1988) have pointed out, this innovation is not entirely new: such "junk" bond financings were also widely used in the United States prior to World War I. The estimated $200 billion of these bonds currently outstanding provide ample justification for investigating this prime tool in the restructuring of corporate America. However, the purpose for analyzing junk bonds here is not to study their role in restructurings.[17] Instead, we use them to focus on the issue of credit risk and associated public policy questions.

There are no direct government guarantees of junk bonds, and so it would seem that the credit risks surrounding them are entirely a private-sector matter. Perhaps. But, as we all know, thrifts with insured deposit liabilities are among the array of financial institutions that hold junk bonds as assets and hence, at least a portion of the default risk of these bonds is indirectly borne by the government.[18] Moreover, it has recently been argued that the Pension Benefit Guarantee Corporation (PBGC) must insure pension benefits that are backed by annuities issued by insurance companies. Insurance companies are major holders of junk bonds. Thus, this claim of greater PBGC responsibility has led some to speculate that there is an implicit government guarantee covering a wider group of institutional investors in this debt than simply thrifts and that the coverage would be especially broad in the event of a major recession and widespread defaults on junk bonds. Even in the absence of such direct concerns, analysis of junk bonds can provide general insights about the properties of debt claims with significant chances for default. Such knowledge is an essential prerequisite for the analysis and understanding of loan guarantees, including deposit insurance which is, of course, a major public policy issue and the subject of study in section 3.

In this section, we try our hand at separating fact from misperception about risky bond pricing and return patterns.[19] We also investigate the compatibility and conflicts of interests between the debt and equityholders of the firm with emphasis on the effects of changes in investment and financing policies of the firm. Issues of public policy surrounding junk bonds are discussed, and we conclude with a discussion of "no-fault" default as a possible response to some of the public policy concerns. Since the intent here is to provide a basic functional understanding of the properties of risky debt, a hypothetical example of great simplicity is used for the analysis. Nevertheless, the properties illustrated by this example are not pathological and indeed, apply to real-world debt.[20]

2.2. A hypothetical example

To study the effect of changes in investment policy, the firm in our hypothetical example must have at least two choices for assets it can own. Therefore, a natural starting point for the analysis is a description of the two types of assets available to the firm. The assets are characterized by a schedule of their values in one-year's time, contingent on the state of the economy at that time. As shown in table 1, the various realizations of value are partitioned into five possible conditions for the economy: *normal, weak, strong, very weak,* and *very strong.* The contingent values of the assets are further classified by whether they are continued in their intended use ("going-concern" value) or sold for their salvage value ("liquidation" value).

For expositional simplicity, we assume that the five possible conditions for the economy are equally likely events (i.e., a probability of one out of five for each). The average of the end-of-year contingent values therefore is equal to the expected value of the asset at that time. Further simplification is gained by neglecting compensation to investors for either the time value of money or risk-bearing. Under these conditions, the current market price of each asset will equal its expected end-of-year value. The assumptions of a zero riskless interest rate and a zero risk premium cause no material distortions in the analysis.

In table 1, the range of possible values specified for asset type 1 (if continued in its intended use) is from 30 to 170, with an average value of 106 and a standard deviation of 48 around that average. The current price of the asset is thus 106, which implies a zero expected rate of return from investing in the asset. The volatility of the rate of return on investment as measured by its standard deviation is 48/106 or 46 percent.

Table 1. Valuation of assets

| | In one year | | | |
| | Asset type 1 values | | Asset type 2 values | |
Condition of economy	Going-concern	Liquidation	Going-concern	Liquidation
Very Weak	30	50	20	40
Weak	80	60	70	50
Normal	110	80	110	80
Strong	140	110	150	120
Very Strong	170	140	180	150
Average Value	106	88	106	88
Expected Value	106	88	106	88
Standard Deviation	48	33	57	42
Current Price	106	88	106	88
Expected Return	0%	0%	0%	0%
Standard Deviation of Return	46%	37%	54%	47%

From table 1, the average or expected performance of type 2 assets is the same as for type 1 assets. Thus, each has the same current price. However, type 2 assets will have superior performance to type 1 assets if the economy is stronger than expected and will have inferior performance if the economy is weaker than expected. Type 2 asset values are thus more volatile than type 1s. Using standard deviation as a quantitative measure of volatility, we have that type 2 assets on a going-concern basis are about 19 percent more volatile than type 1 assets.

With these properties of the assets established, consider now a firm that holds the assets and finances them by a combination of debt and equity. Table 2 displays the price and return patterns of debt and equity for both low-leverage and high-leverage financing strategies when the firm holds type 1 assets. Table 3 presents the price and return patterns for the identical financing strategies when the firm holds type 2 assets. In both tables, the "Value" and "Return" columns under "Assets type" present the values and returns for the whole firm. Therefore, these are also the price and return patterns for "unleveraged" equity if the firm had no debt.

By inspection of table 1, the going-concern values one year from now for both type 1 and type 2 assets exceed their corresponding liquidation values under all conditions for the economy except *very weak*. Liquidation values in that state are 20 larger than going-concern values for both types of assets. The listing of firm values and returns in both tables 2 and 3 assume that management will choose the largest-value use for the assets. Hence, the firm is liquidated if the very weak state of the economy obtains.[21]

In the case of the low-leverage strategy and type 1 assets, the total promised payment of 50 on the debt is made in all states of the economy, and hence this debt is default-free. Equity bears all the risk of the firm, and thus fits the classic analysis of leverage in which the volatility or standard deviation of the levered equity is proportional to the standard deviation of unlevered equity and the proportionality factor is (1 + debt-to-equity ratio), [e.g., (1 + .83) × 38 percent = 70 percent]. In contrast, under the high-leverage policy with twice the face value (and a total promised payment of 100) on the debt, the debt is no longer default-free. Indeed, default, and thus bankruptcy, now occurs whenever the economy underperforms expectations which in our example happens, on average, two times out of five, or 40 percent of the time. Equity bears only a portion of the risk of the firm, and thus the volatility of the equity return is less than proportional to (1 + debt-to-equity ratio), [e.g., (1 + 3.58) × 38 percent = 174 percent > 113 percent]. The balance of the firm's risk is borne by the debt which now has a 23 percent standard deviation. Much the same pattern obtains in table 3 when the firm holds the more volatile type 2 assets. Although the debt is no longer default-free under the low-leverage policy, bankruptcy occurs only when the economy is very weak and the losses in that case are a relatively modest 16 percent.

2.3. *Junk bond price and expected return properties*

The debt return patterns under the low-leverage policy in tables 2 and 3 characterize what is typically called "investment-grade" debt whereas the high-leverage policy captures the behavior of "low-grade" or junk debt. Many of the common misperceptions about the

Table 2. Debt and equity return characteristics for alternative financing policies

| | Assets type 1 | | Low-leverage policy Promised payment to debt = 50 | | | | High-leverage policy Promised payment to debt = 100 | | | |
| | | | Debt | | Equity | | Debt | | Equity | |
Condition of economy	Value	Return	Value	Return	Value	Return	Value	Return	Value	Return
Very Weak	50*	(55)%	50	0%	0	(100)%	50**	(42)%	0	(100)%
Weak	80	(27)%	50	0%	30	(50)%	80***	(7)%	0	(100)%
Normal	110	0%	50	0%	60	0%	100	16%	10	(58)%
Strong	140	27%	50	0%	90	50%	100	16%	40	67%
Very Strong	170	55%	50	0%	120	100%	100	16%	70	192%
Average (Current Price)	110	0%	50	0%	60	0%	86	0%	24	0%
Standard Deviation	42	38%	0	0%	42	70%	20	23%	27	113%
Promised	—	—	50	0%	—	—	100	16%	—	—
			Debt-to-Equity Ratio = 0.83				Debt-to-Equity Ratio = 3.58			

* Liquidation of assets.
** Bankruptcy and liquidation.
*** Bankruptcy only.

Table 3. Debt and equity return characteristics for alternative financing policies

| | Assets type 2 | | Low-leverage policy Promised payment to debt = 50 | | | | High-leverage policy Promised payment to debt = 100 | | | |
| | | | Debt | | Equity | | Debt | | Equity | |
Condition of economy	Value	Return	Value	Return	Value	Return	Value	Return	Value	Return
Very Weak	40*	(64)%	40**	(16)%	0	(100)%	40**	(51)%	0	(100)%
Weak	70	(36)%	50	4%	20	(68)%	70***	(15)%	0	(100)%
Normal	110	0%	50	4%	60	(3)%	100	22%	10	(64)%
Strong	150	36%	50	4%	100	61%	100	22%	50	79%
Very Strong	180	64%	50	4%	130	110%	100	22%	80	185%
Average (Current Price)	110	0%	48	0%	62	0%	82	0%	28	0%
Standard Deviation	51	46%	4	8%	48	78%	24	29%	32	114%
Promised	—	—	50	4%	—	—	100	22%	—	—
			Debt-to-Equity Ratio = 0.77				Debt-to-Equity Ratio = 2.93			

*Liquidation of assets.
**Bankruptcy and liquidation.
***Bankruptcy only.

return properties of junk debt arise from the mistake of treating this debt as if it behaves like investment-grade debt except for a somewhat larger probability of default.

Misperception 1. *The promised yield on a bond provides a reasonable approximation to its expected return and hence, bonds with higher promised yields will have correspondingly higher expected returns.* By assumption in constructing the examples in tables 2 and 3, the bonds are all priced to have the same expected rate of return (0 percent). In general, the promised yield on a bond (figured by calculating the return earned if the promised payments on the bond are made) is the *maximum* yield (or return) that the bond can earn. Therefore, unless the bond is riskless, the expected return on the bond will be less than the promised yield. In the low-leverage policy of table 2, where the debt is riskless, the promised yield equals the expected return. In table 3, the promised yield for that policy is 4 percent, which is somewhat larger than the 0 percent expected return. But, for the high-leverage cases, the promised yields are considerably larger (16 and 22 percent, respectively) and yet the expected return from holding either of these bonds is still zero. Note further that the promised payment (100) and maturity date (one year) as well as the current value of the underlying total assets (110) are the same for the high-leverage bonds of the firms in tables 2 and 3. Nevertheless, the bond with a 22 percent promised yield has the same expected return as the one with the 16 percent promised yield.

Misperception 2. *The probability of default, together with the promised yield, provide a reasonable surrogate for expected return.* By inspection of tables 2 and 3, the bonds under the high-leverage policy each have the same probability of default (i.e., two times out of five, or 40 percent) and indeed, the event of default for each is perfectly correlated with the other. As already noted, they have identical promised payments and maturity dates. If the probability of default were a sufficient statistic for the risk differences among bonds, then it would seem that both bonds should have the same promised yield to produce the same expected return. But, as we see, this is not the case: one bond has a promised yield of 22 percent and the other, a promised yield of 16 percent. Nevertheless, each has the same expected return, 0 percent.

Probability of default is an inadequate statistic because it does not take account of the magnitude of the loss to the debtholder if default occurs. For instance, with the debt on the firm with type 1 assets, the loss is 7 percent if the economy is weak and 42 percent if it is very weak. For debt on the firm with type 2 assets, the losses under corresponding conditions are 15 percent and 51 percent. The larger (22 versus 16 percent) return on these bonds in the event of no default is simply offsetting compensation for the smaller returns (larger losses) in the event of default.[22]

Two other important features of the return patterns on junk bonds, skewness and relative volatility, are illustrated by the examples of tables 2 and 3. By inspection, more often than not (three out of five times on average) the debt will earn a realized return in excess of its expected return. In the case of debt of the firm with type 1 assets, the excess return is substantial, 16 percent versus 0 percent. Even in the less frequent (two out of five) case of default, half the time the loss to the debtholder is a modest 7 percent. It is only the relatively infrequent event (one in five) of a very weak economy, with a corresponding major loss on the debt of 42 percent, that finally "drags" the long-run average return down to its ex ante expectation. Note that even with a one-in-five chance of a major recession each year, there is approximately a one-in-three probability of no major recession during a five-year period and that probability is still above one in ten for a ten-year period. Thus, whether or not realized junk bond returns greatly exceed their ex ante expected values over a specific period will be quite sensitive to the number of relatively rare events, such as major recessions, actually experienced during that period. This pronounced negative skewness in the return distribution therefore requires special attention when evaluating studies that use historical junk-bond returns to estimate ex ante expected returns. In this regard, beware of pronouncements such as "With the exception of a very few and unusual periods, the long-run average returns on junk bonds have otherwise been consistently larger than on other, comparable-risk investments," or "That total returns on junk bonds have been significantly larger than the returns on comparable duration investment-grade bonds in each year of the last ten is strong evidence that expected returns on junk bonds exceed expected returns on investment-grade ones." As a closing parenthetical remark on skewness, note that the returns on equity exhibit the opposite pattern of positive skewness in which, more often than not, the realized returns are below their ex ante expected value, and occasionally they are very much larger. As demonstrated in tables 2 and 3, the size of the positive skewness increases with the amount of leverage.

2.4. Volatility and risk effects of high leverage

The volatility of junk-bond returns will in general exceed the volatility of higher-grade fixed-income securities. Inspection of tables 2 and 3 shows that the standard deviations of debt prices and returns increase with increasing leverage and with increasing volatility in the underlying assets of the firm. However, on occasion, stronger claims about the relative riskiness of bonds are made, such as "Junk bonds are too risky for the typical investor. The investor should instead hold equity shares in conservatively financed firms." As we now show, such unqualified claims about relative riskiness are unfounded. Inspection of tables 2 and 3 shows that the standard deviation of the returns on the debt is always less than the standard deviation of the returns on the underlying assets (e.g., for a high-leverage policy, 23 percent on the debt < 38 percent on type 1 assets and 29 percent on the debt < 46 percent on type 2 assets). But, as already noted, the returns listed in the "Assets" column are the same as for unleveraged equity. Thus, it follows that *for any amount of leverage, the volatility of the returns on the debt is always less than the volatility of the returns on unleveraged equity in a firm with comparable assets and no debt outstanding.*[23]

On the matter of return volatility, it has often been pointed out that as the result of a large substitution of debt for equity financing in the United States during the 1980s, the riskiness of both corporate debt and equity has increased substantially. This essentially correct observation has, however, led to:

Misperception 3. *Because of increased leverage, corporate debt and equity are riskier and therefore, investors' holdings of corporate securities in total have become riskier.* Since the total of corporate securities held by investors is debt plus equity, it would perhaps seem almost a truism that if the returns on each become more volatile, the returns on their sum must also. However, using tables 2 and 3, we show that no such inference can be validly drawn. In table 2, consider first the case of a low-leverage policy: the standard deviation of return is 0 percent on the debt and 70 percent on the equity. Note that as an identity, the market value of the firm's total of debt and equity always equals the market value of its assets. It follows from this identity that the standard deviation of the return from holding the total of corporate investment (i.e., the debt and equity in proportion to the amount outstanding) is always the same as the standard deviation of the return on assets, which in this case is 38 percent. Suppose, retaining the same assets, the firm restructures by swapping debt for equity to achieve the high-leverage policy. As a result of the increase in leverage, the standard deviation of the return on debt increases to 23 percent and on equity increases to 113 percent. Despite the large increase in the volatility of each security, the return volatility of the total holdings of both remains unchanged at 38 percent, because the assets are the same.

To make the point more strongly, consider a firm holding type 2 assets and following a low-leverage policy. From table 3, the standard deviation of return is 8 percent on debt, 78 percent on equity, and 46 percent on holding the total of debt plus equity. Suppose the firm were simultaneously to change its investment policy by exchanging its type 2 assets for type 1 assets *and* change its financing policy to high leverage by swapping debt for equity. From table 2, the effect of this combined change is to increase the standard deviation of the return on debt from 8 to 23 percent and to increase the standard deviation of the return on equity from 78 to 113 percent. However, as a result of a shift to less volatile assets, the standard deviation of the return from holding the total of debt and equity actually *declines* from 46 to 38 percent.

To understand this seemingly paradoxical result, note first that the volatility of debt return is always less than the volatility of total return, which is less than the volatility of (leveraged) equity return. In the process of increasing leverage, the volatility *per dollar* of both debt and equity increases. However, the volatility of the total is a weighted average of the two, and as leverage increases, the weights shift to more on debt and less on equity. Thus, if the weight shift from high-volatility equity to lower-volatility debt increases more rapidly than the rise in volatility of each, then the weighted average of volatility can remain the same or even fall.

2.5. High leverage, bankruptcy, and asset liquidation

Two issues of public concern surrounding the widespread use of junk bonds and the leveraging of corporate America are that firms have become riskier and that, as a result of this increase in risk, the institutional investors in corporate securities are taking on more risk, which in turn makes them more vulnerable. Perhaps. Surely such complex and sweeping concerns cannot be entirely resolved by analysis of a simple hypothetical case. Nevertheless, if the primary empirical evidence for these beliefs is the dramatic increase in leverage and an observed secular increase in both corporate-bond and stock-market return volatilities, then we have shown that such evidence is hardly conclusive for inferring that firms have become riskier. On the investor side, if institutional investors tend to hold the whole of corporate securities, then with a change in financing policy they will still hold the same whole, but partitioned in a different way. For instance, with increased leverage, they will hold more corporate debt and less equity. Hence, even if each separate security has become more volatile, we cannot infer that the whole of institutional investors' portfolios has also become more volatile.

Historically, before the widespread issuing of low-grade bonds, a firm going bankrupt and the subsequent liquidation of its assets were often coincident events. Simple extrapolation of this observation leads to:

Misperception 4. *The substantial increase in the frequency of bankruptcy caused by a substantial increase in corporate leverage will lead to (approximately) the same increase in the frequency of asset liquidations. Hence, a major cost to the economy of high leverage is the resulting destruction of going-concern values of firms caused by liquidations.* If the volatility of asset values is not reduced and the amount of leverage used by firms increases, then the frequency of default will increase. However, declaring bankruptcy and liquidating assets are economically and legally separate decisions, and therefore the two need not coincide. Moreover, if the increase in bankruptcies is the result of higher-leverage policies by firms, then there is reason to believe that the frequency of liquidations will not grow in proportion to the frequency of bankruptcies.

As modeled for our hypothetical example in table 1, going-concern values for assets typically exceed their liquidation values, except when the economic environment turns out to be especially unfavorable for the intended use of the assets. If liquidation decisions are generally driven by attempts to receive the largest-value use of assets, then one would expect liquidations to occur only after a substantial decline in the value of the assets. This appears to be the case empirically.

Consider a firm with a total market value of 100 and financed by a low-leverage strategy with a 1:3 debt-to-equity ratio or market values for debt of 25 and for equity of 75. Neglecting interest accumulation, this firm will not go bankrupt, unless the market value of its assets falls by more than 75 percent to below 25. In contrast, consider a firm with the same assets, but financed by a high-leverage strategy, with a 3:1 debt-to-equity ratio and a debt value of 75 and equity worth 25. This firm can go bankrupt with only a relatively modest decline of 25 percent in the market value of its assets. It is obvious that the *likelihood* of bankruptcy is much greater for the second firm. However, because bankruptcy in the first firm only occurs for very low asset values, *given that bankruptcy has occurred,* it is much more likely that the going-concern value will be below salvage value for the first firm than for the second. Hence, the empirical fraction of bankruptcies that lead to liquidations, estimated from a period of relatively low-leverage financing policies, will provide a biased-high prediction of that fraction in a period of high-leverage policies.[24] This point is illustrated in tables 2 and 3. The frequency of bankruptcy is greater for high-leverage policies than low ones, 0 percent versus 40 percent in table 2 and 20 percent versus 40 percent in table 3. However, given that bankruptcy occurs, liquidation always occurs for the low-leverage firm in contrast to only half of the cases for the high-leverage firm. Thus, in table 3, a shift to a high-leverage policy doubles the frequency of bankruptcy from 20 to 40 percent, but leaves the frequency of liquidation unchanged at 20 percent.

2.6. Conflicts between debt and equity in high-leverage firms

We now turn to a brief analysis of the compatible and conflicting interests of debtholders and equityholders as they apply to investment and financing decisions by the firm. As will be shown in the next section on loan guarantees, these same conflicts will occur between the guarantors of debt and equityholders.

By inspection of tables 2 and 3, the realized prices and returns for both debt and equity are in all cases nondecreasing functions of the realized prices and returns of the firm's assets. In this sense, both debtholders and equityholders have a common interest in having the firm "do well." However, a finer analysis of the patterns shows that if the firm does not do poorly, the returns to the debt are insensitive to how well the firm does (the returns are the same in the *normal, strong,* and *very strong* states). On the other hand, the debt returns are quite sensitive if the firm does poorly (cf. the payoffs in the *weak* and *very weak* states). Equity return patterns are the reverse: the returns are the same whether the realization is *weak* or *very weak*. They increase dramatically as one moves from the *normal* to the *strong* to the *very strong* conditions. Thus, by the structure of their respective contingent payoffs (independently of their personal preferences about risk taking), debtholders focus more on the downside risks of the firm and equityholders are more concerned with its upside potential. It is this contract-induced difference in focus that is the source of conflicting interests over investment and financing policies.

Ceteris paribus, both holders prefer larger asset values for the firm. We thus investigate these conflicts by considering only changes that keep the current total market value of the firm unchanged. To illustrate the effects of changes in investment policy, suppose that a firm with type 1 assets worth 110 exchanges them for more-volatile type 2 assets with equal current value. If this exchange were entirely unanticipated, its effect on the current price of debt and equity can be determined from tables 2 and 3 by comparing firms with the same financing policies. As summarized in part A of table 4, the shift to more volatile assets always reduces the value of debt and increases the value of equity by a corresponding amount.

The managers and board of directors of the firm choose investment and financing policy. They are also elected by the equityholders, and they have a fiduciary responsibility to make decisions in the best interests of the equityholders. Thus, the existence of outstanding debt provides management with a structurally induced incentive to shift investment policy toward more volatile assets and thereby increase the value of equity. Moreover, the incentive is stronger for higher-leverage firms because the magnitude of the value transfer is larger.

To analyze the effect of a change in financing policy, consider a firm with a face amount of 50 in outstanding debt and a low-leverage policy. Suppose that it now shifts to a high-leverage policy by issuing an additional 50 in face amount of new debt (with identical

Table 4. Value transfers between debt and equity: changes in investment and financing policies

A. Increase in asset volatility: firm exchanges type 1 assets for type 2 assets

	Low-leverage policy		High-leverage policy	
	Debt	Equity	Debt	Equity
Initial Value	50	60	86	24
Final Value	48	62	82	28
Value Change	(2)	2	(4)	4
Gain (Loss)	(2)	2	(4)	4
% Gain (Loss)	(4.0)%	3.3%	(4.7)%	16.7%

B. Increase in leverage: firm exchanges debt for equity

	Type 1 assets		Type 2 assets	
	Debt	Equity	Debt	Equity
Initial Value	50	60	48	62
Final Value	86	24	82	28
Value Change	36	(36)	34	(34)
Debt Issued	—	43	—	41
Dilution	(43)	—	(41)	—
Gain (Loss)	(7)	7	(7)	7
% Gain (Loss)	(14.0)%	11.7%	(14.6)%	11.3%

C. Both increase in asset volatility and increase in leverage

	Debt	Equity
Initial Value	50	60
Final Value	82	28
Value Change	32	(32)
Debt Issued	—	41
Dilution	(41)	—
Gain (Loss)	(9)	9
% Gain (Loss)	(18.0)%	15.0%

terms and *pari passu* standing to the old debt) to its equityholders as a dividend. This transaction is economically equivalent to selling the new debt and using the proceeds to either pay a cash dividend or repurchase shares. Another equivalent alternative is to exchange the new debt on a pro rata basis for a portion of the outstanding shares. After the new debt is distributed, the market values of both the old debt and the equity will be lower than they were before the change in financing policy. However, the loss in equity value is more than offset by the value of the distribution to the equityholders which, in this case, equals half the post-distribution market value of the firm's total debt. Thus, as shown in part B of table 4, the equityholders gain from an unanticipated increase in leverage at the expense of the old debtholders.

Part C of table 4 summarizes the value transfer from simultaneous and unanticipated changes in both investment and financing policies that lead to increases in asset value volatility and leverage. Since management, acting in the best interests of equityholders, has an incentive to transfer value from debtholders to equityholders, debtholders look to general law, regulation, and specific contractual restrictions ("covenants") for protection. As our analysis suggests, we do find real-world covenants that attempt to restrict major changes in business activities (asset types), distributions to equityholders, and increases in leverage. Since these restrictions are incentive-incompatible with manager objectives, the debtholders must expend resources to monitor the firm's compliance and to pursue compensation and penalties if violations occur. As already noted, an understanding of these incentive incompatibilities is essential in the analysis of loan guarantees and deposit insurance.

2.7. Junk bonds, public policy, and the feasibility of "no-fault" default

Impact on the health of the financial system and the imposition of losses of real resources, as well as distortions of the allocation of resources in the nonfinancial sectors of the economy, broadly cover the public policy concerns surrounding high-leverage financing of corporations. Included within these are potential corporate tax revenue losses from interest deductions and the losses from government bailouts and loan guarantees.

On the impact of junk bonds on the riskiness of the financial system, our analysis demonstrates that leverage-induced increases in risk and volatility of stock and corporate bond returns does not imply that institutional investors' total portfolios have become any riskier. Moreover, while junk bonds can be far more risky than investment-grade bonds, they are less risky than equity in comparable asset-type firms. Specific financial institutions that shift their portfolios from less-volatile securities to hold junk bonds will, of course, increase the riskiness of their assets. If failure of these institutions would lead to a government bailout, then such shifts in asset risk should be of public concern. But, as the analysis of loan guarantees will show, this issue is not specific to junk bonds.

Financial institutions as investors in junk bonds will clearly be more vulnerable if they do not understand the risk characteristics of these bonds or if they cannot rapidly and efficiently seize ownership and control of assets in the event of default. Beyond education and disclosure requirements, public regulation and policy can do little to protect against incompetent managers who do not understand the risk properties of their investments or who have not had the foresight to develop the structure and expertise necessary either to manage efficiently or dispose of assets of the type that might be acquired as the result of default on bonds held in the portfolio. However, regulations and accounting conventions, such as differential capital requirements and book-value measurements for capital, can create distorting incentives for financial institutions not to seize assets when they should. Thus, policy on junk bonds should focus on minimizing the costs of implementing contractual obligations, particularly the transfer of ownership from equityholders to creditors.

Our analysis has addressed in part the concerns about widespread liquidations destroying going-concern values and production activities in the nonfinancial sector. This analysis did, however, assume that assets were immediately transferred to the debtholders in the event of default and that there are no costs to bankruptcy, either direct, as with legal fees, or indirect, as with disruptions of the operations of the firm. As we know, managers in the real world can place the firm in Chapter 11 bankruptcy and thereby protect the firm from creditor claims for a protracted period of time. This option opens the door to considerable bargaining activities—both before formal default and after, with "workouts" and swap offers of new financial packages for the existing debt. Hence, unlike the perfect "me-first" rules for debt assumed in our hypothetical example, neither debtholders nor equityholders at the time of their investments know with confidence their state-contingent payment schedules. This "zero-sum" uncertainty about the sharing rules for the firm should, ex ante, make both the debt and equity securities less desirable.

I do not know, as an empirical matter, whether these dead-weight losses and distortions of risk-sharing patterns are important problems. However, if they are, there is a solution, namely, "no-fault" default. To illustrate, consider a hypothetical company that owns operating assets and is financed entirely by equity (and trade debt, if necessary). Call the shares of this company *Op. A.* To generate the junk-bond and leveraged-equity patterns for investors, create a holding company whose only assets are all of Op. A shares and finance it by issuing a unit package of two securities called *A.1* and *A.2*, one unit for each share of Op. A owned. The owners of A.2 are entitled to vote to elect the management of the holding company and are also entitled in one year to choose one of three actions: exchange their security plus $100 for one share of Op. A or exchange their security plus one unit of A.1 for one share of Op. A, or do nothing, in which case the security becomes worthless. Owners of A.1 are entitled in one year to a payment of either $100 or one share of Op. A, where the choice of payment is made by the management of the company.

Straightforward analysis reveals that, if the value of Op. A shares is $100 or more in a year's time, then A.2 owners will all choose to exchange their security plus $100 for one share of Op. A. With all shares of Op. A acquired by these owners, the management of the holding company will have exactly enough cash to pay the A.1 owners $100 for each unit. If instead, the Op. A shares in one year are worth less than $100, then the A.2 owners will simply do nothing. The holding company will have no cash and will distribute one share of Op. A for each unit of A.1. In symbols, if V denotes the value of one share of Op. A, the contingent payoff schedules for A.1 and A.2 are $\min[100,V]$ and $\max[0,V-100]$, respectively. If, for instance, Op. A's share price were identical to type 1 assets in table 2, then the contingent payout schedule to A.1 is identical to the debt for the high-leverage policy and the contingent payout to A.2 is identical to the equity.

Note, however, that nowhere were formal bankruptcy proceedings required.[25] Thus, the trade debt of the operating firm is in no way jeopardized by the extensive leverage of the holding company. Moreover, although corporate control of the operating company would change from the A.2 owners to the A.1 owners, this change is no different in impact on the operating company than a change in owners if it were all-equity financed. Hence, the event of default has no disruptive effect on the operating business and does not precipitate liquidation.

Creation of securities like A.1 and A.2 is entirely feasible, and indeed they exist today. The "Prime" and "Score" securities of the Americus Trusts traded on the American Stock Exchange provide A.1 and A.2 type securities on some of the best known operating companies in the United States. The "Super Shares" securities created by Leland O'Brien and Rubinstein Associates provide the equivalent of junk bonds and leveraged equity on the Standard & Poor's 500 portfolio of stocks. Furthermore, the "fully-covered" call writing strategy, in which an investor buys a share of stock and writes a call option against it, produces a contingent payoff pattern at expiration equal to the minimum of either the stock price or the exercise price, a pattern identical to the A.1 security, which receives in value the minimum of either the Op. A stock price or $100. Therefore, every time a call option expires unexercised, we have the economic equivalent of no-fault default, and such expirations do not appear to have any effect on the underlying companies.

If potential bankruptcy costs for junk bonds loom large, why then haven't these alternative no-fault structures superseded them? One possibility is the corporate tax code and regulations restricting securities that various financial institutions can hold. Under current tax and regulatory rules, the A.1 security would not qualify as debt. Hence, payments to A.1 could not be deducted as interest against corporate income. Institutions that regulations permit to hold only debt instruments can invest in junk bonds, but could not invest in A.1 securities, although they are functionally equivalent. There are, of course, other possible explanations for the absence of those structures that have nothing to do with taxes and regulation. Nevertheless, this possibility provides an instance for application of functional analysis to regulatory issues. To encourage disruptive and costly bankruptcies is surely an unintended consequence of the tax code. An even greater paradox is regulation designed to protect institutions against excessive risk-taking that leads to the current junk-bond design, instead of the functionally equivalent but lower-risk design of no-fault default securities.

3. Loan guarantees

3.1. Introduction

Third-party guarantees of financial performance on loans and other debt-related contracts are widely used throughout the United States and in international financial systems. Commercial banks, AAA-rated insurance companies, and, on occasion, sovereigns offer guarantees in return for fees on a broad spectrum of financial instruments ranging from traditional letters of credit to interest rate and currency swaps and even put warrants on stock indices. More specialized firms sell guarantees of interest and principal payments on tax-exempt municipal bonds. Parent corporations routinely guarantee the debt obligations of their subsidiaries. The federal and provincial governments of Canada have in the past made extensive use of loan guarantees to subsidize local corporations.

The U.S. government, either directly or through its agencies, is almost certainly the largest provider of financial guarantees in the world. I need hardly mention that the most important of its liability guarantees, both economically and politically, is deposit insurance. However, guarantees are also used extensively elsewhere. In the corporate sector, the government has guaranteed loans to small businesses, and on occasion, as with Lockheed Aircraft and the Chrysler Corporation, it has done so for very large businesses. Established in 1980, the United States Synthetic Fuels Corporation was empowered to grant loan guarantees to assist the financing of commercial projects that involve the development of alternative fuel technologies. The Pension Benefit Guarantee Corporation (PBGC) provides limited insurance of corporate pension-plan benefits.[26] Residential mortgages and farm and student loans are examples of noncorporate obligations that the government has guaranteed.

Both private-market and government guarantees have great importance in international and domestic finance. Government guarantees, however, warrant special attention. As noted in section 2, with respect to the PBGC, the issue of de facto or implicit guarantees in contrast to contractual or explicit guarantees is far more significant for government than the private sector. Indeed, "What are or should be the limits of government obligations to provide insurance?" is a question bound to be touched on by all the articles in this issue. As we know, there are "off balance sheet" transactions for private companies and there are government expenditures that are not reflected either as current expenses or as additions to liabilities. Guarantees are prime examples of "off budget/off balance sheet" liabilities. If, for example, government provides a cash subsidy to a firm which then uses it to purchase a loan guarantee for its debt, the subsidy is charged to the budget (or is booked as a liability amortized over multiple years). But, if the government provides the guarantee directly, there is no current or future budget impact, unless and until the loan defaults and the creditors are paid. To put this practice into perspective, the treatment is analogous to an insurance company giving away an insurance policy and not booking this transfer of tangible value as either an expense or a liability, unless or until damages are collected on the policy.

The current accounting practice for government guarantees thus provides a powerful incentive to use them for subsidies or transfers. Issuing guarantees has no immediate impact on either the measured budget deficit or the stock of government liabilities. Losses, if any, will occur (often far) in the future. Since the guarantee is not purchased, and since there is no requirement to book a liability or expense, there is neither a price nor a need for an appraisal of the guarantee. Without either, it is difficult to assess the size of the subsidy, a characteristic which some may see as providing additional noneconomic flexibility. In their analysis of the Canadian experience, Baldwin, Lessard, and Mason (1983) provide an excellent discussion of how a guarantee system can go out of control as a result of such "off-budget" incentives. The thrift bailout crisis is, of course, a prime exemplifying case in the United States. Despite those recent experiences, a prospective view suggests that there could be pressures to expand again the use of government loan guarantees, especially in the international financial arena. With ongoing concerns over budget deficits, some may see loan guarantees as an ideal way to provide foreign assistance, especially to the recently opened Eastern European countries, without seeming to pay for it.

With these brief background remarks as motivation, we turn now to a functional analysis of loan guarantees. As in the analysis of junk bonds, we use a simple hypothetical example to identify the factors that influence the value of guarantees and to highlight the types of expertise and controls essential for the successful operation of any guarantor, whether private or government. We then use actual market prices to show that the values of loan guarantees (and hence, the magnitude of the liability they represent to the guarantors) are large. We relate this generic analysis of guarantees to the specifics of policy issues in a concluding brief discussion.

3.2. Analyzing loan guarantees: a hypothetical example

In our analysis of below-investment-grade debt in section 2, we developed the various conflicts of interest between debtholders and equityholders and, from these, derived some guidelines for controls and monitoring by debtholders. Once such debt is guaranteed, the economic responsibility for monitoring and imposing controls on the firm's activities shifts from the firm's debtholders to the guarantor. As with the junk bond analysis, the intent here is to provide a basic functional understanding of the properties of guarantees. Thus, we do so by building on the hypothetical example developed in that section. Again, for emphasis, the properties illustrated by this simple example are not pathological.

The asset investment alternatives and debt financing choices available to the firm are the same as in tables 1, 2, and 3. We add now a guarantor that issues a loan guarantee that insures the promised payment on the debt. The mechanism is that in the event that the firm does not pay the promised amount on the debt, the guarantor pays the full amount to the debtholders and seizes the assets of the firm as a (partial) recovery. If, as we assume, the guarantor will not default on its obligation, then a package of the firm's (non-guaranteed) debt plus a loan guarantee is economically equivalent to a default-free or riskless debt claim with the same promised terms as the non-guaranteed debt. Thus, the guaranteed debt's market price will equal the price of a U.S. government bond of the same terms.

Table 5, panel A displays the price and payoff patterns of debt, equity, and the loan guarantee when the firm in our hypothetical example chooses a high-leverage financing strategy and holds type 1 assets. Table 5, panel B provides the same analysis for the case where the firm holds type 2 assets. The analysis assumes that the guarantee has already been issued and thus the debt sells at its default-free price. Following the convention that

Table 5. Value of debt, equity, and loan guarantee for different asset choices (promised payment on debt = 100)

	A. Asset type 1						
	Value of firm				Guarantor		
Condition of economy	Assets	Loan guarantee	Debt	Equity	Assets seized	(Payment made to debt)	(Net loss)
Very Weak	50	50	100	0	50	(100)	(50)
Weak	80	20	100	0	80	(100)	(20)
Normal	110	0	100	10	0	0	0
Strong	140	0	100	40	0	0	0
Very Strong	170	0	100	70	0	0	0
Average (Current Price)	110	14	100	24	26	(40)	(14)
Standard Deviation	42	20	0	27	33	49	20
	B. Asset type 2						
Very Weak	40	60	100	0	40	(100)	(60)
Weak	70	30	100	0	70	(100)	(30)
Normal	110	0	100	10	0	0	0
Strong	150	0	100	50	0	0	0
Very Strong	180	0	100	80	0	0	0
Average (Current Price)	110	18	100	28	22	(40)	(18)
Standard Deviation	51	24	0	32	29	49	24

the value of the firm equals the sum of the values of its liabilities, debt plus equity, we have that the value of the firm equals the value of its operating assets plus the value of the loan guarantee. In table 5, we also evaluate the contingent liability to the guarantor as the result of issuing the guarantee. We do not show as an asset of the guarantor, the fee if any, paid by the firm for the guarantee.

By comparison of tables 2 and 3 with table 5, the patterns of equity prices and payoffs are the same, with or without the guarantee. Although the event of default affects in one case the debtholders and in the other the guarantor, the economic impact on the equity-holders is the same. The value of the debt (and thus the firm) is larger than in tables 2 and 3 by the amount of the value of the guarantee. If the guarantee is given as an unexpected subsidy to the firm, the beneficiary of the subsidy will depend on whether the debt was previously issued ("old" debt) or not ("new" debt). In the case of the firm with type 1 assets, from table 2, the current values of the (non-guaranteed) debt and equity are 86 and 24, respectively. After the guarantee is given, the debt jumps in value to 100 and the equity value remains unchanged. Old debt gains the entire benefit. If, instead, the firm were initially all-equity financed with a value of 110, then the receipt of the guarantee would allow the firm to distribute debt worth 100 (instead of 86) to its equityholders and with the same post-distribution equity value of 24, the total value to equityholders becomes 124. In either case, the subsidy value given by the guarantor is 14.

By inspection of table 5, both guarantor and equityholder have as a common interest that the firm "do well." But, this common interest is the same as between (non-guaranteed) debtholders and equityholders in section 2.6: namely, the guarantor's losses are quite sensitive to how poorly the firm does and insensitive to how well the firm does, whereas the sensitivity of equity is the reverse.

Table 5 can also be used to analyze the effect of changing firm investment policy after the issue of the guarantee. If the firm were to exchange its type 1 assets with a value of 110 for more volatile type 2 assets of equal value, the effect is to move from panel A to panel B in table 5. The value of debt remains unchanged because its payments are guaranteed in either case. The value of the loan guarantee increases by 4 for a 28.6 percent increase, and this causes an increase in equity value of 16.7 percent. Managers of the firm, repre-senting equityholders' interests, thus have an incentive to increase the volatility of the firm's portfolio of assets. However, the induced increase in the value of the loan guarantee to the firm represents a corresponding loss to the guarantor because its liability increases (without any offsetting fee compensation). Hence, this incentive-incompatibility between managers of the firm and the guarantor on the choice of the risk of the firm's portfolio of assets implies that for the loan guarantee to be a viable contract arrangement, the guarantor must set bounds or other controls that limit the asset choices available to the firm, and this is the case whether the guarantor is a private-sector firm or the government.

In the context of thrifts and government deposit insurance, we have, from even this simple example, a clear ex ante prediction of the impact of relaxing restrictions and widening the menu of assets that thrifts can hold. Our analysis predicts that when choos-ing from among asset portfolios with equal current value, rational, well-informed man-agers, acting in the interest of equityholders, will tend to select the portfolio with the greatest volatility in its returns. By continuity, they would, if necessary, even pay a premium for volatility and choose a portfolio with somewhat lower current value in exchange for more volatility. But, expanding the list of assets that can be held cannot decrease, and will in general increase, the maximum amount of portfolio volatility available at each level of current portfolio value. Hence, such an expansion, ceteris paribus, would be expected to cause an increase in the volatility of thrifts' portfolios. Without offsetting increases in the deposit insurance fees charged, this contractually induced reaction to expansion of permissible asset choices causes an increase in thrift equity value, and a corresponding loss to the government deposit insurer through an increase in liability value. Note that this predicted result occurs even if every thrift manager is neither incompetent nor dishonest.

There were surely some thrift managers in the 1980s who chose more volatile asset portfolios because they believed that higher promised yields implied higher expected returns and profits. Indeed, there were perhaps some regulators with thoughts along the same lines and who further concluded that this increased expected profitability would lead to healthier thrifts and thereby reduce the burden on the deposit insurer.[27] As our analysis demonstrates, such beliefs were not on a sound ex ante foundation. Misperception 1 in section 2.3 on the analysis of junk bonds demonstrates that higher promised yield is not a reliable indicator of higher expected return. Furthermore, *even if* these assets had higher expected returns, if these higher expected returns were only fair compensation for bearing greater risk, then the same result obtains from the shift to a more volatile portfolio of assets: the value of equity increases and the liability of the deposit insurer increases.

The intuition as to why higher expected profitability achieved in this way leads to losses to the guarantor comes from examining the contingent payoff patterns in table 5 and the discussion in section 2.6. Higher expected returns and higher volatility tend to increase the size of asset returns when things go well but also produce lower asset returns when things go poorly. Even if the magnitude of increase in good times is larger than the magnitude of the decrease in bad times, so that the average or expected return increases, the asymmetry of the loan guarantor's contingent liability structure does not capture this benefit. Instead, the guarantor suffers the larger losses in bad times and receives none of the additional gains in good times. Recall the characterization of this asymmetric pattern in our discussion of junk bonds: debtholders and loan guarantors worry about the downside of the firm, and equityholders focus on its upside potential. The only possible offset to this ex ante loss to the guarantor would be if the expanded menu permitted thrifts to buy "undervalued" assets (e.g., buy for $100 an asset worth $110). But, there is absolutely no reason to believe, either ex ante or ex post, that the assets available to thrifts were in general underpriced.

One way that loan guarantors can reduce the value of their loan-guarantee liabilities is to combine more frequent monitoring of the firm with the contractual right to seize the firm's assets (or its equity interest) whenever the value of assets is below the value of its guaranteed debt. Indeed, in a frictionless world, with only liquid assets and no surveillance costs, the guarantor could continuously monitor the value of the firm's assets in relation to its debt value. It could thereby avoid any losses by simply seizing and selling the assets before the insolvency point is reached. As we know, this is the basic model of operation for stock and bond margin loans. As we also know, deposit insurance does not operate this way, even though the insurer has the right to seize before formal default on the debt. Nevertheless, we can use our simple example to analyze the effect of more frequent monitoring.

Suppose, for instance, that at six months through the year, it becomes known whether the economy will experience a boom by year-end. A *boom* is defined as either the strong or very strong states of the economy occurring (cf. the listing in table 5). Maintaining the equal-probability feature for each possible state of the economy, we posit that given a boom will occur, the probabilities are one out of two for strong and one out of two for very strong. Given that a boom will not occur, the probabilities are one out of three each for normal, weak, and very weak. Moreover, viewed from the beginning of the year, the probability of a boom is two out of five and of no boom is three out of five.

It follows for a firm with type 1 assets that if it is learned at six months that a boom will occur, then the revised price of the assets is $\frac{1}{2} \times 140 + \frac{1}{2} \times 170$ or 155, which is larger than the firm's debt of 100. Moreover, since the guarantor only has to pay if at year-end, the economy is in the weak or very weak states, the revised value of the loan guarantee (i.e., the guarantor's liability) is 0. If, however, it is learned at six months that a boom state will not occur at year-end, then the asset value will decline from its original 110 to 80, which is below the value of the guaranteed debt. Table 6 displays the analysis, with panel A the case where the guarantor does not seize the equity and panel B the case where it does. The essential difference is that without seizure, equity has a positive value of $3\frac{1}{3}$, whereas with seizure, equity becomes worthless, the $3\frac{1}{3}$ value now accruing to the guarantor.[28]

If the guarantor does not seize when it should, then there is no purpose for monitoring the firm before year-end, and so the valuation of the guarantor's liability at the beginning of the year is 14, the same as in table 5. If the guarantor does seize, then the price of the loan guarantee at the beginning of the year is $.4 \times 0 + .6 \times 20 = 12$. Hence, more frequent monitoring in this example reduces the liability of the loan guarantee by more than 14 percent.

Table 6. Effect of more-frequent monitoring on cost of loan guarantee (promised payment on debt = 100)

If at six months it is determined that there will be no economic boom at year-end and:

A. Guarantor does not seize the equity interest

Condition of economy	Value of firm				Guarantor		
	Assets	Loan guarantee	Debt	Equity	Assets seized	(Payment made to debt)	(Net loss)
Very Weak	50	50	100	0	50	(100)	(50)
Weak	80	20	100	0	80	(100)	(20)
Normal	110	0	100	10	0	0	0
Average (Current Price)	80	23⅓	100	3⅓	43⅓	(66⅔)	(23⅓)
B. Guarantor does seize the equity interest							
Very Weak	50	50	100	0	50	(100)	(50)
Weak	80	20	100	0	80	(100)	(20)
Normal	110	(10)	100	0	10	0	10
Average (Current Price)	80	20	100	0	46⅔	(66⅔)	(20)

The seizure of equity interest and realization of value for the guarantor in table 6 can be accomplished in three ways: (1) seize the equity, resell it for 3⅓, and use the proceeds to reduce the net losses to 16⅔ and 46⅔ if the weak or very weak state occurs at year-end and to add a small gain of 3⅓ if the normal state obtains; (2) seize the equity and hold it, the losses are not reduced in the weak or very weak states, but the gain is now 10 if the normal state occurs and is an offset to other loan guarantee losses; (3) seize the equity, pay off the debt, and sell the assets,[29] which produces a sure loss of 20, but no further exposure to loss. All three have the same ex ante, actuarial value, but each has a quite different ex post payoff pattern to the guarantor. Each also requires a different expertise: (1) requires that the guarantor has the skills to place equity shares quickly and at low cost; (2) requires an ability to manage the type of assets held by the firm; (3) requires the facility to sell assets of the type held by the firm. An example of (1) might be the transfer of equity of one bank to another by the deposit insurer. For guarantors of firms with very illiquid real estate projects with considerable going-concern values, (2) might be the best route. Route (3) might be the best for junk bond assets, selling them as either a standard package or in strips as a collateralized bond obligation.

Table 6 also demonstrates the error in reasoning (and the cost) of not seizing equity interest early because there is a chance that conditions will change and the guarantor will not have to pay. For example, a comparison of (3) with no seizing has a sure loss of 20 against a one in three chance that the economy will be in a normal condition by year-end with no loss to the guarantor, a one in three chance of a weak state with a loss of 20, and a one in three chance of a loss of 50 in the very weak state. Note, however, that the no-seizure policy is dominated by either early-seizure strategy (1) or (2), since each actually produces positive cash to the guarantor in the one state in which it would not have to pay under the no-seizure strategy.

In sum, guarantors, whether public or private, remain viable only by controlling losses. As we have seen, there are essentially three types of controls: restrictions on the assets that can be held by the firm whose debt is guaranteed; monitoring the value of assets more frequently and/or more carefully and seizing assets swiftly and efficiently; charging adequate fees for the guarantees. There are obviously many different combinations of the three that can produce a viable guarantee system, and the most efficient combination will surely depend on the individual application and will change with changing economic conditions.[30]

It is, however, evident that if the guarantor weakens the restrictions on assets that can be held, decreases the frequency and resources spent on monitoring, and does not change the fees charged for the guarantee, then the losses to the guarantor will rise. For instance, in our hypothetical example, a guarantee of 100 of one-year debt on a firm restricted to type 1 assets and monitored at six-month intervals has an initial value of 12, which is the "break-even" fee to be charged by the guarantor. If the firm is permitted to switch to type 2 assets (which are about 19 percent more volatile than type 1) and if the guarantor eliminates monitoring and seizure of assets at six months, then the break-even cost of the loan guarantee increases by 50 percent to 18. Thus, with these shifts and no fee changes, a loan guarantor goes from viable to vastly underfunded. Although fee increases were eventually introduced, this description is roughly that for thrift deposit insurance during the early to mid-1980s.

3.3. Estimating the value of loan guarantees

Unlike stock and bond market prices, price data on different types of loan guarantees are not readily available, although there are some price quotations available for credit enhancement of commercial paper and swap agreements. Attempts to estimate the value of loan guarantees from historical loss experience suffer from the same problem of extreme negative skewness as the estimation of junk bond returns in section 2.3. In our hypothetical examples in tables 5 and 6, there are, on average, no losses to the guarantor 60 percent of the time. With an ongoing one in five chance of the big-loss, very weak state occurring each year, there is nevertheless about a one in three chance of no occurrences in any five-year period. Hence, the sample estimate of loss experience on loan guarantees is quite sensitive to the particular number of these relatively rare events that occur during the period. It is thus no simple matter to estimate accurately the expected loss rate by using historical experience.

There is a substantial and sophisticated academic literature on estimating the value of loan guarantees and deposit insurance.[31] However, to provide a sense of the private-sector market prices for loan guarantees, we choose a simpler route. As discussed at the outset, the price of nonguaranteed debt plus the price of a loan guarantee for the debt is equal to the price of default-free debt with the same terms. It follows as a matter of subtraction that the value of the loan guarantee is equal to the difference in the price of the two bonds. There are many corporate bonds traded that are not guaranteed. Hence, by estimating the prices for those bonds if they were default-free and subtracting, we have implied prices for the guarantees.

This analysis is carried out for a sample of 10 bonds and the results are presented in table 7. The selection criteria were nothing more than picking lower-grade bonds issued by companies with names that are probably recognizable by most. On the selection date,

Table 7. Estimates of loan guarantee values derived from corporate bond prices (value of loan guarantee = guaranteed debt price − nonguaranteed debt price)

		Corporate bond prices		Loan guarantee value	
Company	Years to maturity	With guarantee[1]	No guarantee[2]	Implied price	Percentage of no-guarantee price
Continental Airlines	6	$109.12	$66.00	$43.12	65.3%
MGM/UA	6	118.24	63.38	54.86	86.6
Mesa Capital	9	127.36	95.50	31.86	33.4
Navistar	14	100.00	89.00	11.00	12.4
Pan Am	14	147.23	58.63	88.60	151.1
RJR	11	88.80	70.88	17.92	25.3
RJR Nabisco	11	141.35	76.88	64.47	83.9
Revlon	20	117.25	80.75	36.50	45.2
Union Carbide	9	102.89	92.25	10.64	11.5
Warner Communications	23	124.11	97.00	27.11	27.9

1. Assumes UST yield curve flat at 9 percent and no adjustment for call provisions. Guarantee covers both principal amount and coupons.
2. Closing market price, *Wall Street Journal*, 5-11-90; no adjustment for cumulative interest.

May 10, 1990, none of the bonds was in default. The estimates of their corresponding default-free prices are derived by discounting promised coupon and principal payments at 9 percent, which approximates the U.S. Treasury bond and note rate on the selection date. Since the purpose of the table is to provide an indicated range of implied market prices for guarantees, no adjustments are made for either cumulative interest or call provisions. Such adjustments would not change the central point that the prices of loan guarantees can be quite large. Pan Am stands out as an extreme with a $89 price for the guarantee which is 150 percent of the bond's nonguaranteed price of $59. However, as indicated by the other entries in table 7, loan guarantee prices in excess of 50 percent of the bond price without the guarantee are not uncommon.

Not only are loan guarantee values large but so are their variations over time. To demonstrate this volatility, we present in table 8 implied guarantee prices derived for the same sample of bonds as in table 7 using bond market prices on August 2, 1990. During the approximately 12-week period, U.S. Treasury interest rates fell by about 40 basis points to 8.60 percent; the value of the guarantees declined for three companies, increased for six companies, and was unchanged for one company. The percentage changes range from a 18.8 percent decline for Union Carbide to a 33.5 percent increase for Pan Am. The average for the sample is a 5.1 percent increase. The cross-sectional standard deviation of the changes is 14.9 percent.

3.4. Loan guarantees and policy issues

Our functional analysis of loan guarantees by necessity makes enormous abstractions. Nevertheless, it does suggest some thoughts on policy.[32] Although fraud and managerial incompetence may be major factors in the cost of the thrift bailout, too much focus on these could mask other, more structural problems.[33] As we have seen, the incentive

Table 8. Changes in loan guarantee values derived from corporate bond prices (May 10, 1990 to August 2, 1990; value of loan guarantee = guaranteed debt price − nonguaranteed debt price)

Company	Years to maturity	Loan guarantee value		Change in loan guarantee value	
		Implied price[1] 5-10-90	Implied price[2] 8-2-90	Dollar change	Percentage change
Continental Airlines	6	$43.12	$49.07	$5.95	13.8%
MGM/UA	6	54.86	61.79	6.93	12.6
Mesa Capital	9	31.86	28.77	(3.09)	(9.7)
Navistar	14	11.00	12.59	1.59	14.5
Pan Am	14	88.60	118.27	29.67	33.5
RJR	11	17.92	17.89	(.03)	0.0
RJR Nabisco	11	64.47	56.43	(8.04)	(12.5)
Revlon	20	36.50	41.29	4.79	13.1
Union Carbide	9	10.64	8.64	(2.00)	(18.8)
Warner Communications	23	27.11	28.24	1.13	4.2

1. As computed in table 7.
2. Closing bond price, Wall Street Journal, 8-3-90; no adjustment for cumulative interest. Assumes UST yield curve flat at 8.60 percent and no adjustment for call provisions. Guarantee covers both principal amount and coupons.

structure surrounding guarantees can lead honest and competent recipients to undertake unintended and undesirable actions in response to changes in the rules governing guarantees. Reductions in asset restrictions and monitoring, a lack of willingness or ability to seize and dispose of assets rapidly and efficiently, and inadequate premiums for deposit guarantees are also important contributors to the cost of the bailout, and these were predictable in advance. If those structural problems are not addressed, the thrift problem can happen again. A parenthetical remark on rhetoric: if taken as *given* that the government requires and provides deposit insurance, then reductions or increases in asset restrictions and monitoring of thrifts should not be classified as acts of deregulation or reregulation. As we have seen, all guarantors, whether government or private-sector providers in a competitive market, must apply those same controls to remain viable.

Prospectively, our analysis points to potential problems from other types of loan guarantees under the current system. As indicated by table 7, the value of a loan guarantee can be a significant fraction of the size of the loan. Furthermore, as shown in table 8, the magnitude of exposure for the guarantor can change substantially in a rather short period of time. Systematic and realistic appraisals for both the initial liability *and* subsequent material changes in value for government-issued guarantees would provide important information for monitoring the guarantee system. Disclosure of the values of guarantees reduces incentives to use them as "hidden" subsidies. To control their use further, these appraised values could be used to treat grants of guarantees as equivalent to a cash transaction for budget purposes with the guarantee carried as a booked liability of the government. Along these same lines of reasoning, it is appropriate to impose similar valuation and accounting treatments of private-sector guarantees issued by institutions with liabilities that are guaranteed by the government.

Notes

1. See R. K. Merton (1987) for the development of the strategic research site concept as a general analytical tool. Examples of other topics in finance not addressed here but that could also serve this function are the stock market and macroeconomic performance (Fischer and Merton, 1984); facts and misperceptions surrounding the cost of capital differences between Japan and the United States (Ando and Auerbach, 1988, 1990; Kester and Luehrman, 1989, 1990); and speculative market efficiency, excess volatility, and economic performance (Duffee, Kupiec, and White, 1990; Grossman, 1988; Grossman and Miller, 1988; Harris, Sofianos, and Shapiro, 1990; King, Sentana, and Wadhwani, 1990; Merton, 1987a, 1987b; Poterba and Summers, 1986; Roll, 1989; Ross, 1989a; Schwert, 1989a, 1989b; Shiller, 1989; Stiglitz, 1989; Stoll and Whaley, 1988). Summaries of recent legislative and regulatory proposals surrounding these issues are provided in Becker, Gira, and Underhill (1989). See also *Market Volatility and Investor Confidence: Report to the Board of Directors of the New York Stock Exchange, Inc.,* June 7, 1990.
2. Various issues and perspectives on financial innovations are represented in Allen (1989), Allen and Gale (1988), Benston and Smith (1976), Black and Scholes (1974), Bodie (1989), Dewing (1934), Finnerty (1985, 1988), Folkerts-Landau and Mathieson (1988), Friedman (1980), Hakansson (1976), Kwast (1986), Merton (1989, 1990), Miller (1986), Mishkin (1990), Silber (1975, 1983), Smith and Taggart (1989), Tufano (1989), and Van Horne (1985).
3. See the comprehensive listings in Finnerty (1988), Mishkin (1990), and Tufano (1989).
4. For examples see Adler and Dumas (1983), Branson and Henderson (1984), Grauer and Hakansson (1987), Perold and Schulman (1988), Solnik (1988), and Solnik and Noetzlin (1982).

5. Cf. Tobin (1978) on using controls to avoid the hardships caused by large movements of capital in and out of a country. See Cole and Obstfeld (1989) and Brennan and Solnik (1989) for attempts to measure the welfare losses from capital controls by using capital flow data.

6. See Bicksler and Chen (1986), Hull (1989, ch. 11), and Smith, Smithson, and Wakeman (1986, 1988) for discussion, analysis, and further references on swap contracts.

7. Shares are assumed to be freely traded on the domestic exchange, and they are therefore priced to earn a competitive rate of return to the marginal investor. If the marginal investor is a domestic investor with no access to world stock markets, then the welfare loss is a higher cost of capital for domestic shares (and lower stock prices) than with an open economy because some of the risk perceived as systematic by constrained domestic investors would be diversifiable from a world-investor perspective. If the marginal investor is a world investor, then the welfare loss is the uncompensated excess volatility from inefficient diversification borne by domestic investors. The transfer of risk by the swap addresses both cases.

8. For incentive reasons, owners of domestic shares should have an economic interest in the firms. Hence, a significant amount but not all of the domestic risk can be swapped to non-voting foreign investors.

9. See also Finnerty (1985, 1988) and Folkerts-Landau and Mathieson (1988).

10. No credit is given to innovations that improve welfare by thwarting regulations that would otherwise impose more cost than benefit on society, because such welfare losses can, at least in principle, be eliminated more efficiently by simply changing the offending regulations.

11. See Merton (1989, pp. 237–247; 1990, pp. 441–447) for descriptions and analyses of these trading strategies as part of a broader theory of production for financial intermediaries.

12. This observation and the analogy to follow are taken from Merton (1989, 1990).

13. See Fischer (1983), Merton (1983a, 1983b, 1990, ch. 18) and Munnell and Grolnic (1986).

14. As I have discussed at length elsewhere (1979, 1989, 1990), controlling default risk for customer-held liabilities of financial intermediaries is a key element in the theory of efficient intermediation and economic performance. Furthermore, much the same point applies for the integrity of markets that trade standardized instruments, such as options, futures, and swaps. Thus, in this specific sense, the theory supports the belief that credit risk is a major macro issue for the international financial markets.

15. I doubt that many oppose the abstract concept of a level playing field. Concrete implementation of that concept is, however, quite another matter. If, for example, economies of scale or scope provide advantages to institutional investors over retail investors in the stock market, should we impose additional costs on the institutions to offset their comparative advantage? Or, if other countries' corporate tax rates are lower than in the United States and thereby foreign financial institutions have lower pre-tax costs of capital, then do we either impose incremental "tariffs" on these institutions or provide subsidies to their U.S. counterparts in order to create a level playing field?

16. Although the data are not drawn from the financial-service industry, Porter's (1990) recent analysis of the efficiency tradeoffs between competition and collaboration might also prove useful in addressing that question for international financial-market regulation.

17. Jensen (1986, 1988, 1989) provides discussion and additional references on the importance of junk bonds in the restructuring of corporations. Friedman (1990) explores the potential influence on macro and monetary policy from the enormous increase in corporate debt in the 1980s.

18. Although banks are not permitted to hold junk bonds directly in their portfolios, they can own them as a member of a partnership, at least at the holding company level. Moreover, some of the direct bank loans made to finance corporate restructurings and takeovers appear to share many of the essential risk characteristics of junk bonds. Thus, as with thrifts, the government is also exposed to default risk on junk-bond-type assets through its insurance for bank deposits.

19. See Altman (1989), Altman and Nammacher (1987), Asquith, Mullins, and Wolff (1989), Blume, Keim, and Patel (1989), Kaplan and Stein (1990), and Weinstein (1987) for empirical evaluations of historical returns on junk bonds.

20. For a more complex and realistic contingent-claims model of risky debt pricing that exhibits the same properties as the example presented here, see Merton (1974, 1990, ch. 12).

21. It should be underscored that in a structural sense, it is the state of the *firm* and not the *economy* which is directly linked to the decision to liquidate or not. However, because the firm's assets in our hypothetical example are posited to be perfectly pro-cyclical, a very weak state of the economy corresponds to a very weak state of the firm.

22. Thus, care must be exercised in using historical default-frequency experience [as reported, for example, in Altman (1989) and Asquith et al. (1989)] to draw inferences about expected returns on junk bonds.

23. See also Merton (1990, pp. 403–404). Note that this result applies to the aggregate of the firm's debt. Obviously, with multiple classes of debt outstanding, it is possible for one or more individual subordinated issues to have greater volatility than a comparable firm's equity with no debt issued.

24. This point has been made on a number of occasions by Michael Jensen, Harvard University, and Mark Wolfson, Stanford University.

25. The management representing the A.2 holders might still threaten to put the firm in Chapter 11 bankruptcy (even though there is no default) in an attempt to extort some positive payoff. If such extortion is legal, it may be more efficient to "pay" it in advance by changing the original terms of the A.2 security to provide a minimum payment (e.g., $2 a unit), conditional on the firm not being in bankruptcy proceedings. Under these terms, the contingent payoff schedules for A.1 and A.2 become $\min[100, \max(0,V - 2)]$ and $\max[\min(2,V), V - 100]$, respectively.

26. For analysis of PBGC guarantees, see Harrison and Sharpe (1983), Marcus (1987), and Sharpe (1976).

27. Another argument for expanding the permissible asset class is to allow thrifts to diversify better and thereby reduce the volatility of their portfolios. But, absent other regulatory actions, there is no incentive for thrift managers to pursue such diversification. Indeed, as we have shown, the incentives created by deposit insurance favor increasing portfolio volatility.

28. In table 6, the calculation of losses from not seizing the equity and control at six months implicitly assumes that the going-concern value of 80 under the "no-boom" state exceeds the liquidation or salvage value of the assets. Otherwise, there would be an additional non-seizure cost to the guarantor equal to the difference between the salvage and going-concern values.

29. As discussed in the previous note, calculations in table 6 assume that going-concern value equals or exceeds liquidation value. Sale of the assets here means selling them for their highest-value use. Thus, seizure option (3) under this condition means selling the assets as a going-concern but without any encumbrance of debt. Since the guarantor gains control of the firm, at least temporarily, under all three seizure options, it would always be in its interest to liquidate the firm if the salvage value of the assets exceeds the going-concern value.

30. See Benston and Kaufman (1988) who recommend higher equity requirements to curb incentives for excessive risk-taking and Ely (1990) who proposes privatizing a portion of the insurance activity through cross-guarantees provided by a consortium of banks. For a study and recommendations on strategies for liquidations of thrifts, see Kormendi et al. (1989).

31. See, for example, Acharya and Dreyfus (1988), Jones and Mason (1980), Marcus and Shaked (1984), Merton (1977, 1978, 1990), Osborne and Mishra (1989), Pennacchi (1987a, 1987b), Ronn and Verma (1986), Selby, Franks, and Karki (1988), Sharpe (1978), Sosin (1980), and Thomson (1987).

32. See also Benston and Kaufman (1988), Buser, Chen, and Kane (1987), Campbell and Glenn (1984), Diamond and Dybvig (1983), Ely (1990), Fama (1980, 1985), Flannery (1988), Kane (1985, 1990), Maisel (1981), Merton (1979), and Pyle (1984).

33. According to the *Wall Street Journal*, July 20, 1990, Bert Ely of Ely & Company estimates fraud losses at $5 billion or only 3.4 percent of his $147 billion total estimated cost of the thrift bailout, excluding future interest payments on current borrowings. Losses on junk bond holdings are estimated at $3 billion or 2 percent of the total.

References

Acharya, S. and J. Dreyfus. "Optimal Bank Reorganization Policies and the Pricing of Federal Deposit Insurance." Unpublished manuscript, Graduate School of Business Administration, New York University, April 1988.

Adler, M. and B. Dumas. "International Portfolio Choice and Corporation Finance: A Survey." *Journal of Finance* 38 (June 1983), 925–984.

Allen, F. "The Changing Nature of Debt and Equity: A Financial Perspective." In R. W. Kopeke and E. S. Rosengre, eds., *Are the Distinctions Between Debt and Equity Disappearing?* Conference Series No. 33, Federal Reserve Bank of Boston, MA 1989.

Allen, F. and D. Gale. "Optimal Security Design." *Review of Financial Studies* 1(Fall 1988), 229–263.

Altman, E. I. "Measuring Corporate Bond Mortality and Performance." *Journal of Finance* 44 (September 1989), 909–922.

Altman, E. I. and S. A. Nammacher. *Investing in Junk Bonds.* New York: John Wiley, 1987.

Ando, A. and A. J. Auerbach. "The Cost of Capital in the United States and Japan: A Comparison." *Journal of the Japanese and International Economies* 2 (June 1988), 134–158.

Ando, A. and A. J. Auerbach. "The Cost of Capital in Japan: Recent Evidence and Further Results." Working Paper No. 3371, National Bureau of Economic Research, Cambridge, MA, May 1990.

Asquith, P., D. W. Mullins, and E. Wolff. "Original Issue High Yield Bonds: Aging Analyses of Defaults, Exchanges, and Calls." *Journal of Finance* 44 (September 1989), 923–952.

Baldwin, C., D. Lessard, and S. Mason. "Budgetary Time Bombs: Controlling Government Loan Guarantees." *Canadian Public Policy* 9 (1983), 338–346.

Becker, B., T. R. Gira, and D. L. Underhill. "Market Reform Proposals and Actions." Unpublished manuscript, Twelfth Annual Commodities Law Institute, IIT Chicago-Kent College of Law, Chicago, September 1989.

Benston, G. J. and G. C. Kaufman. "Regulating Bank Safety and Performance." In W. S. Haraf and R. M. Kushmeider, eds. *Restructuring Banking and Financial Services in America.* Washington, DC.: American Enterprise Institute for Public Policy Research, 1988.

Benston, G. J. and C. Smith. "A Transaction Cost Approach to the Theory of Financial Intermediation," *Journal of Finance* 31 (May 1976), 215–231.

Bicksler, J. and A. H. Chen. "An Economic Analysis of Interest Rate Swaps." *Journal of Finance* 41 (July 1986), 645–655.

Black, F. and M. Scholes. "From Theory to New Financial Product." *Journal of Finance* 29 (May 1974), 399–412.

Blume, M., D. Keim, and S. Patel. "Returns and Volatility of Low-Grade Bonds 1977–1988." Working Paper No. 38–89, The Wharton School, University of Pennsylvania, Philadelphia, December 1989.

Bodie, Z. "Pension Funds and Financial Innovation." Working Paper No. 3101, National Bureau of Economic Research, Cambridge, MA, September 1989.

Branson, W. and D. Henderson. "The Specification and Influence of Asset Markets." In R. Jones and P. Kenen, eds., *Handbook of International Economics.* Amsterdam: North-Holland, 1984.

Brennan, M. J. and B. Solnik. "International Risk Sharing and Capital Mobility." *Journal of International Money and Finance* 8 (September 1989), 359–373.

Buser, S. A., A. H. Chen, and E. J. Kane. "Federal Deposit Insurance, Regulating Policy, and Optimal Bank Capital." *Journal of Finance* 35 (March 1987), 51–60.

Campbell, T. and D. Glenn. "Deposit Insurance in a Deregulated Environment." *Journal of Finance* 39 (July 1984), 775–785.

Cole, H. L. and M. Obstfeld. "Commodity Trade and International Risk Sharing: How Much Do Financial Markets Matter?" Working Paper No. 3027, National Bureau of Economic Research, Cambridge, MA, July 1989.

Dewing, A. S. *A Study of Corporation Securities: Their Nature and Uses in Finance.* New York: Ronald Press Co., 1934.

Diamond, D. W. and P. H. Dybvig. "Bank Runs, Deposit Insurance, and Liquidity." *Journal of Political Economy* 91 (June 1983), 547–566.

Duffee, G., P. Kupiec, and A. P. White. "A Primer on Program Trading and Stock Price Volatility: A Survey of the Issues and the Evidence." Working Paper, Board of Governors of the Federal Reserve System, Washington, DC, 1990.

Ely, B. "Making Deposit Insurance Safe Through 100% Cross-Guarantees." Unpublished manuscript, Ely and Company, Alexandria, VA, 1990.

Fama, E. F. "Banking in the Theory of Finance." *Journal of Monetary Economics* 6 (January 1980), 39–57.

Fama, E. F. "What's Different About Banks?" *Journal of Monetary Economics* 15 (January 1985), 29–39.

Finnerty, J. D. "Zero Coupon Bond Arbitrage: An Illustration of the Regulatory Dialectic at Work." *Financial Management* 14 (Winter 1985), 13–17.

Finnerty, J. D. "Financial Engineering in Corporate Finance: An Overview." *Financial Management* 17 (Winter 1988), 14–33.

Fischer, S. "Welfare Aspects of Government Issue of Indexed Bonds." In R. Dornbusch and M. H. Simonsen, eds., *Inflation, Debt, and Indexation.* Cambridge, MA: MIT Press, 1983.

Fischer, S. and R. C. Merton. "Macroeconomics and Finance: The Role of the Stock Market." In K. Brunner and A. H. Meltzer, eds., *Essays on Macroeconomic Implications of Financial and Labor Markets and Political Processes,* Vol. 21. Amsterdam: North-Holland, 1984.

Flannery, M. J. "Payments System Risk and Public Policy." In W. S. Haraf and R. M. Kushmeider, eds., *Restructuring Banking and Financial Services in America.* Washington, DC: American Enterprise Institute for Public Policy Research, 1988.

Folkerts-Landau, D. and D. J. Mathieson. "Innovation, Institutional Changes, and Regulatory Response in International Financial Markets." In W. S. Haraf and R. M. Kushmeider, eds., *Restructuring Banking and Financial Services in America.* Washington, DC: American Enterprise Institute for Public Policy Research, 1988.

Friedman, B. "Postwar Changes in the American Financial Markets." In M. Feldstein, ed., *The American Economy in Transition.* Chicago: University of Chicago Press, 1980.

Friedman, B. "Implications of Increasing Corporate Indebtedness for Monetary Policy." *Group of Thirty Occasional Papers* 29 (1990), 1–40.

Gammill, J. and A. Perold. "The Changing Character of Stock Market Liquidity." *Journal of Portfolio Management* 13 (Spring 1989), 13–17.

Grauer, R. and N. H. Hakansson. "Gains From International Diversification: 1968–85 Returns on Portfolios of Stocks and Bonds." *Journal of Finance* 42 (July 1987), 721–738.

Grossman, S. "Program Trading and Market Volatility: A Report on Interday Relationships." *Financial Analysts Journal* (July–August 1988), 18–28.

Grossman, S. and M. H. Miller. "Liquidity and Market Structure." *Journal of Finance* 43 (July 1988), 617–637.

Hakansson, N. H. "The Purchasing Power Fund: A New Kind of Financial Intermediary." *Financial Analysts Journal* 32 (November-December 1976), 49–59.

Haraf, W. S. and R. M. Kushmeider, eds. *Restructuring Banking and Financial Services in America.* Washington, DC: American Enterprise Institute for Public Policy Research, 1988.

Harris, L., G. Sofianos, and J. E. Shapiro. "Program Trading and Intraday Volatility." Working Paper No. 90–03, New York Stock Exchange, New York, 1990.

Harrison, M. J. and W. F. Sharpe. "Optimal Funding and Asset Allocation Rules for Defined Benefit Pension Plans." In Z. Bodie and J. Shoven, eds., *Financial Aspects of the U. S. Pension System.* Chicago: University of Chicago Press, 1983.

Herring, R. J. and P. Van Kudre. "Growth Opportunities and Risk-Taking by Financial Intermediaries." *Journal of Finance* 42 (July 1987), 583–599.

Hull, J. *Options, Futures, and Other Derivative Securities.* Englewood Cliffs, NJ: Prentice-Hall, 1989.

Jensen, M. C. "Agency Costs of Free Cash Flow, Corporate Finance and Takeovers." *American Economic Review* 76 (May 1986), 323–329.

Jensen, M. C. "Takeovers: Their Causes and Consequences." *Journal of Economic Perspectives* 2 (Winter 1988), 21–48.

Jenson, M. C. "Eclipse of the Public Corporation." *Harvard Business Review* 67 (September/October 1989), 61–74.

Jones, E. P. and S. Mason. "Valuation of Loan Guarantees." *Journal of Banking and Finance* 4 (March 1980), 89–107.

Kane, E. J. "Good Intentions and Unintended Evil: The Case Against Selective Credit Allocation." *Journal of Money, Credit and Banking* 9 (February 1977), 55–69.

Kane, E. J. "Technological and Regulatory Forces in the Developing Fusion of Financial-Services Competition." *Journal of Finance* 39 (July 1984), 759–772.

Kane, E. J. *The Gathering Crisis in Federal Deposit Insurance.* Cambridge, MA: MIT Press, 1985.

Kane, E. J. "How Market Forces Influence the Structure of Financial Regulation." In W. S. Haraf and R. M. Kushmeider, eds., *Restructuring Banking and Financial Services in America.* Washington, DC: American Enterprise Institute for Public Policy Research, 1988.

Kane, E. J. "Incentive Conflict in the International Regulatory Agreement on Risk-Based Capital." Working Paper No. 3308, National Bureau of Economic Research, Cambridge, MA, March 1990.

Kaplan, S. and J. Stein. "How Risky is the Debt in Highly Leveraged Transactions? Evidence From Public Recapitalizations." Working Paper No. 3390, National Bureau of Economic Research, Cambridge, MA, June 1990.

Kester, W. C. and T. A. Luehrman. "Real Interest Rates and the Cost of Capital: A Comparison of the United States and Japan." *Japan and the World Economy* 1 (1989), 279–301.

Kester, W. C. and T. A. Luehrman. "The Price of Risk in the United States and Japan." Working Paper No. 90–050, Harvard Graduate School of Business Administration, Boston, MA, February 1990.

King, M., E. Sentana, and S. Wadhwani. "Volatility and Links Between National Stock Markets." Working Paper No. 3357, National Bureau of Economic Research, Cambridge, MA, May 1990.

Kormendi, R., V. Bernard, S. Pirrong, and S. Snyder. "Crisis Resolution in the Thrift Industry: Beyond the December Deals." Mid-America Institute for Public Policy Research, Chicago, 1989.

Kwast, M. L., ed. *Financial Futures and Options in the U. S. Economy.* Washington, DC: Board of Governors of the Federal Reserve System, December 1986.

Maisel, S. J., ed. *Risk and Capital Adequacy in Commercial Banks.* Chicago: University of Chicago Press, 1981.

Marcus, A. J. "Corporate Pension Policy and the Value of PBGC Insurance." In Z. Bodie, J. B. Shoven, and D. A. Wise, eds., *Issues in Pension Economics.* Chicago: University of Chicago Press, 1987.

Marcus, A. and I. Shaked. "The Valuation of FDIC Deposit Insurance Using Option-Pricing Estimates." *Journal of Money, Credit and Banking* 16 (November 1984), 446–460.

Merton, R. C. "On the Pricing of Corporate Debt: The Risk Structure of Interest Rates." *Journal of Finance* 29 (May 1974), 449–470.

Merton, R. C. "An Analytic Derivation of the Cost of Deposit Insurance and Loan Guarantees: An Application of Modern Option Pricing Theory." *Journal of Banking and Finance* 1 (June 1977), 3–11.

Merton, R. C. "On the Cost of Deposit Insurance When There Are Surveillance Costs." *Journal of Business* 51 (July 1978), 439–452.

Merton, R. C. "Discussion: Risk and Capital Adequacy in Banks." In *The Regulation of Financial Institutions.* Conference Series No. 21, Federal Reserve Bank of Boston, Boston, MA 1979.

Merton, R. C. "On Consumption-Indexed Public Pension Plans." In Z. Bodie and J. Shoven, eds., *Financial Aspects of the U. S. Pension System.* Chicago: University of Chicago Press, 1983a.

Merton, R. C. "On the Role of Social Security as a Means for Efficient Risk-Bearing in an Economy Where Human Capital Is Not Tradeable." In Z. Bodie and J. Shoven, eds., *Financial Aspects of the U. S. Pension System.* Chicago: University of Chicago Press, 1983b.

Merton, R. C. "A Simple Model of Capital Market Equilibrium with Incomplete Information." *Journal of Finance* 42 (July 1987a), 483–510.

Merton, R. C. "On the Current State of the Stock Market Rationality Hypothesis." In R. Dornbusch, S. Fischer, and J. Bossons, eds., *Macroeconomics and Finance: Essays in Honor of Franco Modigliani.* Cambridge, MA: MIT Press, 1987b.

Merton, R. C. "On the Application of the Continuous-Time Theory of Finance to Financial Intermediation and Insurance." *Geneva Papers on Risk and Insurance* 14 (July 1989), 225–262.

Merton, R. C. *Continuous-Time Finance.* Oxford: Basil Blackwell, 1990.

Merton, R. K. "Three Fragments From a Sociologist's Notebook: Establishing the Phenomenon, Specified Ignorance, and Strategic Research Materials." *The Annual Review of Sociology* (1987).

Miller, M. H. "Financial Innovation: The Last Twenty Years and The Next." *Journal of Financial and Quantitative Analysis* 21 (December 1986), 459–471.

Mishkin, F. S. "Financial Innovation and Current Trends in U. S. Financial Markets." Working Paper No. 3323, National Bureau of Economic Research, Cambridge, MA, April 1990.

Munnell, A. and J. Grolnic. "Should the U. S. Government Issue Index Bonds?" *New England Economic Review* (September-October 1986), 3–21.

Osborne, D. and C. Mishra. "Deposit Insurance as an Exchange Option, Public or Private." Unpublished manuscript, School of Management, University of Texas at Dallas, Richardson, TX, November 1989.

Pennacchi, G. "Alternative Forms of Deposit Insurance: Pricing and Bank Incentive Issues." *Journal of Banking and Finance* 11 (June 1987a), 291–312.

Pennacchi, G. "A Reexamination of the Over- (or Under-) Pricing of Deposit Insurance." *Journal of Money, Credit and Banking* 19 (August 1987b), 340–360.

Perold, A. F. and E. C. Schulman. "The Free Lunch in Currency Hedging: Implications for Investment Policy and Performance Standards." *Financial Analysts Journal* 44 (May/June 1988), 45–50.

Porter, M. *The Competitive Advantage of Nations.* New York: Free Press, 1990.

Poterba, J. and L. Summers. "The Persistence of Volatility and Stock Market Fluctuations." *American Economic Review* 76 (December 1986), 1142–1151.

Pyle, D. H. "Deregulation and Deposit Insurance Reform." *Economic Review* 2 (Spring 1984), 5–15.

Roll, R. "Price Volatility, International Market Links and Implications for Regulatory Policies." *Journal of Financial Services Research* 3 (1989), 211–246.

Ronn, E. I. and A. K. Verma. "Pricing Risk-Adjusted Deposit Insurance: An Option-Based Model." *Journal of Finance* 41 (September 1986), 871–895.

Ross, S. A. "Comment on 'Using Tax Policy to Curb Speculative Short-Term Trading'." Conference on Regulatory Reform of Stock and Futures Markets, Columbia University, New York, May 1989a.

Ross, S. A. "Institutional Markets, Financial Marketing, and Financial Innovation." *Journal of Finance* 44 (July 1989b), 541–556.

Schwert, G. W. "Business Cycles, Financial Crises, and Stock Volatility." *Carnegie-Rochester Conference Series on Public Policy,* Vol. 31. Amsterdam: North-Holland, 1989a.

Schwert, G. W. "Stock Market Volatility." Working Paper No. 89–02, New York Stock Exchange, New York, December 1989b.

Selby, M. J. P., J. R. Franks, and J. P. Karki. "Loan Guarantees, Wealth Transfers and Incentives to Invest." *Journal of Industrial Economics* 37 (September 1988), 47–65.

Sharpe, W. F. "Corporate Pension Funding Policy." *Journal of Financial Economics* 3 (June 1976), 183–193.

Sharpe, W. F. "Bank Capital Adequacy, Deposit Insurance and Security Values." *Journal of Financial and Quantitative Analysis* 13 (November 1978), 701–718.

Shiller, R. J. *Market Volatility.* Cambridge, MA: MIT Press, 1989.

Silber, W., ed. *Financial Innovation.* Lexington, MA: Lexington Books, 1975.

Silber, W. "The Process of Financial Innovation." *American Economic Review* 73 (May 1983), 89–95.

Smith, C. W., Jr., C. W. Smithson, and L. M. Wakeman. "The Evolving Market for Swaps." *Midland Corporate Finance Journal* 4 (Winter 1986), 20–32.

Smith, C. W., Jr., C. W. Smithson, and L. M. Wakeman. "The Market for Interest Rate Swaps." *Financial Management* 17 (Winter 1988), 34–44.

Smith, D. J. and R. A. Taggart. "Innovations in the Bond Market and the Changing Business of Financial Intermediaries." Unpublished manuscript, School of Management, Boston College, Chestnut Hill, MA, June 1989.

Solnik, B. *International Investments.* Reading, MA: Addison-Wesley, 1988.

Solnik, B. and B. Noetzlin. "Optimal International Asset Allocation." *Journal of Portfolio Management* 9 (Fall 1982), 11–21.

Sosin, H. "On the Valuation of Federal Loan Guarantees to Corporations." *Journal of Finance* 35 (December 1980), 1209–1221.

Stiglitz, J. E. "Using Tax Policy to Curb Speculative Short-Term Trading." Conference on Regulatory Reform of Stock and Futures Markets, Columbia University, New York, May 1989.

Stoll, H. R. and R. E. Whaley. "Stock Index Futures and Options: Economic Impact and Policy Issues." *Journal of International Securities Markets* 2 (Spring 1988), 3–18.

Taggart, R. and K. J. Perry. "The Growing Role of Junk Bonds in Corporate Finance." *Continental Bank: Journal of Applied Corporate Finance* 1 (Spring 1988), 37–45.

Thomson, J. B. "The Use of Market Information in Pricing Deposit Insurance." *Journal of Money, Credit and Banking* 19 (November 1987), 528–537.

Tobin, J. "A Proposal for International Monetary Reform." *Eastern Economic Journal* 4 (July/October 1978), 153–159.

Tufano, P. "Three Essays on Financial Innovation." Ph. D. dissertation, Business Economics, Harvard University, Cambridge, MA, 1989.

Van Horne, J. C. "Of Financial Innovations and Excesses." *Journal of Finance* 40 (July 1985), 621–631.

de la Vega, J. P. *Confusión de Confusiones* (1688). English translation by H. Kallenbenz, No. 13, The Kress Library Series of Publications, The Kress Library of Business and Economics, Harvard University, Cambridge, MA, 1957.

Weinstein, M. I. "A Curmudgeon's View of Junk Bonds." *Journal of Portfolio Management* 13 (Spring 1987), 76–80.

Journal of Financial Services Research 4:301–305 (1990)
© 1990 Kluwer Academic Publishers

Commentary: *The Financial System and Economic Performance*

ALLAN H. MELTZER
John M. Olin Professor of Political Economy and Public Policy
Carnegie-Mellon University
Pittsburgh, PA 15213
and Visiting Scholar
American Enterprise Institute for Public Policy Research
1150 17th St., NW
Washington, DC 20036

Robert Merton's article should be read by anyone who is interested in the past or future evolution of financial markets. Merton develops parts of finance theory and their implications for financial markets and financial policy in a clear, crisp, and informative way. It is an excellent piece, well worth a reader's investment of time.

The article starts with a broad overview of the services provided by financial institutions in a market economy: the efficient allocation of savings, the development of signals or information in the form of market clearing interest rates, asset prices, and risk premiums that guide resource allocation. It also includes the provision of a payments system that facilitates transactions by reducing the time and effort that households, corporations, and governments devote to purchasing and processing payments for purchases.

The body of the article discusses three main issues: innovation, below investment grade debt (so-called junk bonds), and loan guarantees or insurance. Merton provides a thorough discussion of each topic.

There are two types of innovation. Some innovations provide clear social benefits by lowering transactions costs, reducing costs of acquiring information, lowering risk, or increasing liquidity. These innovations increase wealth and asset values or raise the utility of a given stock of wealth. Other innovations that circumvent regulations are usually presented as posing a conflict between individual benefit and social objective. Merton gives an example, however, of a government imposing exchange controls that reduce individuals' opportunities to diversify their portfolios. He shows how financial innovation can restore many of the benefits of diversification while maintaining the spirit, if not the letter, of the regulation. Although I accept his point in principle, I find his example a bit misleading. Often exchange controls are imposed to prevent capital flight by asset owners concerned about below market returns, taxation, or confiscation. Why would external investors choose to include these assets, or a claim on these returns in their portfolio, as is required for Merton's innovation to work?

A main implication of the section on innovation is that market regulation should be functional instead of institutional. Merton also favors international coordination if regulations are socially optimal. He recognizes that this is a big if, particularly in an innovative financial system. I will return to this topic.

Junk bonds—below investment grade debt—are one of the most widely discussed innovations of recent years. Many of these securities have a relatively high probability of default. The longest section of the article presents a careful, non-mathematical exposition of some basic principles of default risk with application to the policy issues raised by the recent increase in junk bonds.

Merton uses his running example to show that with high leverage, debt acquires part of the default risk that fell entirely on equity in his low leverage example. He then explores several common misperceptions about expected return and shows the fallacy involved in using the historical difference between interest earnings on high grade and junk bonds as a measure of the payment that one can expect for bearing the additional risk. A conclusion often drawn is that the payment for default risk has exceeded the amount required to compensate for default losses. Merton shows that this fact, if true, says nothing about the expected return on junk bonds.

The section ends with a proposal to reduce or avoid bankruptcy costs while providing the functional equivalent of debt, including junk bonds, and equity. The proposal suggests one of the ways in which financial innovation can raise social welfare.

One of the attractive features of the article is the way Merton is able to develop many of his points by building on a single example. The third section carries forward the example of debt and equity finance of risky portfolios to consider government guarantees, of which deposit insurance is one example.

Under many government insurance programs, the federal government issues a guarantee but does not record the value of the expected loss as an expense. Expenses are reported only when the losses are realized, a form of accounting that would not satisfy many current and prospective private sector accounting rules. The fact that no current charge is recorded probably leads politicians to overuse guarantees. Charges deferred to some uncertain future date do not appear in the budget. Charges deferred are usually charges denied by governments; the long delay in admitting the expected losses in the thrift industry is an example.

What is the effect of the guarantee on the owners of the financial firm? Merton extends his example to show that the owners will choose a more volatile portfolio. The reason is that the risk of failure has been shifted to the government, so the owner's expected loss in the event of failure is reduced and the value of the owner's equity is increased commensurately. The added incentive to take on risk arises even if the firm is not bankrupt. In our recent experience with deposit insurance at savings and loans, many firms were allowed to operate after they were technically bankrupt; for these firms the incentive to purchase high risk assets with volatile returns was often overwhelming. Subsequent realization of the losses on these portfolios wiped out the Federal Savings and Loan Insurance fund and shifted the loss to the taxpayers. Moral: an improperly designed insurance system can be costly.

Merton concludes that if there is to be insurance, whether private or public, there must be regulation to control losses. He suggests that the restrictions can take three possible forms: (1) portfolio restrictions that prevent insured firms from holding volatile assets; (2) frequent monitoring by the regulator and prompt seizure of assets; and (3) charging proper fees for the guarantees.

In a 1967 article, I argued that the basic premise of the deposit insurance system is incorrect (Meltzer, 1967). The reason I gave is that government does not have a comparative advantage in insuring commercial banks. I suggested that government became the insurer of banks and other intermediaries because the Federal Reserve failed to prevent the collapse of large parts of the banking and financial systems during the Great Depression. The principal mistake, I argued, was to confuse the solvency of an individual bank or financial institution with the solvency of the financial system. Insurance can protect an individual bank, not the system. But, as Merton emphasizes, insurance must be correctly priced and that, I suggested, was more likely to happen if the insurance system is privately owned and managed.

There is a role for government. Private insurers cannot insure against systemic risks, particularly risks arising from government policy mistakes, as in the 1930s depression. To reduce the risk of systemwide failures, a lender of last resort must have the power to create money. An insurance company, private or public, cannot create money. The task falls to the central bank.

Looking again at the insurance problem after 25 years, I would make one change in my earlier discussion and in Merton's. There is some benefit to the public in using checks as instruments of payment. Risks of loss and theft are larger for currency than for deposits, so risk can be reduced by encouraging the use of checking deposits. But relatively small depositors cannot be expected to monitor the safety or soundness of their bank, and there is a social benefit in avoiding runs on bank deposits to convert deposits into currency during periods of alarm.

An institutional change would eliminate monitoring costs on some deposits. In place of deposit insurance, let privately owned banks or money market funds offer deposits fully collateralized by portfolios of short-term government securities that are marked to market. Anyone who wants to avoid loss on all or part of his money balances can hold the relevant amount in these deposits. All other deposits would be either uninsured or privately insured. This does not require a new "narrow bank." Money funds limited to holding only short-term government securities currently exist.

Government does not have a comparative advantage in the insurance business. Governments can best reduce risk by establishing institutions that give proper incentive to decisionmakers. The lender of last resort function is an example. Maintaining stability of the anticipated price level is another. Offering indexed bonds may be a third. Many government insurance programs redistribute risk bearing across time or across groups. The thrift industry bailout is one example of such redistribution. The problems posed by Medicare insurance funding are another.

The conclusion I draw from Merton's analysis is, once again, that public policy should distinguish between risk shifting and government actions that reduce the risks that society bears. There are net social benefits from the latter but generally not from the former. As I see it, the issue is not whether deposits or brokerage accounts should be insured *and* regulated, as Merton suggests. Ideally, government activity would be limited to those actions that provide net social benefits – actions where government has a comparative advantage. Merton includes promoting competition, ensuring integrity, providing public goods; I would add, for emphasis, reducing risks to the minimum inherent in nature and trading practices.

Merton recommends that financial regulations should be coordinated internationally only if the regulations are socially optimal. I would add that even if regulations are socially optimal at one time, they are unlikely to remain optimal in a dynamic industry like the financial industry. Furthermore, I see no clear presumption that a regulatory cartel is an optimal arrangement. Here, as elsewhere, competition has benefits.

One area in which government has a role is in maintaining a stable real value of money. Economists argue over whether governments should maintain stable domestic value or stable external value. In the postwar era, most governments have done neither. Neither price levels nor exchange rates have been stable.

Consider the problem faced by a representative person who works until 60 or 65 and lives for 15 or 20 years on a pension. With a stable domestic price level, he can invest his pension in bonds with stable purchasing power and a fixed rate of return. He knows what his income will be and can estimate the size of the estate he will leave to his heirs. In an economy subject to variable inflation, he runs the risk that his real income will be reduced and that he will face poverty before he dies. This risk can be reduced by increasing saving during his working years, but this is unlikely to happen. Inflation shortens horizons and reduces saving, which adds to the problem. Part of the risk of inflation can be avoided by holding real assets or equities but, as Merton's analysis shows, the decision to hold equities requires that he accept a risk of a different kind. And, in practice, capital gains taxes fall on nominal values, reducing their attraction as a hedge against inflation.

Government could solve part of this problem by issuing indexed bonds and by indexing capital gains taxes. Government can reduce the risk of inflation by pursuing policies that maintain anticipated price stability. This is a valuable service that only government, or its monetary authority, can provide.

Finally, I would like to comment briefly on one paramount issue: whether there are advantages to a country in having a strong financial sector. Several of the articles in this issue point out that a principal product of the financial sector is information as reflected not only in efficient markets for financial assets but also in customized lending and borrowing arrangements where markets are not organized. The accumulation of information about borrowers, the skill and knowledge with which competitive lenders assess risks and opportunities, and the innovations that create standardized, tradeable assets from heterogeneous loans are part of the process by which information is used efficiently. More efficient use of information, reductions in the cost of acquiring information and transacting, and better resource allocation are the result. These are the source of productivity gains from the use of money and financial assets (Brunner and Meltzer, 1971).

Much public discussion is based on the incorrect assessment of the nature of these activities. Financial innovators are often pilloried by the regulators, in Congress, in the press, in many parts of the business community, and by the public. Financial innovators are often treated as parasites or worse, concerned only with the minute-to-minute happenings on markets. This view fails to distinguish between the rapidly vanishing value of a particular item of information and the value of an efficient system for producing information and change. The latter is a source of productivity, growth, and economic welfare. Regulation of the financial system should not ignore this relation of the financial system to economic performance. Robert Merton's article brings out some of the reasons why.

References

Brunner, K. and A. H. Meltzer. "The Uses of Money: Money in the Theory of an Exchange Economy." *American Economic Review* 61, 784–805. Reprinted in Brunner and Meltzer, eds., *Monetary Economics.* Oxford: Basil Blackwell, 1989, pp. 230–258.

Meltzer, A. H. "Major Issues in the Regulation of Financial Institutions." *Journal of Political Economy* 75 (suppl. August 1967), 482–501.

Journal of Financial Services Research 4:307–309 (1990)
© 1990 Kluwer Academic Publishers

Commentary: *The Financial System and Economic Performance*

JOHN B. TAYLOR
Member
President's Council of Economic Advisors
Old Executive office Building
Room 314
Washington, DC 20500

Robert Merton's article gives an excellent and successful overview of many topics included in the area of international competitiveness in financial services. I like the way he focused on three particular issues: financial innovation, junk bonds, and loan guarantees. He develops these issues with the use of simple examples—abstract examples, to be sure—but examples that highlight the problems at hand.

I completely agree with his conclusion on loan guarantees—that they are potentially a big and costly problem for the government. In fact, in the President's budget submitted earlier this year, there was extensive discussion of loan guarantee issues and how we might control the risks and their costs. We discussed not only the issues associated with deposit insurance that are highlighted by Merton in his article but also issues related to guarantees in the housing area, the student loan area, and so on.

It would be possible in principle to score these loan guarantees on the budget the way that Merton suggests, and this is one possibility for reform that is rightfully being considered. Another possibility is simply to put outright limits on the extension of loan guarantees. These are possibilities that I support wholeheartedly, as does the Administration.

The issues that I would like to focus on here are the other two that Merton develops—financial innovation in general and a particular type of financial innovation, junk bonds. I will describe how I see these innovations evolving and affecting the financial intermediary sector, and discuss some of their implications for possible reform activity.

It seems to me that most of the recent developments in financial innovation and their effect on the financial system are best thought of in terms of one single trend—the trend toward direct financing as distinct from intermediated financing. Nonfinancial corporate paper outstanding has grown at an 18 percent rate since 1972, for example, compared to growth of 10 percent for commercial and industrial loans. Over this same period of time, the share of bank loans in short-term and intermediate-term credit has shrunk from about 80 percent to 50 percent. This reflects the predominant trend toward direct loans as distinct from intermediated credit. About a third of all mortgage activity now takes place through mortgage-backed securities. Junk bonds, which are discussed in Merton's article, are another aspect of the ability for many firms, in addition to the very large firms, to obtain credit without going through financial intermediaries.

These developments reflect technological improvement, both in the information area and the communication area. Banks and banking-type institutions do not have as much of a comparative advantage as they once had in developing the kind of information they need to generate loans. This is, perhaps, one of the main reasons why bank profitability has declined throughout the 1980s. This decline is noticeable in almost all the figures on bank performances.

To be sure, financial institutions are adapting to these changes in their circumstances. New lines of business are being developed at the financial intermediaries. Standby letters of credit, for example—through which banks actually provide a credit analysis even though they are not providing the funds—separate the credit analysis from the funding. Standby letters of credit have grown by 26 percent per year through the 1980s, a substantial increase in this activity.

This is not the only new line of business that banks have developed. If we measure the trend away from direct bank lending by looking at earnings generated by fees as distinct from interest earnings, fees relative to interest earnings have increased substantially during the 1980s. These financial innovations have had substantial effects on financial intermediaries, on nonbank firms as well as on banks.

For an industry, or for any firm in the industry, to adapt to these kinds of innovations, it is important for the firms, in this case the banks, to have flexibility to make changes. In industries that are not heavily regulated, adaptation to change is relatively easy. In industries that are extensively regulated, adaptation can be much more difficult. I think this is probably the best way to think about the greatest challenge we face with respect to regulatory policy in the financial sector of the economy.

Deposit insurance probably has slowed the adaptation of banks by permitting the continuation of less profitable lines of activity than otherwise would have occurred. The ability to continue doing business in relatively unprofitable areas has slowed down the speed with which banks and nonbank financial institutions have adapted to change. The challenge in thinking about regulation is to find ways for banks to adapt to these changes.

Some possibilities worth mentioning are referred to by Merton in his article. The notion of functional regulation as distinct from institutional regulation is one way to think about providing flexibility for banks to change. Developing risk-based capital requirements as a way to allow institutions to choose among types of financial activities is another being discussed actively. Risk-based deposit insurance would offer still another way for financial institutions to choose among lines of activity that they want to pursue, with differences in risks reflected by differences in costs to the firms involved.

There are, in fact, some features of the Financial Institution Reform, Recovery and Enforcement Act (FIRREA) that permit financial firms to opt for particular activities. Separately capitalized subsidiaries of S&Ls, for example, can go into a broader range of activities, as long as these activities are not supported by insured deposits. This is an example of the application of the risk-based deposit insurance premiums idea.

Finally, in terms of flexibility, I think we need to re-examine whether we should continue to maintain the distinction between investment banking and commercial banking, the so-called Glass-Steagall regulation. Of course, a great deal of relaxation of this distinction has occurred already, but we are actively considering that more could be permitted. Any kind of relaxation should certainly take into account the potential for uneconomic diversification made possible by the continuation of deposit insurance. The issues of deposit insurance and possible revisions of Glass-Steagall need to both be considered together in an effort to reach the goal of more flexibility in regulation of financial institutions.

The appropriate way to think about the activities of financial institutions that Merton so nicely illustrates with examples in his article is, I believe, to consider how more flexibility for adaptation to change could be introduced into our regulatory policy. One approach is to allow financial institutions a greater choice in opting for more risky or less risky activities, as long as the risks are borne by the firms and not transferred to taxpayers. Firms would then be better able to adapt to the changing financial environment and continue to operate profitably in areas where they can provide financial services efficiently.

Journal of Financial Services Research 4:311–339 (1990)
© 1990 Kluwer Academic Publishers

U.S. Banking in an Increasingly Integrated and Competitive World Economy

GEORGE J. BENSTON
John H. Harland Professor of Finance, Accounting, and Economics
School of Business
Emory University
Atlanta, GA 30322

1. Introduction

It is almost trite to say that the world has become increasingly integrated commercially since the Second World War. Trade in producer and consumer products has expanded as the costs of transporting goods, services, and information have declined, as consumers' tastes have expanded to include products made and used in other countries, and as technologies that developed in one country have been adopted worldwide. Banking services have both reflected and led this movement. The services provided by banks in most countries are very similar, and money or access to credit can be transported quickly and cheaply across great distances and national boundaries, particularly when laws and regulations do not impede such movements. Hence, it is not surprising that banking has become increasingly international.[1] Indeed, one of the historically important products offered by banks is facilitation of international trade with credit instruments such as acceptances and letters of credit.

World trade has increased considerably in the past two decades. As shown in table 1, international trade in goods and services has increased more than in proportion to world (excluding the Soviet bloc) gross domestic product (GDP). In 1964, international trade was 11.7 percent of world gross domestic product. This percentage increased to 21.1 percent in 1980 and went down slightly to 17.1 percent in 1985. International banking increased relatively even more. As a percentage of international trade, international banking gross or net of interbank redepositing has gone from 10.6 percent (gross) and 6.4 percent (net) in 1964 to 118.6 and 67.8 percent in 1985.

Furthermore, as the world economy has become more integrated, the risks to which many firms are subject have increased. Prices in many countries have increased considerably both in level and variance. With the breakdown of the Bretton Woods Agreement, exchange rates among currencies, rather than exchange reserves, reflect these changes. Consequently, the net profits of many firms doing business in more than one country are

This article benefited from helpful comments by Allan Meltzer of Carnegie Mellon University, Jeffrey Rosensweig of Emory University, Henry Terrell of the Federal Reserve Board, and especially Cynthia Lichtenstein of Boston College Law School.

determined as much by price and exchange rate changes as by their attainments in production and marketing. Even purely domestic firms are affected, as their competitors may sell foreign-produced goods or domestically produced goods that use foreign materials, or sell materials that are affected by the prices of foreign materials (see Smith, Smithson, and Wilford, 1989). As a result, the market for financial products that allow firms to hedge against these risks has increased greatly. These instruments include currency swaps, interest-rate swaps, currency and interest-rate options, and forward rate agreements.[2]

A cursory review of some statistics suggests that U.S. banks are not faring well in this "new" world. Table 2 gives the nationality of the 10 and 50 largest banks in the world in terms of total deposits converted to U.S. dollars in 1956, 1960, 1970, 1979, and 1988. It appears that U.S. banks have dropped from being among the leaders to positions well

Table 1. Growth of international trade and international banking: 1964–1985*

	1964	1972	1980	1983	1985
Billions of Current Dollars					
Gross Domestic Product (GDP)	$1,605	$3,336	$10,172	$10,140	$12,825
International Trade in Goods and Services (IT)	$188	$463	$2,150	$1,986	$2,190
International Banking (IB):					
net (note a)	$12	$122	$810	$1,240	$1,485
gross (note b)	$20	$208	$1,559	$2,253	$2,598
Percentages					
IT/GDP	11.7%	13.9%	21.1%	19.6%	17.1%
IB net/IT	6.4%	26.3%	37.7%	62.4%	67.8%
IB gross/IT	10.6%	44.9%	72.5%	113.4%	118.6%

*Excludes Soviet block.
[a]Bank for International Settlement series, which nets out interbank redepositing.
[b]Morgan Guarantee series; also includes more countries than BIS series.
Source: Bryant (1987, table 3-1).

Table 2. Nationality of the world's largest banks by deposit size

Country	Number of banks in top 10					Number of banks in top 50				
	1956	1960	1970	1979	1988	1956	1960	1970	1979	1988
United States	5	6	4	2	0	25	19	13	6	2
United Kingdom	3	3	2	2	0	7	5	4	4	4
Canada	2	1	1	0	0	6	5	5	4	1
France	0	0	1	4	0	3	3	3	4	4
Germany	0	0	1	2	0	0	3	4	7	7
Italy	0	0	1	0	0	3	5	4	2	1
Japan					10	3	8	11	16	25
Australia						1	1	1	0	0
Netherlands						0	0	1	3	2
Switzerland						0	0	3	3	3
Belgium						0	0	0	1	0
Other						2	1	1	0	1

Source: American Banker, "500 Largest Banks in the World" (1956 through 1979 from Goddin and Weiss, 1981, table 1).

behind banks in other countries, particularly Japan. For example, five U.S. banks were among the largest ten in 1956 and six in 1960, but this number dropped to four in 1970 and two in 1979. By 1988, all ten largest banks were Japanese. U.S. banks made up half of the largest 50 banks in 1956, and were still a quarter of the total in 1970. However, by 1988, only two U.S. banks were among the largest 50 banks in the world, while half were Japanese.

Does the present position of U.S. banks in lists of the world's largest banks indicate that our banks are losing or have lost their competitive edge? In particular, have the Japanese displaced the United States as the world's bankers? Furthermore, after 1992, financial institutions incorporated in any European Community (E.C.) country will be able to offer services in any other E.C. country: Western Europe will become an integrated market area. Does this mean that U.S. banks are likely to play an even smaller role in the world? What can and should be done to alter this situation?

2. Analysis of the reasons that U.S. banks are no longer among the world's largest

There are many reasons for not taking lists of the world's largest banks very seriously or, at the least, for urging caution in drawing conclusions from such data. At least five reasons can be delineated.

First, deposit size is an inadequate measure of competitiveness, strategic position, and profitability. Banks' off balance sheet activities have increased over the past decade, particularly for U.S. banks. U.S. banks have been the leaders in developing interest and foreign exchange rate swaps, futures, and options for customers to allow them to deal with the increasing variability of interest rates, exchange rates, and other prices. Furthermore, as U.S. banks have increasingly been criticized by the banking authorities for having low book-equity-to-asset ratios, they have had incentives to engage in off-balance sheet activities. Thus, gains and fees from securitization of bank loans and direct intermediation through such instruments as Eurocommercial paper and note issue facilities have partially replaced banks' returns from assets funded with deposits. Unfortunately, it does not appear possible to determine the extent to which U.S. banks have become smaller in deposit size compared to other countries' banks as a result of this off-balance-sheet activity.

Second, deposit size is not an adequate measure of banks' ability to lend or offer services to customers. Lending limits are determined by equity measured by traditional accounting, and bank safety is related to the market value of banks' equity, which (assuming that the stock market is efficient) provides an unbiased estimate of the ability of the bank to absorb losses before imposing costs on depositors and other creditors. In this regard, however, there is reason to believe that U.S. banks are weaker than other international banks. Losses on loans (particularly foreign loans and, more recently, real-estate loans) have reduced international banks' book equity. Furthermore, unlike the situation for banks in some other countries, particularly Japan, the market value of U.S. banks' equities is lower than the book values of their shares. When equity is measured in terms of market values, Baer (1990, p. 26)[3] shows that Japanese banks have capital-to-asset ratios averaging 15 percent, compared to the ratios for U.S. banks of under 5 percent. Indeed, the ratios are higher for Swiss, West German, and U.K. banks (the only other countries shown), and there is a uniformly positive association between market capitalization ratios and growth in holding of foreign assets over 1984–1986. Baer (1990, p. 27) concludes that this relationship suggests that "banks that have high market capitalization ratios have made greater inroads in foreign markets than have banks with relatively low market capitalization ratios."

Third, the list of the world's largest banks includes institutions that are not at all in competition with U.S. banks and does not distinguish between banks' domestic and foreign operations. For example, Goddin and Weiss (1981, pp. 204–205) point out that the largest bank in the world in 1979 (Caisse Nationale de Credit Agricole) is an agglomeration of "94 fairly autonomous regional agricultural banks and over 3,000 local co-operative banks. . . . Similarly, seven of the fourteen German banks appearing in the world's top 100 banks list in 1979 are central giro institutions which act as clearing centers for over 650 savings banks."[4] Thus, a bank's large size may be due primarily to the growth of its domestic operations rather than to its success as an international competitor.

Fourth, banks sometimes become very large merely by merging with other large banks. Goddin and Weiss (1981, p. 205) mention that the world's fifth largest bank in 1971 resulted from the merger of the 40th and 46th largest banks. Similarly, the number of U.K. clearing banks declined from 11 to 6 through mergers during the 1970s, and major mergers occurred during this period in Spain, Sweden, Canada, and the Netherlands. In contrast, the United States' antitrust and anti-branching laws discourage or prohibit mergers of large banks and the creation of nationwide banks. Thus, the reduction in relative size of U.S. banks may be, in part, a reflection of U.S. laws that virtually prohibit large-scale consolidations.

Fifth, the necessary translation of foreign banks' assets (or deposits) to dollars results in an obfuscation of real exchange rate effects. If exchange rate differences reflected only differences in purchasing power, the translation of foreign bank assets to dollars with current dollar-foreign currency exchange rates would be a valid correction for inflation. But, because exchange rates also reflect real differences among countries that persist because of restraints on the movement of capital, goods, and labor, this procedure can under- or over-state banks' relative sizes. For example, when the real value of the yen increases relative to the dollar a Japanese bank would appear to get larger than a U.S. bank, ceteris paribus, even when the size of neither bank changed. (And, to the extent that both hold each other's country assets, the U.S. bank gains and the Japanese bank loses.) Furthermore, this distortion exists even for banks in the same country, because banks hold varying proportions of assets already denominated in dollars. Thus, a bank with no dollar-denominated assets would suffer the full effects of the real exchange rate distortion, while another bank with some dollar-denominated assets would be only partially affected.

The last three of these problems were substantially "solved" by Dohner and Terrell (1988). They examined the growth from 1972 through 1986 of a sample of 33 banks that appeared among the world's largest 100 banks every year during the period, were continuously either privately or governmentally owned over the entire period, and were primarily engaged in commercial banking. The sample also was limited to developed countries with at least three banks that met the criteria, and the sample for each country was limited to seven banks to avoid overweighting. Thus, the sample included Canada (five banks), France (three banks), Japan (seven banks), Switzerland (three banks), the United Kingdom (four banks), Germany (four banks), and the United States (seven banks).[5]

Figure 1 (derived from Dohner and Terrell's table 1, which I updated for 1987–1989) shows the growth in total assets (net of contra accounts) measured in U.S. dollars of the average bank in each of seven countries from 1972 through 1989 (1972 = 100). It is clear that the U.S. banks grew the least over virtually the entire period. The Swiss, German, and French banks grew the most rapidly through 1979-1980, declined through 1984, then grew rapidly again through 1989. The U.K. and Canadian banks followed a roughly similar pattern, although they did not grow as rapidly after 1985. But the Japanese banks out-paced them all after 1982, with growth being particularly great after 1985. Thus, this chart appears to confirm the impression that the U.S. banks lost their world position, at least with respect to size.

An important determinant of the growth of banks is the growth of the economies of their home countries. Figure 2 (derived from Dohner and Terrell's table 2, which I updated for 1987–1989) plots the ratio of the banks' total assets to their countries' gross national product (GNP), with 1972 = 100 so that changes over time are standardized. This figure shows a much more mixed picture than does figure 1. The German, Swiss, French, Canadian, and (to a lesser extent) U.S. banks experienced the greatest growth relative to GNP through 1980. All except the U.S. banks grew rapidly through 1982. Thereafter, all except the U.S. and Canadian banks continued their growth, although much more erratically, while the U.S. and Canadian banks declined in size relative to GNP. Thus, once account is taken of the growth of domestic economies, it appears that the U.S. banks, alone among the banks in the seven countries studied with the exception of Canada since 1982, increased very little in size and the dominant current position of the Japanese banks is seen as due mostly to the growth and amount of their country's GNP in U.S. dollar terms.

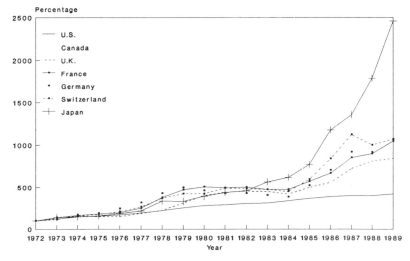

Figure 1. Total assets of multinational banking organizations by headquarter country (1972 = 100)
Source: Dohner and Terrell (1988, table 1), updated for 1987–1989.

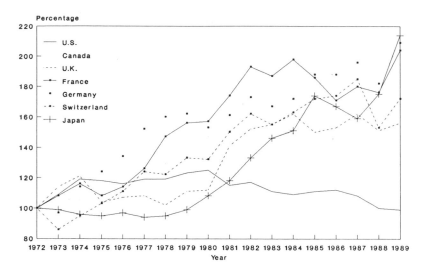

Figure 2. Total assets of multinational banking organizations relative to GNP (1972 = 100)
Source: Dohner and Terrell (1988, table 2), updated for 1987–1989.

The differential growth patterns shown by figure 1 also closely mirror the respective upturn of the six countries' currencies against the U.S. dollar. Japan's yen started rising in 1982, but accelerated in late 1985 when the European currencies also started gaining rapidly in dollar terms. The British pound and particularly the Canadian dollar advanced less rapidly than the yen and continental European currencies after 1985 (Rosensweig, 1986). Thus, both the growth in national economies and the exchange rate of the U.S. dollar appear to explain most, perhaps all, of the relative growth of U.S. international banks.

Dohner and Terrell conducted a formal analysis of the determinants of the difference between the growth of the United States' and other countries' banks. They first disaggregated the banks' holdings of foreign and domestic currency assets, because only foreign asset growth might affect the competitive position of U.S. banks. They then measured the extent to which the growth of domestic deposits (relative to the U.S. banks' growth) was due to (1) real exchange rate changes, (2) faster economic growth, (3) the extent to which the large banks sampled grew relative to other banks in their country, and (4) the interaction of these variables. Their estimates are presented in table 3.

Table 3 shows (in the first number column) the higher growth of the foreign banks over the U.S. banks over the entire 1972–1986 period and three subperiods, 1972–1980, 1980–1984, and 1984–1986. The next three number columns show the proportions (in percentages) of this growth differential that is due to foreign and domestic currency assets.[6] For example, over 1972–1986 the Japanese banks' growth exceeded the U.S. banks' growth by 792.5 percent. Foreign asset growth accounted for 16 percent of total differential growth, with domestic assets responsible for 84 percent. The last three number columns show the percentage of the domestic growth that was due to specified factors. For example, over 1972–1986 the relative importance of the sources of the Japanese banks' higher growth in domestic assets is estimated as 36 percent due to real exchange rate changes, 16 percent due to faster economic growth, and 48 percent due to large bank intermediation.[7]

Table 3. Multinational banking organizations' growth over U.S. banks and factors responsible

Banks headquartered in:	Percentage growth (decline) over U.S. banks	Percentage of growth (decline) over U.S. banks due to:		Percentage of domestic currency asset growth (decline) due to:		
		Foreign assets	Domestic currency assets	Real exchange rate changes	Faster domestic economic growth	Large bank intermediation
1972–1986						
Japan	792.5	16	84	36	16	48
Germany	320.4	(3)	103	20	(10)	89
U.K.	172.6	87	13	186	(109)	23
France	151.5	90	10	326	78	(304)
Canada	86.2	117	(17)	108	(9)	1
1972–1980						
Japan	111.2	(61)	161	55	22	24
Germany	181.1	(11)	111	38	0	61
U.K.	121.0	56	44	(1,226)	266	1,060
France	118.4	31	69	92	8	(1)
Canada	71.6	20	80	(17)	34	84
1980–1984						
Japan	37.2	48	52	(101)	35	167
Germany	(37.4)	20	80	123	9	(33)
U.K.	(16.6)	(445)	545	156	(9)	(46)
France	(26.9)	(61)	161	93	2	6
Canada	7.1	798	(698)	19	5	75
1984–1986						
Japan	76.4	17	83	58	6	36
Germany	69.7	17	83	73	(3)	30
U.K.	19.6	(30)	130	62	(3)	41
France	26.7	(3)	103	112	3	(15)
Canada	(9.2)	44	56	63	(16)	53

Source: Dohner and Terrell (1988, tables 9 and 10).
Note: "Other" sources of growth and "interaction correction" allocated to remaining variables in proportion to their amounts.

Over the entire 1972–1986 period, foreign asset growth appears responsible for much of the relatively higher growth for banks in Canada, France, and the United Kingdom. The countries with the greatest growth relative to the U.S. banks—Japan and Germany— owe their better performance mostly to domestic factors, primarily the position of the large banks studied relative to other banks in their countries (large bank intermediation) and, for Japanese banks, real exchange rate changes. This conclusion also holds for the three subperiods, particularly the 1984–1986 period.

The situation with respect to the Japanese banks was studied in greater detail by Dohner (1989) and Terrell, Dohner, and Lowrey (1989). As noted above, much of the Japanese domestic growth is due to the large banks studied maintaining their share of bank assets while the share of the U.S. banks declined by 21 percent (Dohner, 1989, p. 7).[8] The growth in the Japanese banks' foreign assets, Dohner (p. 9) finds, is "in large part

59

because of peculiarities in Japanese financial regulation that have, in effect, pushed transactions offshore." These "peculiarities" include interest rate controls that made it necessary for Japanese firms to borrow overseas if they wanted to obtain funds, except for those low-risk and favored companies that could benefit from lower domestic interest rates. Interest rate controls on bank deposits restrain the ability of Japanese banks to obtain funds domestically.[9] As banks lost personal savings to other financial institutions that were less constrained, they sought funds from overseas. Indeed, Dohner (1989, p. 10) finds that "[s]tarting in 1984, the Japanese banking sector has become a substantial net capital importer, in amounts as high as \$70 billion per year."

Although a large portion of the relative growth of Japanese and other countries' banks can be explained by conditions in their countries, the recent decline (relative to other countries' banks) and earlier growth of U.S. banks' foreign activities and the position of foreign banks in the United States deserves further exploration. For this purpose, I review next the factors explaining overseas operations of U.S. banks and banking activities in the United States by foreign banks.

3. A brief review of overseas banking by U.S. banks and activities in the United States by foreign banks

3.1. U.S. banks' overseas activities

World War I was responsible for the first major overseas expansion of U.S. banks. National banks were first given the authority to accept drafts and establish foreign branches by the Federal Reserve Act. A 1919 amendment to the Act allowed member banks to establish federally chartered banking entities, called Edge corporations, that were limited to international banking and financial activities and were exempted from U.S. domestic reserve requirements and interest-rate ceilings (Key, 1985, p. 268).

After the Second World War until the 1960s, U.S. banks' international activities were devoted primarily to financing trade between their U.S. clients and foreigners (Dahl, 1967). In 1960, only nine U.S. banks had foreign branches, totalling 139; only three of these banks had substantial foreign branch networks. Then, during the 1960s, U.S. banks' overseas activities expanded considerably. Key (1985, p. 269) reports that by 1970 "80 U.S. banking organizations operated 540 foreign branches in 66 countries." Key identifies three factors as contributing to this change. One is the "emergence of the United States as the principal economic and financial power in the world economy" as world trade and capital flows rapidly expanded and U.S. banks followed their customers abroad (1985, p. 271). Second, "restrictions on geographic expansion and permissible activities of banks in the United States limited the potential for domestic growth" (Key, 1985, p. 271). Third, changes in U.S. laws encouraged and facilitated overseas banking. Some of this activity was designed to avoid the Federal Reserve Board's reserve requirements, interest rate restrictions, minimum maturity requirements on time deposits, and borrowing limits imposed on nondeposit liabilities. Government actions in the mid-1960s to restrain capital movements—the Interest Equalization Tax, Voluntary Foreign Credit Restraint program, and Foreign Direct Investment program—and avoidance of state taxes made foreign banking more attractive to U.S. banks. These laws (particularly the Interest Equalization Tax) were instrumental in the development of the Eurodollar market.

Overseas banking was facilitated by two amendments to the Federal Reserve Act. A 1962 amendment allowed national banks to exercise such powers as are usual in the countries in which their branches are located, other than engaging in nonfinancial commercial business and nongovernment-securities underwriting. (Securities underwriting can be conducted in a bank holding company's foreign subsidiaries to a maximum $15 million in total and no more than 20 percent of an issuer's equity, unlike the absolute prohibition in the United States and for foreign branches.)[10] A 1966 amendment allowed national banks to hold the stock of foreign banks directly and removed strict collateral requirements on loans to foreign banking affiliates. Finally, in the late 1960s the Federal Reserve Board permitted banks without foreign branches to participate in the Eurodollar market by allowing them to establish shell branches. Most of these are located in the Caribbean islands. In 1981 banks in the United States were permitted to establish international banking facilities (IBFs) in their United States offices. IBFs can conduct loan and deposit business with foreign residents without being subject to reserve requirements and interest rate ceilings. IBFs also are exempt from federal and state income taxes.[11] As a result, U.S. banks did not have to establish foreign branches to participate in the Eurocurrency market. However, IBFs have been used primarily by foreign banks (particularly Japanese banks) with U.S. operations (Key and Terrell, 1988, pp. 15–16).

During the 1970s, U.S. banks' overseas operations and foreign lending increased substantially, as U.S. banks served as important conduits through which funds deposited by oil-exporting countries were loaned to developing countries, especially those that were net oil importers (Teeters and Terrell, 1983). The increased variability of interest rates during this period encouraged the development of long-term loans with adjustable or rollover interest rates and syndicated medium-term Eurocurrency credit. The International Banking Act of 1978 further liberalized U.S. law by directing the Federal Reserve to permit domestic expansion of U.S. banks' international banking subsidiaries (Edge corporations). The Fed subsequently permitted these Edge corporations to establish interstate branches, which permitted them to increase their lending limits and conserve on capital. (Previously, each Edge corporation had to be separately capitalized with a minimum of $2 million.)

The process by which U.S. banks have expanded overseas is described well by Houpt (1988). "First," he says, "most banks establish 'correspondent' banking relations with large U.S. and foreign money center banks and rely on them for most international banking services. . . . As a bank's commitment to international business grows, the bank soon creates its own international banking department . . . [generally] located in the head office of the parent bank" (1988, p. 4). It usually creates a shell branch or IBF to participate in the Eurocurrency market. Next, "a bank typically establishes or expands its representative offices in major banking centers" (1988, p. 5). Full-service branches follow, and it may complete "its international banking network by creating or acquiring foreign companies to tap foreign retail markets, or take advantage of foreign tax laws, and to surmount official or de facto barriers to entry" (1988, p. 5).

Houpt provides an extensive discussion of the overseas activities of U.S. banks, supplemented with copious statistics. He reports (1988, table 2) that the number of Federal

Reserve member banks with foreign branches grew steadily from seven in 1955 to 107 in 1972. The number increased to 125 in 1973, then grew gradually to 139 in 1979. After an increase to 159 in 1980, the number with foreign branches topped off at 166 in 1983, then declined to 153 in 1987. The number of foreign branches followed a similar pattern: 115 in 1955, 627 in 1972, 789 in 1979, 892 in 1980, and 902 in 1987. The growth pattern of gross assets is roughly similar. These large numbers may obscure the fact that international activity is concentrated in few banks: 25 banks account for three-quarters of all international assets of U.S. banks (1988, p. 19). The top seven (listed in footnote 4) held 73 percent of the total international assets held by the top 25 banks (1988, table 12).

The principal assets of the top 25 international banks in 1987 (the last year given) are claims on banks (31 percent) and loans (41 percent), most of which are foreign commercial and industrial loans (61 percent of loans in 1987, down from 73 percent in 1978) (1988, table 13). The top 25 banks obtained a large proportion of their income from international activities, ranging from 36 to 47 percent of total net income between 1978 and 1984. In 1985 the percentage dropped to 27 percent, recovered to 32 percent in 1986, and in 1987 losses were reported for the first time. The aggregate loss of $7.9 billion compares to the annual aggregate net income ranging from $4.0 to $4.7 billion between 1980 and 1986 (1988, table 14).

3.2. Foreign banks' U.S. activities

The presence of foreign banks in the United States also increased substantially during the 1970s and 1980s. In 1975, 79 foreign banks had 147 branches or agencies in the United States. This number increased to 153 banks operating 328 outlets in 1980 and then increased steadily to 246 banks operating 514 outlets in 1987. About 40 percent of the banks are Western European or Asian and Middle Eastern. The greatest number of banks are from Japan (32), Brazil (15), Germany (13), Italy (12), France (12), the U.K. (10), and Hong Kong (10) (Houpt, 1988, table 19). Among the 25 banks with the most assets in the United States in 1987, 15 are Japanese, 3 are from the U.K., 2 each are Canadian and Italian, and one each is from Hong Kong, Switzerland, and France (1988, table 22).

Prior to passage of the International Banking Act of 1978, foreign banks that wanted to establish branches or agencies had to obtain permission from individual states. Following the expansion of foreign banking interests in the 1920s, some states enacted laws forbidding branching by foreign-owned banks. In part for this reason, but primarily because of the location of foreign-owned firms and financial activities generally, the main locations for foreign bank activities are New York, California, Illinois, Texas, and Florida.

Because they were not subject to federal regulation before 1978, foreign banks were less regulated than many of their U.S. counterparts; they were not subject to reserve requirements, federal deposit insurance, or deposit interest rate ceilings, and they could operate branches in more than one state. However, foreign banks were subject to the laws of states in which they were licensed. These laws could be more restrictive than the federal law for national banks. For example, New York required that assets be kept within the state, which could be more expensive than the requirement for noninterest-bearing reserves. The International Banking Act of 1978 essentially imposed the same regulations and restrictions on foreign as on domestic banks, with the exception that branches of foreign banks with no deposit accounts under $100,000 need not have deposit insurance.[12]

Houpt notes that "one-half of the U.S. branch and agency assets [of foreign banks] were booked in IBFs, requiring that they be foreign or interbank balances. Some foreign banks have established offices that cater to local consumers (often their ethnic groups), just as U.S. banks have pursued similar strategies abroad" (1988, pp. 30–31). However, he notes, "[m]uch of the activity of their U.S. offices is with other banks and with foreign parties— often from the bank's home country. . . . A full majority of their assets are interbank; credit to U.S. companies accounts for only 23 percent. Their liabilities emphasize this point: over 70 percent are interbank, and only about 13 percent are to private U.S. depositors" (1988, pp. 30–31).

4. Competitive and comparative advantages and disadvantages of U.S. compared to foreign banks

4.1. Foreign banks' operations in the United States

Because the United States imposes the same regulations and restrictions on foreign and U.S. chartered banks, neither group has a competitive legal advantage, with one present and one potential exception. Prior to passage of the International Banking Act of 1978, under certain limited conditions foreign banks could have branches in more than one state. These banks were allowed to keep their branches, which gives them an advantage over domestic banks, with two exceptions. Some Western banks were similarly "grandfathered," and the Depository Institutions (Garn-St. Germain) Act of 1982 provides an exception to the Douglas Amendment of the Bank Holding Company Act for the acquisition of failing banks by out-of-state banks. The potential exception is due to the Glass-Steagall and the Bank Holding Company acts, which prohibit banks operating in the United States from directly or indirectly engaging in most nongovernment securities and insurance activities (among other restrictions). Presently, and to a greater extent after 1992, European Community banks are permitted to merge with or own insurance companies and other enterprises. Should such combinations be interpreted as disqualifying a foreign financial conglomerate from participating in U.S. banking markets, these institutions would have to choose between forgoing opportunities in Europe or in the United States.[13] Otherwise, U.S.- and foreign-chartered banks are treated equally in the United States.

However, as just noted, the position of foreign bank branches in the U.S. banking market, particularly Japanese banks, has increased substantially in recent years. I consider five explanations of this situation: comparative operating advantages of foreign banks; subsidization by foreign governments; lower cost of capital; less profitable domestic compared to U.S. lending; and servicing home-country customers.[14] I then consider the concerns of some U.S. bankers that their foreign competitors might be able to underprice them and, as a result, dominate some U.S. markets.

4.1.1. Comparative operating advantages.   These may take the form of greater efficiency, innovation, marketing, and risk reduction. Some crude evidence on efficiency, as measured by the number of employees per dollar of assets, is provided by Hunter and Timme (1990). They used 1986 data to update previous studies of employment in 150 of the world's largest banks in 1967 and 1979. These researchers used multiple regression to "explain" the number of employees per bank as a function of total assets (in constant dollars), number of branches, and dummy variables representing selected countries and groups of countries. They found significant overall increases in efficiency with respect to total assets, with the number of employees per million dollars of assets dropping from 1.22 in 1967 to 0.66 in 1979 and to 0.34 in 1986. With total assets and number of branches accounted for, the number of employees at the U.S. banks was significantly higher than in banks in other countries in 1979 by 5,592 and in 1986 by 11,236. Higher numbers of employees also were found for Brazil and India (as a group) and the U.K., Canada, Australia, and South Africa (as a group) in all three years, with the number increasingly higher over time and as compared to the U.S. banks. In contrast, Japanese banks had significantly more employees in 1967, but insignificantly fewer employees in 1979 ($-1,689$) and 1986 ($-4,215$) (Hunter and Timme, 1990, table 1). Hunter and Timme conducted a further analysis of changes in employment over the period 1980–1986 at 112 of the world's largest 200 banks.[15] They found statistically significant changes at the U.S., Japanese, and U.K. banks. The U.S. banks increased employment by 2.3 percent a year, the Japanese banks decreased employment by 5.9 percent annually, and the U.K. banks decreased employment by 4.4 percent annually, with total assets and number of branches held constant (1990, table 3). They also note that the U.K. banks "exhibited one of the highest ratios of employees to total assets among banks headquartered in the industrialized countries" (1990, p. 9). Although, as the authors admit, such factors as differences in product mix (and off-balance-sheet activities) could explain these differences in employment, it does appear that the U.S. banks are less efficient with respect to numbers of employees than are the Japanese banks. This research, however, does not distinguish between the domestic and international operations of the large banks studied.

I am not aware of any formal studies of innovation and marketing. Casual observation and informal interviews, though, give no reason to believe that foreign banks have been more innovative; indeed, U.S. banks are said to have pioneered the development of financial instruments and creative financing vehicles.[16] Nor have foreign banks captured much of the U.S. retail market, with the possible exception of Japanese banks in California that are said to have increased their market share by employing the innovative device of being polite to customers.

An additional form of marketing that should be considered is higher bank capital, which reduces the risk to depositors (and, to a lesser extent, to borrowers and other customers). This explanation of the growth of international banks was put forth by Baer (1990). After considering several explanations for the low growth of U.S. banks' foreign assets, he concludes (p. 28):

> The rapid growth of foreign banking organizations in the U.S. is best understood as a result of three events. First, Japanese banking organizations experienced a rapid increase in market capitalization due to rapid increases in the value of their equity

portfolios. Second, the increasing importance of large-value highly leveraged transactions conveyed an advantage to well-capitalized banks able to lend large amounts of money quickly. Third, the market capitalization of the largest U.S. banks suffered repeated reverses due to a series of regional downturns and the failure of many LDC borrowers to repay loans as scheduled.

As noted above, Baer (1990, figure 6) bases this conclusion on a uniformly positive relationship between growth in holdings of foreign assets over 1984–1986 and market capitalization as a percent of assets by banks in Japan, West Germany, the United Kingdom, and the United States; Switzerland is the exception, as banks there have higher capital ratios but less foreign asset growth than West German banks. For this explanation to be correct, depositors in the lesser capitalized U.S. and U.K. banks would have to believe that the banks of other countries are safer because the U.S. and U.K. governments would permit their international banks to fail.

The advantage to banks of risk reduction from diversification does appear to play a role in the desire of foreign banks to expand into the United States. The United States offers a politically and economically stable environment, and the U.S. dollar is the principal international currency. For these reasons and because of the size of this market, the United States offers foreign bank investors and depositors the opportunity of diversifying their assets and reducing the variance of earnings. A few studies present evidence that is consistent with this hypothesis. Goodman (1981) uses proxy variables showing that unsystematic risk is largely reduced when loans from different countries are combined into portfolios. Unfortunately, events following Goodman's study revealed that risk is not distributed independently among countries. The fortunes of countries dependent on commodity exports declined at the same time. Eastern European countries were similarly unable to repay their debts. Hence, what appeared to Goodman to be diversified portfolios turned out to be quite risky. Banks that invested in such portfolios absorbed considerable default costs.

Cosset and Lampron (1982, cited by Rugman and Kamath, 1986, p. 42) report data for Canadian banks that are consistent with the country-diversification explanation. They compare the rate of return on assets of the five multinational Canadian banks with smaller domestic banks over 1971–1979, and find higher returns for the multinationals. Although the multinationals' returns on domestic assets are higher and the standard deviation of returns is lower than those on their international assets, the total standard deviation of returns is lower than each of the components.[17] Unfortunately, I am not aware of country-risk-diversification studies covering the 1980s. I also should note that the studies cited assume implicitly that foreign banks invest in obligations of domestic companies, even though foreign banks' loans tend to be made to divisions of companies headquartered in their countries.

4.1.2. Government subsidies.   Subsidies provided by their governments may give foreign banks a competitive advantage over their U.S. rivals. The subsidies could be paid in the form of below-market interest rates on borrowings from the central bank and government deposits on which banks pay less than market rates. An American Bankers Association (ABA) monograph (1990a, p. 78) states that in 1986 central bank borrowings comprised the following percentages (over 1 percent) of banks' assets: 4.2 for German banks, 1.8 percent for Netherland banks, 1.7 percent for Swiss banks, and 1.2 percent for Japanese banks.[18] This monograph also states that "federal funds [are] held in banks at below-market interest rates" in Belgium, Canada, France, Italy, and Japan (p. 85). On the other hand, foreign banks in the United States complain that they have to pay more than their U.S. rivals for borrowings from the Federal Reserve.

Taxes paid by foreign banks also may be lower. The requirement that U.S. banks keep reserves in noninterest-bearing accounts at the Federal Reserve represents a considerable tax when nominal interest rates are high, as they have been for over a decade.[19] With respect to income taxation, the ABA monograph presents a table showing that United States banks have about the lowest average tax rate in 1988 (p. 84). But the authors correctly point out, "[c]omparing the tax environments of banks in different nations is extremely difficult . . . [in part because] each tax bears an implicit cost to the bank even if the bank avoids the tax—simply because the bank is effectively assessed for the tax to the extent that it forgoes otherwise more lucrative activities" (p. 76).

Finally, I believe that all governments implicitly guarantee the deposits of their international banks. Although many governments charge banks premiums for the insurance and explicitly limit coverage, the charge imposed on U.S. banks is about the highest.[20]

On balance, the magnitude of subsidies does not appear to be very great. In any event, to the extent that foreign banks are subsidized by their governments, the cost is borne by the other taxpayers of these countries. The benefits from the subsidies either are kept by the owners of the foreign banks or reduce the amounts paid by their customers.

4.1.3. Lower costs of capital.

Lower capital costs would permit foreign banks to underprice their U.S. rivals, all other things equal. This situation could occur when the following conditions were present. First, the foreign public has a relatively high demand and possibly a low interest elasticity for saving, perhaps because of favorable tax treatment for saving relative to consumption, custom, age distribution of the population, or restraints on domestic lending that forces nonfavored people (such as would-be entrepreneurs and small businesses) to save rather than borrow. Cartelized or poorly developed financial markets also would increase the cost to investors of borrowing or of issuing equities, while entry by alternative and more efficient suppliers of capital was effectively restricted or investors were unable to obtain capital in less expensive markets. Second, savers tend to put their funds with banks because they are constrained, perhaps by capital controls, taxation, or costly information, from engaging in direct lending or investments. Third, constraints on competition, especially cartel- or government-imposed ceilings on interest rates on deposits and restrictions on alternative investments, allowed banks to pay below-market rates for funds. In this situation, banks obtain funds relatively cheaply and have more on hand than they want to invest domestically. This condition is enhanced if they are able to form a cartel to set lending rates and, thus, limit the amount of domestic lending. Consequently, they will have excess funds to invest in the United States.[21]

Several of these conditions appear applicable, at least in part, to Japan. Cargill (1986, p. 43) states that before 1974 "[h]ouseholds were essentially restricted to holding deposits, bank debentures, and money in trust accounts at controlled interest rates. Even as late as 1978, consumer and mortgage credit in Japan was only 17.5 percent of the gross national product (GNP) compared to 68.1 percent in the United States." However, after 1974 the public shifted substantial amounts from bank deposits to the government postal savings system, which paid a higher interest rate that was, essentially, tax free (1986, p. 49). Cargill also states that, although the financial markets have undergone some degree of deregulation, as of 1985 "[d]eposit rates for the majority of deposit holders remain constrained [and] . . . [l]ending rates remain indirectly tied to the Bank of Japan discount rate" (p. 54). The conditions described apply even more to the Taiwanese banking system, which is highly controlled by the government (it owns nearly all the domestic banks) (Cheng, 1986, p. 148). Nevertheless, savings have been high. [Cheng speculates that the unofficial "curb" market, "although crude and primitive, may have been the unsung hero behind high savings and investment rates" (p. 157).] The explanation, though, does not appear valid for European banks.

A careful study of the cost of capital in the United States, Japan, Germany, and the United Kingdom by McCauley and Zimmer (1989) found significantly lower capital costs in Japan and Germany. The authors reject income tax structures as an important explanation of lower capital costs. Rather, they conclude (p. 7) that "higher household savings in Japan and Germany and more successful policies for maintaining stable growth in Japan and stable prices in Germany" are primarily responsible for the gap. In addition, they ascribe lower capital costs to government policy and business practice in Japan and to the universal banking system of Germany that allows and encourages banks to rescue failing firms, thereby reducing the cost of capital through greater use of debt at lower risk premia. Prowse (1990) provides evidence that supports this conclusion, at least with respect to Japan, where banks can and do hold substantial equity as well as debt positions in firms. His study of 110 Japanese firms reveals approximately equal holdings of debt and equity by the largest debtholders, which reduces the expectation (expressed formally by finance agency theory) that the stockholders might expropriate debtholders by shifting to riskier assets. Prowse finds a statistically significant positive correlation between the amount of debt and equity held by an institution, "a correlation which becomes stronger in those firms which are measured to have greater scope for shareholders to engage in opportunistic behavior at the expense of debtholders" (p. 30). He also compared the leverage ratios of U.S. and Japanese firms. Where agency problems are the greatest, the U.S. firms tend to have lower leverage (less debt). But the Japanese firms' leverage not only is higher overall, but the "ratios do not vary as much (and sometimes vary in the opposite direction to US firms) between firms divided on the basis of the postulated severity of the agency conflict" (p. 30). Prowse concludes that his work "suggests that Japanese financial institutions take on an active monitoring role in the firms in which they invest that US banks are precluded from doing owing to a more restrictive legal and regulatory environment in the US" (p. 31).

4.1.4. Less profitable domestic compared to U.S. lending. Lending in the United States could be more profitable than domestic lending for at least four important reasons: lending cartels, as just discussed; effective competition from government institutions; reduced domestic economic activity; and greater investment returns in the United States. These conditions appear to apply to Japan. Feldman (1986, p. 29) states that "[w]ith the decline in real investment demand after the first oil crisis, rates of return available on the loan market weakened, and alternative uses of funds had to be found." Beginning in 1977, he states (p. 25), banks shifted out of domestic loans toward foreign assets. Suzuki (1986, pp. 17, 41) points out that the banks' major domestic competitors, Japanese government institutions, offer below-market financing to favored borrowers (exporters and export-related investments) and that these institutions' share of fund flows to final borrowers increased from between 16 and 19 percent from 1965 through 1973 to 29 and 27 percent in 1982 and 1983, respectively (the last years given). This situation, together with the high savings rate relative to investment in Japan, encouraged Japanese banks to look to foreign markets.

The opposite situation characterized the United States. The great increase in U.S. government borrowing in the 1980s together with a relatively low savings rate made the United States a net importer of capital. This demand and the stability of the U.S. economy during the 1980s made lending in the United States relatively desirable.

4.1.5. Service to home-country customers.

Demands from home-country customers who have established or are planning to establish a presence in the United States appears to be a very important determinant of foreign bank expansion in the United States. Banks have a comparative advantage in dealing with their own nationals. They specialize in knowing their own country's legal system and their government's rules (official and unofficial) on capital flows, exchange restrictions, tariffs and quotas, taxation, and the like. They also specialize in preparing and administering documents necessary for international trade. When they have a presence in a country, they can more easily obtain similar information about that country. In addition, they are familiar with the customs, language, and relationships of their countrymen. Furthermore, banks that want to keep their customers often must offer them services in countries in which those customers do business, or the customers will shift their business to banks that provide these services.

As noted above, Houpt (1988, p. 31) finds that "[m]uch of the activity of [foreign banks' U.S. branches] is with other banks and with foreign parties—often from the bank's home country." In particular, at year-end 1987, 62 percent of the assets held by Japanese bank branches and agencies in the United States were direct claims on residents of Japan or claims on companies or individuals with Japanese home offices or guarantors (Dohner, 1989, p. 9).

4.1.6. Underpricing by foreign banks.

There is little evidence to support the fear that Japanese or other foreign-owned banks have greatly superior advantages over U.S. banks. Nevertheless, let us assume they enjoy lower costs or are willing to absorb low returns on capital or even losses. If these banks price loans and guarantees at rates lower than those that their U.S. competitors can offer, consumers of these products will benefit even though the U.S. banks lose. Should the products be priced below marginal opportunity costs, the foreign banks also will lose.

Assume further that, as a result of this possibly predatory pricing, the U.S. banks withdraw from the market. The foreign banks might then attempt to exploit this situation by raising their prices. However, there is little to prevent other foreign banks (perhaps those headquartered in another country) from taking business from them by not following their lead. Nor can the foreign banks prevent U.S. banks or other kinds of financial institutions (such as investment banks and insurance companies) from reentering the market. Two facts (in addition to U.S. laws that make monopolization illegal) support this conclusion. First, financial products are almost if not entirely fungible and can be produced with little fixed investment. Second, although a firm or group of firms might dominate the production of a financial product because of some overwhelming comparative advantage, alternative suppliers of financial products abound. These suppliers can develop and offer the product should the sole supplier significantly increase its price to consumers.

4.2. U.S. banks' overseas operations

Analogues of the same five explanations of foreign-bank activity in the United States—comparative operating advantages of U.S. banks, subsidization by the U.S. government, lower cost of capital, less profitable domestic compared to foreign banking, and service to domestic customers—might explain U.S. banks' overseas activities. In addition, I consider the existence and effects of constraints on competition by foreign governments.

Two of these possible explanations can be dismissed rather quickly. There is no reason to believe that the U.S. government has subsidized banks or that U.S. banks have lower costs of capital than their foreign competitors. Indeed, considering that U.S. banks are subject to noninterest-bearing required reserves on their domestic deposits and to deposit insurance premiums rather than noncharged de facto government guarantees, there is some reason to believe that the U.S. government has penalized its banks (or, rather, users of bank money) somewhat. The considerable competitiveness of the U.S. banking system, particularly for money-center international banks, and the legal prohibition of nationwide and universal banking make it unlikely that banks with foreign operations enjoy lower costs of capital, as might be the situation for Japanese banks. Consequently, the analysis is limited to the other three reasons.

4.2.1. Comparative operating advantages and disadvantages. U.S. banks' experience in marketing and in tailoring financial arrangements to meet consumers' demands appear to have been important factors supporting U.S. banks' overseas operations. Before the last decade or so, the financial markets of many countries (such as Japan and France) were characterized by private and government cartels. Unlike the situation in the United States, banks in many countries were not very interested in serving consumers. In these markets, U.S. bankers had much to offer, and they were effective in getting profitable business in some locations. The opportunity to offer services to consumers, though, is limited by difficulties in dealing with foreign cultural mores and by government-imposed restrictions. Even with respect to business-oriented banking, U.S. banks often found it difficult to obtain permission to enter some markets. One means by which entry was facilitated and continued operations were assured was for U.S. banks to make loans on favorable terms to foreign governments and to enterprises that government officials favored. Hence, the benefits from U.S. banks' operations in some countries (including fees and the value of concessions) should be measured net of the losses absorbed on these loans, on a present value basis.[22]

Reduction of risk is another operating advantage of foreign activities. Khoury (1980, ch. 7) examined the financial statements of 13 U.S. international banks over the period 1970–1977. He found that the returns and variance of returns on their foreign and domestic assets were similar. But, because the returns on these two groups of assets were negatively correlated, the combination had lower variance. Thus, international diversification enabled the banks studied to reduce risk without sacrificing return.[23] However, as noted above, the study precedes the losses incurred by U.S. banks on their loans to less developed countries.

These comparative operating advantages (with the possible exception of lower risk) have been reduced and may be completely eliminated. Liberalization of regulations in the Pacific Basin, in particular, have reduced U.S. banks' comparative advantage. Domestic banks in such countries as Japan and Korea have benefited from being in a more competitive environment. Australia and New Zealand also have deregulated their banking markets, and their banks have considerably improved their operations.[24] Much earlier, banks in England and in some other European countries learned much from U.S. banks, particularly with respect to serving consumers.[25]

With the reduction in restrictive regulations expected throughout the European Community after 1992, U.S. banks may find themselves suffering from a comparative disadvantage. The E.C.'s Second Banking Directive will permit an E.C.-chartered bank to conduct any activity allowed in its home country in any other E.C. country. Hence, it is likely that universal banking, in which a bank can conduct virtually any financial activity and own almost any asset (with some limitations), will dominate, although probably not characterize, European banking. U.S. banks' subsidiaries will be allowed to operate in the E.C. on the same terms as other E.C.-chartered banks. It is expected that other U.S. banks will be able to offer the same services as E.C. banks in Europe even though the E.C. banks' U.S. branches and subsidiaries must conform to the more restrictive U.S. laws. But because the Glass-Steagall Act and other laws prohibit most U.S. banks from being directly involved in the United States in such activities as corporate securities underwriting, insurance, and real estate, some U.S. bankers (in particular, those who have not had overseas branches or subsidiaries where such activities can be conducted) may lack the skills to compete effectively with many European bankers.[26] Furthermore, European banks have geographic and language advantages, in addition to experience with universal banking and nationwide branching, that give them a comparative advantage over U.S. banks in serving customers in the E.C.[27]

U.S. banks nevertheless have comparative advantages, at least for the moment, in designing and marketing financial instruments that allow companies to reduce risk. Perhaps because the United States experienced large unexpected changes in interest rates in the late 1970s and early 1980s, many large U.S. financial institutions have become adept at dealing with this situation. As noted above, demand for such instruments is likely to increase in the future as the world economy becomes more integrated. However, much of this expertise is located in investment banks. Were the Glass-Steagall Act's provisions separating commercial and investment banking repealed, a pooling of knowledge and facilities could be beneficial to U.S. institutions.

4.2.2. Less profitable U.S. compared to overseas banking.   Banking in the United States has been less attractive at times than banking in Europe because of costs imposed by U.S. laws and regulations. As previously described, U.S. regulations (particularly the Interest Equalization Tax and required reserves on U.S. deposits) made European banking more profitable for some banks than domestic banking in the 1970s. U.S. banks also could partially escape the Glass-Steagall Act's prohibition against nongovernment securities underwriting by establishing overseas subsidiaries. As discussed above, this has been an important determinant of expansion of U.S. banks into European markets.

4.2.3. Service to domestic customers.   Paralleling the situation for foreign banks, U.S. banks tend to follow their customers as they expand overseas. Again, this appears to be a major reason for international banking.

4.2.4. Constraints on competition by foreign governments.   Several countries (such as Taiwan) limit competition by foreign banks, including U.S. banks. At present, such limitations are almost completely removed from most Western European countries, Canada, New Zealand, Australia, and Japan.[28] Hence, U.S. banks are at a legal disadvantage in these countries only as a result of constraints imposed by the U.S. government. However, as is explained by Cargill and Royama (1990), U.S. banks have found entry into the Japanese domestic market very difficult due to the "main bank system," in which affiliations of firms (*keiretsu*) are led by a large city bank and in which low-risk members borrow from banks and then lend to higher risk members with trade credit (1990, p. 9). Consequently, they say, "[w]hile the number of foreign banks has increased from 64 in 1980 to 82 in 1988, foreign banks represent less than 0.47 percent of all bank deposits. Most of their activities have been confined to interbank and money market transactions" (p. 17). Cargill and Royama also point to the difficulty of U.S. banks to shift from an open market to negotiated pricing, Japanese restrictions on banking, deposit ceiling rates which make competition for household deposits difficult for new entrants, and competition among Japanese institutions which has left few exploitable markets in Japan (pp. 18–19).

In any event, it would not be in the interest of U.S. consumers to restrict competition by foreign banks in retaliation for restraints on U.S. banks, were such restraints responsible for the U.S. banks' lack of success in the foreign banks' countries. Nor would U.S. consumers and taxpayers benefit from subsidies given to U.S. banks that enable them to compete more effectively with foreign banks.

5. Domestic and international banking regulation and supervision

Concerns about bank safety and financial market stability affect U.S. banks in three principal ways: foreign banks may be less restrictively regulated or inadequately supervised, which may give them an advantage over U.S. banks and may impose an externality on U.S. banks; U.S. banks may be subjected to excessively costly domestic regulation and supervision that impedes their competitiveness; and the capital standards formulated by the Basle Committee of central bankers, including the Federal Reserve, may impose greater costs on U.S. than on foreign banks.

5.1. Foreign bank supervision and regulation and externalities

Two consequences might follow if foreign banks were subjected to a lesser degree of supervision and prudential regulation than U.S. banks: U.S. banks would lose business to those banks and an externality costly to U.S. banks might result from foreign banks' failing. The first possible consequence is based on the assumption that a poorly supervised bank would deliberately take great risks and that customers would prefer to do business with such a bank. Neither assumption makes much sense. Depositors who place their funds in such a risk-taking bank either are ignorant of the risks they face or are compensated for those risks with higher interest payments or other rewards. Ignorant or miscalculating depositors who lose when a risk-taking bank fails will either be compensated by their governments (that is to say, by other taxpayers of their countries) or will absorb the loss.[29] In either event, the cost is not borne by U.S. taxpayers and is analogous to the situation (discussed above) of foreign banks being subsidized by their governments. Borrowers and other customers of such risk-taking banks risk losing bank-specific knowledge should their banks fail. Consequently, unless they are direct beneficiaries of the banks' risk-taking, they are likely to do business with safer banks.

Second, two kinds of possibly costly externality might affect U.S. banks when poorly supervised and regulated foreign banks fail. The first is disruption of the international payments system and losses imposed on banks to which failed banks are indebted. This risk, however, is no different than the risks faced by a bank in lending to any customer, except that the amount outstanding can be larger than that permitted under the "loans to one borrower" limitation. Indeed, the risk is lower because most countries tend implicitly to guarantee their domestic banks' deposits. Nevertheless, the cost of disruption can be great if the legal responsibilities of the parties are not set in advance. Consequently, the supervisory agencies in countries with interdependent clearing systems might direct their attention to specifying the parties' legal rights and a means by which these rights can be adjudicated, should the necessity arise.

The second externality is disruption to international financial markets as a result of a "loss of confidence." Presumably, financial market participants would withdraw from doing business with banks if they thought the system might collapse. But where would they go? They could only shift their funds and business to banks perceived as sound. Thus, well-capitalized and well-managed banks would benefit when depositors run from banks thought to be insolvent, which should give banks positive incentives to avoid being perceived as weak. Furthermore, unlike a domestic situation, there cannot be a multiple contraction of world money as a result of people taking funds out of a fractional reserve banking system by hoarding specie or currency. The reason is that there is no world money. Although there could be a temporary reduction of liquidity if the money supply of an important country declined greatly, the central banks of other countries could deal with this situation by expanding their money supplies.

Therefore, I conclude that lax supervision and insufficient regulation of foreign banks, should that occur, might be of concern to taxpayers in their countries, but not to U.S. taxpayers. It also is doubtful that U.S. banks would permanently lose customers with whom they want to do business to failure-prone foreign banks.[30]

5.2. Excessive U.S. supervision and regulation

The ABA monograph (1990a, p. 2) expresses this concern as follows: "U.S. banks operate under more costly and restrictive regulations than do institutions in other industrialized countries. As a consequence of our less flexible regulatory framework, U.S. banks are less able to meet the changing needs of both domestic and foreign customers." The ABA points to restrictions on the financial services that U.S. banks can provide to their customers, particularly securities and insurance underwriting and sales. With respect to regulation, it identifies U.S. banks as having higher reserve requirements, higher-cost deposit insurance, compliance regulation, multiple jurisdictions, and more formal reporting requirements.[31] Each is considered in turn.

5.2.1. Restrictions on financial services—securities and insurance.
Legal prohibitions that prevent U.S. banks from offering their customers complete securities and insurance underwriting and sales reduce those banks' ability to serve their customers and to diversify their activities. As a result, U.S. banks' are somewhat less profitable and possibly more risky than they would be in the absence of these restrictions.[32] As noted above, some U.S. bankers also are disadvantaged because they do not have the opportunity to develop the skills required to compete with foreign banks outside of the United States. Within the United States, however, all banks are similarly disadvantaged.

5.2.2. Reserve requirements.
The noninterest-bearing reserves required against deposits represent a tax on U.S. banks and on users of bank money, but one that also is imposed on foreign banks doing business in the United States. Deposits in overseas branches and subsidiaries of U.S. banks are subject to the reserve requirements of the countries in which they are located. Deposits in overseas branches are subject to the U.S. Eurocurrency reserve requirement of 3 percent on the net amount of (1) total branch loans made to U.S. residents, and (2) advances, less amounts due to their head office. Foreign banks that lend to U.S. residents from outside the United States are not subject to this 3 percent requirement. Hence, U.S. banks are at a disadvantage to the extent of the interest they forgo on these noninterest-bearing reserves that support loans to U.S. residents made by their foreign branches. More importantly, U.S. depositors and the domestic operations of U.S. banks are disadvantaged by this "tax."

5.2.3. Deposit insurance.
Premiums for federal deposit insurance are not charged against deposits held by U.S. banks outside of the country. Nevertheless, these depositors are implicitly protected by the banking agencies' policy of not permitting depositors in

very large banks to absorb losses. Thus, U.S. international banks are, to an extent, subsidized by other banks. However, large U.S. banks that are very unlikely to fail probably
overpay for deposit insurance. In addition, they must pay part of the cost of bailing out
depositors in insolvent savings and loan associations. Hence, these banks should be
interested in reforming the U.S. deposit insurance system to reduce future costs that
might be imposed by risk-prone and risk-preferring depository institutions.

It should be noted that the proposal for partial deposit insurance for accounts over
$100,000 put forth by the ABA (1990b), among others, would tend to disadvantage U.S.
international banks, if it were adopted. Under this proposal, should a bank become
insolvent and be closed by the authorities, domestic deposit accounts over $100,000 and
the total amount of accounts held outside the United States would be reduced immediately by 12 percent (or some other number) to pay for those depositors' share of the
expected costs of the failure. In contrast, the deposits of the foreign banks with which U.S.
banks compete overseas are de facto totally insured by their governments as a result
of those governments' policies of not allowing very large banks to fail with losses imposed
on depositors.

There is an alternative solution, however. It is to impose a capital requirement that is
sufficiently high to absorb most losses, together with a predetermined procedure for
restructuring banks that are likely to fail. To illustrate, banks with over, say, 10 percent
capital to assets, would be supervised generally. Should a bank's capital ratio decline
below 10 percent to, say, 6 percent, the authorities would have the discretion to require its
management to suspend dividends and interest payments on subordinated debt that
serves as capital, forbid the bank from growing, and closely supervise the bank's operations. At this point, market discipline is likely to correct the situation. If the capital
deficiency is not repaired and the ratio declines below 6 percent, the authorities *must*
prohibit the bank from paying dividends and interest on subordinated debt, and not
permit it to expand. Should capital go below 3 percent, the bank would be taken over.
Capital should be measured in terms of market values.[33] As is discussed under international capital standards below, this procedure would not be costly to banks that did not
expect to take advantage of the present U.S. deposit insurance system.

5.2.4. Compliance regulation, multiple jurisdictions, and more formal reporting require-
ments.   U.S. banks are subject to more extensive and expensive examination and supervision than are banks in many countries. Few, if any, countries examine their banks to
determine that anti-discrimination laws and consumer information requirements are
being followed. Few, if any, countries have a Community Reinvestment Act that permits
people to object to bank mergers and branching on the grounds that the banks involved
have not served their local communities well. Only the United States prohibits nationwide
branching; indeed, after 1992 branching throughout the European Community will be
permitted for E.C.-chartered banks. Most countries do not demand as extensive public
and regulatory reporting of financial data as is the situation in the United States. These
often costly requirements do, indeed, increase the U.S. banks' operating costs. To the extent
that these requirements do not benefit the public, they should be removed or reduced.

Banks in other countries also are subject to costly regulation, particularly with respect to labor. Some European countries restrain banks (and other corporations) from reducing their work force and prescribe vacations and other fringe benefits. These requirements impose costs on bank shareholders and customers.

5.3. Basle Accord capital standards

In July 1988, the Basle Committee on Banking Regulations and Supervisory Practices (also known as the Cooke Committee, after its then chairman) published a proposal for a risk-based capital standard that was endorsed by the central banks of the Group of Ten (G-10) Countries plus two.[34] The standard specifies two tiers of capital and four asset risk classes. It is to be applied to banks on a consolidated basis that includes subsidiaries undertaking banking and financial business. By year-end 1992 banks must have capital equal to at least 8 percent of risk-adjusted assets. At least half must be "core capital"—primarily equity shares and retained earnings. The balance is "supplementary capital"—primarily subordinated debt with a minimum original maturity of over five years, loan-loss reserves, undisclosed (secret) reserves, and asset revaluation reserves. The loan-loss reserve portion of supplementary capital is limited and is to be phased out. Subordinated debt is subject to certain qualifying limitations, including being only partially counted as capital as its maturity decreases and being limited to 50 percent of supplementary capital. Four categories of assets are specified for the risk adjustment. A weight of zero is applied to cash, claims on central governments and banks, and (at national discretion) claims on and loans guaranteed by domestic public-sector entities. A 20 percent weight applies to claims on banks chartered by OECD (Organization for European Economic Cooperation) member countries and public sector entities and loans guaranteed by them and cash items in the process of collection. A 50 percent weight applies to mortgage loans on borrower-owned or rented property. All other assets carry a 100 percent weight. Off-balance-sheet exposures are risk-classified and included with similarly classified assets. No consideration is given to interest-rate risk, foreign-exchange risk, and inadequate-diversification risk (among others) or to distinctions among nongovernmental and other-than-OECD-bank loans with the exception of residential mortgages.

The Basle Accord standard imposes costs on banks to the extent that they will have to hold capital in excess of the amount they otherwise would keep. Banks might want to hold less capital for three reasons: limited investment opportunities, taxes, and higher returns from risk-taking. Each of these is described and their effects delineated.

Banks may not be able to invest profitably the assets represented by the capital they are required to keep when they are restrained from undertaking some activities, such as holding equity investments in properties and enterprises. This limitation applies to a much lesser extent to universal banks, as their investments are largely unconstrained.[35] Thus, this possible cost of the Basle Accord capital standard does not affect most European and, to a large extent, Canadian international banks. Japanese banks apparently will not be affected because they can invest in affiliates that can invest in other companies.[36]

Furthermore, Japanese and European banks hold securities and properties with market values considerably in excess of book values. Their banking authorities could permit them to revalue these assets (up to a maximum of 45 percent of unrealized appreciation), thereby increasing their supplementary capital. Therefore, the only banks that might be affected adversely are those in the United States.

Debt allows banks (and other corporations) to reduce income taxes because, in the United States and some other countries, interest paid on debt reduces taxable income while dividends declared on equity does not. Thus, the Basle Accord capital standard that restricts the amount of subordinated debt that can count as capital can impose higher taxes on banks.

Banks may want to hold less capital to take advantage of deposit insurance, as the interest rate they must pay for government-insured deposits does not reflect the risks taken, the benefits from which accrue to shareholders. In this regard, it is important to note that governments in most countries (perhaps all) without formal deposit insurance implicitly guarantee the nonequity liabilities of their large, international banks. Hence, these banking authorities have reason to exclude subordinated debt from capital as they most likely will have to guarantee it should a large bank become insolvent.

The Basle Accord (or another) capital standard could be costless to all U.S. banks except those that want to take excessive risks if subordinated debentures were counted fully as core capital and if banks' activities were not restrained. Subordinated debentures are, in essence, explicitly nongovernment-guaranteed deposits that cannot be repaid until after the authorities have had the time to reorganize or close an insolvent or nearly insolvent bank. For this purpose, subordinated debentures must not be redeemable at the option of the holder or bank and have *remaining* maturities of no less than one or two years. Holders of such debt cannot gain from risk-taking by banks, as they are not residual claimants. Because they can lose, they have great incentives to monitor banks' activities. When such debt is traded, the market-clearing interest rate provides the authorities with early warnings of a banks' deterioration. Difficulties a bank might face in refinancing maturing debt also provide evidence of problems.

6. Conclusions

Pavel and McElravey (1990, p. 3) sum up well the changes that are taking place in international financial markets:

> Financial globalization is being driven by advances in data processing and telecommunications, liberalization of restrictions on cross-border capital flows, deregulation of domestic capital markets, and greater competition among these markets for a share of the world's trading volume.

A quick reading of the lists of the world's largest banks can generate the misleading conclusion that U.S. banks have been losing their previously important position in this growing international marketplace to the Japanese. A close analysis of the data shows that the domination of the list by Japanese banks is due primarily to their domestic economic situation rather than to their prowess in international banking. Furthermore, as U.S. banks earn substantial net revenues from services rather than from loans and other investments, size, as such, is less meaningful.

Within the United States, domestic and foreign banks are equally well and badly constrained by laws and regulations. If better service to consumers were desired, restrictions on interstate branching and on the products banks could offer (particularly securities underwriting and insurance sales) should be removed. These restrictions also reduce the profitability and increase the riskiness of U.S. banks, which disadvantages them in conducting both their U.S. and overseas operations. Noninterest-bearing reserve requirements also are costly to users of bank services. Foreign competitors have an advantage over U.S. banks in this regard because their non-U.S. branches are not subject to reserve requirements as are the overseas branches of U.S. banks.

U.S. banks expanded overseas for much the same reasons that foreign banks operate in the United States. The U.S. banks followed their customers as those customers established overseas operations. The banks exploited comparative advantages in dealing with consumers and in developing and marketing financial products. Financial transactions were moved out of the country as banks and their customers sought to avoid costly and restrictive regulations, such as the Interest Equalization Tax.

The future of U.S. banks' international operations depends, in large measure, on those banks' managements and on the extent to which United States', rather than foreign countries', regulations restrict their ability to be profitable. U.S. regulations not only restrict the activities that U.S. banks can conduct abroad but make it more difficult and expensive to serve their customers at home, thereby weakening them. The movement toward economic integration that the E.C. is adopting is unlikely to affect adversely U.S. banks that already are established in the E.C. Banks not established there probably will not be restrained by the E.C., as long as the United States continues to subject European banks to the same regulations that constrain U.S. banks. However, the U.S. restrictions on banks engaging fully in securities and insurance underwriting and sales not only adversely affects banks in the United States from serving business and consumers well, but restricts somewhat the banks' ability to serve customers elsewhere. The Basle Accord capital standard is likely to be more costly to U.S. than to many other countries' banks, because the United States restricts the assets in which our banks can invest and the products they can offer to the public. Were subordinated debentures counted fully as capital, a large part of this cost could be avoided.

Notes

1. See Bryant (1987), particularly chapter 3, for a description of the "progressive internationalization of financial intermediation."
2. See Bank for International Settlements (1986, part II) for a description of these instruments.

3. Baer does not list the banks included or indicate whether both assets and equity were adjusted to market values. He gives as the source of his data "Bank for International Settlements and Salomon Brothers."

4. It is interesting to note that Caisse Nationale de Credit Agricole is now considered an international bank.

5. The U.S. banks are Citicorp, BankAmerica, Chase Manhattan, Manufacturers Hanover, J. P. Morgan, Chemical Bank, and Bankers Trust.

6. So that the relationship between the variables of interest could be seen easily, I allocated growth due to differing initial shares of domestic and foreign currency assets and statistical prediction error (which Dohner and Terrell label "other") to foreign and domestic assets in proportion to the amounts initially estimated.

7. I similarly allocated Dohner and Terrell's "interaction factor" to each of the three named variables. (The "interaction factor" was particularly high for the Japanese banks.)

8. Citations are to Dohner (1989), although Terrell, Dohner, and Lowrey (1989) present very similar results and use similar language.

9. Yamada (1990) reports that between 1979 and 1984, interest payments on from 93 to 87 percent of deposits were constrained. This percentage declined to 82 percent in 1985, and thereafter by about eight percentage points a year, reaching 46 percent in 1989.

10. Regulation K; an August 1990 proposal amendment to Regulation K would increase this limit to $60 million or 25 percent of the parent financial institution's Tier-1 (essentially common and preferred stock) capital, whichever is less.

11. See Key and Terrell (1988) for an extensive description and analysis of IBFs.

12. See Key and Welsh (1988) for a fulsome description of the activities and regulation of the U.S. offices and branches of foreign banking organizations.

13. See Institute of International Bankers (1990) for an extended discussion. In August 1990, the Federal Reserve proposed excluding ownership of life insurance companies from the "qualifying foreign bank organization" test, which requires a foreign bank doing business in the United States to derive more than half its total revenues from banking activities.

14. Aliber (1984) surveys theories of and empirical work on international banking. He finds little persuasive support for any theory, except perhaps lower cost of capital and, possibly, escape from regulation.

15. The banks included are those headquartered in developed countries with complete data over the period, as reported in the *American Banker*.

16. Bank for International Settlements (1986), which gives a comprehensive listing and valuable discussion of recent financial instruments, identifies most of them as originating with U.S. commercial and investment banks.

17. Rugman and Kamath (1986) review other studies, but they are of U.S. and Canadian banks. Their own study does not compare domestic with international banks. Hence their finding, which indicates relatively low systematic risk for most of the "thirty-seven of the world's largest banks having considerable international operations" (p. 54), is, at most, not inconsistent with the risk-reduction hypothesis.

18. The definition of "bank" and source of the data are not given.

19. Foreign banks' U.S. branches are subject to the same reserve requirements as are U.S.-chartered banks.

20. See Barthomew and Vanderhoff (1990) for a comprehensive discussion of deposit insurance in 27 countries. They report (table 2) that Japan charges .008 percent on deposit balances up to about $60,000, West Germany charges .03 percent of total deposits, the United Kingdom imposes a collective levy not to exceed .3 percent of domestic sterling deposits and limits coverage to 75 percent of deposit balances up to about $12,000, and Switzerland's, France's, and Italy's plans are unfunded.

21. Aliber (1984, pp. 669–670) emphasizes lower costs of capital as an important reason for the expansion of banks into other countries. He supports this conclusion with ratios of the market value of banks in various countries to their book values (q ratio). He says that "banks headquartered in countries with higher q ratios would be in a more favorable position to expand abroad than banks headquartered in countries with lower q ratios" (p. 670). Unfortunately, the q ratio is affected by accounting conventions and inflation as much, if not more, than by the cost of capital. Hence, little can be drawn from the numbers. (He finds higher-than-one q ratios for banks in Canada, Germany, Italy, and especially Japan, and less-than-one q ratios for banks in France, the Netherlands, the United Kingdom, and the United States.)

22. I am not aware of a careful study documenting the benefits and costs.
23. A study of more current data might show a lesser advantage because of the increased integration of world financial markets.
24. See essays on the Pacific Basin countries in Cheng, ed. (1986).
25. However, as Hunter and Timme (1990) find, although U.K. banks appear to have improved their performance in recent years, they appear to have much yet to learn about efficient operations.
26. U.S. investment banks have been successful competitors in European markets. Pavel and McElravey (1990, p. 16) report that "[a]ccording to a 1988 survey, U.S. firms accounted for slightly more than half of all cross-border merger and acquisition activity [in 1988]. . . . U.S. investment banks represented about 12 percent of all mergers and acquisitions for European clients in 1988. . . . Seven of the top underwriters of debt and equity securities worldwide are U.S. firms."
27. See Horvitz and Pettit (1990) for a thorough discussion of the implications of the post-1992 E.C. change for U.S. financial markets and institutions.
28. See Yamada (1990) for a very good review of Japanese deregulation since 1980.
29. U.S. branches of foreign banks must be covered by deposit insurance unless they have no deposits with balances under $100,000. Banks with insured deposits are subject to supervision by the FDIC and state banking authorities.
30. Dale (1984) claims that banks are likely to locate or establish subsidiaries in countries that have lax supervisory standards. However, the only examples he provides are of banks attempting to avoid taxes and government restrictions on capital movements.
31. The monograph also mentions liquidity requirements, which are not imposed on U.S. banks, and capital requirements, which are discussed below.
32. See Benston (1989) for a review of studies and an analysis supporting this conclusion with respect to securities activities.
33. See Benston and Kaufman (1988) for more details.
34. Belgium, Canada, France, Germany, Italy, Japan, Netherlands, Sweden, United Kingdom, and United States plus Luxembourg and Switzerland.
35. After 1992 EC banks will be limited in the proportion of the capital of nonfinancial enterprises they can own.
36. The ABA (1990a, p. 50) monograph provides an example: "Mitsubishi Bank, together with its affiliates, owns more than 76 percent of the outstanding shares of Ryoko Securities. The bank owns its maximum five percent share, and through 29 of its affiliates, such as Mitsubishi Heavy Industry and Tokyo Marine and Fire Insurance, over 70 percent of the securities firm's shares are owned."

References

ABA. *International Banking Competitiveness . . . Why It Matters*. A Report of the Economic Advisory Committee of the American Bankers Association, Washington, DC, 1990a.

ABA. *Federal Deposit Insurance: A Program for Reform*. American Bankers Association, Washington, DC, March, 1990b.

Aliber, Robert Z. "International Banking: A Survey." *Journal of Money, Credit and Banking* 16 (November 1984, Part 2), 661–678.

Bank for International Settlements. *Recent Developments in International Banking*. 1986.

Barthomew, Philip F. and Vicki A. Vanderhoff. "Foreign Deposit Insurance Systems: A Comparison." *Consumer Finance Law Quarterly Report*, forthcoming 1990.

Baer, Herbert L. "Foreign Competition in U.S. Banking Markets." *Economic Perspectives* (Federal Reserve Bank of Chicago) 14 (May/June 1990), 22–29.

Bank for International Settlements. *Recent Innovations in International Banking*. Prepared by a Study Group established by the Central Banks of the Group of Ten Countries, no city of publication, April 1986.

Benston, George J. "The Federal 'Safety Net' and the Repeal of the Glass-Steagall Act's Separation of Commercial and Investment Banking." *Journal of Financial Services Research* 2 (1989), 287–305.

Benston, George J. and George G. Kaufman. "Regulating Bank Safety and Performance." In William S. Haraf and Rose Marie Kushmeider, eds., *Restructuring Banking & Financial Services in America*. Washington, DC: American Enterprise Institute for Public Policy Research, 1988, pp. 63–99.

Bryant, R.C. *International Financial Intermediation*. Washington, DC: The Brookings Institution, 1987.

Cargill, Thomas F. "Financial Reform in the United States and Japan: Comparative View." In Hang-Sheng Cheng, ed., *Financial Policy and Reform in Pacific Basin Countries*. Lexington, MA: Lexington Books, 1986, pp. 39–57.

Cargill, Thomas F. and Shoichi Royama. "The Evolution of Japanese Banking: Isolation to Globalization." *Proceedings of the 26th Conference on Bank Structure and Competition*. Chicago: Federal Reserve Bank of Chicago, May, forthcoming 1990.

Cheng, Hang-Sheng. "Financial Policy and Reform in Taiwan, China." In Hang-Sheng Cheng, ed., *Financial Policy and Reform in Pacific Basin Countries*. Lexington, MA: Lexington Books, 1986, pp. 143–159.

Dahl, F. R. "International Operations of U.S. Banks: Growth and Public Policy Implications." *Law and Contemporary Problems* 32 (Winter 1964), 100–130.

Dale, Richard. *The Regulation of International Banking*. Cambridge, UK: Woodhead-Faulkner, 1984.

Dohner, Robert S. and Henry S. Terrell. "The Determinants of the Growth of Multinational Banking Organizations: 1972–86." *International Finance Discussion Papers*, Number 326 (June). Washington, DC: Board of Governors of the Federal Reserve System, 1988.

Dohner, Robert S. "Japanese Financial Deregulation and the Growth of Japanese International Bank Activity." *USJP Occasional Paper* 98-05. Cambridge, MA: Harvard University Center for International Affairs and the Reischauer Institute of Japanese Studies, 1989.

Goodman, Laurie S. "Bank Lending to Non-OPEC LDCs: Are Risks Diversifiable?" *Federal Reserve Bank of New York Quarterly Review* (Summer 1981), 10–20.

Feldman, Robert Alan. *Japanese Financial Market: Deficits, Dilemmas, and Deregulation*. Cambridge, MA: MIT Press, 1986.

Goodin, C. Stewart and Stephen J. Weiss. "U.S. Banks' Loss of Global Standing." In *Foreign Acquisitions of U.S. Banks*. Richmond: Robert F. Dame, Inc., 1981, pp. 191–229.

Horvitz, Paul and R. Richardson Pettit. "Financial Services in the European Community: Implications for U.S. Financial Markets and Institutions." American Enterprise Institute for Public Policy Research Conference: *The United States and Europe in the 1990s*. March 5–8, 1990.

Houpt, James V. "International Trends for U.S. Banks and Banking Markets." Summarized in the *Federal Reserve Bulletin* (May 1988), 156.

Hunter, William C. and Stephen G. Timme. "Employment in the World's Largest Banks." *Economic Review* (Federal Reserve Bank of Atlanta) (January/February 1990), 2–11.

Institute of International Bankers. *Impact of U.S. Regulation on Bank and Insurance Affiliations Taking Place in Europe in Connection with the Formation of a Single Market in 1992*, February 1990 (no address).

Key, Sidney J. "The Internationalization of U.S. Banking." In Richard C. Aspinwall and Robert A. Eisenbeis, eds., *Handbook for Banking Strategy*. New York: John Wiley & Sons, 1985, pp. 267–292.

Key, Sidney J. and Gary M. Welsh. "Foreign Banks in the United States." In William H. Baughn et al., eds., *The Bankers' Handbook*. New York: Dow-Jones Irwin, 1988, ch. 5, pp. 58–71.

Key, Sidney J. and Henry S. Terrell. "International Banking Facilities." *International Finance Discussion Papers*, Number 333. Washington, DC: Board of Governors of the Federal Reserve System, September 1988.

Khoury, Sarkis. *The Dynamics of International Banking*. New York: Praeger, 1980.

McCauley, Robert N. and Steven A. Zimmer. "Explaining International Differences in the Cost of Capital." *Quarterly Review* (Federal Reserve Bank of New York) (Summer 1989), 7–28.

Pavel, Christine and John N. McElravey. "Globalization in the Financial Services Industry." *Economic Perspectives* (Federal Reserve Bank of Chicago) 14 (May/June 1990), 3–18.

Prowse, Stephen D. "Institutional Investment Patterns and Corporate Financial Behavior in the U.S. and Japan." Finance and Economics Discussion Series, Division of Research and Statistics, Division of Monetary Affairs, No. 108. Washington, DC: Board of Governors of the Federal Reserve System, January 1990.

Rosensweig, Jeffrey. "A New Dollar Index: Capturing a More Global Perspective." *Economic Review* (Federal Reserve Bank of Atlanta) (June/July 1986), 12–22.

Rugman, Alan M. and Shyan J. Kamath. "International Diversification and Multinational Banking." In Sarkis J. Khoury and Alo Ghosh, eds., *Recent Developments in International Banking and Finance*. Vol. 1. Lexington, MA: D.C. Heath and Company, 1986, pp. 35–39.

Smith, Clifford, Charles Smithson, and D. Sykes Wilford. *Managing Financial Risks*. New York: Harper & Row, 1989.

Suzuki, Yoshio. *Money, Finance, and Macroeconomic Performance in Japan*. New Haven, CT: Yale University Press, 1986.

Teeters, Nancy H. and Henry S. Terrell. "The Role of Banks in the International Financial System." *Federal Reserve Bulletin* (September 1983), 663–671.

Terrell, Henry S., Robert S. Dohner and Barbara R. Lowrey. "The U.S. and U.K. Activities of Japanese Banks: 1980-88." *International Finance Discussion Papers*, Number 361. Washington, DC: Board of Governors of the Federal Reserve System, September 1989.

Yamada, Shohei. "Does Competitive Equality Exist in the Japanese Financial Markets?" Paper presented at the *Conference on Regulating Financial Markets: Issues and Policies*. Columbia University, May 14–15, 1990.

Journal of Financial Services Research 4:341–344 (1990)
© 1990 Kluwer Academic Publishers

Commentary: *U.S. Banking in an Increasingly Integrated and Competitive World Economy*

ROBERT LITAN
Senior Fellow
Economic Studies Program
The Brookings Institution
1775 Massachusetts Ave., NW
Washington, DC 20036

George Benston has done his usual masterful job in laying out a basic structure of how we should think about the competitiveness of U.S. banks. As I understand his article, he reaches three major conclusions. First, the efficiency of U.S. banks appears to be declining. Second, our banks continue to be on the cutting edge of innovation and new product development—developing new financial instruments, new hedging strategies, and so on. Third, unnecessary flaws in our bank regulatory system are holding our banks back—the Glass-Steagall Act, the McFadden Act, and the Bank Holding Company Act, among others. If these flaws were corrected, U.S. banks would be more competitive.

The article does not take up the question, however, of how our banks are likely to fare in either our domestic or international markets during the next decade. I want to provide some thoughts about that, but before I give my views on the outlook, I will comment on several points that he discusses.

Although George correctly identifies a number of factors that explain the significant drop in asset rankings by our banks relative to those in the rest of the world—including faster economic growth abroad, depreciation of the dollar, and our domestic restrictions against interstate banking—he does not dwell on another significant reason: our banks' self-inflicted wounds. These include, for example, a series of bad lending decisions dating from the late 1970s, mainly loans to less developed countries, and in the late 1980s, when real estate loans and loans to finance leveraged buyouts became sources of problems. Lending mistakes clearly hurt the ranking of two of our major banks—Continental Illinois and Bank of America. To be sure, these banks are now on the mend, but their problems in the 1980s cost them a decade, if not more, in the race to keep up with competitors.

Lending mistakes have hurt the asset rankings of other banks as well. George rightly points out that one should not obsessively focus on asset rankings because they include only items on the balance sheet while U.S. banks have increasingly expanded through off-balance-sheet activities. Some interesting data on this subject were recently presented in a study by the Federal Reserve Bank of New York attached to Gerald Corrigan's May 3, 1990, testimony before the Senate Banking Committee. According to these data, the on-balance-sheet assets of money center banks were three times their off-balance-sheet liabilities in 1980. During the 1980s this was totally reversed. It turns out that by 1989 their off-balance-sheet liabilities, according to this study, were five times their on-balance-sheet assets.

One of the reasons for this change is the explosion in standby letters of credit. Essentially, banks have been relegated to guaranteeing the commercial paper issues of a lot of high-grade corporate borrowers who are no longer borrowing from banks. The reason why banks have been relegated to this position, of course, is that their credit ratings have deteriorated because of lending mistakes. In other words, they are not in the lending market largely because of self-inflicted wounds. I think this has had a major effect on the decline in their relative position as measured by their on-balance-sheet activities and, at the same time, it has contributed to an explosion of their off-balance-sheet liabilities. The weakness of our banks—the erosion of their capital because of past lending mistakes— also has important implications for their competitive posture in the future.

The second point I want to discuss is the obsession of the moment in financial services—namely, the success of the Japanese banks. Benston focuses on several reasons for their rapid ascent, but he attributes most of their rise in the international rankings to the growth of their domestic market, coupled with a rise in the yen. I think this is fundamentally correct.

What concerns most policymakers here, however, is the tremendous increase in Japanese bank penetration into the U.S. banking market both in deposits and lending (to 10 percent of all U.S. commercial and industrial loans). The key question is why this has occurred.

The most frequently given answer is the allegation that the Japanese banks have low-cost funds because of the regulation of deposit interest rates at home, and they are able to shift those funds to the United States, so the allegation goes, in effect to subsidize their U.S. operations.

I do not think the data bear this out. A recent Federal Reserve Board study published in the *Federal Reserve Bulletin* indicates that only 16 percent of the $113 billion in U.S. deposits in Japanese banks in 1988 came from their parent corporations or from their parent banks. The largest source of their funding was other U.S. banks, and the second largest source of funding was U.S. residents. In other words, Japanese banks are raising most of the money in our market, not in their home market.

These data, of course are averages, but data on changes from 1986 to 1988 suggest the same pattern at the margin. From 1986 to 1988, total U.S. deposits in Japanese banks grew by about $40 billion. Of that growth, $6 billion came from parent banks at home, while some $30 billion of it was from American banks and American residents.

I would argue on the basis of these data that Japanese banks as a group are not shipping low-cost funds from their home market to the American market and, consequently, I do not think you can argue that they have a big cost advantage because their domestic interest rates are kept down.

These data should not really be surprising. If it is true that Japanese banks have low funding costs because of interest rate controls, it also means they have a hard time attracting funds from depositors, especially at a time like the last decade when alternative stock market investments paid off so handsomely. This means that if Japanese banks want to make money abroad they must raise funds abroad. In short, domestic interest rate regulations in Japan have driven Japanese banks to fund themselves offshore. As a result, the marginal cost of funding for Japanese banks looks very close to that for U.S. banks. And any difference should narrow in the future as the Japanese government completes interest rate decontrol.

There is, however, a second component of the cost of capital argument, which focuses on the allegation that Japanese banks have access to low-cost equity capital, which is reflected in their high price/earnings ratios.[1] The reported P/E ratios, however, can be deceiving. The earnings of Japanese banks are vastly understated by conventional accounting principles, which do not include the unrealized capital gains Japanese banks have had on their shareholdings of other corporations. Nor do the bank earnings figures include unrealized capital gains in their real estate.

These omissions are important. My colleague, Barry Bosworth at Brookings, calculates that these two factors largely explain the high P/Es in the nonbank sector in Japan. I suspect that, to a significant extent, the same is true of Japanese banks. In effect, their price/earnings ratios are not as high as they appear to be if you take into account their cross-shareholdings and real estate. But since Japanese banks have been able to earn very high profits on their shareholdings, they can afford low spreads on their lending activities.

This does not mean that Japanese banks are engaging in predatory pricing, however. Predatory pricing would imply that they are actually selling loans in our market "below cost," or below the marginal cost of funds in the U.S. market. I do not think that is what they are doing, nor do I think that is the main concern of those who have complained about the asserted Japanese cost of capital advantage. The charge is that they have a very low cost of equity and can, therefore, afford to have low lending spreads in the U.S. market.[2]

In short, my tentative theory is that the reason why Japanese banks have had low spreads and low apparent returns on equity in the U.S. lending market is that they have extensive cross-shareholdings at home that generate very high earnings. Consequently, when you look at the overall profit performance of the Japanese banks, they are doing quite well. If my interpretation is correct, of course, the cooling off of the Japanese stock market and of their real estate market, if sustained, will slow their penetration of the U.S. market. They may need to jack up their lending spreads in the United States, and this would imply a slowdown in the expansion of Japanese banks.

Another way of stating this is to suggest that the hidden reserves of Japanese banks have fallen substantially because of the large drop in the Japanese stock market. Many of the Japanese banks may be capital constrained and, therefore, will not be able to expand in the United States. This is equivalent to the argument that the rate of return on equity has been vastly understated because of unrealized capital gains.

Let me turn to some final comments about the outlook for the future. We have now had a decade of growing internationalization. Paradoxically, what I see in the future is that many multinational banks here and abroad will probably place more emphasis on sticking to their knitting at home than on expanding their international activities.

Why do I say that? Let us look first at the United States. We are going to be moving toward, in effect, nationwide interstate banking over the next ten years. The "super-regional" banks will be expanding into new markets, in many cases by acquiring failed thrifts. But many of our banks, especially our larger ones, have limited capital to support expansion. My suspicion is they are going to focus much more on the U.S. market than abroad.

A major exception, of course, is Citicorp, which seems to be active virtually everywhere around the world. But most of the rest of American banks do not seem to be focused abroad.

Next consider the Japanese market. Interest rate deregulation is proceeding in this market, which should bring much stronger competition among Japanese banks on their home turf. I have already pointed out the cooling off of the Japanese real estate and stock markets. These changes, in combination, suggest that Japanese banks will be paying more attention to their home market than abroad.

Finally, if you look at Europe, obviously the further integration of that market in 1992 and beyond implies that many of the European banks are going to be spending their time and energy diversifying and consolidating within Europe and paying less attention to the U.S. market. So I suspect we are going to have less internationalization in the sense of slower expansion of foreign banks in other countries' markets in the 1990s.

What does this suggest for our own markets? If I am right about the Japanese banks slowing down their activities here in the United States because of the decline in the Japanese stock market and the cooling off of real estate there, and if I am also right that interest rate deregulation in Japan will cause Japanese banks to pay more attention to the home market, then our banks probably will face less competition at the margin than they would have otherwise from Japanese banks.

The countervailing argument, of course, rests on the fact that Japanese banks have expanded rapidly in our market largely by following transplants of Japanese manufacturing companies to the United States. These Japanese transplants are likely to increase their activity here in the United States, especially if we get trade restrictions, which will be increasingly likely if the trade deficit quits improving (as it should this year). If you look at the 1990s, therefore, the more trade frictions we have and the more Japanese transplants expand here, the more expansion opportunities there will be for Japanese banks.

In the end, I suspect that the "transplant effect" will dominate, causing our banks to continue to lose domestic market share in the lending market to Japanese and other foreign banks, but probably at a much slower pace than they have in the 1980s. That's the bad news. The good news is that we will be going through a decade of rapid consolidation in our own market. We are going to have nationwide interstate banking, probably by the end of the decade. In ten years, our banking system will be a lot trimmer—and hopefully safer—than it is now. In such an environment, many U.S. banks should have a better chance of withstanding foreign competition in our home market in the 1990s than during the rocky 1980s.

Notes

1. The implicit notion is that earnings of Japanese banks (and other corporations) are capitalized by the Japanese stock market at a very low rate.
2. Of course, it is possible to view the Japanese banks as "investing" their unrealized profits in shareholdings into gaining market share in the lending market in the United States. To this extent, the banks may be subsidizing their U.S. lending operations with above-normal stock returns at home. However, there is little evidence that the lending spreads in the United States are actually so low that the banks are losing money in the U.S. market. In any event, with the decline in Japanese stock market prices since the end of 1989, Japanese banks have not been in a position to engage in this subsidization, assuming they ever did.

Journal of Financial Services Research 4:345–348 (1990)
© 1990 Kluwer Academic Publishers

Commentary: *U.S. Banking in an Increasingly Integrated and Competitive World Economy*

KATHLEEN B. COOPER
Chief Economist
Exxon Corporation
Dallas, TX 75062

Not surprisingly, I agree with the thrust of what George Benston had to say. His article essentially argues that U.S. bankers are still innovative despite their higher cost of capital and heavier regulatory burden and that U.S. banks need to be able to offer a broader set of products over wider geographical regions. My intention, therefore, is simply to emphasize a few points that I believe are particularly important.[0]

Benston begins by telling us why the remarkable decline in U.S. banks' rankings (by assets) does not necessarily mean that U.S. banks have lost competitiveness to that same degree. I cannot argue too much with his reasons.

Off-balance-sheet activities in the early 1980s and asset sales in the late 1980s allowed banks to control overall asset growth—which they certainly wanted to do in order to boost capital ratios. It is also a fact that U.S. banks pulled in their horns during the 1980s with regard to international business. In part, we were recovering from LDC losses and, more recently, from international securities market losses (primarily in London). In part, this occurred because we had rediscovered domestic retail banking and figured out how to make it very profitable.

It is nevertheless true that U.S. banks are losing out to foreign competition. And, if you have any doubt that this statement is true, you need only consider that American companies—our most likely customers—use fewer American banks today and more foreign banks than five years ago. Indeed, American companies used 10 American banks and 5 foreign banks in 1988 (versus 15 American and 3 foreign banks five years previously). In other words, the usage of foreign banks among U.S. firms has gone from a 17 percent market share to 33 percent.

Four key factors have clearly made it more difficult for U.S. banks to compete effectively with their foreign brethren:

- Higher regulatory costs.
- Geographic restrictions.
- Narrower product offerings.
- Lower price/earnings ratios.

Work on this article was completed while the author was Executive Vice President and Chief Economist at Security Pacific National Bank, Los Angeles.

The remainder of my remarks will focus on these four factors—how they hurt U.S. bank competitiveness and/or what corrections are needed—and on one key change in trend that is currently underway.

Higher regulatory costs

A critical element detracting from U.S. bank performance is the cost of regulation. These costs will become even more important in the 1990s as our competition internationally obtains still broader charters. According to a recent American Bankers Association study, U.S. banks have the heaviest overall regulatory burden of all G-10 countries. We certainly have very high costs with regard to reserve requirements, deposit guarantees, reporting requirements, and compliance regulations. Furthermore, the multiplicity of legal jurisdictions within the United States adds significantly to the cost of doing business.

Geographic restrictions

Geographic restrictions, without question, prevent U.S. banks from fully exploiting scale economies. Our structure is clearly vastly different from that of other major industrial countries. We have roughly 50 banks per million population versus 11 banks (per million population) in the United Kingdom, 5 in Germany, 3 in Canada, and only 1 in Japan.

Economic studies argued for years that there were no economies of scale for banks above the $100–$500 million mark. Technology and the erosion of market monopolies have changed all that, if it were ever true. Security Pacific and other banks have been able to save very large sums by consolidating smaller banks into their activities—driving more product through the same infrastructure.

Progress is being made in breaking down geographic boundaries and will continue to be made over the next several years. But the slow pace will further inhibit the U.S. banking industry's position relative to its international competition.

Narrower product offerings

All of the compilations of products that can be offered by banking companies in different countries show how much more limited charters U.S. banks have than do European banks and, in reality, Japanese banks. And, of course, universal banking will be widespread in Europe soon and more flexibility is coming in Japan. Without significant change in the United States, American banking institutions will fall farther behind.

I do believe that customers still think of U.S. banks as innovative—perhaps *the* most innovative—with regard to the products that we *can* offer and combine. However, continued restrictions on U.S. banks' ability to combine insurance, securities, and banking products to create the best products for our customers' changing needs will preclude us from remaining the most innovative. Our competition will step in and take our place.

Being able to offer a flexible product mix would provide the opportunity for economies of *scope*—just as banks are increasingly able to take advantage of significant economies of *scale*. For example, we would be able to use our current customer base to add sales of insurance and securities products, as well as to add innovative combinations of such products.

It would be a rare firm that would perform well in foreign markets if it could not innovate within its *home* market. A number of banks learned through their experiences in London that it is difficult to develop innovative new products that can be sold profitably to a small list of customers if they have been unable to develop and learn how to market them in their large home market. American banks were able to hone their skills at marketing swaps in America and have been very successful both domestically and internationally. But we did not do as well at corporate debt and equity underwriting—products that could not be "practiced" in our home market.

Lower price/earnings ratios

Foreign assets already account for 20 percent of U.S. banking assets versus 4 percent in the early 1970s. This sharp increase is certainly the flip side of our investments overseas in the 1960s and 1970s. Nonetheless, it is disconcerting. In California, Japanese-owned assets account for more than 25 percent of all banking assets. In his article, George Benston quipped that Japanese banks apparently achieved this through the innovation of being polite. The real truth, however, is that they did it the old fashioned way: they bought their way in.

Five years ago, Japanese bank presence in California was negligible; but high price/earnings ratios, a strong domestic Japanese economy, and a highly valued yen have allowed purchases of several middle-sized California banks. Up until now, Japanese banks in California have not performed particularly well, that is, have not been leaders in the market. They are active and visible in real estate, and they are trying ever harder in retail and middle-market banking. I believe, however, that Japanese banks will achieve better results over time and that they will drive returns lower.

Employment and efficiency

Finally, I want to emphasize one development that has occurred during the 1980s—a trend that was missed in the studies cited by Benston due to its relative newness. The studies cited by Benston indicate that U.S. banks expanded their employment base much more rapidly than their foreign competitors for the period 1980–1986. The point I want to highlight is the end of that trend.

As figure 1 demonstrates, U.S. commercial bank employment expanded rapidly for the decade 1972–1982 but slowed enormously thereafter. Employment moved from 1 to 1.5 million from 1972 to 1982; expansion continued but at a slower pace until 1986 but has since halted. This phenomenon, which occurred despite continued asset growth and

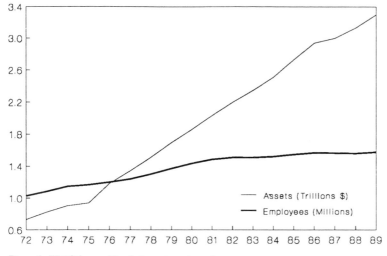

Figure 1. FDIC-insured banks' assets and employees

dramatic increases in service provision, is the result of the relentless push for efficiencies by U.S. commercial banks in recent years and will continue for the foreseeable future through the geographic consolidation phase that lies ahead.

Conclusion

U.S. banks have lost some of their competitive edge vis-a-vis foreign competitors. This loss is due partly to their damaged flexibility as a result of low price/earnings ratios and to the fact that the United States does not have nationwide banking nor as varied a product list as is needed. Looking forward, U.S. banks will have an ever tougher time competing because banks in all other major industrial nations will have an even broader product list than today. If our banks are not allowed to offer that same list, then other countries' banks will be the ones developing new and innovative products from a combination of insurance, securities, and banking products. Then, U.S. banks will clearly have lost their competitiveness and will have become higher risk institutions than is true today.

Journal of Financial Services Research 4:349-378 (1990)
© 1990 Kluwer Academic Publishers

Internationalization of the World's Securities Markets: Economic Causes and Regulatory Consequences

JOSEPH A. GRUNDFEST
Associate Professor of Law
Stanford Law School
Stanford, CA 94305
Commissioner
United States Securities and Exchange Commission (1985-1990)

Not long ago, Americans traded in New York, British traded in London, and Japanese traded in Tokyo. It was a simple world in which the flow of securities transactions respected political geography.

The essentially domestic character of securities markets made regulation a rather straightforward task. There was little concern that traders would move their business offshore if they disliked restrictions imposed by domestic authorities. There was also little concern that international transactions would be used as means to violate domestic securities regulations. Each market was an island—or so it seemed to regulators who had effective monopoly power and little reason to look beyond their own shores.

That world is dead and gone. The demise of domestic securities markets began during the 1960s and 1970s, and the notion of predominantly domestic markets clearly passed from the scene in the 1980s. Indeed, today's markets are international with a vengeance. Japanese investors trade in New York and London as easily as they trade in Tokyo or Osaka. London plays host to brokerage houses and investment banks from the world over. The internationalization of the U.S. markets is so well established that domestic exchanges actively market instruments tailored to meet the demands of domestic investors who seek to calibrate their exposure to foreign securities market risk.

Indeed, in 1988 alone, "a staggering $10 trillion of securitized funds moved across national frontiers" (Heimann, 1989, p. 76).[1] Moreover, "global financial transactions currently account for an historically high multiple of the volume of world trade" (Heimann, 1989). These data strongly suggest that the movement of capital for investment-related purposes, and not simply for the financing of trade, "is driving the economic and financial world" (Heimann, 1989).

Additional funding support for this study was provided by the Kendyl K. Monroe Research Fund and the John M. Olin Program in Law and Economics at the Stanford Law School. I would like to thank Martin Gonzalez, Theodore Meisel, and Jan Van Eck for excellent research assistance.

No doubt, substantial barriers remain to complete internationalization of the world's securities markets, and there is reason to believe that markets will retain a comparative advantage in trading local securities. In particular, local markets have a comparative advantage in generating and interpreting information about local firms. Accounting standards, reporting requirements, and informal information-sharing mechanisms also differ dramatically across markets, and these institutional factors create further biases toward local trading. In addition, local investors may want to maintain disproportionately large portfolios of domestic securities because those instruments can provide a better match for the investor's liabilities or intended consumption stream. It is, therefore, unlikely that markets will ever reach a state of perfect internationalization, in which investors are totally indifferent among the geographic markets in which investments are traded. Nonetheless, the evidence shows that international investment activity has grown tremendously over the past decade, and there is reason to believe that international trading will continue to expand vigorously in the future.

As one example of the inroads made by internationalization, consider the fact that today, even the smallest U.S. investor can ride the internationalization wave. Several mutual funds now market foreign securities portfolios, often on a country-specific basis and in extremely small denominations. Aunt Minnie in Omaha can thus buy shares in the Japan, Germany, France, Italy, and Thailand funds, with an investment as small as $1,000 in each (Kahn, 1990, p.1).[2] The profound implications of this simple form of internationalization are often overlooked—particularly from a regulatory perspective. When Aunt Minnie buys $1,000 of the Japan Fund, she effectively decides to leave the United States' market, where her investments are fully governed by provisions of the Securities Act of 1933 and the Securities and Exchange Act of 1934.[3] Instead, through the Fund, her purchases and sales take place in Japan's markets where Japanese issuers are not required to make disclosures with the detail prescribed by U.S. securities laws. Secondary market transactions in Japan are also not subject to the vast panoply of legal restrictions found in United States' markets.[4] Accordingly, in today's internationalized securities markets, even the smallest investor can treat national regulatory regimes as partially discretionary constraints on investment activity.

Sophisticated investors have even greater latitude to structure their transactions to take advantage of international differences in regulatory regimes. Thus, U.S. traders who anticipate a change in stock prices might engage in an "exchange for physicals" transaction in the London market that could not be executed in the United States. They might also enter the Eurobond market or purchase other securities not offered for sale in the United States.[5]

As we head into the next decade, internationalization will increase investors' freedom to arrange their business affairs in order to select the regulatory environment most suitable for their financial goals. This freedom to choose among competing regulatory structures presents regulators with a series of challenges that were not contemplated at the time domestic regulatory regimes were initially crafted. In particular, most regulatory regimes are based on an implicitly autarkic model of the world's capital markets in which competition among regulators can safely be ignored. That assumption was quite reasonable during the 1930s, the time at which the U.S. regulatory structure was put in place. The world was then in the throes of a depression, and the notion of massive international capital flows was inconceivable.

But the autarky assumption no longer holds, even as a rough first approximation. Today's borders are sieves through which financial transactions flow like water through cheesecloth. As the pace of internationalization increases, so will the challenge to the basic foundation upon which current domestic regulatory regimes are constructed. This article focuses on those challenges, and on potential regulatory responses.

Part 1 of this article begins with an analysis of the extent and composition of internationalization in the world's equity securities markets during the decade of the eighties, viewed primarily from the United States' perspective. A major conclusion of this analysis is that much of the data commonly relied upon for the measurement of international capital market flows is highly deficient. Thus, despite clear evidence that internationalization is rapidly increasing, it is dangerous to put too much faith in the accuracy or relevance of many officially reported statistics.

Part 2 of this article explores the underlying economic, technological, and political forces that gave rise to internationalization. Part 3 suggests that the fundamental forces giving rise to internationalization are likely to grow in strength during the coming decade. Thus, whatever the current magnitude of internationalization, international trading is likely to become an even more significant factor in the world's securities markets.

Part 4 provides an overview of the challenges that internationalization poses for the world's securities regulators. It categorizes those challenges into three distinct forms: enforcement difficulties caused by internationalization of the world's markets; opportunities for efficiency-enhancing coordination that reduces the costs of international investing (as opposed to inefficient forms of standardization that, by reducing potentially beneficial variance in regulatory regimes, could actually increase the cost of capital); and opportunities for quality competition among regulators who legitimately set different regulatory standards for different markets. Part 5 explores the enforcement difficulties generated by internationalization and argues that investigatory cooperation is a legitimate response to a difficult externality problem. Part 6 considers the incentives for coordination of certain regulatory requirements. Part 7 analyzes the prospect for beneficial quality competition between markets with differing regulatory standards. Part 8 concludes the analysis with a brief summary of problems posed and likely solutions.

The bottom-line conclusion of the regulatory analysis is that great care must be exercised when evaluating arguments for greater standardization of world securities market regulation. From an economic perspective, the ultimate rationale for capital market regulation is the existence of a market failure that can be cured by regulation. The simple observation that different jurisdictions have different regulatory regimes does not in and of itself identify a market failure. Indeed, because a diversity of regulatory regimes can promote valuable experimentation and innovation, as well as act as a safety-valve against excessive regulation in specific markets, "too much" international standardization can actually harm the world's capital markets. Thus, while it is possible to support international enforcement cooperation designed to protect the domestic integrity of each sovereign's legal regime, and it is possible to support measures that coordinate regulatory requirements so as to minimize duplicative informational and filing burdens, measures that pursue more aggressive standardization must be viewed more cautiously and often deserve more immediate analysis than immediate support.

1. Internationalization: the facts

It is easier to describe internationalization of the world's securities markets in aggregate, qualitative terms than it is to detail internationalization in a careful quantitative manner. Quantitative measurement and international comparison raise interesting problems of price change and exchange rate adjustment. In addition, many key government statistics are maintained on the basis of historic book values that make it difficult to compare stocks and flows over time. Reliance on book values also makes it difficult to relate reported statistics to observed market values. Furthermore, funds often flow through several different markets as they travel from their initial source to their final investment destination. Middle Eastern deposits in European institutions that are invested in the United States might, for example, be measured as European, not Middle Eastern, investments. The circuitous flow of investment funds also creates an opportunity for double counting investment dollars as they flow through several markets. Moreover, an accurate quantitative portrayal of the state of securities market internationalization would require the use of data series prepared by several different governments: these data are not prepared in a manner designed to promote consistent comparability across time or over time.

Accordingly, there is good reason simply to observe that internationalization is "big" and to leave matters at that. Despite the wisdom inherent in that concise observation, this section attempts to quantify the growth of internationalization measured in terms of foreign investors transacting in U.S. equity securities markets, as well as U.S. investors transacting in foreign equity securities markets. The analysis is restricted to the period spanning 1980 through 1989, the most recent years for which full data are available. Moreover, as explained below, these calculations are subject to significant caveats.

1.1. Foreign transactions in U.S. equity securities markets

As an initial matter, it is important to recognize that purchases of U.S. equity securities by foreigners can be reported either as securities transactions or as direct foreign investments. When foreigners acquire less than 10 percent of a firm's equity, the acquisition is reported as a securities transaction. When a foreigner crosses the 10 percent threshold, the transaction is measured as direct foreign investment. A coherent assessment of foreign investment activity in U.S. equity securities markets thus requires simultaneous consideration of both forms of transactions.[6]

1.1.1. Equity securities transactions.   As illustrated in table 1 and figure 1, aggregate foreign purchases and sales in U.S. equity securities markets, a measure of the volume of trading activity in U.S. markets rather than of net inflows or outflows from U.S. markets, stood at $75.1 billion at the beginning of the decade. By 1989, the volume of those transactions had more than quintupled to $416 billion. The peak 1987 volume of $482 billion in foreign transactions represents a sixfold increase in foreign trading activity. Measured over the ten-year span, foreign transactions in U.S. equity securities markets grew at compound annual growth rate of 21.0 percent.

Table 1. Aggregate foreign purchases and sales of securities in U.S. markets, by geographic origin, 1980–1989 ($ billions)

	1980	1981	1982	1983	1984	1985	1986	1987	1988	1989	1980–1989 CAGR[1]	1989 Mkt shr
Canada	11.8	11.5	10.0	16.4	16.9	22.1	34.6	49.9	33.9	45.4	16.1%	10.9%
Total Europe	46.0	42.8	46.7	80.5	69.1	82.5	141.8	232.5	154.3	203.8	18.0%	48.9%
United Kingdom	12.4	13.4	18.8	29.2	28.3	37.6	64.6	103.9	73.4	97.2	25.7%	23.4%
Switzerland	17.9	14.9	14.2	26.2	20.3	21.6	37.0	59.5	34.9	42.6	10.1%	10.2%
Other Europe	15.7	14.6	13.8	25.1	20.5	23.3	40.2	69.0	46.0	64.0	16.9%	15.4%
Total Asia	9.8	12.9	14.9	21.3	18.7	25.1	55.3	142.4	129.7	98.0	29.1%	23.5%
Japan	1.9	1.4	2.0	3.3	2.7	7.8	26.9	102.6	104.6	60.8	47.0%	14.6%
Other Asia	7.9	11.5	12.9	18.1	15.9	17.3	28.4	39.8	25.1	37.2	18.7%	8.9%
Latin America	7.1	7.7	7.6	14.3	17.3	25.8	39.2	46.9	38.3	61.3	27.2%	14.7%
All other	0.4	0.5	0.7	1.6	2.4	3.5	6.6	10.3	7.8	7.8	39.3%	1.9%
Total	75.1	75.4	79.9	134.1	124.3	159.0	277.5	482.0	364.1	416.3	21.0%	100.0%

Source: Office of the Secretary, U.S. Department of Treasury, *Treasury Bulletin,* table CM-V-5, Spring issues.
[1]CAGR is the cumulative annual growth rate.

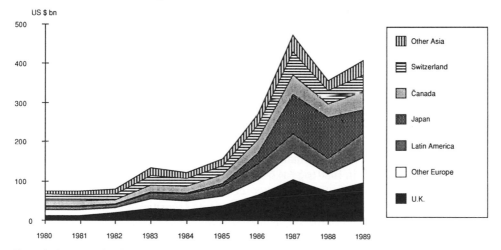

Figure 1. Aggregate foreign transactions in U.S. equities markets, by geographic origin, 1980–1989
Note: "Aggregate Foreign Transactions" is the sum of purchases and sales.
Source: U.S. Treasury Bulletin, various issues.

Though figure 1 hints that Japanese investment played a major role in the growth of foreign investment in the U.S. market, figure 2 illustrates this point more graphically. The horizontal axis of figure 2 measures the share of a particular nation's 1989 trading activity as a percentage of all foreign trading activity in that year. The vertical axis measures the compound annual growth rate between 1980 and 1989 for each nation's trading activity in U.S. equity securities markets. The areas of the circles, and the figures entered in the centers of those circles, describe the difference between purchases and sales aggregated over the nine-year period. Shaded areas indicate an excess of sales over purchases.[7]

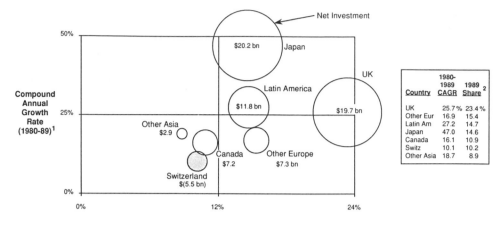

Figure 2. Growth rates, market shares, and net investment of foreigners in U.S. equities markets, by geographic origin, 1980–1989

[1]Based on 1980 and 1989 cumulative investment position.

[2]Does not add to 100 due to the omission of selected countries.

Note: Circle size represents net cumulative investment, 1980–1989.

Source: Survey of Current Business, various issues.

Figure 2 suggests quite clearly that Japan was a dominant force in the international-ization of the United States' equity securities markets. The compound annual growth rate of Japan's trading in U.S. markets, 47.0 percent, was substantially greater than Britain's 25.7 percent rate. Indeed, that remarkable growth rate rocketed Japanese transactions from a mere $1.9 billion in 1980 to $104.6 billion in 1988, though volume declined to $60.8 billion in 1989. Measured in terms of cross-sectional share, Japan's 1989 trading consti-tutes 14.6 percent of all foreign trading in U.S. equity securities markets—a figure that trails Britain's 23.4 percent share. These annual market share data can, however, be quite volatile; in 1988, Japan's share of foreign trading was 28.7 percent, well ahead of Britain's 23.4 percent. Japan's net balance of $20.2 billion in purchases over sales over the course of the decade was the largest flow measured into the market, though here the lead was slim over Britain's $19.7 billion net inflow.

Although the growth of foreign trading in the United States has been impressive, the data must be interpreted with a grain of salt because the total volume of all trading on U.S. securities exchanges also increased dramatically in the 1980s. Using the New York Stock Exchange as an index, the dollar value of transactions volume grew by 307 percent from $382 billion in 1980 to $1,556 billion in 1989 (*New York Stock Exchange Fact Book: 1990*, p. 80). Comparing this growth in total trading volume with the 454 percent growth in foreign activity over the same period suggests that foreign activity in the United States' equity markets has, over the span of the decade, grown at a pace roughly 48 percent faster than that of the U.S. market as a whole.

Table 2. Foreign direct investment in the United States, by geographic origin, 1980–1989 ($ billions)

	1980	1981	1982	1983	1984	1985	1986	1987	1988	1989	1980–1989 CAGR[1]	1989 Share	Net Growth[2]
Canada	9.8	9.9	9.8	11.4	15.3	17.1	20.3	21.7	27.4	31.5	13.9%	7.9%	21.7
Total Europe	43.5	60.5	68.5	92.9	108.2	121.4	144.2	178.0	216.4	262.0	22.1%	65.4%	218.5
United Kingdom	11.3	15.6	23.3	32.2	38.4	43.6	55.9	74.9	101.9	119.1	29.9%	29.7%	107.8
Netherlands	16.2	23.1	21.5	29.2	33.7	37.1	40.7	47.0	49.0	60.5	15.8%	15.1%	44.3
Germany	5.3	7.2	8.2	10.8	12.3	14.8	17.3	19.6	23.8	28.2	20.4%	7.0%	22.9
Other Europe	10.7	14.6	15.5	20.7	23.8	25.9	30.3	36.5	41.7	54.2	19.7%	13.5%	43.5
Japan	4.2	7.0	8.7	11.3	16.0	19.3	26.8	33.4	53.4	69.7	36.6%	17.4%	65.5
Latin America	6.7	8.5	9.2	15.0	16.2	16.8	16.8	15.3	17.0	20.3	13.1%	5.1%	13.6
Middle East	0.7	3.6	4.5	4.4	5.3	5.0	4.9	5.1	5.8	6.4	27.1%	1.6%	5.7
Other	0.6	0.9	1.1	2.1	3.6	5.0	7.4	8.4	8.9	10.9	39.0%	2.7%	10.3
Total	65.5	90.4	101.8	137.1	164.6	184.6	220.4	261.9	328.9	400.8	22.3%	100.0%	335.3

Source: Bureau of Economic Analysis, Department of Commerce, *Survey of Current Business,* June issues.
[1]CAGR is the cumulative annual growth rate.
[2]Net growth is the absolute difference between foreign direct investment in 1980 and 1989.

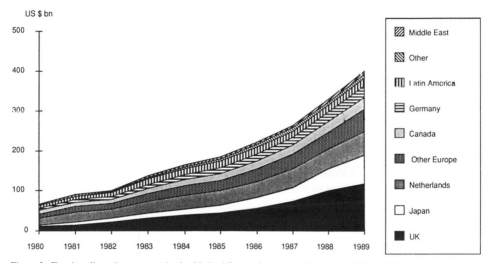

Figure 3. Foreign direct investment in the United States, by geographic origin, 1980–1989
Source: Survey of Current Business, June issues.

1.1.2. Direct investment.

Table 2 and figure 3 describe the increase in foreign direct investment in the United States. From a total of $65.5 billion in 1980, foreign direct investment grew at a compound annual rate of 22.3 percent to $400.8 billion in 1989. This growth rate is roughly comparable to that observed in the securities transations data.

Disaggregation of the data by country of origin, as displayed in figure 4, reveals that Britain and Japan were once again the international market's prime movers. Britain is the

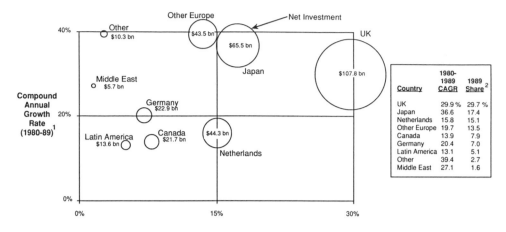

Share of U.S. Direct Investment (1980-89)

Figure 4. Growth rates, market shares, and net foreign direct investment, by geographic origin, 1980–1989
[1]Based on 1980 and 1989 cumulative investment position.
[2]Does not add to 100 due to the omission of selected countries.
Note: Circle size represents net cumulative investment, 1980–1989.
Source: Survey of Current Business, various issues.

largest foreign direct investor in the United States, and during the 1980s increased its direct investment by $107.8 billion to a total of $119.1 billion. Japan began the decade with a smaller direct investment base of only $4.2 billion in the United States, but by 1988 became the second largest foreign direct investor by committing $65.5 billion in new investments for a total direct investment position of $69.7 billion.

Interpreting these data, however, requires an added degree of caution. Although a firm might nominally be considered a U.S. firm, its assets and revenues may in fact be largely foreign. Similarly, many foreign firms have large percentages of their assets and revenues outside their "home" jurisdictions. For example, Nestle, a Swiss firm, has 98 percent of its sales and 95 percent of its assets outside of Switzerland; ICI, the British chemical concern, has 78 percent of its sales and 50 percent of its assets outside Britain; Gillette, a U.S. firm, has 65 percent of its sales and 63 percent of its assets outside the United States; and Cannon, a Japanese firm, has 69 percent of its sales and 32 percent of its assets outside Japan.[8] Thus, the purchase or sale of a U.S., Swiss, British, or other firm does not necessarily mean the purchase or sale of a predominantly U.S., Swiss, British, or other business. In addition, as previously mentioned, because the data measure investments in terms of book value, not market value, they are not dictly comparable over time. Thus, British and Dutch investment positions acquired over a relatively long period, at book prices that are low in comparison to their current market values, could well have a market value far in excess of Japanese holdings which have been acquired more recently at book prices that more closely approximate their market values.

Moreover, despite the growth in foreign direct investment in the United States, U.S. investors continue to control a larger portion of the U.S. economy than is the case abroad.

Foreign owned capital averages over 10 percent of gross national product (GNP) in most industrial countries, but in the United States, "it probably still stands below 7% of GNP" (Morgan Guaranty Trust Co., 1989, p. 3). Thus, a major bank observes that "U.S. investments abroad are far more prominent in foreign economies than are foreign investments in the United States. For example, U.S. investments in the United Kingdom are four times greater as a proportion of U.K. GNP than are U.K. investments in the United States relative to U.S. GNP" (Morgan Guaranty Trust Co., 1989, p. 3).

1.2. U.S. transactions in foreign equity securities markets

1.2.1. Equity securities transactions.   The growth in foreign transactions in U.S. equity markets is mirrored by the growth of U.S. transactions in foreign markets. As illustrated in table 3 and figure 5, U.S. trading in foreign equity securities markets expanded at a cumulative annual growth rate of 32.8 percent, a rate higher than foreign activity growth rates in the United States. Thus, during the years spanning 1980 to 1989, total U.S. purchases and sales of securities abroad grew from $17.9 billion to $230.3 billion.

The international composition of these transactions is more complex, as displayed in figure 6. Again, it is clear that the Japanese and British markets were the dominant sources of growth. Britain attracted 34.8 percent of U.S. trading activity abroad in 1989, while Japan attracted 28.6 percent. Again, these market share data are highly volatile on an annual basis: in 1988, Japan and Britain both attracted roughly a third of U.S. aggregate U.S. transactions abroad. A sharp increase during 1988 in equity sales by U.S. investors in Japan, however, suggests that U.S. investors have been disinvesting in Tokyo securities during the 1980s. That statistic must, however, be interpreted with caution because of the substantial increase in Tokyo share prices. Many of the sales occurring

Table 3. Aggregate U.S. purchases and sales of foreign securities, by geographic region, 1980–1989 ($ billions)

	1980	1981	1982	1983	1984	1985	1986	1987	1988	1989	1980–1989 CAGR[1]	1989 Mkt shr
Canada	6.7	4.9	2.9	5.0	4.4	6.8	9.8	18.9	9.7	10.9	5.5%	4.7%
Total Europe	6.9	5.7	6.5	13.6	13.3	21.5	55.3	101.4	75.6	128.9	38.5%	56.0%
United Kingdom	2.8	2.9	3.6	6.5	7.8	13.3	32.6	67.9	51.2	80.1	45.3%	34.8%
Switzerland	1.6	0.9	0.7	1.8	1.3	1.6	3.2	6.3	5.3	8.5	20.8%	3.7%
Other Europe	2.5	1.9	2.2	5.4	4.2	6.6	19.5	27.2	19.1	40.3	36.0%	17.5%
Total Asia	3.3	6.5	5.1	9.4	10.7	14.0	30.1	56.7	56.2	75.8	41.8%	32.9%
Japan	2.7	5.4	4.3	8.0	9.0	11.6	25.6	47.8	50.4	65.8	42.4%	28.6%
Other Asia	0.6	1.1	0.8	1.4	1.6	2.5	4.5	8.9	5.8	10.1	38.0%	4.3%
Latin America	0.7	1.1	0.8	1.6	0.9	1.2	3.6	7.1	5.3	9.3	33.3%	4.0%
All other	0.3	0.4	0.3	0.8	1.1	2.0	2.7	5.8	4.8	5.4	36.4%	2.3%
Total	17.9	18.6	15.7	30.3	30.4	45.6	101.5	189.8	151.4	230.3	32.8%	100.0%

Source: Office of the Secretary, U.S. Department of Treasury, *Treasury Bulletin*, table CM-V-5, Spring issues.
[1]CARG is the cumulative annual growth rate.

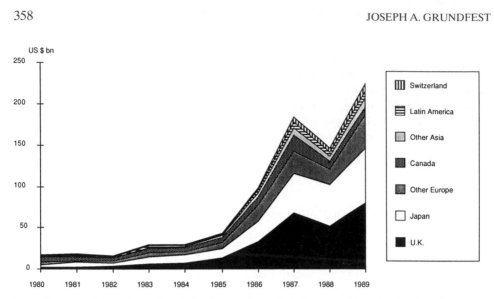

Figure 5. Aggregate U.S. transactions in foreign equities markets, by geographic region, 1980–1989
Note: "Aggregate U.S. Transactions" is the sum of purchases and sales.
Source: U.S. Treasury Bulletin, various issues.

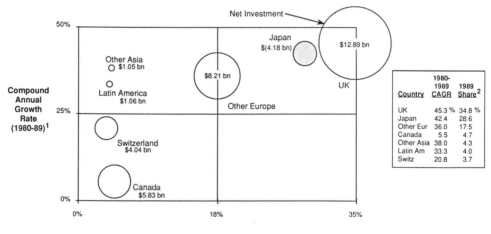

Figure 6. Growth rates, market shares, and net investment of U.S. investors in foreign equities markets, by geographic region, 1980–1989
[1]Based on 1980 and 1989 cumulative investment position.
[2]Does not add to 100 due to the omission of selected countries.
Note: Circle size represents net cumulative investment, 1980–1989.
Source: Survey of Current Business, various issues.

during 1988 may have been of securities acquired at substantially lower prices, and U.S. participants may still hold significant Japanese market positions despite 1988 sales.

1.2.2. Direct investment.   Patterns in U.S. direct investment abroad are, however, quite different from those displayed by other forms of investment analyzed in this article. As suggested by table 4 and figure 7, U.S. direct investment abroad grew at a relatively slow compound annual growth rate of 5.2 percent, roughly a quarter of the growth rates displayed by other forms of securities market activity. Figure 8 indicates that the largest

Table 4. United States direct investment abroad, by geographic region, 1980–1989 ($ billions)

	1980	1981	1982	1983	1984	1985	1986	1987	1988	1989	1980–1989 CAGR[1]	1989 Share	Net Growth[2]
Canada	44.6	45.1	44.5	47.6	50.5	47.1	50.2	58.4	62.6	66.9	4.6%	17.9%	22.3
Total Europe	95.7	101.5	99.9	102.7	103.7	105.4	123.2	146.2	156.9	176.7	7.1%	47.3%	81.0
United Kingdom	28.1	30.3	30.8	30.8	32.1	32.8	35.0	42.0	49.3	60.8	9.0%	16.3%	32.7
Germany	15.4	15.8	15.9	16.0	15.2	16.7	20.3	24.8	21.7	23.1	4.6%	6.2%	7.7
Switzerland	11.3	12.5	13.3	15.0	16.0	15.8	17.5	19.5	18.4	20.0	6.5%	5.4%	8.7
Other Europe	40.9	42.9	39.9	40.9	40.4	40.1	50.4	59.9	67.5	72.8	6.6%	19.5%	31.9
Total Asia	14.7	17.9	19.2	21.5	24.6	24.8	27.3	31.4	36.4	40.3	11.9%	10.8%	25.6
Japan	6.3	6.8	6.9	8.0	8.4	9.2	11.3	14.7	17.9	19.3	13.2%	5.2%	13.0
Other Asia	8.4	11.1	12.3	13.5	16.2	15.6	16.0	16.7	18.5	21.0	10.7%	5.6%	12.6
Latin America	38.3	38.9	33.0	29.7	28.1	27.9	35.0	44.9	51.0	61.4	5.4%	16.4%	23.1
Other	22.1	23.0	24.7	25.5	26.5	24.8	24.3	27.1	26.6	28.1	2.7%	7.5%	6.0
Total	215.4	226.4	221.3	227.0	233.4	230.0	260.0	308.0	333.5	373.4	6.3%	100.0%	158.0

Source: Bureau of Economic Analysis, Department of Commerce, *Survey of Current Business,* June issues.
[1]CAGR is the cumulative annual growth rate.
[2]Net growth is the absolute difference between foreign direct investment in 1980 and 1989.

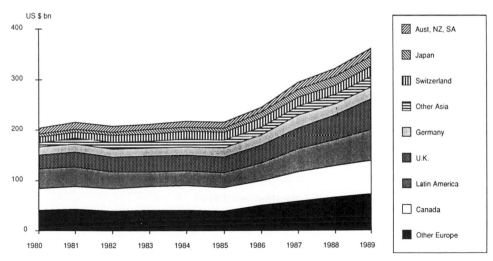

Figure 7. Aggregate U.S. direct investment abroad, by geographic region, 1980–1989
Source: Survey of Current Business, June issues.

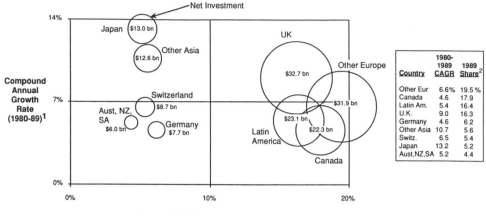

Figure 8. Growth rates, market shares, and net direct investment of U.S. investors abroad, by geographic region, 1980–1989

[1]Based on 1980 and 1989 cumulative investment position.

[2]Does not add to 100 due to the omission of selected countries.

Note: Circle size represents net cumulative investment, 1980–1989.

Source: Survey of Current Business, various issues.

U.S. investments were in Europe (outside of Britain), Britain, and Canada. Although direct investment in Japan displays the highest growth rate, it is measured from an extraordinarily small initial book value of $6.3 billion. Thus, while the aggregate book value of U.S. investments in Japan roughly tripled during the decade, the 1988 book value of U.S. investment in Japan ($19.3 billion) remains a relatively low number.

Again, however, statistics can be quite deceiving. United States' investors have, for decades, been actively acquiring positions abroad, and the market value of their positions far exceeds their stated book value. By one estimate, the market value of U.S. direct investment abroad is at least twice the book value stated in U.S. government statistics (Ulam and Dewald, 1989). A second source suggests that "the relatively older U.S. investments [abroad] have a market value more than three times their book value, while foreign holdings in the United States are worth almost twice their book value. On this basis, the excess of U.S. direct investment assets abroad over foreign assets in the United States probably exceeds $100 billion" (Morgan Guaranty Trust Co., 1989, pp. 3-4).

2. The forces causing internationalization

Internationalization is not a random event. It is the rational consequence of a series of economic, technological, and political forces that grew in strength throughout the 1980s. Although it is possible to identify several distinct developments that are primarily responsible for the growth of internationalization, it is important to recognize that these forces are not wholly independent. Economics, technology, and politics shape each other and interact, often in subtle but profound ways. However, when developments in economics, technology, and politics reinforce each other by moving in a common direction, the effect on the marketplace can be most striking.

That is precisely what happened in the decade of the eighties: the forces of economics, technology, and politics all moved toward internationalization of the world's capital markets. Capital market imbalances, advances in telecommunications and computational capabilities, advances in the technology of finance, the evolution of derivative product markets, and a worldwide move toward capital market deregulation occurred simultaneously. The confluence of these forces inalterably changed the shape of the world's securities markets.

2.1. Capital market imbalances

The first and perhaps most significant force giving rise to internationalization of the world's stock markets is purely economic. Because of international differences in savings rates and investment opportunities, as well as international trade imbalances, the decade of the eighties witnessed the evolution of distinct classes of capital importers and exporters (Morgan Guaranty Trust, 1989, pp. 3–4). On the capital export side of the ledger, OPEC nations were the dominant suppliers of excess capital toward the beginning of the decade. Towards the middle and end of the decade, Japan clearly assumed the role of the world's major capital supplier (Morgan Guaranty Trust, 1989, pp. 3–4).[9]

On the capital import side of the ledger, the emergence of the United States as a major capital importer was the decade's most significant development. Indeed, in the course of the decade, the United States moved from being the world's largest creditor to its largest debtor—a shift in position that could be accomplished only as a result of massive capital flows.[10] The equities traded on the world's securities markets are a particular form of capital. As market theorists have frequently explained, equities represent contingent claims on firm resources that remain after debtholders and other senior claimants are paid off.[11] Worldwide shifts in capital flows would, therefore, naturally be reflected in the world's securities markets.

Given this perspective on the fundamental economic forces underlying internationalization of the world's securities markets, it becomes relatively easy to predict that internationalization is not a passing phase. After all, as long as certain economies have distinct comparative advantages in acting as suppliers and consumers of investable capital, the incentive for cross-border security investment remains. Indeed, in light of the powerful economic and demographic forces suggesting that capital market imbalances are likely to persist, internationalization seems certain to be a permanent fixture of the world's securities markets.

2.2. Technology

The effect of technology on internationalization of the world's securities markets is difficult to overstate. Advances in telecommunication and computation technology have

103

dramatically reduced the cost of trading in both domestic and international markets.[12] Without these technological advances, the cost of obtaining information about market conditions halfway around the world would create a significant barrier to international investment.

Indeed, the central role played by technology becomes obvious when one walks into any modern trading room. The "screen" is the trader's most important tool. Because of the telecommunications links and computational ability behind the screen, traders located anywhere in the world can call up international news and current capital market prices for thousands of instruments traded on any of the world's major markets. Moreover, by combining analytical functions with access to copious data streams, technology offers traders a tool that allows them quickly to solve complex valuation problems and identify potential trading opportunities. Without these tools, the international market would quickly degenerate into a Tower of Babel: a world in which traders in one market would be largely ignorant of developments in other markets and incapable of comprehending the significance of foreign developments for their own investment decisions.

Viewed from this perspective, the remarkable advance in technology between 1980 and 1990 is absolutely critical to the evolution of today's internationalized securities market. It would literally be impossible to operate today's global market with technology that was state of the art in 1980: transmission and computation rates would be too slow, telecommunications costs would be too expensive, and critical analytic tools would be unworkable because the available hardware would simply be unable to support the necessary software.

2.3. Finance theory

Modern finance theory provides powerful insights into the value of portfolio diversification. It also provides techniques for hedging and arbitraging among markets, as well as techniques for redefining and reallocating risk among purchasers and sellers of securities.[13] Each of these insights played a significant role in the evolution of the modern internationalized securities market, either by providing an incentive to engage in international transactions or by providing a tool that improved the pricing and efficiency of international markets.

Portfolio theory, for example, teaches the value of diversification. For many years, investors viewed diversification as an exercise to be conducted within a market or across various investment categories. Thus, investors would diversify by broadening the list of stocks in their portfolios, or balancing their equity investments with investments in bonds, real estate, or venture capital.[14] These investments would, however, take place primarily within domestic markets.

Recently, however, investors have begun considering the benefits of diversification across national markets. Thus, instead of merely diversifying within domestic borders, investors now seek to hedge against domestic market risk by purchasing foreign equities, bonds, real estate, and other assets. Indeed, they are also beginning to view the foreign currency markets not only as a means through which to hedge currency risk but also as an independent investment opportunity.[15] The most obvious evidence of this development is, perhaps, the emergence of "global" mutual funds designed specifically to offer to investors a low-cost means of achieving global market diversification, even with a relatively small investment (see Heimann, 1989). The evolution of portfolio theory has thus provided investors with an incentive to look beyond their own shores and has thereby increased the demand for foreign securities trading.

The ability to arbitrage and hedge across markets is also central to the operation of an international securities marketplace. Investors typically seek assurances that the prices they face in any one market are reasonable in light of the prices available in other markets. Investors also often seek to tailor their risk exposure by buying or selling instruments that provide a useful hedge against undesired risk. Issuers have similar demands. They want assurances that they are not being underpaid for their securities and often want to issue securities with specific risk characteristics that are particularly suited to their financing needs. For example, the purchaser of a Japanese equity warrant would want assurances that the warrant is fairly priced. He might also want to hedge his position against exchange rate or interest rate risk. And, the issuer of those same warrants might want assurances that he can hedge his risk by engaging in a series of fairly priced futures market transactions that have the stability to net out foreign exchange fluctuations.

Providing such price integrity and hedging capability is no simple matter in a world of complex financial instruments denominated in a smorgasbord of currencies. Fortunately, the modern technology of finance provides a broad array of analytical tools that are readily adapted to the challenges posed by international securities markets. The technology of finance now allows traders to calculate complex equilibrium relationships between cash, options, and futures markets, thereby providing the basic tools necessary for traders to arbitrage away inefficient price differences. Similarly, the technology of finance allows investors to craft highly specialized instruments with characteristics that are carefully designed to match the interests of particular buyers and sellers.[16] Without this ability, international and domestic securities markets would be much more rudimentary trading institutions lacking in both liquidity and imagination.

With the current state of the art, the technology of finance is sufficiently evolved that it supports the creation of new trading instruments that are specifically designed to take advantage of opportunities created by the international nature of the market itself. For example, in early 1990 several investment banks designed Nikkei puts that allow retail investors to buy and sell the risk that the Japanese equity market will suffer a decline.[17] The issuers of these instruments often had no direct exposure to the Japanese equity markets. They were able to issue these instruments only because of the availability of futures and other markets that allow them to hedge against specific forms of equity and currency risk. The net result of the transaction was to create a new equity-like instrument that requires, as a condition of its existence, liquid international futures and options markets. Thus, international markets have reached a stage where they provide not only the environment in which trades take place but also the rationale for the creation of new instruments that would not exist but for the international nature of the market itself.

2.4. Derivative markets

Closely related to the changes wrought by advances in finance theory are the benefits created by the evolution of an international network of derivative product markets. In 1980, securities markets were dominated by "plain vanilla" stock exchanges. Securities-related options and futures markets were rare, and their volumes were relatively small. Today, however, each of the world's major trading markets has a troika of equities, options, and futures markets.[18]

The evolution of derivative product markets has particular significance for foreign traders. In many situations, foreign traders have hedging demands that differ significantly from those of domestic traders.[19] These demands can be quite difficult, if not impossible, to satisfy absent an active and liquid derivative products market. The emergence of these markets therefore provides a service that is of particular value to international investors and promotes the internationalization of the world's securities markets.

In many instances, the world's derivative product markets are keenly aware of the intense interest in international trading for hedging and other purposes. In response to this demand, many markets introduced international products specifically designed to allow domestic investors to trade foreign security-related risks. For example, in the United States, investors can trade futures on the Nikkei Stock Average through the Singapore International Monetary Exchange, futures on the Financial Times Stock Index (FT-SE) 100 through the London International Financial Futures Exchange, and futures on the Toronto Stock Exchange 300 through the Toronto Futures Exchange (see Rosenbaum, 1990, p. 50).

2.5. Deregulation

Regulatory barriers have long been an impediment to securities trading on both a domestic and international level. Several countries have, however, recently lowered regulatory barriers that made trading unnecessarily expensive for all market participants. Most notably, in 1987 the London markets eliminated fixed commission rates as part of their "Big Bang."[20] These domestic liberalizations benefit international traders as much as domestic ones and have helped reduce the cost of intermarket capital flows.

On the international trade front, Japanese markets have lowered many of the barriers that traditionally kept foreign firms out of the country (Viner, 1988; Tanji, 1987; Miller, 1990; "Openness, Not Retaliation . . . ," 1990, p. 5). Although these barriers are substantially reduced, and although international firms now have a more than token presence in Tokyo, significant barriers to foreign entry and participation remain. Further progress in opening Japan's markets could thus facilitate even greater internationalization of the world's securities markets.[21]

Most significant, perhaps, is the face that some regulators have begun adjusting their domestic regulatory regimes in response to perceived competition from abroad. The recent decision by the United States Securities and Exchange Commission to adopt Rule 144A—a provision that will allow the free and liquid trading of privately placed foreign instruments among large institutional investors in the United States—was motivated in part by the observation that the United States' financial services industry was being harmed by overly narrow interpretations of the registration requirements of the Securities Act (U.S. SEC, 1990). If Rule 144A operates as some of its proponents expect, capital costs for U.S. issuers should be reduced and many foreign firms should for the first time enter the U.S. market with special "144A placements" offered to institutional investors (Greene and Beller, 1990).

Similarly, the spectre of foreign competition can be used as a weapon in domestic regulatory debates. The Securities and Exchange Commission, for example, recently announced a sweeping review of current U.S. accounting standards to determine whether they are "affecting adversely the ability of U.S. companies to compete internationally with foreign companies whose home country's accounting rules may be less stringent than U.S. standards" ("SEC Launches Extensive Review . . . ," 1990). If the review indicates that current accounting regulations impose costs that disadvantage U.S. firms in international competition, then the Commission may well initiate changes designed to make U.S. reporting requirements more "competitive" in the international marketplace ("SEC Launches Extensive Review . . . ," 1990).

3. The future of internationalization

Given the fact that internationalization did not evolve by chance, it is equally unlikely that its future will be determined by random forces. Though economic prognostication is surely one of the more dangerous hobbies known to man, certain trends that are already well-established in the world's marketplace make it highly likely that tomorrow's securities markets will be even more globalized than today's.

Imbalances between the sources of investable capital and the locations offering the most profitable investment alternatives are likely to continue. Indeed, because of the opening of Eastern Europe, the reunification of Germany, Europe 1992, the aging of the Japanese population, and possible increases in the price of oil, to mention only a few relevant factors, there is a significant chance that the pattern of capital flows in the 1990s will differ materially from the patterns observed during the eighties.[22] These changed patterns do not foretell a decrease in internationalization; instead they suggest changes in capital flows and a new shape to internationalization.

The pace of technological change is also likely to quicken.[23] Advances in computer and telecommunication technology are likely to reduce the costs even further and make available services that are quantitatively and qualitatively quite superior to the level of services that are currently available. Particularly noteworthy is the possibility that electronic trading will mature and come into its own during the coming decade. The Chicago Mercantile Exchange and The Chicago Board of Trade have jointly agreed to develop an after-hours computerized trading system,[24] and the New York Stock Exchange has also announced plans to introduce automated after-hours securities trading.[25] It is a trivial technological step from after-hours electronic trading to electronic trading at all times of the day.[26]

In addition, the introduction of computerized trading systems may bring more fundamental changes to the structure and operation of domestic equity marketplaces. Electronic crossing networks in which large institutional traders are able to transact a portion of their business have already captured a small but potentially significant piece of the market.[27] The possibility of discrete single price clearing auctions is also being actively explored.[28] If only a fraction of these changes come to pass in the nineties, the shape of domestic securities markets is sure to change and the pace of internationalization is certain to be enhanced.

Progress in our understanding of the technology of finance is somewhat more difficult to predict. However, no additional progress is necessary in order to sustain substantial additional internationalization of the world's capital markets. In particular, there is reason to believe that many investors are insufficiently diversified from an international perspective. Thus, even if the nineties bring no analytic breakthroughs leading to greater internationalization, a great deal of internationalization could take place simply as a result of investors' desire to implement lessons that have already been learned.

Additional growth and diversity in the derivative product markets also seems assured in the coming decade. As already mentioned, derivative product markets are actively moving toward electronic trading. Moreover, these marketplaces are introducing new products specifically designed to facilitate the internationalization of the world's capital markets. The net result of this activity is certain to be an increase in interest in international derivative product trading that will be correlated with an increase in international securities trading.

The final and clearly most difficult piece of the puzzle regarding the future of the internationalization concerns the fate of deregulation. If the world's markets are simply able to maintain the status quo, then the opportunity for enhanced internationalization will be preserved. Preservation of the status quo will not, however, generate many of the benefits surely to arise from further reductions of barriers to international capital flows, particularly those that continue to exist in Japan. But if the world's major markets retreat from many of the liberalizations of the past decade and begin penalizing foreign or domestic traders either by introducing new barriers to entry or by increasing transactions costs, then all bets are off.[29] Significant and imprudent steps toward reregulation are the one identifiable force on the horizon that could stall or even reverse the market's trend toward internationalization.

While it seems highly improbable that the world will experience massive reregulation that turns back the hands of time and returns the world's securities markets to a relatively autarkic state, it is worthwhile to remember that the reunification of Germany, which seemed inevitable as of mid-1990, seemed impossible at the beginning of 1989. Politicians are among the most unpredictable forces in nature and can cause a great deal to happen—good and bad—in a relatively short period of time. Ideally, political intervention will have a beneficial effect on the world's securities markets, but politics is one area where prediction is too dangerous even to be ventured.

4. Consequences for regulators: three distinct challenges

Although internationalization is sure to have significant consequences for investors, issuers, securities markets, and the financial services industry, few market participants will find their future as affected by internationalization as the world's securities regulators. During the 1980s, internationalization changed the art of securities trading. In the 1990s, internationalization will revolutionize the art of securities regulation.

This revolution in the art of regulation will occur in three distinct forms. First, there is a set of international cooperative measures that are necessary if domestic regulators are to be able to continue effectively to regulate their own domestic markets. Simply put, internationalization creates an opportunity for the evasion of legitimately adopted domestic regulatory requirements. This opportunity for evasion, which can be considered as a form of externality, can be addressed through cooperative international investigatory measures.

Second, the world's securities markets are beset by a maze of contradictory and incompatible regulatory requirements that often serve no real purpose. Many of these differences are simply the result of historical accident, and they often impose costs that outweigh any benefits. Coordination of these regulatory requirements so as to reduce the compliance burdens associated with international trading would benefit issuers and investors worldwide. For example, coordinated registration and accounting procedures could materially reduce the costs of raising capital in an international market. Coordination is, however, a double-edged sword because if the international marketplace coordinates at a quality level that is too low or too high, or if the imposition of international standards drives efficient diversity out of the market, then the cost of coordination can, in some cases, outweigh its benefits.

Third, there is a set of regulatory standards for which different nations may legitimately wish to adopt different approaches. Diversity in regulation is not necessarily harmful. Diversity can foster beneficial innovation and competition among regulators, and it need not lead to an inexorable race to the bottom. Nations that recognize this point may even wish to establish diverse regulatory regimes even within their own jurisdictions—a foresighted step that the United States recently extended within its own securities market.

The major challenge for regulators will, however, be to distinguish situations in which coordination is desirable from those in which diversity yields greater benefits. The remainder of this article addresses these three sets of regulatory challenges and the progress that has been made addressing each.

5. International cooperation and domestic regulatory integrity

Given the realities of an internationalized securities marketplace, no nation will be able to enforce even its most basic antifraud strictures without the cooperation of a substantial number of its trading partners. To illustrate this new reality, consider the following example. A British subject violates British law in the course of trading British securities with other British subjects in British markets. The violative trades are, however, channeled through the United States, Japan, Switzerland, or other foreign jurisdictions. Under these circumstances, Britain will not be able to enforce its own rules against its own subjects trading its own securities in its own markets without the active cooperation of its international financial market trading partners.

This example is more than hypothetical. The recent revelation of the "Quinn scandals" in Europe suggests that tens of millions of dollars have been stolen from European investors as the result of a scheme based on transactions in United States securities markets (*SEC. v. Arnold Kimmes et al.*, 1989). Without the active cooperation of United States law enforcement agencies, European authorities would be hard pressed to develop a case against a fraud that occurred in their own back yard.[30]

In a similar vein, a recent study by the General Accounting Office determined that trades originating abroad represented more than one-third of all cases of suspected insider trading referred to the United States Securities and Exchange Commission in 1987.[31] As several cases have demonstrated, such trading can be generated by U.S. nationals electing to trade from foreign locales for the express purpose of evading detection by United States authorities (Levine, 1990, p. 80).[32]

Significantly, no nation need impose its philosophy of market regulation on any of its trading partners in order successfully to address this level of fraud. Each nation can continue to define fraud as it likes; each can adopt its own approach to insider trading regulation; and each can set whatever penalties it deems appropriate under the circumstances. All that is needed is a common understanding that the purpose of internationalization is to facilitate legitimate trading. The purpose of internationalization in the world's securities market is not to provide a means of evading the domestic regulations of participating markets, nor is it an excuse for one nation unilaterally to impose its standards on trading that does not involve its own markets.

The problems posed by international fraud can be addressed by cooperation rooted in the simplest form of enlightened self-interest. Putting aside rogue jurisdictions that perceive little benefit from assuring that their market facilities are not used to shelter illegal offshore trading affairs of the world's securities markets, each jurisdiction has a legitimate interest in maintaining its ability to enforce its domestic regulations in its domestic markets. This enforcement capacity can be maintained only if cooperation is forthcoming from trading partners. But cooperation will be forthcoming only if the favor is returned.

This rather straightforward fact of modern commercial life explains a great deal of the success achieved by the Securities and Exchange Commission in negotiating its network of memoranda of understanding, treaties, communiques, and accords. These bilateral understandings today exist between the United States and agencies of the United Kingdom, Japan, Switzerland, France, the Netherlands, Brazil, Ontario, Quebec, Canada, Italy, Turkey, the Cayman Islands, and the International Organization of Securities Commissions. Together they create an effective network through which foreign jurisdictions can obtain information from the United States about activities that might constitute violations abroad.[33] Similarly, they create an effective network whereby U.S. authorities can obtain information about violations in domestic U.S. markets resulting from foreign trades.[34]

In order further to enhance the ability of U.S. authorities to cooperate in investigations of foreign securities law violations, Congress adopted the Insider Trading and Securities Enforcement Act of 1988 (see House of Representatives 5133, 100th Congress, 2nd Session (1988), Section 6). That statute contains a provision empowering the Securities and Exchange Commission to conduct investigations on behalf of foreign securities authorities, even if there is no allegation that U.S. law has been violated. This provision was adopted both in order to assist investigations of foreign securities law violations and to provide an inducement for foreign trading partners to adopt reciprocal cooperative provisions.[35]

The value of a cooperative approach to international enforcement issues is particularly striking in light of the SEC's experience in the early part of the eighties. At that time, the Commission relied primarily on unilateral attempts to obtain foreign-based evidence. Those efforts were often fruitless. In addition, the efforts were "time consuming, expensive, and strained international relations" (Levine and Callcott, 1989, p. 3).[36] In contrast, having invested the effort of explaining to foreign jurisdictions the value of a bilateral understanding that allows each party to protect and promote the interests of the other, the Commission is now reaping the rewards of its more cooperative approach.

Indeed, the value of international enforcement cooperation extends far beyond the operation of the world's securities markets. In late April of 1990 representatives of the Group of Seven (Britain, Canada, France, Italy, Japan, the United States, and West Germany) met with representatives of eight other nations, some of which are known for their bank secrecy laws (including Switzerland, Austria, and Luxembourg), to discuss problems raised by money laundering arising out of international narcotics traffic.[37] The meeting led to the proposal of a broad set of regulatory and banking reforms designed to pierce through the shield erected by bank secrecy laws (Labaton, 1990, p. c1). Evidently, the benefits of international enforcement cooperation are not limited to the world's securities markets, and progress in this direction can be expected along many different fronts.

No doubt, some market participants might object to even this level of enforcement cooperation on the ground that certain domestic regulations are inefficient. By prohibiting foreign trading in violation of these strictures, international enforcement cooperation could thus reduce market efficiency. The difficulty with this argument, however, is that it is essentially lawless. No legal regime can operate in an environment in which compliance is voluntary. Indeed, even when regulations properly address market externalities, some traders will perceive that their interests are adversely affected and will attempt to evade domestic regulations on the premise that those regulations are inefficient. If avoidance can be justified on this rationale, then compliance becomes discretionary, and domestic legal regimes lose their force.

Thus, unless one believes that regulation of capital market transactions is suspect in all circumstances, provisions to protect the enforcement integrity of the legal regime are, at some level, necessary. The socially accepted means of expressing objection to an inefficient regulation is to work within the system to change the regulation, and not to evade the regulation through illegal means. Furthermore, if a regulation is in fact inefficient, it creates opportunities for other markets to establish trading systems that do not suffer from the same inefficiency and through which traders can legitimately interact. International competition thus acts as a potential safety-valve governing the extent to which local regulators can impose inefficient constraints without forcing transactions offshore.

6. International regulatory coordination: when is it efficient?

Enforcement cooperation is not the only area in which regulators will be challenged by the international market. Issuers and investors alike often complain that multiple and inconsistent registration and accounting standards add to the costs of international investing. From this perspective, if regulators can successfully coordinate certain disclosure and accounting requirements, the cost of capital will be reduced and the efficiency of the markets will be enhanced.[38]

Even though it is unrealistic—and perhaps even undesirable—to think of a single registration statement that could be used by all issuers in all markets, there clearly are situations in which a dose of coordination can be accomplished at relatively low cost and with obvious benefit for all market participants. In particular, when the substance of the required disclosures are sufficiently similar, nothing is gained by requiring issuers to replicate those disclosures in separate registration statements. Under those circumstances, it makes sense for securities regulators to consider a single filing that would be acceptable for multiple jurisdictions.

The United States and Ontario have embarked on just such an experiment. In 1989 the Securities and Exchange Commission and the Ontario Securities Commission issued a notice of proposed rulemaking that described a procedure for filing a registration statement that would be jointly acceptable by both authorities.[39] No doubt, this effort was initially undertaken by the United States and a Canadian province because the similarities in their registration requirements made coordination a relatively easy task. However, as regulators learn that the compromises necessary for a meaningful degree of coordination do not require an abdication of basic regulatory principles, the opportunities for cooperation could increase dramatically. In this regard, it is important that regulators not be overly ambitious. Even if wide-scale coordination between two countries turns out to be infeasible, there may be portions of registration statements or other filings that can be standardized much to the market's advantage.

Coordination in the area of international accounting procedures provides special challenges and opportunities.[40] Investors considering a choice between different markets are often confronted with the need to compare financial results reported according to wildly different accounting conventions. In many situations, the first step in reaching an investment decision involves the difficult exercise of translating one set of financial results into another country's accounting convention.[41] To many international investors, there is no innate preference for one reporting system over another. Instead, there is a desire for ready comparability.

To satisfy this market demand, regulators might want to consider adopting domestic conventions specifically designed to facilitate international comparability of financial reports. In some situations these facilitation conventions might be easily implemented:

rules for consolidation of subsidiaries, depreciation, and tax accounting are all areas where comparability can be enhanced with little or no damage to domestic philosophies of accounting and disclosure.

In other situations, however, achieving comparability will be far more difficult. For example, certain European countries allow issuers to maintain hidden reserves that are used to smooth earnings over time.[42] Other nations, such as the United States, would find such accounting practices fundamentally inconsistent with their domestic market philosophies. Accordingly, they are unlikely to accept such reports within their jurisdictions, unless accompanied by "comparability" data that would effectively destroy the fundamental purpose of the hidden reserve account. Under these circumstances, it is probably asking too much to expect markets with such divergent philosophies of accounting easily to achieve some middle-ground accommodation. The existence of such differences does not, however, mean that substantial progress could not be made on several other fronts.

One other area of international coordination deserves special mention. Capital standards are often a point of serious contention because firms subject to more stringent requirements often argue that they are unfairly forced to compete with less creditworthy institutions in a process that is potentially damaging for the stability of the world's financial markets. Such controversy preceded the adoption of the Basle international capital adequacy standards for the banking industry, and some observers have asked whether similar standardized capital requirements are appropriate in the securities industry.[43]

Needless to say, this is a contentious issue. Unlike the banking industry, which is perceived to have government backing on an international scale, the securities industry in the United States is not backed by government insurance, as evidenced by the government's decision to allow Drexel Burnham Lambert to fail (Hershey, 1990, p. 2). Accordingly, the argument for international minimum net capital standards would have to be quite different than the arguments frequently presented in the banking sector.

The process of setting international capital standards would also surely be bloody. Whatever the rule finally adopted, some securities firms would surely see themselves as disadvantaged and would lobby heavily against adoption of the proposed standards. Moreover, the debate would, to say the least, be highly complex and would raise questions involving the valuation of a large array of securities positions, the definition and treatment of hedged positions, and the measurement of risk related to intricate swap market and option positions.[44]

7. Quality competition: the danger of an über-regulator

Having observed that there are several dimensions in which international cooperation and coordination are potentially desirable, it should be emphasized that complete standardization is not necessarily in the world economy's best interest. Put another way, it is doubtful that the world's securities markets would be improved if they were subject to the control of a single über-regulator enforcing a consistent, worldwide set of regulations.

There is value in diversity. Diversity promotes experimentation and innovation in regulation just as it does in product and service competition.[45] Diversity also allows securities market participants to select transaction quality levels that are most suitable given the parties' preferences and prevailing market conditions. Excessive standardization could stifle important forms of innovation and prohibit markets and firms from providing socially desirable quality levels that are inconsistent with worldwide standards.

Indeed, there is an important perspective from which diversity among regulatory regimes can add value to all the world's securities markets. Regulation can increase or decrease the quality of investments and transactions available in any one market. It can increase or decrease disclosure by issuers, speed or slow settlement, and forbid or permit many practices that have the effect of shifting various forms of risk among different classes of investors.

Quality, however, comes at a price. In many situations, investors are willing to pay an additional amount to support a regulatory regime that provides valuable quality safeguards. If, however, investors do not desire the quality level imposed by a particular regulatory regime, or if investors find that the price of the quality generated by regulation is too high relative to other alternatives available in the marketplace, then investors will search out markets that provide preferable price-quality combinations.

International quality competition among regulators thus provides a market mechanism that helps prevent regulators from adopting rules that impose costs in excess of their benefits. Without this disciplining effect of the market, investors would effectively have no recourse in addressing inefficient regulatory structures other than frontal assault on domestic regulations and regulators themselves. Moreover, and perhaps more importantly, domestic regulators can learn from their international peers. If a regulatory approach works well and at relatively low cost in a foreign jurisdiction, might it not also work well in the domestic jurisdiction markets? Excessive standardization would eliminate both of these beneficial mechanisms from the marketplace.

In a world of price-quality competition among securities regulators—a world that is already upon us—it is also valuable to observe that a single jurisdiction can have more than one price-quality combination in its own domestic market. A jurisdiction can achieve this result by having different rules for investors and transactions with different characteristics. In particular, it may be politically or economically reasonable for marketplaces to adopt levels of protection for smaller, less sophisticated investors that differ from the regulations that apply to transactions involving larger investors with greater sophistication.

Interestingly, both the United States and the United Kingdom have recently taken steps in this direction. In the United States, the recent adoption of Rule 144A creates a liquid market for the free secondary trading of privately placed securities among large institutional investors.[46] In Britain, the SIB decided to permit "business investors" to participate in various financial and commodity market transactions without being subject to stricter rules that apply to other, less sophisticated investors. These "business investors" are generally corporations with capital or net assets of at least 500,000 pounds, local governments, or other public bodies.[47]

Regulation, therefore, does not necessarily imply standardization, either on an international level or within a single jurisdiction. Regulations can be carefully tailored to address apparent externalities, and these externalities can vary across jurisdictions, across transactions, and over time. Strong proponents of international standardization across a broad range of market practices thus tend to overstate their case. Instead, the most prudent path for international securities market regulation may involve a balanced approach that relies on basic forms of enforcement cooperation and compliance coordination, rather than adherence to a single trans-national regulatory philosophy.

8. Conclusion

Internationalization of the world's securities markets is here to stay. Internationalization grew quickly during the 1980s because of the confluence of economic, technological, and political forces. The same forces are likely to gather strength during the coming decade. Indeed, if current trends continue, internationalization is certain to increase during the coming decade to levels well above those currently observed in the world's securities markets.

Internationalization will pose a particular challenge for securities regulators. Because of the ease with which international transactions can be used to evade domestic regulatory strictures, regulators have a common incentive to cooperate in international securities enforcement efforts. Significantly, this form of cooperation does not require international agreement as to the substance of any domestic regulatory regime. Each country can, for example, continue to define illegal insider trading in any way it sees fit, and yet cooperate in efforts to identify persons who use the mechanisms of the international marketplace to evade legitimately adopted domestic regulations.

Internationalization will also provide opportunities for efficient coordination of registration and accounting requirements. Such measures can improve information flows to the market, reduce capital formation costs, and enhance secondary market liquidity.

International standardization can, however, be carried too far. Not all transactions need conform to identical standards, and market participants can have perfectly legitimate reasons for desiring to conduct different aspects of their business under different regulatory regimes. Diversity among regulatory regimes can also foster beneficial innovation and experimentation. Most significantly, perhaps, it can provide a form of regulatory competition that prevents regulators from adopting rules that systematically impose costs in excess of their benefits.

Viewed from this perspective, the dominant challenge for the coming decade will be to identify areas in which international regulatory cooperation is beneficial, while avoiding areas in which diversity and competition among regulators is more desirable. No doubt the task will be challenging, and there will be much room for debate and error, but a great deal hinges on regulators getting this distinction just right.

Notes

1. For an extensive analysis of the internatonalization of the world's securities markets see U.S. Securities and Exchange Commission (1987). See also Chuppe, Haworth, and Watkins, 1989b; Chuppe, Haworth, and Watkins, 1989a; Winch, Knight, and Jickling, 1989; Allen, 1986.
2. In 1988 there were 121 mutual funds classified as international, global equity, or global bond funds, whereas in 1983 there were no such funds. (according to the Investment Company Institute's *Mutual Fund Fact Book* 20, 1989; see also Cooper (1990, p. 179) where she argues that there may now be a glut of country funds in the market.)
3. Technically, the investment is made in a United States fund that is subject to U.S. regulations at the fund level, but the fund's managers then invest the fund's assets in offshore markets that are not subject to U.S. regulation.
4. For a description of the differences between U.S. and Japanese approaches to insider trading regulation see Akashi (1989) who indicates a much weaker enforcement of insider trading rules in Japan than in the United States.
5. See, for example, *College Retirement Equities Fund,* U.S. Securities and Exchange Commission, No Action Letter (available February 18, 1987), which permits the College Retirement Equities Fund to participate in French privatization offerings on a private-placement basis. French authorities sought assurances that, by simply selling to U.S. institutional investors, they would not become subject to the registration provisions of U.S. securities laws. See also *Offshore Offers and Sales,* 17 CFR §230.901-04 (May 1990), Securities Act Release No. 6863 (April 24, 1990), 55 *Fed. Reg.* 18306 (May 2, 1990), for the adoption of Regulation S which accepts a territorial principle of jurisdiction regarding the application of U.S. registration requirements to international securities offerings.
6. Because most foreign direct investments in the United States represent blocks averaging 80.2 percent of the affiliate's equity, and because foreign investments tend to be either significantly greater or less than a 10 percent interest in a firm's equity, the data are relatively insensitive to the specific use of a 10 percent threshold to distinguish among these types of transactions (Graham and Krugman, 1989).
7. The figures describing aggregate differences between purchases and sales must be interpreted with particular caution because they are based on book values and fail to adjust for fluctuations in market values over time. Thus, even in situations where the data suggest net disinvestment, as in the case of Switzerland, the market value of securities held in the United States might well have increased because of a general rise in stock market values.
8. Statistics are from "The Stateless World of Manufacturing," *Business Week,* May 14, 1990, p. 103; see also Julius, 1990; and Makin, 1990, forthcoming.
9. Recent data suggest the re-emergence of OPEC as a source of equity market purchases. See Henriques (1990, p. 15).
10. See, for example, United States Congress, Joint Economic Committee, *U.S. Foreign Debt,* 100th Congress, 2nd Session (September 13, 1988).
11. See, for example, Mason and Merton (1985, pp. 7–54).
12. See, for example, Wriston (1988–1989, pp. 63–75), who argues that advances in information technology have fundamentally weakened all governments' ability to control economic policy. See also U.S. Congress, Office of Technology Assessment, 1990; and Ayling (1986) for the effect that technology has on securities markets.
13. See, generally, Copeland and Weston (1988).
14. For a brief discussion of the benefits of diversification viewed from an international perspective see, for example, Sharpe (1985, pp. 706–721). See also Lessaw (1976, p. 32) and Solnik (1977, p. 51), the latter of whom states that an internationally diversified portfolio is one-tenth as risky as a well-diversified portfolio of U.S. stocks.
15. See, for example, Lewis, 1990; Black, 1989.
16. The evolution of the swap market, which now totals more than $1 trillion in notional value, is an excellent example of a market in which instruments are tailored to the highly individual demands of specific market participants. See, for example, Walmsley (1988, pp. 125–147).
17. See, for example, McCarney, 1990, p. c1; Calvey, 1990, p. 1; Hargreaves, 1990, p. 35.
18. See, for example, "Faith in the Future," *Corporate Finance* (July 1990), p. 17, which describes selected new and proposed futures and options contracts in the U.S., European, and Japanese markets.

19. See, generally, Black (1989). See also Rosenbaum (1990, p. 50).
20. See, for example, Poser (1988).
21. See, for example, Brauchli (1990, p. A18).
22. Early evidence of this pattern is already emerging. In the first quarter of 1990, "despite a stable dollar, foreign investors were net sellers of U.S. securities for the first time since the third quarter of 1983. . . . [T]his new development emphasizes that the U.S. can no longer count on an unending supply of foreign capital" (Securities Industry Association, 1990).
23. See, generally, Bollenbacher (1990, p. 22).
24. See, for example, Kollar, 1990, p. 7A; "CBT Throws in the Towel . . . ," 1990, p. 6.
25. Norris (1990, p. c2) describes plans of American and Cincinnati stock exchanges and of the Chicago Board Options Exchange to compete with newly announced after-hours trading system developed by the New York Stock Exchange.
26. "Plans are now under way to set up fully computerized and automated financial exchanges in Japan in the near future" ("Exchange Sets Sights . . . ," 1989).
27. In an electronic crossing network, institutional buyers and sellers meet each other directly on a computer screen without intermediation by specialists or market makers. See, for example, U.S. Securities and Exchange Commission (1989).
28. See, for example, Wunsch (1989).
29. See, for example, Grundfest, 1990.
30. See also Schultz (1990, p. c1) for a description of frauds in the United States involving the sale of foreign securities.
31. See the opening statements of Hon. Douglas Bernard, Jr., and Hon. Gary Montjoy in *Problems With the SEC's Enforcement of the Securities Laws as to Suspicious Foreign Originated Trades:* Hearings before the Subcomm. on Commerce, Consumer, and Monetary Affairs of the House Committee on Government Operations, 100th Congress, 2nd Session (1988). See also Torres and Salwen (1990, p. A3) who note a spate of insider trading inquiries in connection with foreign acquisitions of publicly traded U.S. firms.
32. To maintain secrecy, Levine explains that he opened a numbered Swiss bank account and "went to great lengths to avoid creating a paper trail for investigators to follow. . . . [The bank] sent me no bank statements. I called in my trades from public phones—collect."
33. For an excellent summary of the current state of SEC enforcement efforts on the international front, as well as a summary of international information sharing arrangements, see Mann and Mari (1990).
34. Of interest is the observation that this degree of cooperation is forthcoming even from countries that have a long history of bank secrecy. These jurisdictions often recognize that their secrecy statutes were adopted for reasons that have nothing to do with the facilitation of illegal commerce, whether in the form of securities transactions or the laundering of drug money. Thus, in circumstances where sufficient evidence can be presented that a secrecy jurisdiction is being used for purposes inconsistent with the host jurisdiction's purpose in protecting depositor confidentiality, the host can be persuaded to lift the veil of secrecy.
35. See generally, Levine and Caldicott (1989).
36. See also Rider (1990) for a review that is critical of U.S. attempts to extend the scope of its international securities jurisdiction, particularly as reflected in the SEC's "waiver-by-conduct" proposal (Exchange Act Release No. 21186, 1984). "When somewhat presumptuously questioned as to how far his writ ran, Henry II responded, as far as his arrows reached! Given the developments that have since taken place in ballistics, such an approach to jurisdiction might even accommodate the extraterritorial zeal of our North American cousins."
37. See generally, Walter (1990).
38. See, for example, Note, "Barriers to the International Flow of Capital . . . ," 1987. Variations in regulatory regimes present the "greatest obstacle to internationalization of capital markets."
39. Securities Act Release No. 6, 841 [1989 Transfer Binder] Fed. Sec. L. Rep. (CCH) ¶ 84, 432 (July 26, 1989). See also Karmel, 1990, pp. 3–18; Waitzer, 1989.
40. See, for example, Beresford, 1990, pp. 17–24; Choi and Levich, 1990, forthcoming. See also "SEC Launches Extensive Review . . . ," 1990.
41. See, for example, French and Poterba (1990) who explain half the disparity between U.S. and Japan price/earnings ratios by differences in accounting practices regarding consolidation of earnings from subsidiaries and depreciation of fixed assets. See also Choi and Levich (1990, forthcoming).

42. See, for example, Sychrava (1990, p. 15) who states that Swiss accounting procedures "allow you to hide earnings until you want to reveal them."

43. For a different and provocative view on the reasons for the adoption of international bank capital adequacy standards, see Kane (1990) who describes the Basle accord as a cartel-like arrangement among the world's banking regulators.

44. As an example of the likely parameters of of the controversy, consider the debate accompanying release of Revision Four of the EEC's Draft Capital Adequacy Directive. See Joint Letter of Merrill Lynch International, Morgan Stanley International, Salomon Brothers International, and Shearson, Lehman, Hutton International to the Rt. Hon Sir Leon Brittan, Vice President of The European Commission, Feb. 22, 1990; EEC, Directorate-General, Financial Institutions and Company Law, Discussion Document, *Issues Arising in the Draft Proposal for a Council Directive on Capital Adequacy of Investment Firms Including Credit Institutions* (Revision 4, November 1989); see also "Japan: New Rules Will Tighten Capital Adequacy Requirements," 2 International Securities Regulation Report 1 (August 2, 1989).

45. See, for example, Fischel (1988).

46. See Brauchli (1990).

47. See, for example, *Changes Introduced By the Companies Act, 1989,* Financial Regulation Report (December 1989); *Possible Changes to the FSA and a New Approach by the SIB,* Financial Regulation Report (March 1989).

References

Akashi, Tomoko. "Regulation of Insider Trading in Japan." *Columbia Law Review* 89 (October 1989), 1296.

Allen, Julius W. *The Internationalization of Securities Trading Markets.* Washington, DC: Congressional Research Service, Library of Congress, April 1986.

Ayling, D. *The Internationalization of Stock Markets.* 1986.

Beresford, Dennis R. "What's the FASB Doing About International Accounting Standards?" *Financial Executive* 6 (May-June 1990), 17-24.

Black, Fischer. "Universal Hedging: Optimizing Currency Risk and Reward in International Equity Portfolios." *Financial Analysts Journal* 45 (July–August 1989), 16-22.

Bollenbacher, George. "Financial Technology in the Year 2000." *Investment Dealers Digest* (May 14, 1990), 22.

Brauchli, Marcus W. "U.S. Treasury Aide Assails Japan's Pace in Financial Reform, Warns of Sanctions." *Wall Street Journal* (May 23, 1990), A18.

Calvey, Mark. "Timing Was Right for Nikkei Put Warrants." *Investor's Daily* (March 20, 1990), 1.

"CBT Throws in the Towel, Agrees to Join Globex." *Wall Street Computer Review* (July 1990), 6.

Choi, Frederich D.S. and Richard M. Levich. *The Capital Market Effects of International Accounting Diversity,* Arthur Anderson & Co. and Solomon Bros, Inc. Homewood, IL: Dow Jones-Irwin, 1990, forthcoming.

Chuppe, Terry M., Hugh R. Haworth, and Marvin G. Watkins. "Global Finance: Causes, Consequences and Prospects for the Future." *Global Finance Journal* 1 (Fall 1989a), 1-20.

Chuppe, Terry M., Hugh R. Haworth, and Marvin G. Watkins. *The Securities Markets in the 1980s: A Global Perspective.* Washington, DC: U.S. Securities and Exchange Commission, January 26, 1989b.

Cooper, Wendy. "Too Few Countries, Too Many Funds?" *Institutional Investor* (May 1990), 179.

Copeland, Thomas E. and J. Fred Weston. *Financial Theory and Corporate Policy,* 3rd ed. Reading, MA: Addison-Wesley, 1988.

"Exchange Sets Sights On Fully Automated Trading," *International Securities Regulation Reporter* (BNA) 2 (August 16, 1989), 1.

"Faith in the Future." *Corporate Finance* (July 1990), 17.

Fischel, Daniel R. "Should One Agency Regulate Futures Markets?" In Robert J. Barro et al., eds., *Black Monday and the Future of Financial Markets.* Homewood, IL: Dow Jones-Irwin, 1988.

French, Kenneth and James Poterba. "Are Japanese Stock Prices Too High?" NBER Working Paper No. 3290, March 1990.

Graham, Edward M. and Paul R. Krugman. *Foreign Direct Investment in the United States,* Vol. 10. Washington, DC: Institute for International Economics, 1989.

Greene, Edward F. and Alan L. Beller. "Rule 144A: Keeping the U.S. Competitive in the International Financial Markets." *Insights* 4 (June 1990), 3–13.

Grundfest, Joseph A. "The Damning Facts of a New Stocks Tax." *Wall Street Journal* (July 23, 1990), A12.

Hargreaves, Deborah. "Nikkei Put Warrants Given Enthusiastic Welcome on Amex." *Financial Times* (January 16, 1990), 35.

Heimann, John G., Vice Chairman, Merrill Lynch Capital Markets. Statement in Hearings Before the Subcommittee on Securities of the Committee on Banking, Housing and Urban Affairs, U.S. Senate, *Globalization of the Securities Markets* (June 14, 1989), p. 76.

Henriques, G. "Remember Petrodollars? They're Back." *New York Times* (May 6, 1990), section 3, p. 15.

Hershey, Robert D., Jr. "Greenspan Opposes Rescue of Failing Securities Firms." *The New York Times* (March 2, 1990), section D, p. 2.

Julius, DeAnne. *Global Companies and Public Policy.* London: Royal Institute of International Affairs, 1990.

Kahn, Virginia Munger. "You Can Invest Abroad and Not Leave Home." *Investor's Daily* (February 5, 1990), 1.

Kane, Edward. "Incentive Conflict in the International Regulatory Agreement on Risk-Based Capital." NBER Working Paper No. 3308, March 1990.

Karmel, Roberta. "SEC Regulation of Multijurisdictional Offerings." *Brooklyn Journal of International Law* 16 (1990), 3–18.

Kollar, Mark. "After Three Attempts Globex Will Debut." *Journal of Commerce* (June 25, 1990), 7A.

Labaton, Stephen. "Group of Seven Asks Money-Laundering Curbs." *The New York Times* (April 20, 1990), C1.

Lessaw, S. "World, Country and Industry Relationships in Equity Returns: Implications for Risk Reduction Through International Diversification." *Financial Analyst Journal* (January-February 1976), 32.

Levine, Dennis B. "The Inside Story of an Inside Trader." *Fortune* (May 21, 1990), 80.

Levine, Theodore and W. Hardy Callcott. "The SEC and Foreign Policy: The International Securities Enforcement Cooperation Act of 1988." *Securities Regulation Law Journal* 17 (Summer 1989), 115.

Lewis, Janet. "Currencies: Risk, Opportunity or Just a Wash?" *Institutional Investor* (June 1990), 137–139.

Makin, John H. "National Superpowers Are Obsolete and So Is Managed Trade." *The American Enterprise* (September-October 1990, forthcoming).

Mann, Michael D. and Joseph G. Mari. *Developments in International Securities Law Enforcement.* Washington, DC: U.S. Securities and Exchange Commission, 1990.

Mason, Scott P. and Robert C. Merton. "The Role of Contingent Claims Analysis in Corporate Finance." In Edward Altman and Marti G. Subrahamanyam, eds., *Recent Advances in Corporate Finance.* New York: Irwin, 1985, pp. 7–54.

McCarney, Robert J. "Americans Cash in as Tokyo Shares Fall." *Washington Post* (April 4, 1990), C1.

Miller, Rich. "U.S.-Japan Joust Over Financial Market Deregulation." *The Reuter Library Report* (May 17, 1990).

Morgan Guaranty Trust Co. *World Financial Markets* (June 29, 1989), 3.

Norris, Floyd. "3 Exchanges Set Plan for All-Night Trading." *New York Times* (June 19, 1990), C2.

Note, "Barriers to the International Flow of Capital: The Facilitation of Multinational Securities Offerings." *Vanderbilt Journal of Transnational Law.* 20 (1987), 81.

"Openness, Not Retaliation, Is Key to Competitiveness." *American Banker* (May 21, 1990), 5.

Poser, Norman S. "Big Bang and the Financial Services Act Seen Through American Eyes." *Brooklyn Journal of International Law* 14 (1988), 317–338.

Rider, Barry A. K. "Policing the International Financial Markets: An English Perspective." *Brooklyn Journal of International Law* (1990), 179–221.

Rosenbaum, Amy. "Coming to America: Foreign Products Hit U.S. Shores." *Futures* (May 1990), 50.

Schultz, Ellen. "Overseas Investing Boom Spawns New Wave of Scams." *Wall Street Journal* (May 8, 1990), C1.

"SEC Launches Extensive Review of Cost Effectiveness of FASB Standards." *Securities Regulation & Law Reporter . (BNA)* 22 (July 27, 1990), 1111.

Securities Industry Association. "The Times They Are A-Changin'." *Foreign Activity* 13 (July 24, 1990), 1.

Sharpe, William F. *Investments,* 3rd ed. New York: Prentice Hall, 1985.

Solnik, K. "Why Not Diversify Internationally Rather than Domestically?" *Financial Analyst Journal* (July-August 1977), 51.

Sychrava, Juliet. "Investing in Swiss Securities." *Euromoney* (June 1990), 15.

Tanji, Makoto. "Recent Changes in the Organization and Regulation of the Capital Markets." In *Changes in the Organization and Regulation of Capital Markets.* Basle: Bank for International Settlements, March 1987.

Torres, Craig and Kevin G. Salwen. "Trading in Fund American Prior to News of Deal Raises Suspicion of Insider Moves." *Wall Street Journal* (August 3, 1990), A3.

Ulam, Michael and William G. Dewald. "The U.S. Net International Investment Position: Misstated and Misunderstood." In James A. Dorn and William A. Niskanen, eds., *Dollars, Deficits, and Trade.* Norwell, MA: Kluwer Academic Publishers for the CATO Institute, 1989.

U.S. Congress, Official Technology Assessment. *Trading Around the Clock: Global Securities Markets and Information Technology,* OTA-BP-CIT-66, July 1990.

U.S. Securities and Exchange Commission. *Internationalization of the Securities Markets.* Report of the Staff of the U.S. Securities and Exchange Commission to the Senate Committee on Banking, Housing and Urban Affairs, and for the House Committee on Energy and Commerce, Washington, DC, July 27, 1987.

U.S. Securities and Exchange Commission. *Proprietary Trading Systems,* Securities Act Release No. 34-26708, April 11, 1989.

U.S. Securities and Exchange Commission. Securities Act Release No. 6862, April 23, 1990. *Federal Register* 55 (April 30, 1990), 17933.

Viner, Aaron. *Inside Japanese Financial Markets.* Homewood, IL: Dow Jones-Irwin, 1988.

Waitzer, Edward. "Disclosure Proposals for U.S.-Canada Transactions." *International Security Regulation Report* 2 (October 11, 1989), 7.

Walmsley, Julian. *The New Financial Instruments.* New York: John Wiley & Sons, 1988.

Walter, Inge. *The Secret Money Market: Inside the Dark World of Tax Evasion, Financial Fraud, Insider Trading, Money Laundering, and Capital Flight.* New York: Harper & Row, 1990.

Wriston, Walter B. "Technology and Sovereignty." *Foreign Affairs* 67 (Winter 1988–1989), 63–75.

Winch, Kevin F., Edward Knight, and Mark Jickling. *Globalization of Securities Markets.* Washington, DC: Congressional Research Service, Library of Congress, June 7, 1989.

Wunsch, R. Steven. "The Saga of the Battling Boxes." *Global Custodian* (September 1989), 90–92.

Journal of Financial Services Research 4:379–382 (1990)
© 1990 Kluwer Academic Publishers

Commentary: *Internationalization of the World's Securities Markets: Economic Causes and Regulatory Consequences*

FRANKLIN R. EDWARDS
Arthur F. Burns Chair in Free and Competitive Enterprise
Columbia Business School and Director
Center for Study of Futures Markets, Columbia University, New York, NY 10027

Joseph Grundfest has provided us with a broad-based and perceptive view of international securities markets.

His article can be divided into three parts. The first is a descriptive analysis of the internationalization of securities markets from two perspectives: the activities of foreigners in the United States, and the activities of U.S. citizens in foreign securities markets. A striking statistic is that trading by foreigners on the New York Stock Exchange as a proportion of all trading has nearly doubled during the 1980s, rising from about 8 percent to about 14 percent. Similarly, U.S. trading on foreign securities markets grew at a cumulative annual growth rate of 28.6 percent during the nine years from 1980 to 1988.

Thus, securities trading is becoming increasingly international in scope, and markets are becoming increasingly interlinked. An interesting question, which Grundfest does not address (and on which the evidence is mixed), is whether price movements on securities markets are more highly correlated than in the past. Does greater intermarket participation, for example, result in price shocks in one country's securities markets being more fully transmitted to securities markets in other countries? If so, this could have implications for the regulation of securities markets.

Another striking, but hardly surprising, statistic is that the chief foreign beneficiaries of the recent internationalization have been Japan and the United Kingdom. Securities markets in those countries are now serious competitors to New York as world financial markets. U.S. securities exchanges will have to be more efficient and more innovative in the future if they are to retain their present world position. In particular, exchanges that succeed in adopting superior trading technologies and market governance will see their market shares grow in the future.

In the second part of his article, Grundfest analyzes the causes of the increasing internationalization and makes predictions about its future course. He singles out "capital imbalances" among countries, technology changes, widespread acceptance of advances in finance theory by portfolio managers, and deregulation.

A factor that Grundfest does not discuss, but which I believe to be quite important, is the sharp growth in the role of institutions in securities markets. In the United States, for example, institutions such as pension funds and investment companies now account for 70 to 80 percent of trading on the New York Stock Exchange. A similar "institutionalization of markets" is occurring in foreign securities countries as well. With vast sums to invest, institutions have significant economies of scale in learning about and trading on foreign securities markets, and international diversification promises attractive returns.

The third part of Grundfest's article, and the one which provides the most fertile ground for friendly disagreement, addresses the regulatory implications of securities market internationalization. Grundfest focuses this discussion on three issues: the need for international cooperative regulatory agreements; the need for standardization of regulation; and, as perhaps an antidote to the first two, the benefits of international regulatory competition.

These issues raise several obvious and key questions. When are international cooperative agreements among regulators either necessary or in the public interest? When and why is international standardization of regulation beneficial? When and why is international regulatory competition detrimental? While these issues are not entirely independent of one another, they nevertheless emphasize different aspects of the debate. Although Grundfest provides us with some insight into each of these questions, he does not provide full answers to them. They are not easy questions. International cooperative agreements, he argues, are necessary for domestic regulations to be effective. Without them markets can be used to evade domestic regulations.

Grundfest provides the following illustration: a British subject may be able to trade British securities with other British subjects in British markets by channeling such trades through, say, the United States and Switzerland. In this case British authorities may need access to information available to U.S. authorities but not normally available to British authorities. An exchange of information among U.S. and British regulators, therefore, would enhance enforcement and protect the sanctity of British law. The Securities and Exchange Commission has, in fact, over the past several years negotiated a network of "bilateral understandings" with many countries.

While it is clear that there is a role for international "understandings," Grundfest does not discuss a related issue that may arise as a consequence of internationalization. In particular, let us take U.S. insider trading laws. Suppose that a U.S. subject trades a U.S. stock—say, IBM—on the Tokyo Stock Exchange while in possession of material, non-public ("inside") information about IBM. Furthermore, suppose that in doing so, the U.S. trader deals only with Japanese subjects, and that his actions do not violate any Japanese (insider trading) laws.

Does such trading violate the sanctity of U.S. markets? Are U.S. markets made less efficient? Are U.S. citizens defrauded or harmed in any way? Are U.S. markets less "fair" in any way? If Japanese regulation permits such trading, should U.S. subjects be held to U.S. standards when trading in Japan?

There are, of course, many variations on the example I have given above. It would be useful, therefore, if we formulated a more definitive criterion for when domestic regulators should invoke bilateral understandings in pursuit of criminal activity.

My fear is that without such criteria regulators at times may be overzealous and enforce U.S. regulations in a counterproductive manner. An example of this is the SEC's recent attempt to curtail the exemption to the "uptick" rule that program traders now enjoy. The uptick rule prohibits short-selling of a stock when the stock is on a "downtick." The recent SEC initiative seeks to tighten the exemption in connection with the unwinding of positions established overseas (and in London particularly).

The SEC's 1986 uptick exemption was made to facilitate index arbitrage between stocks and stock index futures, which requires the simultaneous buying and selling of stocks and stock index futures. Without the exemption, such arbitrage would be hampered because it might prove difficult to unwind a position in a declining market by simultaneously selling stocks (on a downtick) and buying futures. If such arbitrage becomes difficult, it could destroy the close link between the cash and futures equity markets.

The SEC is now contending that this exemption should not be permitted in the unwinding of an arbitrage position established overseas. For example, a firm might establish such a position in London when the U.S. stock market is closed at night, in order to accommodate an institutional client who wants to sell stocks immediately. In such cases the firm will acquire stocks and short futures prior to the opening of the U.S. market, and then unwind the position later by selling stocks in New York and simultaneously buying futures. This transaction would become perilous if the arbitraging firm were subject to the uptick rule.

There is absolutely no reason for the SEC to discriminate against arbitrage positions established overseas. The original purpose of the uptick rule was to prevent "bear raids" on companies. Index arbitrage is totally unrelated to this objective. Interfering with index arbitrage, whether at home or abroad, will make markets less efficient. It would, therefore, be counterproductive for the SEC to elicit help from British authorities to enforce its uptick rule against index arbitragers, either in London or New York. By doing so the SEC has lost sight of the objective of the uptick rule, and has interfered with the efficient functioning of international securities markets.

International standardization of regulations, such as disclosure or capital requirements, is more problematic. For standardization to enhance global efficiency the regulations established will have to be better (or "more optimal") than those that arise in the absence of international cooperation. Without standardization, a combination of domestic goals and international competition is likely to determine the regulations adopted by each country. Unless there are significant externalities present, the regulations that individual countries adopt should be the optimal ones.

Grundfest does not provide us with any guidelines as to when such externalities are present and what their nature might be. Furthermore, standardization suggests that what is optimal in one country is optimal in another. This is unlikely. Also, what is optimal at one time is unlikely to be optimal at another time, and regulators are unlikely to be able to renegotiate standardized agreements quickly.

A case in point that presently is occupying regulators is the need to standardize capital requirements for securities firms. The International Organization of Securities Commissions (IOSCO) is spearheading this effort. Those who support this approach argue that there is a risk of systemic failure in securities markets (a form of externality) that can be mitigated by standardizing capital requirements. The nature of the alleged systemic risk is not clear to me, nor is the purported prophylactic effect of standardized capital requirements.

I think Grundfest would agree with me that the case for standardization of securities regulations has not been made effectively. The best way to achieve optimal securities regulation over time is to continue to allow international competition among regulatory jurisdictions. It may not always result in optimal laws, but there is no reason to believe that standardization will be better.

The SEC's most recent Rule 144A is evidence of the benefits of international competition. Rule 144A identifies a category of securities transactions involving large institutions (with portfolios of $100 million or more) that are no longer subject to the SEC's disclosure provisions. More specifically, it permits the resale of such private-placement securities without registration and without having to hold them for two years. The effect of the new rule is to reduce significantly the costs associated with large securities transactions, and make it more attractive to conduct these transactions in the United States as opposed to the Euromarkets.

For years SEC regulations have discouraged foreign issuers from raising capital in the United States and have encouraged U.S. companies to go overseas, helping to create Euromarkets that now rival U.S. markets in size, liquidity, and the quality of market participants. Competition from foreign markets is making the SEC re-think the wisdom of its regulations and, hopefully, is moving it to eliminate unnecessary and costly impediments to the creation of efficient and competitive U.S. securities markets. Rule 144A is a step in the right direction.

In conclusion, Grundfest has provided us with an excellent survey of the growing internationalization of securities markets, and has drawn out some of the key regulatory implications of this development. His article suggests, and I agree, that in the future there will arise a number of new regulatory issues as a result of the increasing internationalization of securities markets.

Journal of Financial Services Research 4:383–385 (1990)

Commentary: *Internationalization of the World's Securities Markets: Economic Causes and Regulatory Consequences*

PETER M. FLANIGAN
Managing Director
Dillon, Read, and Co., Inc.
535 Madison Avenue
New York, NY 10022

Joseph Grundfest has written a very thought-provoking article. I would like to add a couple of ideas to some of the thoughts he put forward.

The very impressive charts in his article deal with only the last decade. When people talk about international capital markets, they almost never go back before the middle of this century. This emphasis on the very recent past denies us the opportunity to learn something from history about international capital markets which, after all, have been active and productive for a long time.

The main reason, I would guess, that we do not go back beyond the 1950s is that there was a 20-year hiatus prior to about 1950. We had blown up much of the world's capital during World War II, except for U.S. capital, and during the war we invested much of our capital in government. For some time before that, we had used up most of our capital, or lost it, during the Depression of the 1930s. But in the hundred years prior to that—without the benefit of new, modern technology in communications and transportation—there was an extraordinary amount of international capital movement, and international capital markets were very active.

I think much of the recent growth in international capital markets has been the result of the increase in capital available for investment. This is suggested by the article's statistics. They show that while the absolute figures were up significantly, the percent of international capital transactions to total transactions was up even more significantly.

My favorite example of early international capital market activity shows that regulation of international capital markets was not a necessary precondition—in fact, the opposite may be more nearly true. My example comes from a time in the early nineteenth century when Napoleon was in a bit of a credit squeeze and he called together whoever were his chief financial advisers and said, "We've got to get out of this." So, probably with the assistance of some "smoke and mirrors" that they provided, he decided he was going to sell assets to reduce the squeeze. The only handy asset was the Louisiana Territory for which they needed to find a buyer. The buyer they approached, the United States, had very little information on what it was buying, had no authority to make the purchase, and did not have any money. So its representatives decided to go to England from France, even though the legendary government regulator, Horatio Hornblower, was stopping that kind of travel. But the buyer's representatives got there anyway and visited Baring Brothers. The Barings agreed to finance this transaction, in spite of the fact that their country was at the same time straining to bring down Mr. Napoleon.

I would submit that Aunt Minnie, in the metaphor of Grundfest's article, living in Brighton instead of Omaha, financed that transaction through her funds in some saving or building society. She accomplished what she wanted, which was to get a higher return with the indirect help of her professional advisers. That same thing went on after the end of the Napoleonic War. As we all know, the British ended up owning most of our assets, we developed our country, and Aunt Minnie got rich (or at least she got a higher return than she otherwise might have). Most, if not all, of that international investment was the result of international capital market activity that occurred without the benefit either of modern technology or of any significant regulation.

The present discussion of financing through international capital markets prompts me to recall my first visits to Japan in the 1950s. It may be hard to believe now, but at that time we were trying to provide them with capital. I learned then that in the 1920s, Dillon-Read had sent people by train to the West Coast and then by boat to Yokohama. They negotiated with Tokyo Electric and Kansai Electric, then got back on the boat at Yokohama, got back on the train at the coast, and came back to New York. They offered a bundle of securities that in today's market would be equal to $300 or $400 million, a big deal even by today's standards. Once again, this international financial transaction was accomplished without benefit of modern technology, communications, or transportation and without benefit—if that is what it is—of regulation.

I think, of course, that important efficiencies have come from modern transportation and communications, from derivative financial products, and from all the other important things that have been discussed in this conference. But I think these efficiencies can probably be measured in basis points—20, 30, or 50 basis points, I do not know how much. I want to emphasize that the driving force for the international capital market is the potential for higher returns that comes from putting capital to work where it can make its most valuable contribution to the development of an economy.

It is a matter of first importance that we keep capital investment and economic development opportunities in place in countries around the world. It is important that we not lose these opportunities as we did in the middle of this century. From the examples that I have given, I would guess that we should try to minimize regulation.

The second point I would make is that Aunt Minnie in Omaha really does not enter into the market; she gives her money to a professional who does that. She does not have to make a decision about the regulatory atmosphere in Tokyo, London, or anywhere else. She chooses people who can make that decision on her behalf.

It is well known that with efficient markets, arbitrage across markets should generate a single price for the same security in different markets. But even though we are talking about global markets, they do not always seem to arbitrage values. And, frankly, I do not understand why. I think the answer may be in the suggestion at the end of Grundfest's article, that we should try to make it easier for people to understand relative values.

Here is an interesting example. Some time ago, you could look at two rather similar companies, both making beer. One, Anheuser-Busch, makes Budweiser which is the largest selling imported beer in Japan, and the stock is traded on the Tokyo Exchange. The second is Sapporo, the second largest beer company in Japan, and not such a strong second, while Anheuser-Busch is a strong first in a market that's almost twice as big.

At the time I looked at the statistics, earnings had recently increased at a single digit rate for Sapporo and at a double digit rate for Anheuser-Busch. The expectation of all the experts was that this trend was going to continue. Yet, Sapporo was selling at 100 times earnings and Anheuser-Busch was selling at 13 or 14 times earnings. Even if you make the most draconian adjustments to the Japanese price/earnings ratio, you get maybe 50 times earnings on a comparable basis. So, Sapporo was selling at, say, three times the value of Anheuser-Busch.

I have to ask myself why. Perhaps a difference in the cost of capital means that the Japanese stock should sell at 50 percent more in value, but not 300 percent more. Part of the answer, of course, is that much of the investment in stocks here and abroad is held by individuals and not by professionals. For Anheuser-Busch, for instance, 50 percent of it is owned by individuals, but most the individuals are not themselves making those markets.

The main point of this example is that I strongly support the suggestion that we look for ways to create commonality in those aspects of our international securities markets that could provide better information across national boundaries, that we try to work toward more common accounting conventions between us, and that we follow more approaches like the SEC's Rule 144A, where the documents are common across markets. We can then hope that, in time, we will truly globalize markets in a way that arbitrages values instead of just single securities. I only wish Grundfest were back at the SEC in order to move forward some of the ideas that are in his excellent article.

Journal of Financial Services Research, 4:387–408 (1990)
© 1990 Kluwer Academic Publishers

International Competitiveness of U.S. Futures Exchanges

MERTON H. MILLER
Robert R. McCormick Distinguished Service Professor
Graduate School of Business
University of Chicago
Chicago, IL 60637

1. Introduction: the U.S. futures industry from a worldwide perspective

Futures exchanges are business organizations providing transaction services and associated clearing and settlement services in a wide variety of products ranging these days from agricultural products (corn, soy beans, beef cattle) to precious metals (gold, silver, platinum) to petroleum products (heating oil, gasoline) and, most important currently, to financial instruments (stock indexes, Treasury bonds, foreign currencies). A breakdown of the futures exchange industry by location and type of product traded for the three years 1980, 1985, and 1990 is presented in table 1.

Although often dubbed "commodity exchanges," the futures exchanges trade not physical commodities, but *contracts*, which are similar in many respects to "insurance policies," where the "hazard" being insured is the change in the price of the underlying commodity over the life of the contract. Because the terms of settlement between the parties to the contract depend on the price of the underlying commodity at the time of settlement, futures and options contracts are often called "derivative instruments." That term can be misleading, however, if it suggests, as some critics of futures and options markets intend it to, that the market for the underlying commodity is the only "real" market, in the sense of the place where value is actually determined. In fact, however, whenever a strong and active futures market exists, the true value of the commodity is much more likely to be "discovered" in the futures market than in the underlying spot market. The lower transactions costs and higher liquidity on the futures exchanges makes those markets the more natural entry port for price-relevant information. Precisely why the costs might be lower and the liquidity higher on futures markets than on spot markets will be explained in due course. Suffice it to say, at this point, that the costs of trading and settlement are lower on the futures exchanges because the essential business strategy of those exchanges is to keep them lower. The futures exchanges are the "discount stores" of the financial services industry.

The author, who is also serving currently as a Public Governor of the Chicago Mercantile Exchange (CME), is indebted to the CME Research Division for compiling the volume estimates presented at several points in the text, and to the Division's Chief Economist Todd Petzel for helpful comments on an earlier draft. Thanks are due also to George Benston, Fischer Black, John P. Davidson, Kenneth French, and Alan Meltzer.

Table 1. Number of futures exchanges

	1980	1985	1990
U.S. commodities	9	10	10
U.S. financial	4	6	6
World commodities	14	13	13
World financial	1	6	16

Source: Chicago Mercantile Exchange Research Division.

The U.S. futures industry is by far the largest in the world at the moment. The Chicago Mercantile Exchange, for example, currently the second largest exchange in terms of volume, as conventionally measured, traded over 100 million contracts last year, mostly in financial instruments and foreign currencies. Multiplying the number of contracts by the nominal value of each—one Standard & Poor (S&P) 500 contract, for example, has a face value of about $175,000 currently and one Eurodollar contract a face value of $1 million— yields impressive dollar totals. The nominal dollar value, so computed, of the S&P 500 contracts traded daily would surely equal or exceed the dollar value of shares traded on the New York Stock Exchange (NYSE). But these purely notional totals can be seriously misleading. The actual *cash* changing hands in a day's trading in S&P 500 contracts at the Chicago Mercantile Exchange (CME) can never be more than a small fraction of the cash flow at the NYSE, for reasons that will become clear later.

A better indicator of the true economic weight of the industry, therefore, may be not a flow measure, like contract volume, but a stock measure, like market value of the enterprise. Exchanges in the United States, of course, do not formally issue common stock. Our law insists that exchanges be organized not as the profit-making corporations they really are, but essentially as country clubs, with those privileged to trade directly on the floor constituting the "members." The posted prices of those memberships can thus constitute one measure, at least, of the franchise values that an exchange embodies. In the case of the CME, for example, whose full membership seats currently sell for $500,000 or so, the combined worth of the stake of the 2,800 or so members of various classes comes to nearly $800 million. That size would put the CME roughly among the lower fifth of the firms listed on the NYSE in terms of capitalization. By comparison, the franchise value of the NYSE is on the order of $500 million. The franchise value of the entire U.S. futures and options industry was about $2.0 billion in mid-year 1989, and that of all overseas exchanges might come to perhaps a fifth of that.

The customer clientele base of the U.S. futures industry is primarily domestic, but the foreign presence is also substantial, running perhaps to 20 percent or more for such internationally relevant contracts as petroleum, gold, and Eurodollars, as well as U.S. Treasury bonds and stock index products. U.S. customer purchases of foreign contracts are still much smaller than foreign purchases of U.S. contracts, but the outflow has grown substantially in recent years, particularly since the introduction of stock index futures and option products in the Tokyo market. A noticeable rise in U.S. customer use of foreign markets, primarily London, has also occurred recently in the special case of so-called

Table 2. Financial market share

	1980	1985	1990
U.S.	100%	94%	63%
Other	0%	6%	37%

Source: CME Research Division.

"exchange for physicals" (EFP's) in connection with the CME's S&P 500 index contract. The London-based EFP's, to be discussed in more detail later, currently amount to somewhere between 1.0 and 1.5 percent of the S&P 500 contract volume.

Some estimates of the relative market shares in financial futures of the U.S. and foreign exchanges are presented in table 2 for three years: 1980, 1985, and 1990. Note the rapid rise in the foreign share in terms of contract volume since 1980. In 1980, the futures industry was almost entirely, and in financials, literally entirely, a U.S. phenomenon. By 1990, however, the rest-of-the-world share in financial contracts had risen to a substantial 37 percent.

That trend in market shares can be expected to continue apace in the years ahead. The essential technology for exchange-based trading of futures and options is no secret; and in the technology of electronic or screen-based trading of options and futures that of some overseas competitors may even be somewhat ahead of ours. In fact, in the normal course of industrial evolution, the U.S. dominance might well have ended long since, save for the enormous advantage that inevitably attaches to all "first movers" in an exchange setting. So great apparently are the economies of scale in liquidity that the trading demand for any contract quickly gravitates to a single exchange. Even a better-designed new competing contract can rarely win away the business of a contract well established at another exchange. The savings in transaction costs and especially in market impact costs in the more liquid market often more than counterbalance the contracts' defects.

The U.S. exchanges will continue to enjoy this advantage on their already well-established contracts, assuming of course—and it is by no means a comfortable assumption to be making these days—that heavy-handed regulatory interventions do not undermine the liquidity of those contracts. But growth in this industry has typically proceeded by the introduction of new contracts that respond to the new pockets of price volatility that turn up, often so unexpectedly, as the domestic and world economies evolve. The 1960s had their pork bellies; the 1970s had their foreign currencies, interest rates, and petroleum contracts; and the 1980s had their stock indexes. As we look ahead to the 1990s, no one knows what the hot new products will turn out to be. But they stand as much chance of making their first appearance abroad as here.

The competitiveness of the U.S. industry involves much more, however, than facing off against foreign futures and options exchanges. Both groups of exchanges must contend with the powerful competition of "off-exchange" or "over-the-counter" products, like "swaps," that are equivalent in many essential respects to exchange-traded futures and options, but subject to very different forms of regulatory supervision. If the futures exchanges are the discount stores, or, perhaps better, the "one-size-fits-all" stores, of the industry, the producers of some of these equivalent products, mostly the large international banks, are the top-of-the-line firms, offering "tailor-made" services to their customers. And, of course, thanks to the wonders of electronic networking, the customers are increasingly able to deal with each other directly, bypassing both the exchanges and the banks.

To forecast where the eventual boundaries will be drawn between these competing segments is at least as difficult for the derivative products as for any other industrial area. Who in 1979, after all, could have predicted the enormous retreat of the U.S. automobile industry in the face of Japanese competition? A better approach to forecasting the competitive future of the U.S. futures exchanges is to focus on their technology and cost structure, highlighting in the process those areas in which the U.S. futures industry might reasonably hope to maintain its edge over its many rivals at home and abroad. That search must begin with a clear understanding of how, and why, exchange-traded futures contracts differ from off-exchange, negotiated forward contracts. That subject is taken up in the next section. Section 3 appraises the competitive strengths of the overseas exchanges. The article concludes in section 4 with some speculations about the impact on futures trading of governmental regulation, the wild card in the competitiveness equation.

2. Exchange-traded futures contracts: demand, supply, and technology

To those unfamiliar with how futures work, transactions in them may well smack of witchcraft. Imagine, if you will, a magician displaying an ingot consisting of 1,000 ounces of 99.9 percent pure silver at a time when silver sells for $7.00 an ounce. The magician announces that by uttering certain magic words he will transmute this silver ingot not into gold—because that sort of alchemy is so old-fashioned—but into U.S. Treasury bills. The magic words he then pronounces are: "Sell silver futures." And sure enough, the Treasury bills suddenly appear in place of the ingot.

"How did he do it?" the audience gasps in wonder. For the answer, take a closer look at the terms of the futures contract. It obligates the magician to deliver 1,000 ounces of silver, three months from today at a price of $7.15 an ounce. Has the magician perhaps found a patsy to pay him the extra 15 cents in Treasury bills?

Not at all. Look again at the contract, this time from the point of view of a buyer who will need 1,000 ounces of silver three months from now. He could, if he chose, buy the silver immediately at $7.00 an ounce and store it for 90 days. That would involve two kinds of costs, however: first, storage costs at, say, $0.01 per ounce, and second, the opportunity costs of the funds needed to buy the silver. After all, if he didn't buy the silver, he could have invested the money in safe Treasury bills, yielding currently, say, 8 percent annually or 2 percent per quarter. Two percent on the $7,000 investment comes to $140 or $0.14 an ounce. Hence the buyer should be indifferent between buying the spot silver now at $7.00 and buying a futures contract obligating him to buy the silver three months from now at $7.15 an ounce. And by the same token, the seller-magician should be indifferent between selling the three-month futures contract for $7.15 an ounce or selling the silver immediately for $7.00, saving the $0.01 storage cost and *investing the $7,000 in Treasury bills*. The effective purchase of the bills is already taken care of, as it were, in the price stipulated in the futures contract.

This parable of the magician transforming silver into Treasury bills is merely a verbal transcription of the so-called "cost-of-carry formula" that defines the equilibrium price of a futures contract in terms of the current spot price of the commodity. In its simplest form, the cost-of-carry can be expressed by the equation:

$$f_{O,T} = P_O(1 + r(T) + s(T) - d(T))$$

where $f_{O,T}$ is the futures price today (i.e., at time O) for a unit of the commodity to be delivered T days from now; P_O is the present spot price of the commodity; $r(T)$ is the cumulative interest opportunity cost over the T days; $s(T)$ is the cumulative storage cost; and $d(T)$ is the cumulative "convenience yield" from holding the commodity over the T-day interval. The latter term was left out of the parable to simplify the story. But its role becomes important when we turn to consider why people choose to buy and sell futures contracts at all. If they want bills, why not just buy them directly and be done with it?

The answer is because the firms and individuals holding (or planning to hold) inventories of commodities or securities, and who constitute the primary clientele of the futures exchanges, want to have their cake and eat it too, so to speak. They want the convenience of having adequate inventory on hand to meet customer or production needs; but they don't want to face the risk that the value of that inventory may suddenly drop on them. To avoid that risk they can "hedge" by mimicking our magician and selling futures against their inventory position.

That selling the futures contract will in fact dispose of the price risk is easily seen by extending the previous example. Suppose that the spot price of silver were to fall over the next three months from its current level at $7.00 an ounce to $5.00 an ounce. Even a magician might be understandably disconcerted by this hit of 28 percent, or $2,000 on his silver holdings. But remember that he has a contract counterparty who has agreed to take the silver off his hands at the end of the three months for $7.15 an ounce. Our hedger has the choice of going ahead with that delivery of the silver, which will bring in $7,150; or of keeping the silver and buying back his contract (or one equivalent to it) which will then be selling at a discount of $2.15 an ounce (i.e., the $5.00 value of the silver on the delivery date minus the delivery price of $7.15). Or, if silver futures were a so-called "cash settled" rather than a "delivery settled" contract, the hedger would keep the silver and merely accept a check from the counterparty in the amount of $2,150. In all three cases, the hedgers' net worth at contract expiration would be $7,140, exactly as if the hedger had put his original $7,000 into riskless Treasury bills.[1]

That the hedgers can insulate themselves from risk by selling futures should be clear enough by now. But where does that risk go? Is the whole futures industry anything more than just a gigantic game of "hot potato"?

The answer offered in many conventional descriptions of futures markets is that the risks are assumed by a special class of investors dubbed "speculators" whose steady nerves make them better able than the hedgers to face the specter of falling prices. But speculators are only part of the risk-transfer story. (And risk-bearing is only part of their function in the grand scheme of things. Speculators, lured by the prospect of trading gains, also help speed the incorporation of new information into prices; and by their trading activity, even when they guess wrong, help to defray the overhead costs of the exchanges.)

In practice, much of the downside risk feared by hedgers like our magician gets shifted to firms and individuals more worried by *upside* risk (as, for example, a manufacturer committed to selling its output of photographic film under fixed price contracts, and now concerned about a possible rise in the cost of a key raw material). Both sides of the trade, in other words, are often business firms using futures contracts not for the pleasures of gambling, but to manage the risks of their inventory positions. And, as profit-oriented business firms, they can be presumed to be managing those risks at the lowest cost possible, a fact crucial for weighing the competitive prospects of futures exchanges.

Those exchanges, of course, are by no means the only alternative for firms in their efforts at risk management. Rather than hold silver in inventory, for example, a "short hedger" (like our magician and so called because he sells and hence takes a short position in the future) might switch to a Japanese-style "just-in-time" inventory strategy. And a "long hedger" like our film manufacturer might abandon selling under fixed price contracts and shift the price risk to his customers. Or the two hedgers might contract with each other directly via expressions of interest on computer bulletin boards and then negotiate a forward contract that fully meets their individual needs. Or, as is particularly likely those days for foreign exchange risks and interest rate risks, they may each find a bank willing to take the opposite side of their risks, either directly as a principal or as a broker by arranging for them to "swap" their positions. Given these and other alternatives available to the firms, what leads them to do it with futures? The answer is, of course, that under certain conditions, though certainly by no means always, risk management with futures happens to be the cheapest way.

2.1. When and why futures exchanges may be cost effective [2]

The parties entering any forward arrangement, whether an exchange-traded futures contract or an over-the-counter forward contract, face the costs of protecting against contract default by the other party (and, of course, also incur the substantial costs and uncertainties of legal redress when a default does occur). Tales surface after every market crash of losers unwilling or unable to fulfill their contractual obligations. Even mere rumors of such defaults by major market traders can lead to self-protective withdrawals from the market by other traders. Such rumors circulated at the height of the panic on October 19, 1987; and similar difficulties arose again more recently, when potential buyers of the assets of the then still technically free-standing brokerage subsidiaries of Drexel, Burnham, Lambert refused to deal with them after the parent company filed for bankruptcy.

2.1.1. *Forward markets and credit monitoring.*   One way of reducing vulnerability to contract default is to obey the ancient dictum: know thy counterparty and check his credit-worthiness thoroughly before signing the contract. And keep checking it thereafter throughout the life of the contract, because a firm's credit worthiness can deteriorate dramatically even in the short span of three months. This time-tested route of credit monitoring is precisely that followed in the huge interbank foreign-exchange and swap markets. It works there as well as it does because this market is essentially an exclusive club with a small number of wealthy and well-known players, each of whom, moreover,

has considerable expertise in checking the credit not only of each other as counterparties but also of their underlying corporate customers who place the orders.

A drawback to the system, however, is its less-than-complete flexibility when, for any of a number of sound business reasons, one of the bank counterparties or one of the underlying corporate customers wants to withdraw from the agreement before the contract expires. In principle, of course, the relevant parties to a forward contract are free to renegotiate the original terms, and in practice they frequently do. The party wanting out, however, would surely prefer not to be constrained to deal solely with the original counterparty, but rather to be able to deal with any third party willing and able to assume the obligations to the original counterparty over the remaining life of the contract. Finding a "willing" third party is often easy enough; but verifying the "able" part requires a new round of credit checking both by the party wanting out, who would presumably have to reassume the obligation if the third party defaulted, and probably also by the original counterparty as well. Rechecking credit-worthiness in this fashion every time a contract obligation is transferred is feasible really only when all the players already know each other and when they deal in contract sizes large enough to spread the fixed costs of credit-checking and negotiation.

2.1.2. *Assuring contract performance in futures markets: the role of the clearing house.*

For the rest of the universe of firms and contract sizes not meeting these conditions, the futures markets have developed an alternative approach that greatly economizes on the amount of credit checking (and of legal pursuit) that might otherwise be needed to assure performance both of the original forward contract and of any subsequent transfers of its obligations. The futures markets do it by setting up a "clearing house" as the counterparty to *both* sides of every contract. Technically, the forward contracts bought or sold on the exchanges are all contracts with the clearing house—an arrangement that not only permits an efficient solution of the credit problem, as we shall see below, but that has other important advantages relative to forward contracts negotiated directly between the parties. With only a single issuer, contract terms can be standardized so that any seller can get out of his original obligation simply by "offsetting" it with the purchase of any other and fully equivalent contract. His accounts on the books of clearing houses would then be in balance at zero, and his obligations to the clearing house to fulfill the original contract are effectively ended. Yet the original buyer need have no concern at that point, or earlier, about the seller carrying out the contract's obligations. The clearing house, and not the original seller, whoever that might happen to be, is the contract counterparty to whom the buyer looks for satisfaction of the contract's terms.

The clearing house, as the counterparty to both sides, thus relieves the credit-risk anxieties of the contracting parties to the trade by substituting its own credit for theirs. But what makes those promises by the clearing house credible enough to permit bargains to be routinely struck on the floor of the exchange between complete strangers? The answer lies in an ingenious multilevel, defense-in depth strategy, long recognized as the hallmark of futures-market trading.[3] The first line of defense for the clearing house consists of the initial "margins" or good faith deposits it requires in advance in cash or cash equivalents from each side of every trade. The initial margins are set high enough to absorb possible trading losses by either party on any days except those with extraordinarily large price changes. The second line of defense is a daily settling up of the accounts. Recall that our cost-of-carry forward price of $7.15 was appropriate when the spot silver was $7.00 an ounce. Should the futures price of silver have risen during the trading day to $7.25—as might happen, say, if the spot price rose to $7.10—anyone who sold silver futures yesterday at $7.15 has already incurred an obligation to pay $100 (i.e., the 10 cent price change times 1,000 ounces) to the buyer at contract expiration, and possibly much more than $100 if the price of silver were to keep rising. To allay any concerns the buyer might have about the satisfaction of his claims (as well as to make sure that the clearing house remains a zero-balance clearing house and not a bank), the clearing house "marks to market" each trader's position at the end of the trading day. The gains and losses of each side to the contract are tabulated, and the winners may withdraw their gains in cash if they so choose, drawing that cash, in effect, from the loser's margin deposits. Losers desiring to hold their positions must deposit more cash if their margin account has dropped below its "maintenance margin" level. Should the shortfall in the margin account not be remedied by the start of the next day's trading, the account will immediately be closed out by offsetting the position in the trading pit at the prevailing price. The same fate can be meted out to losers if they fail to meet the intraday margin calls on days with exceptionally large price moves.[4] The clearing-house defense system, in short, seeks to solve the problems of customer credit risk and of maintaining the credibility of its own guarantees by minimizing the amount of credit in the system. The futures markets aim to be not merely "cash on delivery" markets but "cash before delivery" markets.

Behind these front-line clearing-house defenses, the futures exchanges have erected still others to dampen the impact of any failures to meet obligations within the clearing mechanism itself. Customer margin accounts must be "segregated"; they are not a source of borrowed funds to any brokerage firm, and hence are insulated from any brokerage firm failures. Each so-called "clearing firm" that constitutes the membership of the clearing house must also guarantee the contract performance of the brokerage firms and individual members for which it chooses to serve as clearing agent, and must support that guarantee with margin deposits and frequent intraday margin calls. The clearing houses also have guarantee funds (sometimes called "security deposits" or "clearing corporation stock"), parent corporation guarantees for the trading of clearing member subsidiaries, and substantial committed bank lines of credit to provide emergency liquidity on short notice. The clearing firms themselves are jointly and severally responsible for each other's failure to perform, and the financial integrity of the clearing house itself is sustained ultimately by the full wealth of all the clearing members of the exchange.

That this combined system of defenses is effective is evident in the oft-quoted boast of the CME and the Chicago Board of Trade (CBOT), the two largest exchanges, that no customer of theirs has ever suffered from a contract default.[5] But, of course, there are no free lunches. The system of margins-cum-daily settlements, in particular, does impose costs on the market users and, to that extent, reduces their demand for trading services. Balancing the conflicting needs for transaction volume on the one hand and clearing-house security on the other is a major part of every exchange's business strategy and helps to explain their very hostile reaction to calls for government control over margins—a subject to be taken up again in section 4.

Thanks to their system of bonding traders with margins, the futures exchanges have carved out and maintained a zone of comparative advantage in their competition with directly negotiated forward contracts. But for a wide range of transaction sizes, the trading floors of the exchanges provide another equally important competitive edge.

2.2. Transactions costs and the floor-trading system

Although transaction sizes on futures exchanges are an order of magnitude or more smaller than in the interbank forward foreign exchange market or the dealer Treasury bond market, the differences in *ad valorem* costs of actually effecting transactions in the two market settings are nowhere near as large. The bid/ask spreads in the Chicago Board of Trade's Treasury bond pit, for example, are typically 1/32nd on a contract size of $100,000 or three one-hundredths of 1 percent, with perhaps another one-hundredth of 1 percent or so additional in direct commissions. Large customers can sometimes better that in the spot market, but not always. And the futures market offers an at least partially compensating advantage in the form of its transparency; transactors can see the prices at which trades are actually taking place.

The particular technology that U.S. futures markets use to provide their customers with low-cost and transparent transaction services is that of a centralized, "open-outcry" market with competing market makers. Orders flow from the customers to "floor brokers" or "order fillers" who then auction these orders publicly to the "floor traders" or "locals." The locals, by and large, are not long-term "value buyers" but short-term intermediaries whose trades serve to offset the inevitable lack of perfect synchronization between the arrival of buy orders and sell orders. They provide the users with "immediacy"; and that can be a most valuable service indeed to someone seeking to hedge an inventory, often heavily financed with short-term loans, of an underlying commodity or financial instrument subject to great price volatility.[6] The compensation the market makers expect to receive for supplying this immediacy is the expected difference between the prices at which they buy and resell on the one hand, and the costs they incur in the process.

These costs for the locals are of two major kinds, over and above the direct record-keeping and paper-shuffling costs inevitably incurred in any financial transaction. The first is simply the mirror-side of the same exposure to an adverse price move that the customer gives up by trading with a market maker rather than waiting for the ultimate counterparty to arrive. The market makers may well have greater tolerance for this risk than the individual customer, as noted earlier. But that is only one reason the arrangement remains viable. In a competitive, open-outcry market, the delay-risk is a shared risk. The larger the population of traders in the pit, the lower, on average, the costs to each of assuming the temporary price risks—an example, once again, of the kinds of economies of scale so critical in determining a market's ability to stay competitive.[7]

Why, then, does the number of floor traders not increase to the point where the unit cost of bearing the temporary price risk becomes effectively zero? The answer lies in the second major, and all too often neglected, cost of market making, to wit, the opportunity costs of the financial and human capital necessary to sustain a continuous market presence. Given these costs, the supply of market makers can be expected to adjust until, in equilibrium, the net expected market returns (after adjustment for risk) of the marginal market maker just equals his cost of maintaining a continuous market presence. The higher the costs of maintaining that presence, the fewer the market makers in equilibrium and hence the higher the effective costs of immediacy to the customers. In the limit, when the number of market makers that can recover their fixed costs becomes sufficiently small, the market ceases to be viable.[8]

Recognizing these essentially fixed costs of market making and the adjustments in the supply of market makers they induce can help illuminate both the history and the business strategy of the U.S. futures exchanges. They make clearer, for example, why the futures exchanges found their first natural niche in agricultural commodities. The long chain of handlings and processings of farm commodities on the road to their ultimate consumers creates a continuing demand for *trading* as the processors successively hedge and unhedge their inventories. By contrast, the highly publicized Consumer Price Index futures contract of the Coffee, Sugar, and Cocoa Exchange never found a place, even though many firms had substantial contractual cost-of-living commitments that they might well have wanted to hedge. But those commitments apparently did not change often enough to generate the steady flow of orders needed to sustain the continuing presence of market makers on the trading floor of an exchange.

The overhead costs of maintaining market presence create not only economies of scale but economies of scope as well. Floor trading skills are not strongly contract-specific. Hence futures exchanges have always had many contracts trading simultaneously, giving their market makers more chances to trade enough to meet their overhead expenses. The same inexorable logic of overhead costs also underlay the diversification of the U.S. futures exchanges in the early 1970s beyond their original, and at that time somewhat stagnant, niche in agricultural products to foreign exchange contracts, options, and financial futures generally.

In the course of the 20 years during which the U.S. futures exchanges were diversifying from the agriculturals to the financials they have achieved economies of scale that, at first sight, might make them seem impregnable to direct competition in their successful contracts either from foreign futures and options exchanges or from the off-exchange, forward markets. And, indeed, they probably *would* be impregnable in those contracts, if everything could stay the same. But, of course, it can't. New technology has been developed and new regulatory initiatives have been proposed that could lead to a dramatic redrawing of current competitive boundaries.

3. The competitive threat from overseas futures exchanges

The major threat from overseas to the currently dominant position of U.S. futures markets is probably a technological one: the development and perfection of electronic screen trading. Decentralized electronic screen trading, if it can be made to work efficiently, could undercut the main source of the scale economies and hence the current comparative advantage of U.S. futures exchanges, to wit, the large pool of highly skilled and experienced floor traders. Foreign competitors would need many years, if not generations, to put comparable populations of market traders on their trading floors. But with successful electronic screen trading, the very centralized trading floor itself becomes dispensable, as the example of the post-Big Bang London Stock Exchange so vividly demonstrates.[9]

Electronic trading systems are of two basic kinds at the moment, though inevitably with some overlap. At the one extreme are dealer-quote screens or "bulletin boards" like those of NASDAQ in the United States or SEAQ in London. Execution of small orders at a dealer's posted price is usually guaranteed, but larger orders must be phoned in and negotiated. Some such systems are fully transparent in the sense of reporting all recent transaction prices along with the current dealer quotes; but, on many others, the reporting of large negotiated transactions done off-screen can be delayed until the ending of the trading day or even longer. At the other extreme to the dealer bulletin boards are the more recently developed "order matching" systems in which the screen serves essentially as a visible "limit order" book. Those with access to the network enter their bids and offers subject to a well-specified set of time, price, and size priorities. The posted limit prices are then matched by the computer and when a valid trade is possible, it is executed (and confirmed) directly without need for additional telephone calls. Since the computer executes all trades, the system can easily be made fully transparent, though the use of separate windows on the screen for trade reporting makes for the kind of crowded and busy picture that seems user friendly only to members of the current Nintendo generation.

That electronic market systems of either of these types could win a head-to-head competition with active, high-volume contracts like the CBOT's Treasury Bond pit or the CME's Eurodollar pit either currently or in the foreseeable future is far less likely than many computer enthusiasts seem ready to believe. A pit with several hundred locals offers far more fast, virtually simultaneous transaction-handling capacity. Nor is it simply a matter of waiting until computer technology improves, as it someday surely will, to the point where several hundred simultaneously bidding locals can actually be accommodated on the screen. The problem is not so much technology as motivation. In a screen trading environment, the floor trader loses his "edge," in the sense of the information advantage he draws from being present on the floor and able to observe the incoming order flow. By having to post his quotes in advance on the screen, he must now offer, in effect, a free option to all other traders, and he therefore runs a greater risk of being picked off by someone with better or more up-to-date information. Screen trading systems, in sum, particularly of the order-matching kind, thus are unlikely to attract the services of large numbers of competing market makers and hence to offer levels of immediacy and liquidity comparable to those of the currently most active trading pits.[10]

Barring regulatory upheavals, the U.S. exchanges are likely to feel the competitive impact of overseas screen trading not so much in their main and firmly established markets as in the markets for new products and low-volume products. They might also have faced competitive inroads in the form of screen-trading even of their established products in after-hours trading, had not both the CBOT and CME taken steps to counter such entry—the former by holding additional, after-normal-hours pit trading sessions and the latter by planning a screen-based order-matching system of its own (Globex) for after-hours trading. Nor, once an overseas exchange has successfully launched a new screen-traded contract, can a U.S. exchange automatically hope to capture the business by introducing the contract or a close substitute on its own trading floor. The first-mover advantage in this industry is too strong.[11] Given its economies of scale, floor-trading in an already established contract may well have cost advantages over screen trading; but if a successful screen trading contract comes on the scene first, the floor may never attract enough volume to get up to speed.

The emphasis so far in this section has been on the possible competitive impact of overseas exchanges on the U.S. industry. But competition runs both ways. And, subject, as always, to the important qualification, "regulation aside," the U.S. futures exchanges could also reasonably be expected to increase their penetration of overseas markets.[12] The view, once treated as axiomatic, that each country had a natural and largely unbeatable advantage in the trading of its own domestic instruments can no longer be taken for granted now that more shares of Volvo, to pick one conspicuous example, trade in London than in Stockholm. Derivative instruments are, in the nature of the case, even less firmly tied to any particular country. Any exchange, wherever it happens to be located, can create a futures or option contract on any underlying object, even the Rock of Gibraltar, provided only that it changed in some reasonably objectively measurable dimension. Physical delivery has never really been essential to futures contracts. Until the passage of the Commodity Futures Trading Commission Act in 1974, the possibility of delivery served merely as little more than a legal technicality to keep some state courts from treating commercial futures contracts as unenforceable gambling debts. Very little delivery ever actually took place, though the very possibility of making or taking delivery may have helped to assure the convergence of the futures price to the spot price at the expiration date. The 1974 Act, however, made cash settlement legal for futures contracts, and that has been the route to settlement taken in most, though by no means all, of the new contracts introduced since that time. Not only is physical delivery thus not critical for a viable futures contract but neither is the possibility of direct intermarket arbitrage, although arbitrage by tying the price of the derivative more closely to that of the underlying certainly makes the contract more useful to potential hedgers.

The tabulation below of foreign-source contracts being traded currently and in 1980 and 1985 shows that process of trading contracts involving nondomestic underlyings is already well under way. Particularly noteworthy is the German Bund contract traded not in Frankfurt, but on the London International Financial Futures Exchange (LIFFE) in London. Equally interesting, though not shown in the table, is the Nikkei Stock Index Futures contract, first introduced on the Singapore International Monetary Exchange (SIMEX) in 1988 and taken over by the Osaka Stock Exchange (OSE) in 1989. Nor is the competition in cross-border products a matter of the futures exchanges only. Derivative contracts much in the news recently are the Nikkei warrants (essentially long-term put and call options) traded over-the-counter and on the American Stock Exchange.

Given the ease nowadays of effecting cross-border financial transactions—for most sophisticated customers, nothing more is usually involved than pushing a button or two—trade in futures and options, in a totally free and unregulated environment, could be expected to flow to the cheapest market. And the U.S. industry, given the economies of

Table 3. Trading other countries' products

	1980	1985	1990
U.S.	—	—	Diffs (CME)
			ECU (NYCE)
			Euromark (LIFFE)
			German bund (LIFFE)
			Yen bond (LIFFE)
Other	—	Eurodollar (LIFFE)	Eurodollar (LIFFE)
			Euromark (MATIF)
			U.S. dollar (NZFE)
			Eurodollar (SIMEX)
			Eurodollar (TIFFE)

Source: CME Research Division.

scale and scope that it has already achieved, would be a formidable competitor indeed. But no industry, and certainly not this one, operates internationally in a totally free and unregulated environment. Protectionism, both direct and indirect, is as much a fact of life in financial services as anywhere else. Many of the key issues in international and inter-market regulation have been covered in another article in this issue by former SEC Commissioner Grundfest and need not be repeated here. The concern instead will be with some seemingly purely domestic regulatory policy proposals that would raise the cost of trading on the exchanges, and to that extent would weaken their competitiveness both internationally and relative to their domestic rivals.

4. Regulation and competitiveness: the case of stock index futures margins

Regulation, in practice, affects an industry's competitiveness mainly by lowering it. Reg-ulation, by its very nature, makes cost of production higher than they otherwise would be. Circumstances can always be imagined, of course, in which regulation might actually *improve* an industry's viability on balance. Instituting the SEC in 1934 may perhaps have helped restore confidence in the U.S. stock market to investors demoralized by the Crash of 1929. The same investor-confidence argument is being invoked currently to justify costly new trading regulations for the futures exchanges in the wake of the FBI's sting operation disclosed in January 1989. But the relation of regulation to confidence can easily be oversold. The exchanges themselves have the strongest of commercial motives to maintain the confidence of their customers; but not to overinvest in it. The regulators and congressional overseers face no such cost/revenue tradeoff and thus inevitably overreact to any appearance of scandal. As one wag put it: When a congressman says that his constituents are losing confidence in the market, he really means that his constituents are losing confidence in him!

To say that regulation raises costs of production is not to suggest, of course, that such cost increases are never justified. Externalities, such as pollution, do exist; and imposing compensating costs on those who cause it, and thereby reducing their combined output of product plus pollution, is often clearly in the public interest. But the presumption of social benefit from the added regulatory costs requires a more careful balancing of all the gains and losses, direct and indirect, than our political mechanisms can seem to supply. The result of our efforts to correct for externalities has all too often found the direct costs plus the unintended side consequences of the regulatory intervention substantially outweighing the benefits actually achieved. The proposed transfer to the SEC of margin authority for index futures can serve, perhaps, as an instructive example of how such an imbalance could easily arise despite the best of intentions on the part of the regulators.

4.1. Mandated margins for index futures: the presumed benefits

Proposals to transfer the authority over stock index futures margins from the private-sector exchanges to public-sector regulators first surfaced in earnest, as is so often the case with calls for regulation, after a specific event—in this instance the great market break of October 19 and 20, 1987. The Brady Commission, in its post-mortem study of the Crash, made "harmonization" of stock and futures margins a key recommendation; and while the the term harmonization was nowhere defined, their call for harmonization was everywhere regarded, and was presumably so intended by the Brady Commission, as a code word for federal control over index futures margins. The call by the Brady Commission was taken up subsequently by both the former and the current chairman of the SEC and, of course, their congressional overseers. A bill transferring index futures margin authority to the SEC has, in fact, recently been introduced, with Administration backing.

In the period immediately after the Crash of 1987, the main emphasis of those calling for federal regulation was on the dangers to the safety and integrity of the entire payments system posed by the massive flows of cash margin funds from the losers to the winners after a major market move. The force of this argument was largely undercut, however, by the very fact that the financial system did manage to survive despite the biggest one-day move in U.S. stock market history. The system survived, moreover, despite the almost complete absence at that time of any contingency planning for such emergencies on the part either of the banks or of the monetary authorities. Such contingency plans have since been put into place, and so effectively, apparently, that the much-discussed mini-crash of October 13, 1989—a market break of more than 6 percent—produced virtually no visible signs of strain on the payments system.

Proponents of federal regulation have thus tended to put less stress recently on systemic strain and more on the supposed contribution of low futures margins to market volatility. The high leverage in a futures position is said to encourage excessive speculation in the futures market, causing erratic and unwarranted price moves that then flow from there via index arbitrage to the stock market in damaging bursts of "episodic volatility."

To review in detail the enormous (and still rapidly growing) literature on market volatility and its proximate causes would clearly not be appropriate in an article of the present limited scope. Suffice to say that the Administration's strongly stated views on the contribution of index futures to market volatility find little support in the serious academic literature on the subject. The Administration's arguments, in fact, are little more than modern-dress versions of the charges that have long been raised against futures markets generally, not merely stock index futures markets.

The charge that the futures markets are roiling the spot markets always seems plausible on the surface because the lower cost and greater liquidity of trading futures makes the futures market the natural entry-port for new information. The news once "discovered" or revealed in price changes for futures, flows from there to the cash market by the arbitrage process. In most cash markets, only minor arbitrage flows are actually needed to restore the price relations required by the cost-of-carry formula. Spot market dealers typically "price off the futures"; that is, they observe the current futures price and mark their own quotes up or down accordingly. But in the case of stock index futures, the spot market is not a dispersed dealer-market, but another exchange, and one, moreover, whose official rhetoric stresses the price continuity delivered by its franchised specialists and by the public limit-order book he manages. That very continuity, however, by slowing the adjustment of prices, created both tempting opportunities and much public notoriety for index arbitrage in the early years of the index contract. As the NYSE adjusted to the new realities, prices there have adjusted faster, substantially reducing thereby the profitability of intermarket arbitrage. True arbitrage, never anywhere as large as the public's perceptions of it, has accordingly diminished substantially. But its notoriety lingers on.[13]

The notion that "news" and not futures trading is responsible ultimately for the large price changes in the spot market has also been resisted by many because specific "smoking guns," as it were, can so rarely be tied to big market moves. But news, in the relevant economic sense, is not just "news events," like assassinations or military defeats. The pricing of stocks involves more than merely appraising current and near-term dividends and earnings. Required also are projections of growth rates and risk-adjusted discount rates for earning power far into the distant and uncertain future. Thanks to the nonlinear way that these growth rates and discount rates enter into prices, even small changes in the perception of what might be called the future economic climate can lead investors to rethink their previous decisions about the proper allocation of their wealth between equity and fixed income securities. When a sufficiently large number of them choose, more or less simultaneously, to reduce their equity proportions substantially, then, given the fixity of the supplies of equity and debt securities in the immediate short run, equilibrium can be restored only by a drop in equity values substantial enough to restore the desired equity exposure. Large, economic climate-related readjustments of that kind appear to have occurred in October 1929, October 1987, and, on a smaller scale, in October 1989 (although, in that case, at least, the failure of the United Air Lines buyout can be identified as a specific event that triggered the reappraisal of future buyout prospects more generally). Which October, or perhaps even which May, will see the next major readjustment of equity proportions no one, of course, now can say. But happen someday it surely will, no matter what the regulatory structure.

4.2. Federal margin regulation and the costs of futures trading

No amount of regulation in general or of "oversight" can keep major price moves from taking place when circumstances demand. Even closing down a market altogether will merely shift to another market the volatility flowing from perceived changes in the underlying fundamentals. In the particular case of the regulation of stock market margin requirements by the Federal Reserve System, moreover, a mountain of academic studies testifies to the almost complete absence of any detectable causal relations between the Fed's mandated minimum initial margin requirements and subsequent stock market volatility.[14] Nor is this judgment about underlying market volatility likely to be altered in any way if the authority to set index futures margins were transferred from the exchanges either to the Federal Reserve System (which doesn't want the responsibility) or to the SEC (which very much does). Federalizing control over futures margins will simply raise the cost of trading index futures and lower the quantity of futures contracts traded.

That such must be the case is almost axiomatic. Futures exchanges, as seen earlier, set their margins according to standard business "profit-maximizing" conditions. When they consider raising margins, they weigh the gains from reducing the risks of contract default against the loss of business from customers deterred by the opportunity costs of posting higher margins. No outside regulator can be presumed to set margins in the same way; if they did, why bother with regulation at all? And even if the regulators sought to find the profit-maximizing balance, they are hardly likely to be better at that task than the exchanges themselves. The result in either case must be a departure from the (constantly changing) optimum margin level.

How far the public-sector determined margins will deviate from the exchange's optimum will depend, of course, on the particular objective function followed by the regulators in setting margin levels. That objective function, whatever its precise form, must inevitably be highly asymmetric, in the sense that an active regulator invites heavy criticism for the few bad market days but receives little praise for the many uneventful ones.[15] The indicated strategy, under those circumstances, appears to be that followed by the Federal Reserve System in setting initial stock-market margins over the last 16 years: set the margin level high and keep it there! That way, the regulator can never be blamed either for precipitating a crash by raising margins sharply when the market is surging; or for causing the market to overheat by having set margins too low on the upside. The very fact that the margins had to be raised to stop the overheating, moreover, will be taken by the public and by Congressional overseers as *prima facie* evidence that the margins had been set too low in the first place.

The pressures on the SEC—currently the leading candidate for regulator of index futures margins—to follow the high-and-stable margins policy will be even greater that those that led the Fed to that policy. Unlike the Fed, the SEC (and the Treasury Department) really seems to believe that "excessive speculation" in index futures causes market crashes for which they may be held responsible once they win their highly publicized fight for margin authority. And the SEC, in its long-standing role as guardian of what it sees as the main market, can hardly be expected to be acutely sensitive to any drops in trading volume that high margins might cause in one of the merely derivative markets newly brought under its mantle.[16]

But while index futures margins would thus surely rise under any public-sector regulatory authority, the effective increase in trading costs that results will depend considerably on how the new rules would apply to the various categories of traders. Initial "speculative margins"—in the sense of margins for accounts that do not qualify for the lower "hedger margins"—are currently $21,000 or about 12 percent on a contract with a nominal value of $175,000. Raising these margins to $87,500 to match the 50 percent level currently in force for common stocks—an equalization often suggested by critics of index futures—would make index futures prohibitively expensive for this class of traders. With futures marked to market daily, the five-day (or longer) settlement period for stocks would make them a better buy. Loss of these accounts would represent about 20 percent of the current open interest at the CME. If initial speculative margin levels were to be set not at 50 percent, but only at 20 percent ($35,000), as some on the SEC have hinted, then most of the purely retail portion of the accounts, currently running between 5 and 7 percent of the open interest, would likely still be lost. The nonretail remainder, consisting mainly of commodity pools, can also be expected to reduce participation in index futures substantially, though some of the trading activity might well be shifted to other futures contracts, at the CME or elsewhere, where the opportunity costs of the margin requirements would be lower.

The institutional hedging accounts that make up the bulk of the open interest pose additional problems for the regulators. Some critics interpret the call for harmonization of margins to mean that the special status of hedging margins (currently $6,000 per contract or a bit more than 3 percent of nominal value) be eliminated altogether. After all, no such exemptions apply to margined long or short positions in common stocks. Special exemptions from margin requirements do exist, it is true, for broker-dealers and other stock market professionals, but they must meet capital requirements that have much the same effect. Those capital requirements, which apply both to long and short stock positions, would be equivalent to margin requirements of 20 to 25 percent. If, in the name of harmonization, futures margins for hedgers were to be raised to the same level, the drop in volume for the contract would be virtually total, despite the often-heard claim that margins don't really have a cost to the pension funds and other big institutional traders. True, those institutions *could* post billions of dollars of Treasury bills as collateral with a clearing firm, rather than posting cash, on which no interest is earned, or posting bank letters of credit on which fees must be paid. But holding bills has an opportunity cost in the form of lower yields; and even if it did not, few such institutions would be prepared to give up custody of any major portion of their assets under current customer-account segregation rules. The segregation requirement applies only to a broker's customer accounts taken as a whole; any individual customer would still be exposed to a default by another customer, even if not, perhaps, to a failure of the brokerage firm itself.[17]

Some have argued that the basic goal of harmonization might be achieved in less drastic fashion by restricting the hedging exemption to short hedgers only, that is, to those who actually hold the underlying stock and propose to sell futures against them. The long hedgers, or anticipatory hedgers as they are sometimes called, and who now represent a third or so of the open interest, would be subject to the speculative margins. The benefits to the long-run viability of the market from this seemingly less restrictive definition of hedging are much less, however, than they might seem at first glance. The short hedgers will indeed still be able to sell. But, as the old Wall Street joke goes: "To whom?"

Transferring control over index futures margins from the private sector to the public sector will thus occasion a sizeable drop-off in the volume of contracts traded, ranging from a minimum of perhaps 20 to 25 percent if the increase in margins is confined to so-called speculative margin accounts, to as much as 100 percent if the higher levels were applied also to hedgers (short and long); to floor traders (most of whom now face no margin requirements as such since they typically zero out their positions by the end of the day); and to the margins that clearing firms must maintain with the clearing house. Many have considered the disaster scenario unlikely on the grounds that the SEC, having obtained the margin authority on the promise of being a responsible regulator, would hesitate to be caught murdering the futures market in public. But, in a world where the chairman of the SEC's congressional oversight committee has likened index futures to cockroaches, not even this possibility can safely be ruled out. One way or another, then, the volume of business in index futures will surely contract. Where the lost business is likely to go is the final question to be considered.

4.3. Federal margin controls and international competitiveness

The Eurodollar and Eurobond markets today stand as vivid reminders of how heavy-handed interventions by U.S. regulators can shift the locus of activity in the financial services sector. Federal regulation of index-futures margins will induce similar shifts in trading patterns, though perhaps less dramatically so, at least in the immediate short run. The Euromarkets, after all, are markets only in a generic sense. Their business is basically carried on by separate broker-dealer firms and banks dispersed over virtually the entire world, or at least that part of it beyond U.S. regulatory jurisdiction. Index futures, by contrast, are traded currently on centralized, exchange markets with very specific loca-tional ties. Moving whole business complexes from one location to another is certainly not unthinkable, as is clear from such past examples as the community of skilled glass workers who migrated en masse from Charleroi, Belgium, to found Charleroi, Pennsylvania, in the 1880s; or the more recent displacement of the diamond-cutting industry from the Neth-erlands to New York and to Israel. But no such dramatic translations can be expected in an industry whose products are as generic as index futures even though, as emphasized earlier, the size and skills of its body of trading locals are major sources of its competitive comparative advantage.

The shift in business will take place rather in separate tranches, with the first slice almost certainly going to London. London, as noted earlier, has already made inroads on the CME's S&P 500 index futures contract, thanks to two particular features of U.S. regulatory laws governing stocks and securities. The CFTC Act and related statutes currently allow negotiated, off-exchange transactions in futures only for the transfer of a futures contract in return for delivery of the underlying commodity itself (hence the term exchange-for-physicals, or EFP). At the same time, the SEC-mandated trading rules prohibit the short-selling of stock on any exchange under its jurisdiction except on an uptick. The SEC also prohibits dealers from crossing blocks or portfolios of stocks without first exposing those trades to the floor. The CFTC rules on negotiated block trades are even more restrictive. The consequence: those seeking either to short-sell a portfolio of S&P 500 stocks without violating the uptick rule, or to undertake a negotiated transaction in stock index futures do so, in London, with an EFP after regular U.S. trading hours.

In the normal course of competitive give and take, the CME could surely have been expected to propose counter moves that might win back at least some of the after-hours block business lost to London, for example, by petitioning the CFTC, as it has in fact recently done, to loosen its current restrictions on large-order transactions negotiated off-exchange. That the CME's ability to respond to competitive challenges will be weakened directly by the higher levels of margins mandated by the SEC has already been established. But the SEC could also damage even further both the CME and the NYSE by heeding those urging it to rein in the London EFP's now used for bypassing the uptick rules. Such steps, if successful, would give additional impetus to the direct trading of large-cap U.S. stocks in London; and as the spot market there becomes more liquid, the introduction of a London-based U.S. index-futures contract for after-U.S. hours trading becomes a very real possibility.[18]

Meanwhile, at the other end of the world's time zone in the Far East, the weakened position of the CME would open opportunities for after-hours trading of U.S. index futures that might well be picked up first by SIMEX in Singapore. That exchange, after all, was first off the mark in Japanese stock-index futures when the Japanese markets were hobbled by their own regulators and while the efforts of the U.S. exchanges to fill the gap were still being delayed by the SEC and the CFTC.[19] The SIMEX Japanese index contract never achieved critical mass for a variety of reasons, and the business was eventually absorbed by the immensely strong financial service industry in Japan proper. The same evolution might well be repeated for an after-U.S. hours contract on the U.S. S&P 500 or similar contract.

As after-hours index futures contracts in London and the Far East become rooted and grow more liquid, the overseas exchanges will certainly be tempted to expand into the prime-time hours of the newly high-margin, high-cost U.S. index futures markets. Is it possible that some exchange not under U.S. jurisdiction, but still in the U.S. time zone, might get there first? Toronto might seem the natural candidate, judging by some reactions to its recently introduced Canadian Index Participation Security (IPS)—a contract often cited these days by the SEC and the Treasury as the kind of innovative hybrid futures security supposedly driven abroad by the lack of a unified U.S. regulatory structure. These glowing references to the Toronto IPS by the Treasury and the SEC can be dismissed, however, as merely "negative campaigning" by those agencies against the CFTC from whom they seek to wrest jurisdiction over index futures. The index participation certificates traded in Toronto are essentially fully collateralized warehouse receipts. They do not have the features that led the courts to classify as futures contracts the products of the same name introduced and later withdrawn by the American Stock Exchange and the Philadelphia Stock Exchange.[20] In principle, of course, the Toronto Stock Exchange could choose, at any time, to expand its product line and contest for market share against a weakened U.S. futures industry. Its much-praised computerized trading system, however, appears better suited for the low-volume trading of individual stocks and retail-sized stock baskets than for the high-volume, large-size transactions in futures contracts by institutional investors. Should those institutional customers seek trading alternatives to futures during U.S. trading hours, they are unlikely to find them in Toronto.

Four other possibilities they might turn to come immediately to mind, three already on stream and one as yet only a gleam in the eye of some enterprising financial engineers. Some of the business lost to the futures exchanges will flow back to the NYSE either directly in program trades or as block trades negotiated in the upstairs market and subsequently crossed on the floor. Some of the business will be picked up in off-exchange trades with so-called third market block traders like Jefferies, and some to fourth market crossing networks like INSTINET or POSIT. And some will flow to the index options exchanges. Those exchanges have run, until recently, a far distant second to index futures thanks to the very low position limits imposed by the SEC, which has regulatory jurisdiction over options on stocks. Those limits have now been raised to the point where institutional investors can, and do, seriously consider options an effective substitute for futures in hedging strategies. But that effectiveness of options as a substitute for futures traces in no small part to the ability of options market makers to hedge their own positions quickly and cheaply on the futures exchanges. Without that protection, spreads and commissions in the options market are likely to be forced to levels far larger than institutional investors have become accustomed to paying.

Sooner or later, then, one such disgruntled institutional investor will surely approach the risk-management division of a world-class bank with the following proposition: "You currently swap dollars for yen and swap fixed rate debt for floating rate debt. Can you do a three-month swap for me of, say, $100 million in an indexed portfolio of stocks against $100 million in Treasury bills? I realize that you might have to put up additional bank capital against the swap under the new Bank for International Settlement capital rules, but I will compensate you for that by posting collateral with you up front and adding to it (or subtracting from it) periodically over the life of the agreement your risk exposure changes."

The operation described is, of course, a contract equivalent to an index futures contract in every essential respect but one: it would trade in the interbank forward market and not on an exchange where margins were set by the SEC. No one yet can say which banks in which countries are best positioned to pick up the stock-swap business (and ultimately the commodity-swap business) that the U.S. futures exchanges lose. But if size of bank offers any clue, the flow of business is surely much more likely to be out than in.

Notes

1. The net worth is $7,140 and not the $7,150 of the contract price because we must net out the storage costs. Those costs are in the futures price, it is true, but they were also incurred by the hedger. The same netting out applies to the convenience yield. On that score, note that if the hedger were actually to draw down the inventory during the three months, the original hedge would no longer be exact; but a riskless position could be restored by "lifting" (i.e., buying back) futures contracts in the amount of the inventory sold.
2. Two excellent academic studies of the cost-effectiveness of futures trading are those of Carlton (1984) and Telser and Higginbotham (1977).
3. The system can be traced as far back as the rice futures market in the Tokugawa Japan of the 1730s (Schaede, 1988) and was presumably rediscovered independently by the Chicago grain markets in the 1860s, though the destruction of records in the great Chicago Fire of 1871 makes any exact dating almost impossible. For an economic analysis of the margin system see Telser (1981).
4. As a further precaution against overextended customers, the exchanges (spurred on by the regulators) also impose "position limits." The exchange margins, moreover, are only the minimums. Brokers frequently require some customers to post additional initial margins.
5. On two of the smaller exchanges, however, clearing-member defaults have in fact occurred within the last 20 years—Chicago Discount Brokers on the Mid-American Exchange and Volume Investors on the Commodity Exchange (COMEX). In the latter case, all customers were ultimately made whole, but only after some delay.

6. Immediacy is closely related to, but not quite synonymous with "liquidity." A market is said to be liquid if it not only provides immediacy, but does so for reasonable quantities at little change in price. The futures markets provide liquidity as well as immediacy by having many locals on hand to compete for all or part of each incoming customer order.

7. The delay risk here discussed blends into another risk, to wit, the adverse selection risk in which the market member is disadvantaged by trading with people who have inside, or at least markedly superior, information to his. Risk of this kind is probably more acute in the case of individual stocks, say, where it has been the focus of much study, than for the much less idiosyncratic "commodities" traded on the futures exchanges. The substantially lesser vulnerability of stock index futures to insider information is another reason why market spreads for the futures are substantially smaller than on the separate stocks that make up the index.

8. For a fuller account of the equilibrating process, see Grossman and Miller (1988).

9. Still another example is the fully-electronic New Zealand Futures Exchange (NZFE) market. For a sparsely populated country with no single dominating financial center, a computer network made much more sense than any centralized exchange.

10. Screen networks, if big enough, may not *need* market makers in the traditional sense, however. Big networks may come close to the Walrasian ideal market in which *all* potential buyers and sellers are present and ready to trade.

11. A first-mover advantage also exists for screen-trading computer networks, because the cost of developing a worldwide network is high and because brokerage firms face both space and financial limits on the number of separate computer consoles they can handle. Hence the recently announced decision of the CBOT to join Globex rather than continue its attempts to set up a competing after-hours electronic network of its own.

12. The Nikkei 225 stock index futures contract, now screen-traded in Japan, may some day provide an interesting test case. The U.S. futures exchanges, for reasons to be noted later, have not so far chosen to offer such a contract.

13. For evidence on the speeding up of price adjustment in the NYSE relative to futures prices see Froot, Gammill, and Perold (1990). Rough calculations of the gross and net profitability of index arbitrage suggest, as one would expect, the truly riskless arbitrage operations under current conditions would just barely match the nominal riskless rate of return on Treasury bills. Much of what the NYSE currently classifies as "index arbitrage" must therefore presumably represent similar-looking but actually highly risky strategies such as "legging," in which the futures and offsetting cash legs are set not simultaneously, but with one or the other deliberately lagged.

14. See among many others Schwert (1990), Kupiec (1989), and Hsieh and Miller (1990).

15. Nor, of course, do the regulators derive the same kind of financial benefits that the exchanges do from increases in the volume of contracts traded, though the regulators might conceivably do so indirectly if user fees or charges were levied to defray the regulatory expenses. Otherwise, they feel pressures to expand volume only indirectly via the pressures that the exchange members can bring to bear on the congressional overseers of the regulators.

16. See, among many others, Schwert (1990), Kupiec (1989), and Hsieh and Miller (1990).

17. See, in this connection, Jordan and Morgan (1990).

18. Given the number of large cap stocks from so many countries currently trading in London, that city is also the likely home of the first international stock index future when and if it is ever traded.

   Enactment of the transactions tax recently trial-ballooned in Washington would greatly increase the likelihood of a successful U.S. index futures product in London. The tax would not only accelerate the trading of U.S. stocks in London but, unless very carefully drawn, might would kill the competing U.S. index futures industry altogether.

19. Despite having since received approval from U.S. regulators to offer Japanese index products, both the CME and the CBOT have hesitated to begin trading, mainly because they fear that too few large cap Japanese stocks trade in this country (thanks to the reluctance of Japanese firms to meet the stringent SEC registration requirements).

20. The Philadelphia and American products were withdrawn not because they could not legally be traded, but because trading them would have forced the Philadelphia and American Stock Exchanges to meet the requirements of two separate regulators, the CFTC as well as the SEC. The irony of this complaint by the exchanges has apparently been lost on the SEC, however, which has made the IPS experience a major part of its case to impose the same double burden on the futures exchanges.

References

Carlton, Dennis. "Futures Markets: Their Purpose, Their History, Their Growth, Their Successes and Fail-
    ures." *Journal of Futures Markets* 4, 3 (1984): 237–271.
Froot, Kenneth A., James F. Gammill, Jr., and Andre F. Perold. "New Trading Practices and the Short-Run
    Predictability of the S&P 500 Index." Working paper, Harvard Business School, 1990.
Grossman, Sanford and Merton H. Miller. "Liquidity and Market Structure." *Journal of Finance* 43, 3 (July
    1988): 617–633.
Grundfest, Joseph A. "Securities Markets in International Perspective." In this issue.
Hsieh, David and Merton H. Miller. "Margin Regulation and Stock Market Volatility." *Journal of Finance* 44
    (March 1990): 3–29.
Jordan, James V. and George L. Morgan. "Default Risk in Futures Markets: The Customer-Broker Relation-
    ship." *Journal of Finance* 45 (July 1990): 909–933.
Kupiec, Paul. "Initial Margins Requirements and Stock Returns Volatility: Another Look." *Journal of Financial
    Services Research* 3 (December 1989): 287–301.
Schaede, Ulrike. "Forwards and Futures in Tokugawa-Period Japan: A New Perspective on the Dojima Rice
    Market." Working paper, Universitaet Marburg, May 1988.
Schwert, G. William. "Stock Market Volatility." *Financial Analysts Journal* (1990, forthcoming).
Telser, Lester and Harlow Higginbotham. "Organized Futures Markets: Costs and Benefits." *Journal of Political
    Economy* 85 (October 1977): 969–1000.
Telser, Lester. "Margins and Futures Contracts." *Journal of Futures Markets* 1 (1981): 225–253.

Journal of Financial Services Research, 4:409–413 (1990)

Commentary: *International Competitiveness of U.S. Futures Exchanges*

HANS R. STOLL
*AnneMarie and Thomas B. Walker, Jr., Professor of Finance
and Director, Financial Markets Research Center
Owen Graduate School of Management
Vanderbilt University
Nashville, TN 37203*

In this commentary I am not going to disagree with the "Father of Finance" (and my dissertation advisor to boot). Instead I will make a few comments on Merton Miller's article and then develop in somewhat more depth two issues raised in it.

1. The article

Miller's reputation in finance is as debunker of financial illusions: for example, the illusion that debt or dividends create value. If debt or dividends create value, they do so in much subtler ways than originally thought. In his article, Miller debunks the notion that the U.S. futures markets, the world's dominant futures markets (or, for that matter, all U.S. financial markets, including the stock market), are immune from competition. His thesis is that regulation imposes costs that can divert trading to other countries offering the same contracts, to other domestic markets (the burgeoning forward markets, in particular), or make it difficult to respond to other unforeseen changes.

He convincingly makes the case for futures markets as low-cost trading centers that provide for financial integrity (through the clearing house) and liquidity by attracting many short-term traders. Futures facilitate "trade among strangers" in a way that forward markets cannot.[1]

The regulatory cost he discusses is the cost of high margins, but other costs, such as the proposed turnover tax for stock trading by tax-exempt investors, would do equally well.[2] If there is something to disagree about, it is the severity of the problem. As Miller notes, trading markets, such as futures and stock markets, are natural monopolies, which means it is difficult for another market to compete. One could argue that it is going to take more than an increase in margins to take business away from the world's premier futures markets. Second, other markets have costs imposed on them. For example, most of the European markets have a stock trading tax.

But Miller is correct that in today's financial markets competition is increasing dramatically. Regulatory costs can affect the relative positions of existing and emerging markets.

First, foreign markets are removing taxes and reducing costs. In reaction to competition from London, other European exchanges, such as those in France, Germany, and Sweden, are lowering or eliminating transaction taxes and in other ways improving the efficiency of their exchanges. European markets are improving their ability to compete with U.S. markets.

Second, modern communications technology weakens even a natural monopoly. With real-time dissemination of quotes, a satellite market can assure investors of as good a price as the primary market. If an investor can be assured of a good price, he will trade on a satellite market (at home or abroad) if other costs of trading are less. Even without regulatory cost disadvantages, off-board trading is a problem. Regional markets arise that don't incur costs of establishing a market and yet are able to siphon off business. This is less of a problem in futures markets in which all trades take place on the floor of the exchange.

Third, nonregulated entities, not necessarily foreign, will arise. As Miller notes, the interbank forward market, while less efficient in trading standardized contracts, could take over financial futures and options trading. It may also become profitable for entre-preneurs to develop proprietary trading systems.[3]

Fourth, the erosion of the position of the primary market may take time and is likely to be concentrated in new products. The United States might hold on to existing markets but would find it more difficult to compete in new products.

Over time and with increased communication of prices, trading can move elsewhere. The best chance of avoiding this is to give all exchanges the flexibility to respond quickly and with minimum intervention to competitive threats and opportunities. Indeed, the evident increase in worldwide competition among financial markets lessens the need for regulatory intervention.

Now I want to take the opportunity to discuss some ideas raised in Miller's article.

2. Innovation, organization of exchanges, and regulation

Should exchanges be thought of as businesses with a profit motive? Or should they be quasi-governmental organizations overseeing the markets?

The SEC approach to securities markets has been much more of the latter, while the futures markets have had greater independence and greater ability to capture the profits from their activities. The incentives to innovate are greatly reduced if the profits from innovation cannot be garnered.

Futures markets have innovated primarily in the instruments they trade. They control the issuance, trading, and clearing of contracts. They are able to capture the benefits of innovation. Stock markets have not innovated in instruments. The lack of innovation by stock exchanges is due to a different mentality created in part by regulation and by the fact that stock exchanges traded instruments created by corporations.

A second area of innovation is in trading systems. As Miller points out, futures are efficient trading systems and provide great liquidity and financial integrity. Yet they have been slow to respond to institutional pressures for large blocks and to technological changes that would allow computerization. Both stocks and futures markets are being pushed by their customers to improve speed and efficiency. Futures have greater control over trading and thus have a greater chance of capturing the benefits of automation.

Some of the resistance to automated trading is the concern of members of exchanges that they won't reap the profits from innovations. Again, this appears to be less of a problem in futures than in stocks.

The SEC approach to competing trading systems is that different exchanges should be linked. The SEC recently asked the five option exchanges to devise a link much like the Intermarket Trading System (ITS) that links common stocks. But a trading link gives a competing exchange access to improvements in trading that another exchange creates. The SEC, to its credit, has backed off from imposing a single computerized national market system on equity markets, favoring instead a looser ITS link. This go-slow approach has been criticized by some, but it has the benefit of maintaining competition among exchanges. Various forms of competition among equity exchanges have thus been allowed, even to the extent of permitting the establishment of various proprietary trading systems that have many of the characteristics of organized exchanges. The proprietary (and profit-motivated) systems are important sources of innovation and competition. Others argue that the regulatory restrictions (as in ITS) give proprietary trading systems an unfair advantage over existing markets.

The problem is to find a system under which it is in the interest of exchanges to innovate while at the same time fair prices and efficient trading are available to investors. If they can't capture the benefits of innovation, innovation won't occur.

3. Stock index futures, margins, and jurisdiction

Mert has devoted a good part of his article to stock index futures in recognition of the continued controversy surrounding them and in recognition of the current jurisdictional dispute between the CFTC and the SEC. How does one approach the critics of stock index futures? What is the problem?

One approach is to examine the data and see if stock index futures cause volatility, if index arbitrage is a problem, and the like. To quote from another of Miller's recent articles, "God is in the details." Well, I agree that God is in the details. Having looked at the details, with Bob Whaley of Duke University, around expiration days and over five-minute intervals on other days over a five-year period, I can tell you the details are boring. Anyone who has looked at the recent SEC report on the October 13 crashette can also attest to that. The numbers in the report are boring. The conclusions are not, but the conclusions aren't related to the numbers.

3.1. Volatility

3.1.1. Expiration days. The Stoll and Whaley study examines individual stocks in great detail.[4] On expiration days, volatility induced by unwinding of arbitrage positions is about .30 percent on quarterly expiration, which is of the same order of magnitude as the bid-ask spread on a stock. The change in settlement procedures to use of the opening price has increased volatility at the opening and decreased it slightly at the close. Volatility at the nonquarterly expiration (of index options) is not meaningfully different from that on nonexpiration days or for nonindex stocks. Stoll and Whaley conclude that the concern about expiration day volatility is "much ado about (nearly) nothing." Markets are able to adjust. The observed effect has to do with the cost of doing trades in the stock market. The cost on expiration day is not much different from that on other days, only more observable since all stocks are being sold or bought. Expiration days are something to worry about, but they are not a major problem that requires draconian regulatory measures.

3.1.2. Other days.[5]   With respect to the relation of futures to stocks on nonexpiration days, account has to be taken of the slow-moving nature of a price index. Futures appear to lead the index because the index stocks aren't trading all the time. But when the data are adjusted to account for infrequent trading, Stoll and Whaley find that futures still tend to lead cash more often than they lag. They also find that the link between futures and cash has tightened in the period 1982 to 1987.

Like the wheat futures market, where wheat futures move more quickly than cash wheat prices, stock index futures prices move more quickly and more dramatically than the cash stock prices seem to. Yet processors and handlers price cash "off the futures," as Miller notes. A similar phenomenon is at hand with respect to stocks and bonds and currencies and other financial instruments. As the SEC notes in its recent study of the October 1989 crashette, "[T]he stock index futures market plays a major price discovery function for the stock market, with the futures market leading, rather than following, short term price trends in the underlying equity market."

3.2. Margins

There is not appropriate space here to rehash the arguments against federal margin setting in the futures market or the stock market. Suffice it to say that the Federal Reserve Board appeared ready in 1984 to give up margin-setting authority even for common stocks.[6] The most compelling argument against federal margin setting is perhaps the strong support for it from brokerage firms. Since brokers get to hold customer funds, they tend to benefit from high margins. The cost is greatest for individual investors who find it more difficult to evade margins and who are not eligible for exemptions that apply to dealers.[7]

3.3. Jurisdiction and innovation

The strongest argument for merger of the CFTC and SEC is the controversy over index participations (IP's), which resulted in the courts deciding that IP's were futures and therefore under the exclusive jurisdiction of CFTC. But the problem could be solved by eliminating the exclusivity clause that gives the CFTC exclusive jurisdiction over anything deemed to be a futures contract. Without exclusivity, exchanges could seek approval from the SEC of a hybrid instrument that contains some characteristics of a futures contract.

It is widely agreed that futures and stock markets should be coordinated with respect to such matters as clearing and settlement, regulatory enforcement, and margins. But coordination does not require merger of the agencies or assignment of jurisdiction over stock index futures to the SEC. Competitive regulation makes for more complete discussion of the issues. Merging the CFTC and SEC might cause the two agencies to "speak with one voice," but it would also stifle responsible discussion of important issues. Regulatory competition has benefits like business competition.

Finally, it is worth nothing that implementation of SEC oversight of stock index futures (SIF) poses its own difficulties and problems of coordination. Would, for example, SIF be regulated as securities under securities statutes and held in securities accounts eligible for Securities Investor Protection Corporation insurance? Or would they continue to be treated as commodities (which is the Administration's proposal)? If the latter, what is the purpose of SEC oversight? If SIF continue to be regulated as commodities by the SEC, new problems of coordination arise as futures exchanges and futures commission merchants now must deal with the SEC as well as the CFTC.

4. Conclusion

It is evident to all of us that the future today "ain't what it used to be" in 1980. As Miller points out, free markets that are able to adjust to changing circumstances are the best guarantee of efficient and fair financial markets.

Notes

1. For a discussion of how futures markets facilitate "trade among strangers," see Telser and Higinbotham (1977).
2. For example, the Dole-Kassebaum bill would impose a 10 percent excise tax on gains from sales of assets held less than 30 days and a 5 percent tax on gains from the sale of assets held from 30 to 180 days. The tax would apply to presently tax-exempt institutions such as pension funds.
3. A variety of such systems now exists in stocks.
4. The recent Stoll and Whaley study, covering expiration days in the period 1985 to 1989, is entitled "Expiration Day Effects: What has Changed?" and is forthcoming in the *Financial Analysts Journal*.
5. Stoll and Whaley's "The Dynamics of Stock Index and Stock Index Futures Returns," forthcoming in the *Journal of Financial and Quantitative Analysis*, looks at prices every five minutes for the period 1982 to March 1987.
6. See the Board of Governors of the Federal Reserve System study (1984).
7. See Stoll (1990) for a more complete discussion of margin issues.

References

Board of Governors of the Federal Reserve System. *A Review and Evaluation of Federal Margin Requirements*. A study by the Staff, Washington, D.C., December 1984.

Stoll, H. "Margins on Stock Index Futures Contracts." *Investing* (Summer 1990).

Stoll, H. and R. Whaley. "The Dynamics of Stock Index and Stock Index Futures Returns." *Journal of Financial and Quantitative Analysis* (forthcoming).

Stoll, H. and R. Whaley. "Expiration Day Effects: What Has Changed?" *Financial Analysts Journal* (forthcoming).

Telser, L. G. and H. N. Higinbotham. "Organized Futures Markets: Costs and Benefits." *Journal of Political Economy* 85 (1977), 969–1000.

Journal of Financial Services Research, 4:415–418 (1990)
© 1990 Kluwer Academic Publishers

Commentary: *International Competitiveness of U.S. Futures Exchanges*

BRUCE KOVNER
Chairman, Caxton Corporation
667 Madison Avenue
New York, NY 10021

My comments will reflect the point of view of a practitioner, someone who has been in the futures market more or less every day for the last 13 or 14 years. During that time, I have seen much change and development in the futures market and forward markets and, of course, considerable growth and acceptance in the financial community. From that background, I see the current period as one in which U.S. competitive advantage seems to be diminishing. Such a shift is clearly suggested in Merton Miller's article.

We have seen the development of several futures exchanges outside the United States—in London, in Germany, and especially in Japan. As a matter of fact, Japan now has the largest stock index futures markets in the world. The Osaka exchange, whose stock index futures started in October 1988, has a trading volume of about $10 billion per day in stock index futures; the Chicago Mercantile Exchange has an average daily volume of $6.6 billion.

The Japanese Exchange traded stock index futures products are off limits to U.S. investors. Unlike most other foreign futures contracts, stock index futures on foreign exchanges may not be traded by U.S. investors until the Commodities Futures Trading Commission (CFTC) has specifically approved the contract. This approval has not been forthcoming in the case of Japan. We are permitted to trade Japanese stock index futures on the Singapore exchange which, however, has a trading volume of less than one-thirtieth of the futures contract in Japan. A U.S. investor is thus forced to rely on an exchange with poor liquidity and poor price discovery. He must bear a higher transaction cost, and also higher risks. For example, in the October 1987 crash, the Singapore contract plummeted almost 80 percent on the opening, but recovered to close down 28 percent. The cash market traded down steadily to finish on lows down 15 percent.

We can expect extensive growth in non-U.S. futures markets. Some growth will be in stock index futures trading, and some will be in other financial instruments such as long-term Japanese government bonds on the Japanese exchanges, German, American, and British bonds in London, and French interest rates in France.

I want to make a few points about the advantages and shortcomings of the U.S. futures markets. As a major user, I find myself, on the one hand, a great proponent and defender of U.S. futures markets. On the other hand, I am also acutely aware of their quite serious limitations. Many of these limitations are exacerbated by regulation, and some of them are not present in other markets.

From my point of view, there are at least four major problems in U.S. futures markets right now. First is price discovery. In large trading pits, there are too many people to have uniform pricing. In the New York Mercantile crude oil pit, or at CBOT's U.S. bond market, you can have more than one price in the pit at the same time. You also quite often have delays in reporting those prices.

These kinds of problems can be quite serious when volume is heavy or when there are crises of one kind or another. The price discovery process breaks down, and price differences in the pit can be significant. These problems are less likely to exist in electronic systems on which price discovery is available on all video terminals.

Second, there are problems that result from liquidity limits set under current regulatory policies. There are position limits in every contract which limit the number of contracts any investor can hold. These limits are set remarkably low, certainly low in relation to the positions in related cash markets.

There are limits, in addition, on price movements. When prices move more than a certain amount, the markets are closed for the day in the U.S. case. That means there is a limitation on liquidating or initiating a position for the rest of the day. In my view, a higher degree of emotion and price distress occurs at those times. In any case, American futures markets suffer from these limits on positions and on price movements, whereas cash markets and some non-U.S. futures markets do not.

Third, there are limitations of exchange reliability. Futures markets in the U.S. are, for the most part, more reliable than foreign markets. However, the United States is not immune. In one of the most recent cases of interest, the New York Commodities Exchange (COMEX) had a default in gold trading and was not able to set the problem right for quite a while. A more serious problem developed for tin on the London Metals Exchange, where it took a year or two to solve the problem. Similar problems in France, Hong Kong, and Singapore have, at times, been much more serious.

A related problem arises from regulatory policies. The United States has a policy that requires clearing firms to segregate customer funds, but these funds are segregated in pools that put each customer at risk to other customers. The pool itself cannot be used for other purposes by the clearing house, but if a customer goes bankrupt, the segregated pool may not have enough money in it to meet all obligations. That was the problem at the COMEX, and it took about a year to sort it out.

I should note another problem that pertains to futures markets in general, and also to U.S. markets. You might call it "product arthritis"—the difficulty of getting new products developed to respond to market conditions. I agree with Merton Miller's view that the U.S. futures markets, on the whole, have been quite innovative in developing new contracts while offering the highest quality product in world futures markets. More recently, however, problems have been developing in terms of the high cost and rigidity associated with making innovations as the regulators have attempted to avoid the quality problems that have arisen elsewhere.

One market that does not get the attention in the press that I think it deserves is the interbank foreign exchange market. This is the largest financial market in the world. It is in some respects the first electronic market. With worldwide price discovery by direct electronic feed from participating banks, the basic Reuters screen has created half (and probably the more important half) of the much-sought-after electronic market. The recent addition of the "Reuters Dealing 2000" system extends the electronic component to allow dealing directly on the system. This interbank foreign exchange market is, in my view, the most efficient market in the world, in spite of its not being regulated by any national authority. (I say "in spite of," but perhaps "because of" is more accurate.)

There is a futures market in currencies in Chicago; however, it suffers from a number of disadvantages. First, its liquidity is about an order of magnitude less than the interbank foreign exchange market; and second, it has product disadvantages. Because of the structure of the contracts in the futures market, nondollar transactions, so-called cross-trades, cannot be consummated easily. The exchanges have, at least so far, failed to address this problem.

I agree with Miller's doubts about raising stock index margins or shifting control away from the exchanges. As a participant in this market, I find it very hard to understand how the idea of increasing margins is likely to increase liquidity. If liquidity decreases, which is a much more likely result, we certainly are going to see less efficient price discovery and more volatility in times of pressure. It would seem to me that the appropriate goal is to increase liquidity. Increasing margins to 50 percent is unlikely to accomplish that. I think there is a fairly good chance that increasing margins significantly will drive most of the business out of Chicago. London now does a great deal of this business, and I would argue that London is prepared to increase its role. London does have a structural disadvantage—trading in London now ends at about noon New York time—but with sufficient economic incentive, London traders will stick around for three or four more hours. A great deal of stock business in the underlying securities, as well as futures, could be driven to London.

The efficiencies associated with trading stock index futures are significant, and many institutions have developed useful strategies based on them. I doubt that they will all choose to end such strategies, or to pay much higher costs if alternatives are available. So I would expect that the New York Stock Exchange would be among the losers if margins are increased significantly. It seems clear, whatever happens to the flow of business, that the efficiency of the market would suffer from much higher margins.

As I reflect on Grundfest's and Miller's articles in this issue, I am struck by the fact that the markets make judgments all the time about the efficiency of markets and their relative desirability. One way to observe this vote of confidence is by measuring open interest over time and using other measures of volume. By those standards, the unregulated market—the interbank foreign exchange market—is perhaps doing best. The U.S. futures markets are doing well in financial markets but not very well in the equity index markets. Open interest has not been rising in the U.S. stock index futures, and the relative share of U.S. markets has been falling dramatically. I would expect that trend to continue if the regulatory policies that are currently being supported by the U.S. Treasury and the Securities and Exchange Commission are pursued.

If you do a rank ordering of the exchanges around the world by their growth in open interest and volume, you would find, after the well-established U.S. markets, a very rapidly growing Japanese market. A great deal of business could move from the United States to Japanese markets; it certainly has in some areas already. Then London futures markets are next, followed by some of the other European futures markets that have just started. Much farther down the list are Pacific Rim markets, such as the Singapore market, the Malaysian market, or the Hong Kong market—all of which have had default or other problems that suggest that the integrity of the exchange is at least open to question—and they have, therefore, not had very much growth.

My closing comments are on the regulatory picture. The U.S. regulatory process, by withholding approvals and imposing burdensome regulations, is threatening to impair our competitive advantage in the futures markets. People elsewhere in the world can eventually learn the business and take it away from us. We may see the center of gravity for the financial futures markets shift away from us.

The regulatory policy outlook is clouded right now by the turf battles that are going on between the agencies. Our ability to start new contracts that respond to changing opportunities in developing financial instruments has certainly diminished. But despite that bleak regulatory picture, our financial markets remain very strong and competitive. I only hope we manage to keep them that way by avoiding introduction of regulatory burdens that are too heavy.

Journal of Financial Services Research 4:419–460 (1990)
© 1990 Kluwer Academic Publishers

Managing Pension and Retirement Assets: An International Perspective

ZVI BODIE
Professor of Finance and Economics
Boston University School of Management
Boston, MA 02215

1. Introduction

A major force behind private saving, both in theory and in practice, is the retirement motive. How these savings are invested can have profound effects on capital markets around the world. This article analyzes the institutional forms that private retirement savings take, how they have affected capital markets to date, and how they might affect them in the future.

Common to most of the world's industrialized countries is an aging population, and their retirement income systems face a similar set of policy issues. Countries can learn much from each other, with opportunities to pool resources through the market system in mutually advantageous ways.

In virtually every country, the government plays a critical role in the retirement income system—as provider, insurer, and regulator. Even in the United States, where the private sector is the major source of retirement income, the Social Security and public welfare systems provide a large proportion of retirement income, especially for those at the lower end of the income distribution. This article, however, focuses on the behavior of the private sector.

By far the most important institution in the retirement income market is the employer-sponsored pension plan. These plans vary in form and complexity, but they all share certain common elements in every country. Defined contribution (DC) plans are the easiest to understand, while defined benefit (DB) plans can be exceedingly complex arrangements.

Under a DC plan, each employee has an account into which the employer and the employee (in a contributory plan) make regular contributions. Benefit levels depend on the total contributions and investment earnings of the accumulation in the account. In a DB plan, by contrast, the employee's pension benefit entitlement is determined by a formula that takes into account years of service for the employer and, in most cases, wages or salary. Most private DB plans in the United States are noncontributory. The important

The research in this article was supported by U.S. Department of Labor Contract Number J-9-P-8-0097. Many of the ideas herein are based on work that I have done with Leslie E. Papke on the DOL project and with Robert C. Merton and Alan Marcus as part of a National Bureau of Economic Research project on pensions. I alone am to be held responsible for the interpretation and development of ideas in this article. Any opinions expressed are mine and not those of the Department of Labor or of the NBER.

distinction between the two is that benefits in a DB plan are independent of the performance of the plan's assets.

While DC plans are by definition fully funded, DB plans can be funded to any degree. In France, Germany, and Japan, for example, most corporate pension plans are on a pay-as-you-go basis. Only funded pension plans can have a direct effect on world security markets. This is because in an unfunded plan the retirement savings are locked up in the sponsoring organization—the benefits promised are a liability of the plan sponsor.

Of the total securities held by private pension plans in the nine most industrialized countries in 1986, 70 percent were in the hands of U.S. pension funds.[1] Their investment policy has had a profound effect on the direction and rate of innovation in the U.S. capital markets. In 1988 U.S. pension plan assets amounted to almost $2.5 trillion. Most of this money was invested in debt and equity securities. Pension funds held about 25 percent of the total holdings of common stock and 39 percent of the total of corporate and foreign bonds held by U.S. entities.[2]

The search by pension funds for an improved risk-reward tradeoff has spawned a new branch of the financial services industry—professional asset management. In the past 20 years, advising pension funds about asset allocation, security selection, and portfolio management, including evaluation of professional managers, has grown from virtually nothing to a big business.

These trends prompt a number of questions:

- What are the economic causes and consequences of the funding of pension plans?
- What are the unique features of pension and retirement funds that might cause them to adopt investment policies that differ from those of others investors?
- How have these investment policies affected the capital markets?
- What are the likely future trends in pension plan asset allocation and their likely effects on the capital markets?
- What are the prospects for international competition and cooperation in the market for retirement income products and services?

Pension fund finance is a complicated subject. Much of what has been written about it in the popular press and even in the professional literature is erroneous. A major objective of this article is to expose some of these fallacies and to show how they can lead to bad decisions by households, pension plan sponsors, and government regulators.

2. The retirement income system: Markets and institutions

Almost by definition, the economic function of a country's retirement income system is to replace enough of preretirement employment income to enable people to maintain their standard of living in their old age. In many countries the state-sponsored part of the retirement income system is also used to redistribute income both within and across generations.

In most industrialized countries retirement income comes from three major sources: the government, employee pension plans, and private savings (including family support and home ownership).[3] The role of the government varies across countries, but virtually everywhere it provides a floor of protection through a combination of the national insurance and welfare systems. Often the national insurance scheme provides retirement benefits in the form of cash and medical insurance. In the remainder of this article we will refer to these as Social Security.

Most employer pension plans are integrated with Social Security either explicitly or implicitly. They are usually designed to replace most of preretirement earnings when combined with Social Security.[4] Undoubtedly, private savings are influenced by the combined levels of Social Security and pension income.

The markets and institutions that have developed to provide retirement income products have been heavily influenced by government rules and regulations regarding private pensions and retirement savings. Chief among these is their tax-favored status in virtually all industrialized countries. Below we will explore how this special tax status affects funding and asset allocation decisions.

Some components of retirement income are outside the scope of this article. A major source of retirement income for many households, for example, is home ownership. How this resource is used and how access to it during retirement might be improved is not addressed here.[5] We also do not consider the issue of employer-provided health insurance for the elderly. Instead, we limit the scope of this article to pension plans and retirement funds.

3. Pensions as insurance[6]

There are many sources of retirement income uncertainty that a risk-averse individual would like to insure against. Pension plans offer a convenient way of doing so. Let us briefly consider some of the most important.

3.1. Replacement rate risk

Replacement rate risk is the possibility that the retiree will not have enough income to maintain the same standard of living after retiring as during the preretirement years. For most people the process of saving for an adequate level of retirement income is very difficult. Planning is difficult because of the specialized knowledge it requires. Implementation is difficult because it requires discipline.

People can acquire the expertise by employing a specialist with the requisite training and ability, but acquiring the discipline is more difficult. One of the main arguments in support of the Social Security retirement system is that people want the government to force them to save for retirement through a payroll tax that finances at least a minimal level of benefits in retirement.[7] The reason governments give for providing tax incentives for retirement savings is that without them people are apt to save too little.

Employer pensions can be viewed as a supplement to Social Security designed to insure that the combined income from both sources will enable retirees to maintain their pre-retirement standard of living. By automatic deferment of a portion of earnings through a pension plan, employees benefit from a saving discipline that otherwise might be lacking.

3.2. Longevity risk

Longevity risk is the risk that the retiree will outlive the amount saved for retirement income. One way people insure against the risk of exhausting their savings during retirement is by saving in the form of life annuity contracts. But the private market for life annuities is plagued by the problem of adverse selection: there is a tendency for people with a higher than average life expectancy to have a high demand for this kind of insurance. In the competitive equilibrium the average individual finds the equilibrium price unattractive and tends to self-insure against longevity risk by providing an extra reserve of retirement savings. At least one study of the private annuities market in the United States seems to confirm the theory that private annuities are priced unattractively for the average individual.[8]

Employer pension plans offer a way of overcoming the adverse selection problem. By making participation in the plan mandatory and offering life annuities as the only payout option, the cost of insuring each participant can be kept low.[9]

3.3. Social Security risk

Social Security risk is the risk that the benefits provided by the state-sponsored retirement system will be cut before the individual reaches retirement age. While informed people may know the current rules governing their expected benefits from the Social Security system, those rules have a history of changing in unpredictable ways both in the United States and elsewhere. The integration of employer-provided pensions with Social Security is one method of insuring plan participants against this risk.[10]

The uncertainties associated with Social Security retirement benefits stem primarily from the fact that the objectives of that system are different from those of the private pension system. From its inception, the U.S. Social Security system had an income redistribution goal that was at least as important as the income replacement goal.[11]

Of course, there are risks associated with private pension benefits, too. One can view a mixed public-private system of retirement income provision as a way of reducing the risks of each separate component through diversification across providers. Formal methods of integration vary across countries and across pension plans within each country.

In the United States, formal integration is achieved by having step-rate benefit formulas or formulas with offsets. These formulas are designed to have the sponsor supplement the income from Social Security.[12] In Japan and the United Kingdom, sponsors of private plans can "contract out" of at least part of the Social Security system.

3.4. Investment risk

Investment risk is the possibility that the amount saved for retirement will be inadequate because the assets in which money is invested perform poorly. For most people the question of how much to save for retirement is matched in complexity by the question of how to invest whatever they save. The array of investment choices offered by financial institutions and markets often bewilders the ordinary citizen who is untutored in the fundamentals of finance.

On this issue there is a fundamental difference between defined benefit and defined contribution plans. It is often claimed that a major advantage of the DB form is that it allows the participant to avoid investment risk. In fact, many DC plans offer investment options with minimal risk. What most DC plans do not offer, and all DB plans do, is a guarantee that the combination of plan contributions and investment income will be enough to provide a promised benefit at retirement. This promise is backed up by all the assets of the plan sponsor and in some countries by government insurance.

In the United States, employers whose primary pension plan is of the DB form usually offer their employees additional voluntary tax-deferred savings plans. These supplementary plans, which are always DC in form, usually provide a variety of investment options and often are subsidized by matching contributions from the employer. In this way employers provide a guaranteed floor of retirement income free of investment risk, while maintaining a tax-sheltered environment for additional retirement savings that can be invested as the employee sees fit.

3.5. Inflation risk

Inflation risk is the risk that price increases will erode the purchasing power of retirement savings. While Social Security benefits and pension benefits under some public plans are insured against inflation, the vast majority of private pension plans in the United States offer no automatic inflation protection. Before retirement, pension savings are partially protected against inflation through a variety of means, but virtually no private pension plans offer automatic inflation protection after retirement.[13] The situation is similar in Japan and Canada. Inflation protection is much more common in the European countries.[14]

The supplementary voluntary defined contribution plans offered by many employers in the United States are often viewed as a way of providing inflation insurance. These plans are encouraged both by tax-favored treatment and often by matching employer contributions. While these supplementary plans offer participants the opportunity to save more for retirement, they do not offer cost-of-living guarantees, and in that sense are not, strictly speaking, inflation insurance.[15]

4. The employer as logical provider of retirement income insurance

Within the private sector in the United States, pension coverage is most prevalent in large firms (Andrews, 1985). In small firms unionization is an important correlate of pension coverage. In Japan, too, pension coverage is more widespread in large firms.

In principle there are a variety of ways that people could acquire the different kinds of retirement income insurance discussed above. Why, then, is there a strong tendency for large firms or those with unionized employees to provide it?

4.1. Informational efficiencies

It is costly to acquire the knowledge necessary to prepare and carry out long-run plans for income provision. Each person's lifetime financial plan depends on preferences known only to that person. But people have enough in common in this regard that a standard retirement savings plan can prove suitable to many.

Furthermore, an employer often has better access than the employees themselves to some of the information relevant to preparing long-run financial plans for his employees. In particular, the employer may have better knowledge of the probable path of future labor income of company employees. By providing a basic plan that saves enough to provide for replacement of the likely future stream of labor earnings, the employer can therefore save more efficiently than can each employee.

For a sponsor to provide efficiently for future wage and salary replacement of employees, it is enough to have accurate forecasts of the earnings of the group as a whole and not the individual earnings of each member of the group. It is easier, although by no means easy, to forecast group earnings than it is to forecast an individual's future earnings.

4.2. Agency problems

While employers and employees often have conflicting economic interests, in many respects their interests coincide. Employers who acquire a reputation for taking care of the retirement needs of their employees should find it easier to recruit and retain higher quality employees. If an attitude of trust and good will toward the employer develops in the minds of the employees, then motivation and labor productivity should be enhanced. Employers, therefore, have some economic incentive to act in the best interests of their employees.

Other possible providers of retirement planning services may be less suitable as beneficial agents of the employee. Insurance agents, stock brokers, and others who provide these services to individual households may be less credible than the employer because they may be interested in selling some product or service that people would not choose were they well informed. These other providers may have their own motivation to persuade the individual to save too much for retirement or to invest in inappropriate ways. Anyone who has ever tried to find competent and impartial personal financial planning or investment advice is aware of the difficulties.

When employers provide pension plans, they become responsible for managing the plan's assets. Whether the funds are managed internally or outside, the plan sponsor seeks competent specialists to help in that process. Indeed, the growth of a professional asset management industry in the United States in the past two decades is in large part due to the growth in pension funds.[16]

The trust of the employees is further enhanced when they know that the sponsor's own management team is covered by the same pension plan as the other employees. This is often the case.

4.3. Access to capital markets

Plan sponsors, be they private firms or state or local governments, often have access to capital markets that is unavailable to their employees on an individual basis. Thus while a risk faced by an individual employee may be uninsurable directly through the capital markets, it may be insurable through the employer.

Of course, financial intermediaries such as insurance companies exist precisely for this reason, and for many purposes they provide a suitable vehicle for the insurance needs of employees. But often a financial intermediary will not be willing to provide enough of the insurance desired by the individual at an efficient price because of problems of adverse selection and moral hazard.

Longevity insurance is one important example. In principle, longevity risk is, to a large extent, diversifiable and can be largely eliminated through risk pooling and sharing. But, as described earlier, the problem of adverse selection can make the private insurance market for life annuities inefficient. Group insurance through pension plans is a solution to this problem.

In most cases it is possible to imagine other types of actual or potential financial intermediaries that could offer the kinds of insurance embodied in employer-provided pension plans. In the United States, small employers often contract with financial institutions such as insurance companies or mutual funds to provide some or all aspects of their pension services. But that fact just suggests that when a plan sponsor choose not to provide retirement income insurance through an outside contractor, it views itself as the efficient provider.

5. Defined contribution plans, retirement accounts, and variable annuities

Defined contribution plans are, in effect, tax-deferred retirement savings accounts held in trust for the employees. Contributions usually are specified as a predetermined fraction of salary, although that fraction need not be constant over the course of a career. Contributions from both parties are tax-deductible, and investment income accrues tax-free. At retirement, the employee receives a lump sum or an annuity whose size depends on the accumulated value of the funds in the retirement account and is then taxed as ordinary income.

In the United States, the employee often has some choice as to how the account is to be invested.[17] In principle, contributions may be invested in any security, although in practice most plans limit investment options to various fixed-income, stock, and money market funds. The employee bears all the investment risk; the retirement account is by definition fully funded, and the firm has no obligation beyond making its periodic contribution.

Most covered employees are in DB pension plans. In recent years, however, at least in the United States there has been a pronounced trend toward DC plans.[18] All supplementary retirement savings plans offered by employers in the United States (401k plans, for example) are DC in form.

For defined contribution plans investment policy is not much different from that of an individual deciding how to invest the money in a tax-qualified individual retirement account.[19] Indeed, institutions such as mutual funds and insurance companies that cater to the investment needs of individual investors are the main providers of investment vehicles for DC plans.

5.1. Taxes and efficient diversification

The guiding principle behind investment policy in a retirement account is efficient diversification, that is, achieving the maximum expected return for any given level of risk exposure. Its special feature, however, is the fact that investment earnings are not taxed as long as the money is held in the account. This consideration should cause the investor to tilt the asset mix toward the least tax-advantaged securities—corporate bonds, for example.

Typically an individual may have some investment in the form of tax-qualified retirement accounts and some in the form of ordinary taxable accounts. The basic investment principle is to hold equities in the ordinary account, while holding whatever bonds are wanted in the retirement account. This maximizes the tax advantage of the retirement account.

To see how this works, consider an example. Suppose you have $200,000 of wealth, $100,000 of it in a tax-qualified retirement account. You decide you should invest half of your wealth in bonds and half in stocks, so you allocate half of each account to each. Doing this does not maximize your after-tax return. You could reduce your tax bill with no change in before-tax returns by simply shifting your bonds into the retirement account and holding all your stocks outside the retirement account.

The reason is that most of your return on stocks comes in the form of capital appreciation. In many countries capital gains are taxed at a lower rate than ordinary income. Even in the United States, where the capital gains tax rate is currently the same as on ordinary income, the capital gains tax is payable only when the asset is sold. This means that income taxes on stocks can be deferred indefinitely (except for dividends) even when they are not held in a tax-deferred retirement account.[20]

5.2. Variable annuities

Annuity contracts are sold by life insurance companies and usually are combined with some form of life insurance. The buyer either makes a single payment or a series of payments, and in return gets title to a stream of benefits from the insurance company starting at some future time, usually at retirement age. Most annuity contracts have several withdrawal options, including a lump-sum cash-out at any time.

By definition, a life annuity is one that lasts for as long as you live. Like Social Security, therefore, life annuities offer longevity insurance and would seem to be an ideal asset for someone in the retirement years. Indeed, theory suggests that where there are no bequest motives, it would be optimal for people to invest heavily in actuarially fair life annuities.[21]

There are two types of life annuities, fixed and variable. A fixed annuity pays a fixed nominal sum of money per period (usually each month), while a variable annuity pays a periodic amount linked to the investment performance of some underlying portfolio.

Variable annuities are structured so that the investment risk of the underlying asset portfolio is passed through to the recipient, much as shareholders bear the risk of a mutual fund. There are two stages in a variable annuity contract: an accumulation phase and a payout phase. During the accumulation phase, the investor contributes money periodically to one or more open-end mutual funds and accumulates shares. The second, or payout, stage usually starts at retirement, when the investor typically has several options including:

1. Taking the market value of the shares in a lump-sum payment.
2. Receiving a fixed annuity until death.
3. Receiving a variable amount of money each period that is computed according to a procedure best explained by the example following.

Assume that at retirement you have $100,000 accumulated in a variable annuity contract. The initial annuity payment is determined by setting an assumed investment return (AIR), 4 percent per year in this example, and making additional assumptions about mortality probabilities. Assume you will live for only three years after retirement and will receive three annual payments starting one year from now.

The benefit payment in each year, R_t, is given by the recursive formula:

$$B_t = B_{t-1} \times \frac{(1+R_t)}{(1+\text{AIR})}$$

where R_t is the actual holding period return on the underlying portfolio in year t.

In other words, each year the amount you receive equals the previous year's benefit times a factor that reflects the actual compared to the assumed investment return. In this example, if the actual return equals 4 percent, the factor will be one, and this year's benefit will equal last year's. If R_t is greater than 4 percent, the benefit will increase, and if R_t is less than 4 percent, the benefit will decrease. The starting benefit is found by computing a hypothetical constant payment with a present value of $100,000 using the 4 percent AIR to discount future values and multiplying it by the first year's performance factor.

Table 1 summarizes the computation and shows what the payment will be in each of three years if R_t is 6 percent, then 2 percent, then 4 percent. The last column shows the balance in the fund after each payment.

This method guarantees that the initial $100,000 will be sufficient to pay all benefits due regardless of what actual holding period returns turn out to be. In this way the variable annuity contract passes all portfolio risk through to the annuitant.

By selecting an appropriate mix of underlying assets, such as stocks, bonds, and cash, an investor can create a stream of variable annuity payments with a wide variety of risk-return combinations. Naturally, the investor wants to select a combination that offers the highest expected level of payments for any specified level of risk.[22]

Table 1. Illustration of a variable annuity

t	R_t	B_t	Remaining balance $= A_t = A_{t-1} x(1 + R_t) - B_t$
0			$100,000
1	6%	36,728	69,272
2	2%	36,022	34,635
3	4%	36,022	0

Notes: Starting accumulation = $100,000.

R_t = rate or return on underlying portfolio in year t.

Assumed investment return (AIR) = 4 percent per year.

B_t = benefit received at end of year t = $B_{t-1} \frac{(1+R_t)}{(1+AIR)}$.

B_0 = $36,035. This is the hypothetical constant payment, which has a present value of $100,000, using a discount rate of 4 percent per year.

A_t = Remaining balance after B_t is withdrawn.

Variable annuities are very flexible contracts that combine several insurance and investment features. They have the potential for solving some of the problems associated with traditional defined benefit pension plans. We will return to them later in the article when we discuss the future of defined benefit plans.

5.3. Investing for the long-run

A feature of retirement saving that is commonly thought to have an important effect on the way it is invested is the fact that the investment horizon is long. As many empirical studies have shown, a well-diversified portfolio of U.S. stocks has outperformed bills, bonds, and inflation over holding periods longer than 20 years, for almost any starting date during the past 60 years.[23] From this empirical fact, many people have concluded that stocks are the most appropriate investment for the long-run saver. The conventional wisdom is that younger people should invest more in stocks than older people simply because they have a longer investment horizon.

The following excerpt from the Spring 1990 issue of In the Vanguard, a publication of The Vanguard Group (of mutual funds), is typical:

> Over the past six decades, stocks have achieved an average annual rate of return of 9.7%—far exceeding the 5.2% average return on corporate bonds and the 3.6% average return on U.S. Treasury bills. Yet it's no secret that the stock market is subject to wide and unpredictable price swings in any given year. Consider, however, that the volatility of stock market returns diminishes markedly over time. . . . During any one-year period between 1960 and 1989, the maximum spread in annual returns of stocks (as measured by the unmanaged Standard and Poor's 500 Composite Stock Price Index) was 64% (from a high of 37.2% to a low of -26.5%). Over ten-year holding periods, the difference in annual rates of return decreased to 16% (17.5% to 1.2%) and, over 25 years, less than 2% (10.2% to 8.4%). Note that for ten-year periods and

beyond, the returns were all positive. Clearly, over time, stock market risk hardly seems excessive—even for the most cautious long-term investor. So, take stock of time when investing in stocks.

Paul A. Samuelson and Robert C. Merton have proved this proposition false in a series of articles.[24] They show that, under standard assumptions about the probability distribution of stock returns and investor preferences, the length of an investor's time horizon per se should not affect the optimal asset mix.

5.4. Fallacy 1: stocks are not risky in the long run

An example makes the fallacy clear. Assume that you are choosing between stocks and a risk-free investment paying an interest rate of eight percent per year. Your investment horizon is N years. If you invest in stocks there is some possibility of a shortfall, that is, that you will earn an average compound rate of return less than eight percent per year.

The believability of the fallacy that stocks are not risky in the long run stems from the indisputable fact that the farther in the future the benefit is to be paid, the lower the probability of a shortfall. This is the intuition behind the view that stocks are less risky in the long run. It is also the reason that, when we examine the historical data, we should expect to find that stock returns exceed bond returns for long holding periods. The likelihood of actually observing a 20-year period during which bonds earn more than stocks is very small. This is especially true if the sample consists of only a few statistically independent observations. For example, if the data being examined are drawn from the period 1926–1989, then there are only three truly independent 20-year holding periods in the sample.

But if there is such a small probability of a shortfall when the holding period is long, why should we not invest more in stocks? The answer is that while the probability of earning less than the risk-free rate declines with the length of the holding period, the probability of an *extreme* shortfall actually grows. The probability of a shortfall is a misleading measure of risk.

It is easiest to see this point if we assume that in any one-year period, the rate of return on stocks can take only one of two values. For example, assume that the rate of return will either be 30 percent with probability .72 or −20 percent with probability .28, so that the mean is 16 percent and the standard deviation 22.5 percent.[25] Consider the worst possible outcome for holding periods of increasing length. For a one-year holding period you can lose 20 percent of your initial investment, for a two year period 36 percent, and for a 20-year period as much as 99 percent.[26]

Figures 1 and 2 illustrate what can happen to the value of a portfolio that has a starting value of $1. The upper curve in figure 1 shows the maximum value of the portfolio, and the lower curve shows the minimum value. The middle curve shows its value if invested in a risk-free asset earning 8 percent per year. Figure 2 shows the probability distributions of the value of the portfolio after 5 years and after 20 years. Tables 2 and 3 present the same probabilities in tabular form.

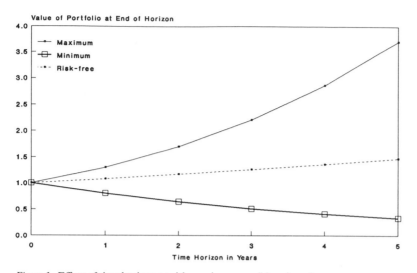

Figure 1. Effect of time horizon on risk: maximum possible gain or loss

Note: Each year the stock market either goes up 30 percent or down 20 percent. The figure shows the maximum and minimum possible values of an initial investment of $1 at the end of the specified number of years. The risk-free interest rate is 8 percent per year. The middle curve shows the value of the portfolio growing at the risk-free rate.

Table 2. Probability distribution of portfolio values after five years

Value	Probability	Cumulative Probability
$0.33	0.0017	0.0017
$0.53	0.0221	0.0238
$0.87	0.1138	0.1376
$1.41	0.2926	0.4303*
$2.28	0.3762	0.8065
$3.71	0.1935	1.0000

Notes: 1. Each year the stock market either goes up 30 percent with probability .72 or down 20 percent with probability .28. The table gives the probability distribution of the value of an initial investment of $1 at the end of five years. If invested at the risk-free interest rate of eight percent per year, the $1 would grow to $1.47 at the end of five years. Anything less than this value is a shortfall. The probability of a shortfall in this case is .43 (indicated by a *).

2. The probabilities were generated using the binomial formula: $\quad f(x) = \binom{N}{x}p^x(1 - p)^{N-x}$ where $N = 5$ and $p = 0.72$.

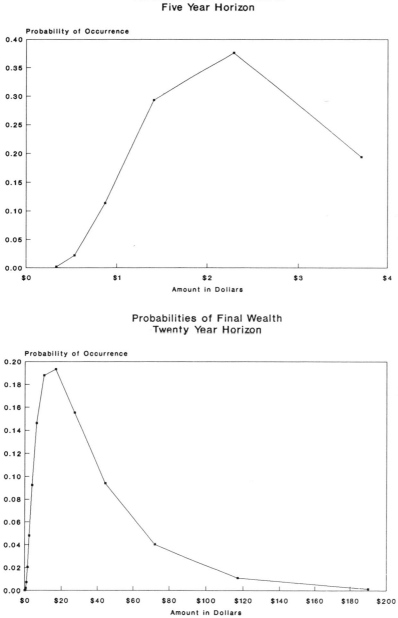

Figure 2. Probability distributions of portfolio value after 5 and 20 years.

Table 3. Probability distribution of portfolio values after 20 years

Value	Probability	Cumulative Probability
$ 0.01	0.0000	0.0000
$ 0.02	0.0000	0.0000
$ 0.03	0.0000	0.0000
$ 0.05	0.0000	0.0000
$ 0.08	0.0000	0.0000
$ 0.13	0.0000	0.0000
$ 0.21	0.0001	0.0001
$ 0.34	0.0005	0.0006
$ 0.56	0.0021	0.0027
$ 0.91	0.0072	0.0100
$ 1.48	0.0205	0.0305
$ 2.41	0.0479	0.0784
$ 3.91	0.0924	0.1707*
$ 6.35	0.1462	0.3169
$ 10.32	0.1879	0.5048
$ 16.77	0.1933	0.6981
$ 27.26	0.1553	0.8534
$ 44.29	0.0940	0.9474
$ 71.97	0.0403	0.9877
$116.95	0.0109	0.9986
$190.05	0.0014	1.0000

Notes: Each year the stock market either goes up 30 percent with probability .72 or down 20 percent with probability .28. The table gives the probability distribution of the value of an initial investment of $1 at the end of 20 years. If invested at the risk-free interest rate of 8 percent per year, the $1 would grow to $4.66 at the end of 20 years. Anything less than this value is a shortfall. The probability of a shortfall in this case is .17. The probabilities were generated using the binomial formula with $N = 20$.

As the time horizon gets longer, the probability of a shortfall gets smaller, but the maximum possible loss grows. Thus, after 5 years you would have $1.47 from investing in the risk-free asset; the probability of a shortfall from investing in stocks would be .43; and the lowest possible value of your portfolio would be $.33. After 20 years, you would have $4.66 from investing in the risk-free asset; the probability of a shortfall would be only .17; but the lowest possible value of your portfolio would be $.01. As we will show later, the cost of insuring against a shortfall is higher the longer the horizon.

Samuelson (1969) and Merton (1969) analyze the case of an individual whose objective is to maximize the expected utility of lifetime consumption. They show that the length of the investment horizon per se has no predictable effect on the optimal proportion to invest in stocks. In fact, for the family of constant relative risk aversion utility functions, the proportion in stocks is independent of the investment horizon.

The proposition that the young should invest more in stocks than the old may still be true—but not because stocks are less risky in the long run. A rational reason for younger people to hold more of their investments in stock is that a larger fraction of a young person's wealth is in the form of human capital.

A person usually faces an expected stream of labor income over the working years. The present value of that stream, one's human capital, is a large proportion of the total wealth (human capital + other wealth) when one is young, and usually decreases as one ages. If it is optimal to hold a constant proportion of total wealth in stocks, stocks as a proportion of nonhuman wealth must then decline as human capital declines over the life cycle.

This rationale for investing more in stocks when one is young is reinforced if the individual has flexibility in labor supply decisions. If one can choose how much to work in each year, and/or delay or accelerate the date of retirement, then one should rationally be willing to tolerate more portfolio risk when one is young. The reason is that one can self-insure against adverse portfolio outcomes by adjusting the amount of labor income one earns over the remainder of one's working years.[27]

5.5. Stocks as a hedge against inflation

A related fallacy is the notion that stocks are a hedge against inflation.

5.6. Fallacy 2: Stocks are a hedge against inflation

The reasoning behind this fallacy is that stocks are an ownership claim over real physical capital. Real profits are either unaffected or enhanced when there is unanticipated inflation, so owners of real capital should not be hurt by it.

Let us assume that this proposition is true, and that the real rate of return on stocks is uncorrelated or slightly positively correlated with inflation. If stocks are to be a good hedge against inflation risk in the conventional sense, however, the nominal return on stocks would have to be *highly* positively correlated with inflation.

To see this, suppose that you are a pensioner living on a money-fixed pension and therefore concerned about inflation risk. You could eliminate this risk to your real income stream by hedging with bonds linked to the consumer price level. You might want to invest some of your money in stocks to increase your expected return, but there is no way to use this investment to reduce your risk in any significant way, because stock returns are not highly correlated with inflation.

To have any valid economic content, the proposition that stocks are a good inflation hedge can mean only that in a regression of stock returns against the rate of inflation, the slope coefficient is 1. Even if this were true, the R^2 in that regression would have to be high for stocks to be useful as a vehicle for hedging against inflation risk.

Thus, even in the best of circumstances, stocks can offer only a limited hedge against inflation risk. Empirical studies show that stock returns have been negatively correlated with inflation in the past with a low R^2. The conclusion is that if you want to use equities to hedge inflation risk, you would have to sell short, and you would not reduce your risk by much.[28]

6. Defined benefit pension plans

In a DB plan, the pension benefit is determined by a formula that takes into account the employee's history of service and wages or salary. The plan sponsor provides this benefit regardless of the investment performance of the pension fund assets. The annuity promised to the employee is the employer's liability.

6.1. The nature of defined benefit pension obligations

The pensions offered under DB plans in the United States are best viewed as annuities that offer a guaranteed minimum nominal benefit determined by the plan's benefit formula. This guaranteed benefit is permanently enriched from time to time, at the discretion of management, depending on the financial condition of the plan sponsor, the increase in the living costs of retirees, and the performance of the fund's assets.[29]

The evidence in support of this "guaranteed minimum" contention is that many plans have voluntarily given ad hoc benefit increases to plan participants in the past.[30] While many have interpreted these increases as evidence of implicit cost-of-living indexation, in actuality they are very different from a formal COLA (cost-of-living adjustment).[31] Rather, they are an implicit claim of the employees on the plan sponsor.

The implicit pension obligation is a complex contingent claim, both in the economic and legal sense. One way to view this contingent claim is as an employee ownership share in the pension fund surplus. In the case of corporate pension plans, it seems clear that if the sponsoring corporation does not do well financially, then employees cannot expect to get anything more than the minimum guaranteed formula benefit.

There is mounting evidence that U.S. corporations facing severe financial difficulties, either because of low profitability or because of a threat of hostile takeover, will terminate their overfunded pension plans and give employees only the legal minimum.[32] On the other hand, if the corporation is doing well financially, and if retired employees face inflation, then there is evidence that the corporation will help them out with ad hoc benefit increases.

6.2. Fallacy 3: final pay pension plans are effectively indexed for inflation

Unlike Social Security benefits, whose starting value is indexed to a general index of wages, private pension benefits even in final pay formula plans are "indexed" only to the extent that (1) the employee continues to work for the same employer, (2) the employee's own wage or salary keeps pace with the general index, and (3) the employer continues to maintain the same plan.

Very few private corporations in the United States offer pension benefits that are automatically indexed for inflation. This lack of inflation indexation gives rise to the portability problem. Workers who change jobs wind up with lower pension benefits at retirement than otherwise identical workers who stay with the same employer, even if the employers have DB plans with the same final-pay benefit formula.

In the United States, both the Financial Accounting Standards Board (FASB) and Congress have adopted the present value of the guaranteed nominal floor as the appropriate measure of a sponsor's pension liability. In FASB Statement 87, the rule-making body of the accounting profession specifies that the measure of corporate pension liabilities to be used on the corporate balance sheet in external reports is the accumulated benefit obligation (ABO)—that is, the present value of pension benefits owed to employees under the plan's benefit formula absent any salary projections and at a nominal rate of interest.[33]

In its Omnibus Budget Reconciliation Act (OBRA) of 1987, Congress defined the current liability as the measure of a corporation's pension liability and set limits on the amount of tax-qualified contributions a corporation could make as a proportion of the current liability. OBRA's definition of the current liability is essentially the same as FASB Statement 87's definition of the ABO.

Statement 87, however, recognizes an additional measure of a defined benefit plan's liability: the projected benefit obligation (PBO). The PBO is a measure of the sponsor's pension liability that includes projected increases in salary up to the expected age of retirement. Statement 87 requires corporations to use the PBO in computing pension expense reported in their income statements. This is useful for financial analysts, in that the amount may help them to derive an appropriate estimate of expected future labor costs for discounted cash flow valuation models of the firm as a going concern. The PBO is not, however, an appropriate measure of the benefits that the employer has guaranteed and therefore not a target to be hedged by pension fund investment policy.[34]

We can clarify the issues involved by considering a numerical example. Suppose the plan pays a benefit equal to 1 percent of final salary per year of service. To keep the mathematics simple, we will make some additional assumptions that will not affect the qualitative results in which we are interested. Plan participants enter the plan at age 25, retire at age 65, and live until age 85. There is immediate vesting, no early retirement option, and no employee turnover.[35] These assumptions allow us to ignore the actuarial adjustments necessary to account for mortality risk and turnover.

We assume that the typical employee's salary increases at the rate of inflation. This implies no change in real wages over an employee's career and allows us to avoid the complications arising from the spread between nominal wage growth and inflation. Finally, we assume that the interest rate appropriate for discounting nominal annuities is 9 percent per year (the riskless real rate of 3 percent per year plus an expected rate of inflation of 5 percent per year plus a risk premium of 1 percent per year).

Under a final-pay formula of this sort there is a wage indexation effect that is critical in understanding the difference between the ABO and the PBO. Suppose that you just turned 26 years old and have received a salary of $30,000. You have therefore accrued a deferred pension annuity of $300 per year for 20 years starting 39 years from now when you retire. The present value of this deferred annuity is $95. This is the ABO.

If you work for another year, assuming inflation of 5 percent, you will receive a salary of $31,500. The pension annuity that you are now entitled to is 2 percent of $31,500, or $630 per year starting 38 years from now. By working for an additional year you have earned an additional percentage point of salary for the additional year of service ($315), and you have increased the salary base for computing your pension benefit ($15), amounting to a

$330 increase. Had you not worked the additional year you would have been entitled to only $300 per year at retirement. Thus, you have earned the indexation increment to your pension benefit ($15) through continued employment.

That this indexation increment to the pension benefit can be achieved only through continued employment is well understood by plan participants facing the retirement decision. They will often delay the date of retirement if they anticipate inflation in the immediate future, in order to raise the salary base for computing their pension benefit.

By contrast, if the pension benefit were automatically indexed for inflation up to the age of retirement, then regardless of what happens in the future your projected pension

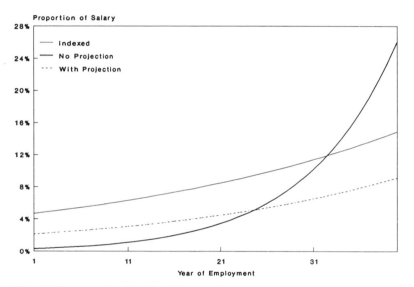

Figure 3. Present value of new benefits earned

Assumptions: The plan pays a benefit equal to 1 percent of final salary per year of service. Plan participants enter the plan at age 25, retire at age 65, and live until age 85. The employee's salary grows at the rate of inflation, which is 5 percent per year. The interest rate used for discounting nominal annuities is 9 percent per year.

Table 4. Present value of new benefits earned (as a proportion of salary)

Year of Employment	Without Salary Projection	With Salary Projection	Fully Indexed Pension
1	.32%	2.12%	4.70%
10	.98	2.97	6.13
20	3.10	4.32	8.24
30	9.18	6.28	11.07
40	26.08	9.13	14.88
Steady State	6.40	4.82	8.86

Assumptions: The plan pays a benefit equal to 1 percent of final salary per year of service. Plan participants enter the plan at age 25, retire at age 65, and live until age 85. The employee's salary grows at the rate of inflation, which is five percent per year. The riskless real rate of interest is 3 percent per year, and the nominal rate used for discounting nominal annuities is 9 percent per year. The steady-state values assume an equal age distribution of plan participants (age range from 25 to 85).

benefit after one year of service is 300×1.05^{40} or $2,112 per year. The present value of this deferred annuity is $669. This is the PBO.

Figure 3 and the second column of table 4 show the profile of the present value of new benefits earned (as a proportion of salary) in each year. This is the amount the sponsor (or the sponsor and the beneficiary in a contributory DB plan) would have to contribute to the pension fund in order to provide the eventual benefit earned in that year. Figure 4 and table 5 show the value of the employee's accrued benefits (as a proportion of salary) at the end of each year. This represents the amount of money that the employee would be entitled to if the plan were terminated or if the employee left at that time.

The different columns in tables 4 and 5 and the curves in figures 3 and 4 correspond to three different assumptions about how benefits are adjusted for inflation. The first assumes no inflation adjustment other than through the final pay benefit formula (labeled

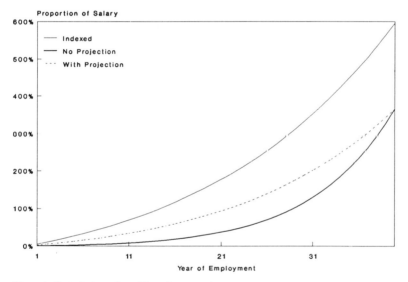

Figure 4. Cumulative value of benefits earned

Notes: Indexed = Indexed Benefit Obligation (IBO)
No Projection = Accumulated Benefit Obligation (ABO)
With Projection = Projected Benefit Obligation (PBO)

Table 5. Cumulative value of benefits earned (as a proportion of salary)

Year of Employment	ABO	PBO	IBO
1	.32%	2.12%	4.70%
10	6.88	29.74	61.29
20	32.58	86.43	164.75
30	115.68	188.43	332.11
40	365.14	365.14	595.10
Steady State	128.33	155.84	247.66

Assumptions: Same as for table 4.

"no projection" and ABO). The second assumes that benefits are indexed for inflation up to the age of retirement regardless of whether the employee continues to accrue new benefits (labeled "with projection" and PBO). The third assumes that there is full indexation of benefits both before and after retirement (labeled "indexed" and IBO).

All three accrual profiles in figure 3 are "backloaded," that is, the present value of pension benefits earned is a much larger proportion of salary in the later years than in the earlier years. This backloading is attributable to two factors: the time value of money and inflation. The older the worker, the closer the date of retirement, and therefore the higher the present value of an additional dollar of pension benefits.

For the indexed plan, the degree of backloading and the value of benefits earned over a career are independent of the rate of inflation. In the other two plans, however, inflation both increases backloading and reduces the value of benefits earned.

Inflation increases backloading of the first two plans for two reasons. First, it increases the nominal rate of interest, thus accentuating the time value of money factor already mentioned. Second, given the benefit formula and our assumption that salary increases at the rate of inflation, inflation creates an indexation component in the benefit earned each year. With each year of continued employment, the present value of the benefit earned increases both because the number of years of service increases and because the nominal salary base increases.

Note that at retirement the ABO and the PBO have the same value. They differ only in how much the sponsor is assumed to owe the worker before retirement. The PBO would be the correct number to use if benefits were tied to some index of prices or wages up to the age of retirement independently of whether the employee stays with the employer. Because private plans in the United States do not offer such automatic indexation, however, it is a mistake to use the PBO as the measure of what the sponsor owes.[36]

In contrast to the situation in the United States, current law in the United Kingdom requires pension sponsors to index accrued pension benefits for inflation to the age of retirement.[37] Thus even a terminated employee has indexation for general inflation up to retirement age, as long as the benefit is vested. Under the U.K. system, the PBO is the appropriate measure of the sponsor's liability.

The indexed benefit obligation or IBO is the present value of the pension liability assuming indexation for inflation both before and after retirement. Figures 3 and 4 and tables 4 and 5 show that inflation indexation makes an enormous difference to the value of pension benefits, even when the rate of inflation is a modest 5 percent per year. Without indexation, at retirement a plan participant would have benefits with a lump-sum equivalent value of 3.65 times final salary. With indexation it would be 5.95 times final salary, an increase of 63 percent.

Figures 3 and 4 and tables 4 and 5 give some useful insights into the costs of providing deferred annuities under DB plans both with and without indexation for inflation. In contributory DB plans the pattern of employee contributions often does not match the backloaded pattern of the economic costs of providing the accruing benefits.

The Social Security system in the United States is an example of a DB plan in which the level and pattern of contributions do not match the accrual pattern of benefits. There can be incentives for individuals to exploit such a system when given a choice about when to join. By not joining until late in their working careers when the present value of the benefits to be earned exceeds the present value of the contributions to be paid, they can gain a great advantage. The same would be true in a private contributory DB plan in which the contribution rate is independent of age.[38]

6.3. Funding Policy

While DC plans are by definition fully funded, DB plans can be funded to any degree. In some countries, most notably West Germany and Japan, corporations fund their pension liabilities to a very limited extent—private DB plans are "pay-as-you-go." In the United States, plan sponsors can fund their DB plans either by insuring them through an insurance company or by setting up a special pension trust.

Why and how does funding matter? Funding matters a great deal, but not for the reason usually offered by proponents of funded pensions—namely, that it increases national saving. First, funding can affect benefit security, or at least it can determine who bears the cost of providing benefit security. Funding also affects pension investment policy. Without funding there are no pension assets to be managed because the pension savings are all invested in the sponsoring corporation. Let us examine these issues more closely.

How does pension funding affect benefit security? First, consider why it might not matter.[39] Suppose sponsors have completely unfunded DB pension plans. Each year benefits accrue to the plan participants. These benefits are guaranteed by the sponsor. This means the pension plan beneficiaries have a claim on the sponsor similar to the claim of other creditors—a pension liability collateralized by the assets of the sponsor. If the plan sponsor is a good credit risk, then the promised benefits are secure. Even if the sponsor is not a good credit risk, though, the promised benefits can be secure if they are guaranteed by a third party such as the Pension Benefit Guaranty Corporation (PBGC) in the United States.

Now assume full funding of the plans. Assume that sponsors fund their plans by issuing stocks and bonds to other sponsors. Each pension trust will now hold a diversified portfolio of securities issued by the other plan sponsors. In the aggregate, no new saving takes place, and no new real assets are created as a result of funding. Funding simply amounts to the transfer of securities among plan sponsors, but does not change the value of the benefits. If the government is insuring pension benefits, funding will shift much of the cost of providing this insurance away from the government to the plan sponsors.

How, then, can funding affect benefit security? Suppose benefits can be represented as a perpetual annuity of b per year. The present value of that perpetual annuity is $b/(r + \delta)$ where r is the risk-free interest rate and δ a risk premium reflecting the default risk of the benefits. Funding can increase the present value of benefits in two ways.

First, if there is funding, the pension obligation is collateralized by a more diversified portfolio of assets, thus reducing the risk of default on the pension obligation. Therefore, δ is reduced, and the present value of benefits increases. This assumes that government insurance of pension benefits is only partial. If government insurance is complete, then once again funding just shifts the cost of providing it from the government to the sponsors.

Second, if the plan is funded, it is possible that the sponsor will increase benefits voluntarily. For example, ad hoc benefit increases during periods of high inflation may be related to the pension surplus. If true, this would also increase the present value of benefits.

It should be clear from this discussion that the funding of defined benefit liabilities has no impact on personal saving except insofar as it affects the present value of promised benefits. Many of the critics of unfunded public pension systems have argued that private pensions increase national saving because they are funded.[40] The debate has been clouded by the following fallacy.

6.4. Fallacy 4: pension benefits are part of saving only if they are funded

From an economic point of view, a pension benefit entitlement is part of labor compensation when it is earned, and the present value of the accrued benefit is part of personal wealth whether or not it is funded. The fallacious belief that it is not stems from the way benefits under DB plans are treated in the national accounts.

In the United States, only contributions by plan sponsors are treated as part of labor compensation and personal saving.[41] This accounting practice does not make sense, for when employees earn an additional dollar in present value of pension benefits, they are lending that amount to the sponsoring corporation. Conceptually, the obligation is exactly the same as accrued wages. Funding the accrued benefit by making a contribution to the pension fund merely collateralizes the sponsor's obligation; it does not alter its amount or nature.

Clearly, with unfunded pension plans there are no pension assets to be managed. The pension fund is, in effect, a captive insurance subsidiary of the sponsoring corporation. This has an important implication: there can be no competition in the international pension asset management market if all pension funds are completely unfunded.

Why do employers fund their DB plans? Reasons can vary across countries. Let us consider the case of a U.S. pension fund. In this country, there are at least four reasons why firms fund their defined benefit pension plans.

First, there are minimum standards imposed by law. The purpose of these standards is to insure the promised pension benefits against the risk of default by the corporate sponsor and to protect the government (and therefore the taxpayer) from abuse of the insurance provided by the government. Recent changes in the law in the United States have made the insurance premium charged by the PBGC a function of the degree of underfunding and eliminated the possibility of voluntary termination of an underfunded pension plan.[42]

Second, there are big tax incentives for plan sponsors to fund their DB plans. Black (1980) and Tepper (1981) have shown that the tax advantage to pension funding stems from the ability of the sponsor to earn the pretax interest rate on pension investments. To maximize the value of this tax shelter, it is necessary to invest entirely in assets offering the highest pretax interest rate. Because dividends from investment in common and preferred stock are taxed at a much lower rate than interest on bonds, corporate pension funds, therefore, should invest entirely in taxable bonds and other fixed-income investments. Recent changes in U.S. tax laws have reduced the ability of pension plans to overfund, but sponsors still are allowed to make additional tax-qualified contributions as long as pension assets represent less than 150 percent of the current liability.[43]

Third, funding its pension plan provides the sponsoring corporation with financial "slack" that can be used in case of possible financial difficulties the firm may face in the future.[44] Because the law still allows plan sponsors facing financial distress to draw upon excess pension assets by reduced funding or, in the extreme case, voluntary plan termination, the pension fund effectively serves as a tax-sheltered corporate contingency fund.

Finally, in the United States, PBGC insurance covers only a portion of the promised benefits for the highly compensated plan participants. Funding provides a cushion of safety for this group, which includes top corporate management.[45]

Most pension plans in the United States are overfunded. Bodie and Papke (1990) estimate that in 1986, 76 percent of single employer pension plans had assets whose market value exceeded the present value of accumulated benefits. After adjusting to a common interest rate, the average asset to liability ratio in the sample is 1.74.

6.5. Pension investment strategies

If a corporate pension fund has an ABO that exceeds the market value of its assets, FASB Statement 87 requires that the corporation recognize the unfunded liability on its balance sheet. If, however, the pension assets exceed the ABO, the corporation cannot include the surplus on its balance sheet.

This asymmetric accounting treatment expresses a deeply held view about DB pension funds. Representatives of organized labor, some politicians, and even a few pension professionals believe that, as guarantor of the accumulated pension benefits, the sponsoring corporation is liable for pension asset shortfalls but does not have a clear right to the entire surplus in case of pension overfunding.

The question of ownership of the pension surplus is a central issue in the theory of corporate pension policy. Current law specifies that the employer owns the surplus as long as specific standards are satisfied.[46] Most of the academic finance literature has assumed that the sponsoring corporation owns the entire surplus, and therefore that the pension fund balance sheet can be consolidated with the balance sheet of the sponsoring corporation. According to this approach, the economic significance of the pension trust is that it provides shareholders with an opportunity for tax arbitrage and the possibility of exploiting PBGC insurance under certain circumstances.[47]

The case for viewing the surplus as belonging entirely to the shareholders rests on the idea that even if a sponsor cannot immediately get the entire pension surplus through a plan termination, in the long run a sponsor can always get the pension surplus out by reducing its future level of funding. The case for viewing shareholder ownership of the pension surplus as less than complete is that virtually all parties to the pension contract view plan beneficiaries as having some claim to the pension surplus.

In the United States, there are now substantial tax penalties for terminating an overfunded pension plan. Some legislators have proposed measures that would require sponsors to use surplus pension assets to provide retroactive inflation protection of benefits. But even in the absence of such legislation, sponsors behave as if the corporation's shareholders and the plan beneficiaries actually share ownership.[48]

What are the economic consequences of shareholders owning less than 100 percent of the pension surplus? The corporate guarantee of the ABO is in effect a put option on the investments of the pension fund with an exercise price equal to the present value of the ABO. The pension fund net worth is analogous to a call option.

According to the theory of option pricing, if the volatility of the underlying security's price increases, then the put and the corresponding call option will both increase in value by the same amount.[49] In the case of a defined benefit pension fund, if the value of both the corporate pension guarantee (a corporate liability) and the pension fund net worth (only partially a corporate asset) increase by the same amount, the value of corporate equity must go down.

One way to minimize the cost of the benefit guarantee to the corporation's shareholders is to immunize the pension liability.[50] If the plan sponsor has to pay $100 per year for the next five years, it can hedge (immunize) this stream of benefit obligations by buying a set of five zero-coupon bonds each with a face value of $100 and each maturing sequentially starting one year from now. Once having purchased the five zeros, the plan sponsor could put them away and forget about its obligation. There is no risk of a shortfall and therefore no cost to the sponsor of insuring the plan participants against it.

Pension fund pursuit of such immunization strategies is in some ways behind the innovations of the past ten years. It has created a demand for fixed-income instruments with a guaranteed duration. Financial instruments such as zero coupon bonds, collateralized mortgage obligations (CMOs), guaranteed investment contracts (GICs), and interest rate future contracts can be viewed, at least in part, as a market response to this demand. These products all offer ways to eliminate duration uncertainty from traditional bonds and mortgages.

If the pension fund is overfunded, then a 100 percent fixed-income portfolio is no longer required to minimize the cost of the corporate pension guarantee. Management can invest surplus pension assets in equities, provided it reduces the proportion so invested when the market value of pension assets comes close to the value of the ABO. Such an investment strategy is a type of portfolio insurance known as contingent immunization.

To understand how contingent immunization works, consider a simple version of it that makes use of a stop-loss order. Imagine that the ABO is $100 and that the fund has $120 of assets entirely invested in equities. The fund can protect itself against downside risk by maintaining a stop-loss order on all its equities at a price of $100. This means that should the price of the stocks fall to $100, the fund manager would liquidate all the stocks and immunize the ABO. A stop-loss order at $100 is not a perfect hedge because there is no guarantee that the sell order can be executed at a price of $100. The result of a series of stop-loss orders at prices starting well above $100 is even better protection against downside risk.

Even without PBGC insurance, an underfunded pension plan has less incentive to immunize than a fully funded plan. This is because the sensitivity of the value of the corporate pension guarantee to the volatility of the fund's investment portfolio is greatest when the ABO equals the value of the pension assets and declines as the level of funding falls.

In the United States, PBGC insurance creates an additional incentive for an under-funded pension fund to invest in risky assets. Briefly, the PBGC's insurance of pension benefits in effect gives the sponsoring firm a put option. The value of this PBGC put increases with the risk of the underlying asset, but the cost of the insurance to the sponsor does not.

Before the Single-Employer Pension Plan Amendments Act of 1986, even healthy firms with underfunded pension plans had some incentive to exploit this PBGC put by volun-tarily terminating an underfunded plan.[51] The new law has eliminated this possibility. Firms in financial distress, however, still have an incentive to invest pension fund money in the riskiest assets, just as troubled thrift institutions insured by the Federal Savings and Loan Insurance Corporation (FSLIC) have had similar motivation with respect to their loan portfolios.

If the only goal guiding corporate pension policy were shareholder wealth maximization, it would be hard to understand why a financially sound pension sponsor would invest in equities at all. A policy of 100 percent bond investment would both maximize the tax advan-tage of funding the pension plan and minimize the cost of guaranteeing the defined benefits.

Yet we know that in general pension funds invest from 40 percent to 60 percent of their portfolios in equity securities.[52] There are at least four possible explanations.

The first is that corporate management views the pension plan as a trust for the employees and manages the fund as if it were a defined contribution plan. Management may be willing to subordinate the goal of shareholder value maximization to the goal of satisfying the risk-return preferences of plan participants.

The second possible explanation is that management believes that through superior market timing and security selection it is possible to create value in excess of management fees and expenses. This would be seen as reducing pension costs through superior invest-ment performance. Many executives in nonfinancial corporations are used to creating value in excess of cost in their businesses, and they assume this can also be done in the area of portfolio management. Of course, if that is true, one must ask why they do not do it on corporate account rather than in the pension fund. That way they could have their tax shelter cake and eat it, too.

The third possible explanation is that management has a mistaken view of the suitabil-ity of equity securities as a hedge. Some plan sponsors and money managers think that investing in equities provides a hedge against inflation. We have already explained the fallacy associated with this view.

The fourth possible explanation is that plan sponsors hold the fallacious view that they can reduce ex ante plan costs by investing in equities even if they do not outper-form the market.

6.6. Fallacy 5: a pension sponsor can reduce ex ante plan costs by investing more in stocks

The reasoning behind this fallacy is as follows. A pension plan sponsor must make contributions to the pension fund in order to produce enough of a cash flow in the future to pay benefits promised to employees. These contributions are called the plan's costs.

To compute the contributions required to fund the pension plan, actuaries assume a certain expected rate of return on the pension fund investment portfolio. If the sponsor increases the expected return by investing a higher proportion in stocks, presumably it can reduce contributions, that is, the ex ante plan costs.

The problem with this reasoning is that it ignores the fact that increasing the proportion invested in stocks also increases the risk of the portfolio. In an efficient capital market, where risk is appropriately priced, there is no way to reduce ex ante risk-adjusted pension costs. Many actuaries nevertheless claim that one can perform this portfolio magic because pension funds have very long investment horizons, and, therefore, for them stocks are not really risky. So we are back to Fallacy 1.

To see the fallacy in assuming that a sponsor can reduce its ex ante plan costs simply by investing in stocks instead of bonds, consider the case of a pension fund with an obligation to pay $2,054 nine years from now. At a continuously compounded interest rate of 8 percent per year, this obligation has a present value of $1,000. In order to immunize the liability the sponsor could invest $1,000 in a default-free zero coupon bonds maturing in nine years. According to the fallacious view, if it invests in stocks with an expected return of 16 percent per year, the sponsor can fund the liability by investing only $487 ($2,054$e^{-.16*9}$).

But suppose the sponsor wants to eliminate the risk of a shortfall. It can eliminate all uncertainty about the future value of the stock portfolio by buying a put option and selling a call option both maturing in nine years with an exercise price of $2,054. The net cost of doing this would be $513, so the total cost today of providing the $2,054 in nine years would be $1,000 (that is, $486 invested in stocks plus $536 for the put less $23 that it gets for selling the call).[53] In other words, the sponsor would be indifferent between investing $1,000 in zero coupon bonds maturing in nine years or investing in a completely insured stock portfolio that would produce the same end result.

There is one sense in which the long-run nature of a pension fund's liabilities might legitimately influence their investment policies in a way that would earn them a higher risk-adjusted return. Pension funds usually have less of a need for liquidity than other investors. Therefore, they should tilt their investment portfolio toward those investments that offer a liquidity premium. Rather than invest in U.S. Treasury bonds, pension funds should prefer U.S. Agency bonds, which are less liquid and offer a slightly higher return. Similarly, pension funds should prefer privately placed bonds and mortgages to publicly traded ones.

7. U.S. pension funds and the capital markets

In the last fifteen years, the investment policies of pension funds have had a profound effect on the U.S. capital markets. They have affected the rate and direction of financial innovations, the behavior of security prices and rates of return, and the policies of the corporations whose securities they hold. Let us consider some of these effects.

7.1. Financial innovation as a response to the investment demands of pension funds

Most of the innovations in the fixed-income securities markets since the early 1970s have come in response to an underlying increase in the level and volatility of interest rates. These interest rate developments were triggered largely by the inflationary trend that began in the late 1960s.

Figure 5 shows the history of the 10-year moving average inflation rate and the interest rate on 10-year Treasury bonds from 1958 to 1988. If we take the moving average of past inflation rates as a proxy for the expected rate of inflation, we can explain the trend in long-term interest rates almost entirely by the trend in expected inflation.

The initial response to the high and unpredictable interest rates of the early 1970s was the emergence of an active market for floating rate debt, as both borrowers and lenders shied away from long-term commitments at fixed rates. Smith and Taggart (1989) point to Citicorp's $850 million issue in 1974 as the key development in this area. Many bond market analysts at that time were predicting a permanent shortening of the maturity structure of fixed rate debt and a complete transition to floating rate corporate debt and adjustable rate mortgages. The last thing they imagined was a surge in the exact opposite direction.

But then came ERISA. In 1974 Congress passed the Employee Retirement Income Security Act and in one bold stroke transformed the structure of institutional demand for fixed-income securities. Two critical features of ERISA for the capital markets are its codification of the legal status of corporate defined benefit pension obligations and its

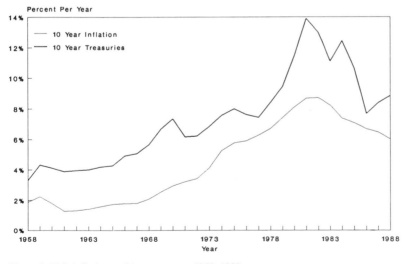

Figure 5. U.S. inflation and interest rates: 1958–1988

Note: The inflation rate is a 10-year moving average of the annual change in the CPI.
Source: The 10-year Treasury bond interest rate—*Economic Report of the President 1989*, table B-71. The rate of inflation—Bureau of Labor Statistics.

imposition of minimum funding requirements. Both provisions of the new law created strong incentives for pension sponsors to hedge. The new age of bond immunization and duration matching began, creating a demand for fixed-income securities with a known duration.

The demand for long duration fixed-income securities was not new. Life insurance companies always had an investment demand for long-term fixed-income securities to hedge their whole-life and annuity products. But consumer demand for these products went into eclipse in the 1970s because of the inflationary bulge and resulting high interest rates. Sales of new policies fell sharply, and loans to policyholders at contractual interest rates as low as 4 percent per year were siphoning funds away at a pace that alarmed insurance executives.

Eventually, the inflation and interest rate uncertainty of the 1970s led the insurance industry to innovate in the retail market of the 1980s. Companies designed universal life and variable life insurance policies offering interest rates that were both higher and more adjustable than those embodied in traditional whole-life policies. Joining forces with mutual funds, the life insurance industry also started offering insured savings plans that allowed a broader spectrum of investment instruments, including money market funds and common stocks. Thus retail demand in the insurance market has led to a shortening of the maturity structure of life insurance company investments.

The more recent demand for long-term fixed-income securities has come primarily from pension funds. Life insurance companies have played an important role in this market both by directly assuming pension fund liabilities and by providing guaranteed investment contracts (GICs) to pension funds.[54] Thus life insurance company demand for long duration debt securities derives ultimately from the demand by pension funds.

The development of collateralized mortgage obligations (CMO's) is a good example of how the demand for fixed-income securities with a known duration has led to the creation of new markets. CMOs came about because of the problem of prepayment risk associated with mortgage-backed securities. The CMO reduces this risk by dividing the cash flows from mortgage-backed securities into a series of classes called tranches. The fast-pay tranche receives all the principal payments made on the entire mortgage pool until the total investment of the investors in the tranche is repaid. In the meantime, investors in the other tranches receive only the interest on their investment. In this way, the fast-pay tranche is retired first and is the shortest-term mortgage-backed security. The next tranche then receives all of the principal payments until it is retired, and so on, until the slow-pay tranche, the longest-term class, finally receives payback of principal after all other tranches have been retired.

While the immunization strategies of pension funds have spurred innovation in the fixed-income securities markets, contingent immunization strategies have created a market for index options and futures contracts. These contracts offer two types of advantages to pension funds. First, it is often cheaper to implement dynamic hedging strategies in derivative securities markets, and second, there is often a tax advantage to doing so.

The tax advantage stems from the way options and futures trades are taxed in the United States. Trading gains on options and futures are taxed at a higher effective rate than those on stocks. An investor can replicate the payoff to a stock portfolio by investing in bonds and taking a long position in stock index futures. Because they are tax-exempt, pension funds can earn a higher return using the bonds-plus-futures approach.[55]

7.2. Market indexing and program trading

A practice that has become very popular among pension funds in the last 10 years, especially those engaging in contingent immunization, is market indexing. Indexing consists of managing a portfolio so as to match the performance of some broad market index of either stocks, bonds, or a combination of both.

Index trading does not necessarily mean that pension funds have stopped trying to beat the market. Indeed, active market timing strategies can most readily be implemented using broad market indexes. Managers seeking to find mispriced individual securities might still want to invest their core portfolio in broad market indexes.

The growing popularity of indexing among pension funds has fueled the development of new markets for index futures and options contracts. It has proven to be much cheaper and more convenient to implement index trades on these derivative markets rather than on the conventional security exchanges.

The existence of markets for derivative securities means that, at times, arbitrage is possible if relative prices get out of line. In order to exploit arbitrage opportunities, it has been necessary to develop sophisticated computer software and trading technology. The techniques developed by securities firms for themselves and for their institutional clients have come to be known as program trading. The term is often used synonymously with index arbitrage.

Some have criticized pension funds and their professional money managers for these new trading practices and market innovations. When directed at index arbitrage, the criticism is unjustified. In fact, index arbitrage enhances economic efficiency by insuring that the prices of the underlying securities and their derivatives stay in line.

Competition from the futures and options markets has forced the conventional exchanges to introduce some innovations. Recently, for example, the New York Stock Exchange started to allow basket trading of stocks. Eventually, an increase in basket trading will eliminate the profitability of program trading by making it less costly to do index arbitrage.

7.3. Portfolio insurance and market volatility

Program trading has been blamed for increasing stock market volatility. The criticism, however, should not be directed at program trading per se but rather at the dynamic hedging strategies used by pension funds to provide protection against shortfall risk. If funds automatically liquidate their stock portfolios when the market starts to go down, this is likely to accentuate a market downturn. Many critics of portfolio insurance have pointed out that massive selling by pension funds may have contributed to the severity of the October 1987 stock market crash.

The crash of 1987 taught pension funds a valuable lesson about the difference between true insurance against shortfall risk (a put option) and "synthetic" insurance produced through dynamic hedging. For many institutions, the synthetic insurance did not work as well as expected. One effect may be to encourage greater use of index puts in the future.[56]

7.4. Excessive churning and speculation

Pension funds have also come under criticism for excessive churning and short-sightedness involving dire consequences for the national economy. Senator Kassebaum and others, for example, maintain that the investment practices of pension funds are partly responsible for American business myopia. They argue that American productivity and the U.S. competitive position in the world economy are jeopardized by this situation.[57]

It is difficult for most finance professionals to go along with these criticisms. Most pension fund equity managers search for stocks whose intrinsic values (based on long-run expectations of cash flow) exceed their current price, and they sell them when they believe their prices exceed intrinsic value. Professional equity managers usually employ discounted cash flow models that incorporate estimates of corporate outflows and inflows well into the future.[58] In these circumstances it is not unusual for firms with little or no current earnings or net cash inflow to command substantial prices for their stock. Biotech firms are a good example.

Professional equity managers tend to be well informed. There is overwhelming evidence that stock prices react to new information very quickly. Indeed, stock prices often start to move in response to new information even before such information is officially announced.[59] Often, investment professionals have a more accurate understanding of the prospects of a firm or a whole industry than do the managers of the firm. That is why reporters frequently interview security analysts when they want to assess the economic significance of some new technological discovery.

Corporate managers usually try to smooth reported earnings through a judicious choice of accepted accounting alternatives. A negative earnings report is, therefore, taken as a signal that the company's managers were not able to conceal the bad news despite their best efforts.

Typically, an active investment manager will set a target price for a stock thought to be undervalued. If and when that target is reached, the stock is reevaluated. If the stock is thought to be overvalued, it is sold. The Kassebaum bill would discourage this process of active management. The government would instead encourage low-turnover, passive strategies, at the expense of high-turnover active strategies. This would make the stock market less useful as a guide to what the investment community thinks of a firm's future prospects.

7.5. Pension funds and corporate control

A more substantive criticism of pension funds and other institutional investors is that they do not become involved enough in the management of the corporations whose stock they own. Typically, if a pension fund disapproves of a corporation's actions, it will simply sell its stock rather than challenge the corporation's top executives.

In the recent environment of hostile takeovers, the fear of losing shareholder support has been a powerful force pushing management of target firms to take actions to please their institutional investors. At the same time, it is not at all clear that either the national interest or the interests of plan beneficiaries would be better served if pension funds became more actively involved in corporate management.

Excess pension assets have been called a possible lure for corporate raiders. Mitchell and Mulherin (1989) analyze pension plan terminations associated with corporate take-overs during 1980–1987. Citing Jensen's (1986) free cash flow idea and the market for corporate control, the authors argue that excess funds may represent inactive assets and that plan terminations are another aspect of efficient financial restructuring.

7.6. Social investing

Some people have suggested even more ambitious objectives for the management of pension fund assets. They see an opportunity to use pension funds as a means of achieving social and political objectives that are seemingly unrelated to the primary goal of provid-ing retirement benefits. Some examples are: to promote economic growth in depressed regions or industries, to protect the environment against pollution, to fight apartheid in South Africa, or to strengthen trade unions. Pursuit of goals like these is called social investing.

Social investing has had its greatest impact on government and union pension funds.[60] Even there, it has had very limited impact. One study notes that union trustees "become more concerned with the business aspects of the pension fund than with the economic impact."[61]

A recent experiment by TIAA-CREF, a very large DC plan for college faculty and administrators, represents an interesting approach to the issue of social investing. Indi-vidual participants in the plan now can direct any proportion of their pension accumula-tion to a specially designated social investing fund. Thus members are free to make their own tradeoffs between personal retirement income goals and other social goals. The amount of money that will be allocated to this special fund will be watched by all those interested in social investing.

8. The Japanese pension system[62]

It would be inappropriate here to survey the pension systems of every country in the world, or even every major country. Instead, we focus on Japan. The Japanese pension system is an example of one with both important similarities to and differences from the U.S. system. What we learn from this comparison can be extended to any other country.

Most Japanese workers make provision for old age through individual savings. Pension benefits typically are taken as a lump sum and added to these personal savings.

It is customary for employers in the private sector to pay a lump sum benefit to employees on termination of employment regardless of whether termination is due to retirement, death, disability, layoff, or resignation. While not mandatory, these programs cover about 90 percent of employees. The major exceptions are very small firms. A 1976 law established government insurance of these termination benefits up to certain limits, financed through Workmen's Compensation Insurance.

Traditionally, employer-provided termination benefits are financed on a pay-as-you-go basis. The sponsoring company creates a special reserve account on the balance sheet as benefits are accrued. The tax law of 1952 made the benefits partially tax deductible when booked.

Legislation passed in 1962 established Tax-Qualified Pension Plans (TQPPP's), which are very similar to funded pension plans in the United State. In 1989, these funded plans covered about 8.5 million employees or roughly 28 percent of the private sector work force.

In 1966, an amendment of the Employees Pension Insurance Law permitted private companies to "contract out" of the earnings-related portion of Social Security by establishing Employee Pension Funds (EPFs). These plans must be funded. The benefit consists of two components. The first, an "equivalent benefit" equal to the amount payable under Social Security, is financed by joint contributions of employer and employee, and is to be paid in the form of a life annuity. The second part, "the excess benefit," differs by fund, is mostly financed by the employer, and can be taken in a lump sum.

When the law was passed in 1966, there was no inflation indexation of Social Security. An amendment in 1973 introduced indexation, but cost-of-living supplements are payable by the government and not by the contracting-out sponsor. In 1989, EPFs covered roughly 8 million employees, or about 26 percent of those eligible.

Japan also has a defined contribution plan called the Smaller Enterprise Retirement Allowance Mutual Aid Plan, established under a 1959 law. Only employers with 300 or fewer employees are eligible, and contributions are made exclusively by the employer. The benefit amount is fixed according to a table based on monthly contribution and length of participation, and is payable in a lump sum on termination of employment. In 1989, about 2.3 million workers were covered by this plan.

Until December of 1989 all pension assets had to be managed either by trust banks or life insurance companies according to guidelines established by the Ministry of Finance. Table 8 presents both the limits and the actual mix of EPF assets held in trusts. Pension assets managed by insurance companies are subject to similar limits. An amendment to the law passed in December 1989 allows EPFs to manage a portion of their assets in-house or to entrust them to investment advisors.

9. Inflation protection and other innovations

Full cost-of-living adjustment of private pension benefits is rare both in the United States and Japan. It is more common in Europe.[63] As people rely more and more on pensions and private savings to provide their retirement income, there will surely be a growing demand for protection against inflation.

Table 8. Asset mix of Japanese pension trusts

Type of Asset	Ministry of Finance Guidelines	Actual Mix in 1987
Bonds and other fixed income securities	50% or more	54%
Equities	30% or less	26%
Foreign assets	30% or less	16%
Other	*	4%

*A maximum of 20 percent may be invested in real estate.

In some countries, the government has played an active role in providing default-free bonds linked to the consumer price index for pension funds to use as the basis for inflation-protected retirement annuities. In the United Kingdom, the government has gone so far as to mandate the indexation of the minimum level of employer-provided pension benefits, and has issued bonds tied to the retail price index.[64] The government of the Province of Ontario, Canada, seems on the verge of adopting similar measures.[65]

For many years economists have considered it desirable, if not essential, for the U.S. government to issue inflation-linked bonds in order to lay the foundation for private inflation insurance. Economists such as Milton Friedman, Franco Modigliani, and James Tobin, who hold very different opinions on other issues, have been united in their enthusiastic support for the idea of the U.S. Treasury's issuing CPI-linked bonds. Even now many people think that the only entity that can truly guarantee default-free inflation insurance is the government.

While it is, strictly speaking, true that only the government can issue completely default-free index-linked bonds, it is equally true that private insurance can be almost free of default risk. A private insurance company can offer policies that are virtually free of default risk through a combination of three elements: (1) diversifying the risk of its liabilities through risk-pooling (as life insurance companies do with their life insurance policies), (2) hedging the risk of its liabilities through appropriate investment strategies, and (3) maintaining adequate equity capital so that the residual risk that is not diversified away or hedged away by the company's investment strategy is fully absorbed by the company's shareholders.

Inflation insurance is not a diversifiable risk in the aggregate, so the first of the three elements is not available. But diversifiability of risk is neither a necessary nor a sufficient condition for it to be insurable. An insurance company or other financial intermediary can use a combination of the other two elements to provide nearly complete inflation insurance.

These observations imply that what is necessary for inflation insurance to exist is the presence of players in the economy who are willing to bear some part of the risk of inflation at a fair market price. Natural candidates are people or institutions who are "over-indexed" for inflation. Feldstein (1983) and Summers (1983) have maintained that substantial numbers of households at all stages of the life cycle may find themselves in this position.

During their working years, households have their earning power (or human capital) and often own their own homes. Although these assets are not risk-free, they certainly seem to be protected against inflation risk. Wages tend to keep pace with inflation, and residential real estate often does especially well in times of inflation.

For these two reasons, a promising source of CPI-linked investments for an inflation insurance intermediary is CPI-linked home mortgages. The U.S. Department of Housing and Urban Development (HUD) is seriously considering certifying a variety of price-level-adjusted mortgages (PLAMs) for Federal Housing Administration (FHA) approval.[66] PLAMs have often been discussed as a simultaneous solution to the problems of young people seeking affordable mortgage financing and to the problems of old people on money-fixed incomes seeking inflation protection.

For the young, PLAMs address important problems associated with both the conventional fixed-rate and the standard adjustable-rate mortgage designs. Under both of these plans, the payment schedule is a level nominal stream rather than a level real stream. As a result, the monthly payment is often too high a fraction of initial monthly income for the young to qualify for a home mortgage loan. With an ARM, when the monthly mortgage payment is recalculated periodically at the new adjustable interest rate, the borrower can be subject to large fluctuations in the monthly payment.

PLAMs set a monthly payment that is fixed in real terms. The nominal payment is adjusted monthly according to the realized rate of inflation. This implies a graduated schedule of nominal payments with a much lower starting value. Assuming that a home-buyer's earnings adjust for inflation, the monthly mortgage payment is a relatively stable proportion of income.

Once FHA mortgage insurance is available and the tax status of PLAM's is clarified, they could account for a significant portion of new lending in the home mortgage market. Financial intermediaries, such as insurance companies, could then issue inflation-protected retirement annuities using PLAM's as the base.

Fischer (1986) maintains that many business firms may want to issue price-indexed debt in order to reduce their risk. Nonfinancial businesses have shown some willingness to issue debt securities that are indexed to the prices of their output. A financial intermediary could pool such bonds in order to synthesize an investment that hedges annuities indexed to broader price indexes.[67]

In 1988 several financial institutions issued securities linked to the U.S. consumer price level. The new securities were issued first by the Franklin Savings Association of Ottawa, Kansas, in January 1988 in two different forms.[68]

The first is certificates of deposit, called Inflation-Plus CD's, insured by the Federal Savings and Loan Insurance Corporation (FSLIC), and paying an interest rate tied to the Bureau of Labor Statistics Consumer Price Index (CPI). Interest is paid monthly and is equal to a stated real rate plus the proportional increase in the CPI during the previous month.

The second form is 20-year noncallable collateralized bonds, called Real Yield Securities, or REALs. These offer a floating coupon rate equal to a stated real rate plus the previous year's proportional change in the CPI, adjusted and payable quarterly. Two other financial institutions have followed the lead of Franklin Savings.[69]

Recently, federal regulators seized the assets of Franklin Savings Association on technical grounds having nothing to do with the CPI-linked securities issued by Franklin. This action has made clear that while they were free of default risk, these securities were not free of regulatory risk.

With a large market for price-indexed securities and their derivatives, pension plan sponsors and other financial institutions could then offer annuities with inflation insurance features. Sponsors that already offer their employees several investment options for their supplementary savings plans could simply expand the set of alternatives to include CPI-linked securities.

Merton (1983) has proposed a more radical innovation. Instead of indexing retirement annuities to the cost of living, he suggests indexing them to aggregate per capita consumption. With a CPI-linked annuity, the benefit is fixed in real terms regardless of what happens to the standard of living in the economy. According to Merton's scheme, a retiree would receive a benefit that rises or falls with per capita consumption. The motivating idea is that the elderly care more about preserving their income relative to the rest of the population than they do about preserving its absolute value.

One way to understand Merton's proposal is as a defined contribution plan offering variable annuity contracts based on an underlying portfolio of bonds that are indexed to aggregate per capita consumption. Merton envisions a major role for the government in making this type of product possible by providing consumption-indexed bonds that are free of default risk.

In view of the innovative atmosphere in the world's financial markets in recent years, it is conceivable that the private sector can manage to produce something similar without help from the government. A variable annuity based on an underlying portfolio of assets that are highly correlated with aggregate consumption might be almost as good. Perhaps a variable annuity based on an internationally diversified portfolio of securities (the "world market portfolio") would even be preferable for a large class of people.

10. International portfolio diversification

Despite the attention that Japanese pension fund investments in the United States have attracted in recent years, pension funds (whether American or Japanese) do not currently invest much in foreign securities. The scope for increased international diversification is enormous, but the barriers are substantial.

The U.S. government is the only one that imposes no limits on the amount that pension funds can invest abroad. Ironically, the countries that stand to gain the most from international diversification are the ones that impose the most restrictions—those with small domestic capital markets. These governments have been concerned that if they allowed pension funds to invest abroad, there would no longer be enough domestic investment to promote growth of the national economy.

The potential advantages of international diversification for investors have been documented in numerous studies.[70] Diversifying across stock markets in different countries makes it possible to achieve significantly higher expected returns for any given degree of risk. The development of stock index futures markets is making it relatively convenient and inexpensive to achieve international equity diversification. An example is the IMI futures contract traded on the Coffee, Sugar, and Cocoa Exchange in New York City.

Merton (1990) has advanced the idea of using stock index swaps to achieve the benefits of international diversification without the transfer of capital resources. Swaps are very common today in fixed-income securities and foreign exchange, but the idea has not yet been applied to equities or stock indexes. By separating capital flows from risk-sharing, these contracts make it feasible to achieve the benefits of international diversification without creating massive capital flow imbalances.

One would imagine that the potential welfare gains from international equity swaps would be greatest in small countries where there is limited ability to diversify in the domestic capital market. Often these small countries have pension funds that invest a large fraction of the national wealth. Singapore is a good example. If the governments in these countries were to relax their restrictions on foreign investing to allow swaps, they could reap the benefits of increased diversification without fear of capital flight or foreign intervention in the domestic capital market.

11. Summary and conclusion

This article began with some questions. Let us summarize our answers to those questions and draw some conclusions about pensions and the international capital markets.

What are the economic causes and consequences of the funding of pension plans?

The primary reason for funding pension plans is to enhance benefit security. How the funds accumulated for that purpose are invested can have a major impact not only on benefit security but also on other public and private objectives.

With an unfunded DB pension plan, the retirement savings are, in effect, invested in the sponsoring organization. The corporate obligation to pay benefits is a form of debt, which in many countries is guaranteed by the government.

Funded pension plans have become a major element in the flow of funds in the U.S. economy. The search for an improved risk–reward tradeoff by pension funds has spawned a new branch of the financial services industry—professional asset management. Advising pension funds about all phases of the management of assets is a big business.

What are the unique features of pension and retirement funds that might cause them to adopt investment policies that differ from those of other investors?

DC plans are tax-exempt retirement accounts held in trust for the plan beneficiaries. The guiding principle behind investment policy in such a private retirement account is efficient diversification, that is, achieving the maximum expected return for any given level of risk exposure. Tax considerations should cause the investor to tilt the asset mix toward the least tax-advantaged securities.

The pensions offered under DB plans in the United States are best viewed as participating annuities that offer a guaranteed minimum nominal benefit determined by the plan's benefit formula. This guaranteed benefit is permanently enriched from time to time, at the discretion of management, depending on the financial condition of the plan sponsor, the increase in the living costs of retirees, and the performance of the fund's assets. In order to minimize the cost of providing the guarantee, the sponsor has a strong incentive to invest an amount equal to the present value of the accumulated benefit obligation in fixed-income securities with a matching duration.

How have these investment policies affected the capital markets?

Pension funds have played a critical role in the evolution of the markets for debt and equity securities and their derivatives in the United States over the last 15 years. Many of the innovations in the U.S. financial markets during this period can be interpreted as responses to the hedging demands of pension funds or of life insurance companies operating on their behalf. Some examples are the emergence of the markets for zero coupon bonds, GICs, CMOs, options, and financial futures contracts. Index trading, both in the cash and futures markets, is another manifestation.

What are the likely future trends in pension plan asset allocation and their likely effects on the capital markets?

Both in the United States and elsewhere in the industrialized world, the issue of inflation protection of retirement benefits is likely to be a factor of major importance. The opportunities for financial innovation to deal with the problem of inflation risk through some combination of government and private sector initiatives are great.

As the search for an improved risk reward tradeoff grows, trading by pension funds in indexes of all kinds is likely to grow. This will lead to further rapid development of international markets for futures, options, and swaps. It is also likely that the trend toward the professionalization of the asset management business will continue as the accumulations in retirement funds grow.

The basic retirement annuity design in this future environment is likely to be the variable annuity contract. It is flexible enough to satisfy the needs of households for insurance against the main sources of retirement income risk, and it can be adapted to use in defined benefit and defined contribution pension plans as well as in individual retirement accounts.

What are the prospects for international competition and cooperation in the market for retirement income products and services?

As the population of the industrialized countries of the world continues to age, the growth in funded pension plans will lead to an increasing internationalization of their capital markets. In Japan, for example, a mostly unfunded private pension system has moved in the direction of full funding.

Already, investment on behalf of pension funds by Japanese trust banks and insurance companies has had an impact on U.S. securities and real estate markets. The recent decision by Japan's Ministry of Finance to allow plans to manage their own investments offers opportunities for professional money managers from other countries to compete in the Japanese market. A similar trend toward the liberalization of restrictions on international investing by pension funds seems to be under way in the United Kingdom and Canada.

Notes

1. The U.K. was second with 9 percent, as reported by Dialey and Turner (1989).
2. See Hoffman (1989).
3. By definition, employment income is not counted as part of retirement income.
4. See Merton, Bodie, and Marcus (1987).
5. The interested reader is referred to Scholen (1987).
6. See Bodie [1990a] for a more detailed treatment of the material in this section.
7. Another important reason is income redistribution.
8. See Freidman and Warshawsky (1988).
9. It is worth noting that in Japan pension benefits are generally received as a lump sum rather than an annuity.
10. See Merton, Bodie, and Marcus (1987).
11. Social Security redistributes income both within and across generations. See Blinder (1988).
12. See McGill and Grubbs (1989).
13. The principal means of protecting the real value of benefits accrued during the preretirement years is through a benefit formula that ties the retirement benefit to average earnings during the last few years of employment. This form of wage indexation stops at retirement, however.
14. See Clark (1990a).
15. Bodie (1990b) suggests ways to improve the inflation protection provided by these supplementary plans.
16. Examples of firms that have been formed to offer professional management services to pension funds are Wells Fargo Investment Advisers and Batterymarch Financial Management.
17. In a recent survey, Bankers Trust Company (1987) reports that in half of the plans surveyed the employee has an investment choice over employee contributions only.
18. See Gustman and Steinmeier (1989).
19. In the United States, the two main types of individual retirement accounts are IRAs and Keogh plans.
20. For further details and an illustration of this tax-timing feature of stocks, see Bodie, Kane, and Marcus (1989, p. 844).
21. For an elaboration of this point see Kotlikoff and Spivak (1981).
22. For an elaboration on possible combinations see Bodie (1980) and Bodie and Pesando (1983).
23. The mean one-year rate of return on a diversified stock portfolio, like the S&P 500, exceeds the risk-free rate of interest by about 8.5 percent per year with a standard deviation of about 20 percent per year.
24. See Merton (1969, 1971), Merton and Samuelson (1977), and Samuelson (1963, 1969, 1971, 1989).
25. This is a binomial distribution. The distribution of actual stock returns is more like a lognormal distribution. As the length of the holding period gets longer, however, the binomial distribution approximates the lognormal rather closely.
26. In the worst case scenario, the amount of money you will have left after N years is $.8^N$.
27. See Bodie and W. Samuelson (1989). P. Samuelson (1989) offers two other possible reasons for time horizon effects on risk-taking behavior.
28. See Bodie (1976).
29. Once a sponsor increases the benefit under a DB plan, it is never reduced. This distinguishes it from a variable annuity.
30. See Clark, Allen, and Sumner (1983) for a discussion of these ad hoc increases.
31. See, for example, Cohn and Modigliani (1985) or Ippolito (1986).
32. See, for example, VanDerhei and Harrington (1989), Petersen (1989), and Pontiff, Shleifer, and Weisbach (1989). Mitchell and Mulherin (1989) present evidence that terminations of overfunded plans may reflect efficient corporate restructurings rather than the transfer of wealth from plan participants to shareholders.
33. FASB Statement 87 also requires that U.S. multinational corporations value the liabilities of their foreign pension plans in the same manner as their domestic plans.
34. For an alternative view that sees the projected benefit obligation as at least as appropriate a measure see Black (1989), Arnott and Bernstein (1988), and Ambachtsheer (1987).
35. A benefit is vested if the employee is entitled to it even after terminating employment. Most employers require employees to work for some minimum number of years before their benefits are vested.

36. Note, however, that if a plan sponsor makes contributions to the pension fund each year equal to the amounts in the third column of table 2, corresponding to the PBO, then by the time the employee reaches retirement, the amount accumulated in the fund will equal the amount necessary to pay the pension benefits. The projected benefit method is therefore an acceptable actuarial funding method. See Winklevoss (1977).
37. This so-called preservation of pension benefits is subject to a cap of 5 percent per year.
38. In Israel this problem exists in the Histadrut (Labor Federation) pension plan. See Habib and Factor (1979).
39. Some of the ideas discussed in this section can be found in Tepper (1982).
40. Of course, if unfunded pension obligations of public plans are hidden from the public by inadequate accounting practices, then funding can make a difference by forcing disclosure.
41. See Munnell and Yahn (1990).
42. See Utgoff (1988).
43. The relevant law is the Omnibus Budget Reconciliation Act (OBRA) of 1987.
44. See Bodie and associates (1987) for a more complete discussion of the financial slack motive for funding a pension plan.
45. See Light and Perold (1987) for a more complete discussion of this point.
46. See VanDerhei (1988).
47. See the articles by Sharpe (1976), Treynor (1977), Black (1980), Tepper (1981), Harrison and Sharpe (1983), and Bicksler and Chen (1985).
48. See Bulow and Scholes (1983).
49. See, for example, Bodie, Kane, and Marcus (1989, p. 564).
50. See Leibowitz (1986).
51. See Harrison and Sharpe (1983).
52. According to Bodie and Papke (1990).
53. These values were computed using the Black-Scholes (1973) option pricing model.
54. GIC's are essentially zero coupon bonds issued by insurance companies, who hedge the liability by investing in fixed-income securities. While guaranteeing a nominal rate of interest for up to six years, GIC's typically offer investors the option to withdraw their money early with no penalty. They are, therefore, very popular investments in defined contribution plans.
55. Scholes (1976) has shown this for options. His arguments apply to futures as well.
56. See "Crash Prompts New Look for Portfolio Insurance" in *Futures* magazine, February 1988.
57. The Excessive Churning and Speculation Act of 1989 (S.1654), sponsored by Senators Dole and Kassebaum, is intended to reduce stock market turnover by taxing short-term capital gains of pension funds. In explaining the rationale for the proposed law, Senator Kassebaum has said:

    The legislation is designed to encourage pension fund managers to adopt a better long-term investment strategy. . . . Absent such a change, we face the stark prospect of losing our status as a major industrial player.

58. See chapters 17 and 18 of Bodie, Kane, and Marcus (1989) for an explanation of these models.
59. See Bodie, Kane, and Marcus (1989, ch. 13).
60. See Deaton (1989, table 10.4, p. 326).
61. Taken from Rifkin and Barber (1978, p. 254).
62. The data in this section are taken from Yumiba (1990) and Murakami (1990). For further details on the Japanese system also see Clark (1990b).
63. See Clark (1990a).
64. See Hemming and Kay (1982).
65. See Martin Friedland (1988).
66. See Modigliani and Lessard (1975) for a discussion of these mortgage designs.
67. See Blinder (1976).
68. See Bodie (1990d).
69. In August 1988 Anchor Savings Bank became the second U.S. institution to issue REALs, and in September 1988 JHM Acceptance Corporation issued modified index-linked bonds subject to a nominal interest rate cap of 14 percent per annum. The investment banking firm of Morgan Stanley and Company is the underwriter and market maker for REALs. These bonds are not actively traded, however.
70. See, for example, Solnik (1989).

References

Ambachtsheer, Keith P. "Pension Fund Asset Allocation: In Defense of a 60/40 Equity/Debt Asset Mix." *Financial Analysts Journal* (September/October 1987).

Andrews, Emily. *The Changing Profile of Pensions in America*. Washington, DC: Employee Benefit Research Institute, 1985.

Arnott, Robert D. and Peter L. Bernstein. "The Right Way to Manage Your Pension Fund." *Harvard Business Review* (January–February 1988), 95–102.

Bankers Trust Company. *Corporate Defined Contribution Plans: A Changing Environment*. New York, 1987.

Berkowitz, Logue and Associates, Inc. "Study of the Investment Performance of ERISA Plans." Prepared for the Office of Pension and Welfare Benefits, Department of Labor, July 21, 1986.

Bicksler, James and Andrew Chen. "The Integration of Insurance and Taxes in Corporate Pension Strategy." *Journal of Finance* (July 1985), 943–955.

Black, Fischer. "Should You Use Stocks to Hedge Your Pension Liability?" *Financial Analysts Journal* (January/February 1989), 10–12.

Black, Fischer. "The Tax Consequences of Long-Run Pension Policy." *Financial Analysts Journal* (1980), 21–28.

Binder, Alan S. "Indexing the Economy Through Financial Intermediation." Princeton University Econometric Research Program Research Memorandum No. 196, March 1976.

Binder, Alan S. "Why Is the Government in the Pension Business?" In Susan M. Wachter, ed., *Social Security and Private Pensions*. Lexington, MA: Lexington Books, 1988, ch. 2.

Bodie, Zvi. "Common Stocks As a Hedge Against Inflation." *Journal of Finance* (May 1976).

Bodie, Zvi. "An Innovation for Stable Real Retirement Income." *The Journal of Portfolio Management* (Fall 1980), 5–13.

Bodie, Zvi. "Inflation Insurance." *Journal of Risk and Insurance* (December 1990).

Bodie, Zvi. "Pensions as Retirement Income Insurance." *Journal of Economic Literature* (March 1990a).

Bodie, Zvi. "Inflation Protection for Pension Plans." *Compensation and Benefits Management* (Spring 1990b).

Bodie, Zvi. "The ABO, the PBO, and Pension Investment Policy." *Financial Analysts Journal* (September/October 1990c).

Bodie, Zvi. "Inflation, Index-Linked Bonds, and Asset Allocation." *Journal of Portfolio Management* (Winter 1990d).

Bodie, Zvi, Alex Kane, and Alan Marcus. *Investments*. Homewood, IL: Richard D. Irwin, 1989.

Bodie, Zvi, Jay O. Light, Randall Morck, and Robert A. Taggart, Jr. "Corporate Pension Policy: An Empirical Investigation." In Bodie, Shoven, and Wise, eds., *Issues in Pension Economics*. Chicago: University of Chicago Press, 1987, ch. 2.

Bodie, Zvi, Alan J. Marcus, and Robert C. Merton. "Defined Benefit vs. Defined Contribution Pension Plans: What Are the Real Tradeoffs?" In Bodie, Shoven, and Wise, eds., *Pensions in the U.S. Economy*. Chicago: University of Chicago Press, 1988, ch. 5.

Bodie, Zvi and Leslie E. Papke. "Pension Fund Finance." In Bodie and Munnell, eds., *Pensions and the U.S. Economy: The Need for Good Data*. Philadelphia: University of Pennsylvania Press, forthcoming.

Bodie, Zvi and James Pesando. "Retirement Annuity Design in an Inflationary Climate." In Bodie and Shoven, eds., *Financial Aspects of the U.S. Pension System*. Chicago: University of Chicago Press, 1983, ch. 11.

Bodie, Zvi and William Samuelson. "Labor Supply Flexibility and Portfolio Choice." National Bureau of Economic Research Working Paper Number 3043, July 1989.

Bulow, Jeremy. "What are Corporate Pension Liabilities?" *Quarterly Journal of Economics* 97 (August 1982).

Bulow, Jeremy, Randall Morck, and Lawrence Summers. "How Does the Market Value Unfunded Pension Liabilities?" In Bodie, Shoven, and Wise, eds., *Issues in Pension Economics*. Chicago: University of Chicago Press, 1988, ch. 4.

Bulow, Jeremy and Myron Scholes. "Who Owns the Assets in a Defined-Benefit Pension Plan?" In Bodie and Shoven, eds., *Financial Aspects of the U.S. Pension System*. Chicago: University of Chicago Press, 1983, ch. 1.

Clark, Robert L. "Cost of Living Adjustments in International Perspective." In J.A. Turner, ed., *Pension Policy: An International Perspective*. Washington, D.C.: U.S. Government Printing Office, 1990a.

Clark, Robert L. *Retirement Systems in Japan*. Homewood, IL: Dow Jones/Irwin, 1990b.

Clark, Robert L., Steven G. Allen, and Daniel A. Sumner. "Inflation and Pension Benefits." Final report for the Department of Labor Contract No. J-9-P-1-0074, 1983.

Cohn, Richard A. and Franco Modigliani. "Inflation and Corporate Financial Management." In Altman and Subrahmanyam, eds., *Recent Advances in Corporate Finance*. Homewood, IL: Richard D. Irwin, 1985, ch. 13.

Dailey, Lorna and John Turner. "U.S. Pensions in World Perspective." In John A. Turner and Daniel J. Beller, eds., *Trends in Pensions 1989*. Washington, DC: U.S. Government Printing Office, 1989, ch. 2.

Deaton, Richard L. *The Political Economy of Pensions*. Vancouver, BC: UBC Press, 1989.

Feldstein, Martin. "Should Private Pensions Be Indexed?" In Bodie and Shoren, eds., *Financial Aspects of the U.S. Pension System*. Chicago: University of Chicago Press, 1983, ch. 8.

Fischer, Stanley. "The Demand for Index Bonds." *Journal of Political Economy*, 1975; reprinted in *Indexing, Inflation, and Economic Policy*. Cambridge, MA: MIT Press, 1986.

Fischer, Stanley. "On the Nonexistence of Privately Issued Index Bonds in the U.S. Capital Market." In *Indexing, Inflation, and Economic Policy*. Cambridge, MA: MIT Press, 1986, ch. 10.

Friedland, Martin. *Report of the Task Force on Inflation Protection for Employment Pension Plans*. Ontario Government Publication, January 1988.

Friedman, Benjamin M. and Mark Warshawsky. "Annuity Prices and Saving Behavior in the United States." In Bodie, Shoren, and Wise, eds., *Pensions in the U.S. Economy*. Chicago: University of Chicago Press, 1988, ch. 2.

Greenwich Research Associates. *Report on Large Corporate Pension Plans*. 1988.

Gustman, Alan L. and Thomas L. Steinmeier. "The Stampede Toward Defined Contribution Pension Plans: Fact or Fiction?" Unpublished paper, August 1989.

Habib, Jack and Haim Factor. "The Pension System in Israel." Brookdale Institute of Gerontology in Israel Reprint Series No. R-4-79, 1979.

Harrison, Michael J. and William F. Sharpe. "Optimal Funding and Asset Allocation Rules for Defined Benefit Pension Plans." In Bodie and Shoren, eds., *Financial Aspects of U.S. Pension Systems*. Chicago: University of Chicago Press, 1983, ch. 4.

Hemming, Richard and John Kay. "The Costs of the State Earnings Related Pension Scheme." *Economic Journal* 92, 366 (1982).

Hoffman, A.J. "Pension Assets and the Economy." In J.A. Turner and D.J. Beller, eds., *Trends in Pensions*. Washington, D.C.: U.S. Government Printing Office, 1989.

Ippolito, Richard A. "The Economic Burden of Corporate Pension Liabilities." *Financial Analysts Journal* (January/February 1986), 22–34.

Jensen, Michael C. "Agency Costs of Free Cash Flow, Corporate Finance, and Takeovers." *American Economic Review* 76 (May 1986), 323–329.

Kotlikoff, Laurence J. and Avia Spivak. "The Family as an Incomplete Annuities Market." *Journal of Political Economy* 89 (1981), 372–391.

Langetieg, T.C., M.C. Findlay, and L. da Motta. "Multiperiod Pension Plans and ERISA." *Journal of Financial and Quantitative Analysis* 17 (1982), 603–631.

Leibowitz, Martin L. "The Dedicated Bond Portfolio in Pension Funds." *Financial Analysts Journal* 42, 1 and 2 (January/February and March/April 1986).

Leland, Hayne E. and Mark Rubinstein. "The Evolution of Portfolio Insurance." In Donald Luskin, ed., *Portfolio Insurance*. New York: John Wiley and Sons, 1988, ch. 1.

Light, Jay O. and Andre F. Perold. "Risk Sharing and Corporate Pension Policies." Harvard Business School Working Paper, October 1987.

McGill, Dan M. and Donald Grubbs. *Fundamentals of Private Pensions*, 6th ed. Homewood, IL: Richard D. Irwin, 1989.

Merton, Robert C. "On the Application of the Continuous-Time Theory of Finance to Financial Intermediation and Insurance." The Geneva Papers on Risk and Insurance, Vol. 14, No. 52, July 1989; reprinted in Merton, R.C. *Continuous-Time Finance*. Oxford: Basil Blackwell, 1990.

Merton, Robert C. "The Financial System and Economic Performance." (This issue)

Merton, Robert C. "On Consumption-Indexed Public Pension Plans." In Bodie and Shoven, eds., *Financial Aspects of the U.S. Pension System*. Chicago: University of Chicago Press, 1983, ch. 10.

Merton, Robert C. "Lifetime Portfolio Selection by Dynamic Stochastic Programming: The Continuous Time Case." *Review of Economics and Statistics* 51 (August 1969).

Merton, Robert C. "Lifetime Consumption and Portfolio Rules in a Continuous Time Model." *Journal of Economic Theory* (1971).

Merton, Robert C., Zvi Bodie, and Alan Marcus. "Pension Plan Integration as Insurance Against Social Security Risk." In Bodie, Shoven, and Wise, eds., *Issues in Pension Economics*. Chicago: University of Chicago Press, 1987, ch. 6.

Merton, Robert C. and Paul A. Samuelson. "Fallacy of the Log—Normal Approximation to Portfolio Decision-Making Over Many Periods." *Journal of Financial Economics* 1, pp. 67-94; reprinted in Friend and Bicksler, eds., *Risk and Return in Finance*. New York: Heath Lexington, 1977.

Mitchell, M. L. and J. H. Mulherin. "Pensions and Mergers." In J.A. Turner and D.J. Beller, eds., *Trends in Pensions*. Washington, DC: U.S. Department of Labor, Pension and Welfare Benefits Administration, 1989.

Modigliani, Franco and Donald Lessard, eds., *New Mortgage Designs for Stable Housing in an Inflationary Environment*. Federal Reserve Bank of Boston, Conference Series No. 14, 1975.

Munnell, Alicia and J. Grolnic. "Should the U.S. Government Issue Index Bonds?" *New England Economic Review* (September/October 1986), 3-21.

Munnell, Alicia and F. Yahn. "Pensions and Saving." In Bodie and Munnell, eds., *Pensions and the U.S. Economy: The Need for Good Data*. Philadelphia: University of Pennsylvania Press, forthcoming.

Murakami, Kiyoshi. "Severance and Retirement Benefits in Japan." Paper presented at U.S. Department of Labor International Conference on Private Pension Policy, February 1990.

Petersen, Mitchell. "Pension Terminations and Worker-Stockholder Wealth Transfers." Working Paper, MIT, 1989.

Pontiff, Jeremy, Andrei Shleifer, and Michael Weisbach. "Reversions of Excess Pension Assets After Take-overs." Working Paper, June 1989.

Rifkin, Jeremy and Randy Barber. *The North Will Rise Again: Pensions, Politics, and Power in the 1980s*. Boston: Beacon Press, 1978.

Samuelson, Paul A. "Risk and Uncertainty: A Fallacy of Large Numbers." *Scientia*, 6th Series, 57th year (April–May 1963), 1-6.

Samuelson, Paul A. "Lifetime Portfolio Selection by Dynamic Stochastic Programming." *Review of Economics and Statistics* 51, 3 (August 1969), 239-246.

Samuelson, Paul A. "The Fallacy of Maximizing the Geometric Mean in Long Sequences of Investing or Gambling." *Proceedings of the National Academy of Science* 68 (1971), 207-211.

Samuelson, Paul A. "The Judgement of Economic Science on Rational Portfolio Management: Timing and Long-Horizon Effects." *Journal of Portfolio Management* (Fall 1989), 4-12.

Scholen, Ken. "Home-Made Money: Consumers Guide to Home Equity Conversion." Washington, DC: American Association of Retired Persons, 1987.

Scholes, Myron. "Taxes and the Pricing of Options." *Journal of Finance* (May 1976), 319-332.

Sharpe, William F. "Corporate Pension Funding Policy." *Journal of Financial Economics* 3 (1976), 183-193.

Smith, Donald J. and Robert A. Taggart, Jr. "Innovations in the Bond Market and the Changing Business of Financial Intermediaries." June 1989.

Solnik, Bruno. *International Investment*, 1989.

Summers, Lawrence. "Observations on the Indexation of Old Age Pensions." In Bodie and Shoven, eds., *Financial Aspects of the U.S. Pension System*. Chicago: University of Chicago Press, 1983, ch. 9.

Tepper, Irwin. "Taxation and Corporate Pension Policy." *Journal of Finance* (March 1981), 1-13.

Tepper, Irwin. "The Future of Private Pension Funding." *Financial Analysts Journal* (January/February 1982).

Treynor, Jack L. "The Principles of Corporate Pension Finance." *Journal of Finance* (1977), 627-638.

Turner, John A. and Daniel J. Beller, eds. *Trends in Pensions 1989*. Washington, DC: U.S. Government Printing Office, 1989.

Utgoff, Kathleen P. "Pension Reform Strengthens Defined-Benefit Plans." *Compensation and Benefits Management* (Summer 1988).

VanDerhei, Jack. "Plan Termination Insurance for Single-Employer Pension Plans." In Rosenbloom, ed., *The Handbook of Employee Benefits*, 2nd ed. Homewood, IL: Dow Jones-Irwin, 1988, ch. 51.

VanDerhei, Jack and Scott Harrington. "Pension Asset Reversions." In John A. Turner and Daniel J. Beller, eds., *Trends in Pensions*. Washington, DC: U.S. Government Printing Office, 1989, ch. 10.

Winkelvoss, Howard E. *Pension Mathematics: With Numerical Illustrations*. Homewood, IL: Richard D. Irwin, 1977.

Yumiba, Yoshihiro. "Japanese Private Pension Statistics." Paper presented at U.S. Department of Labor International Conference on Private Pension Policy, February 1990.

Journal of Financial Services Research 4:461–463 (1990)
© 1990 Kluwer Academic Publishers

Commentary: *Managing Pension and Retirement Assets: An International Perspective*

KATHLEEN P. UTGOFF
Economist
Groom and Nordberg, Chartered
1701 Pennsylvania Ave., NW
Washington, DC 20006

The publication of an article like Zvi Bodie's reflects a substantial change that is relatively recent. Until a few years ago, pensions were the purview of a small number of academic economists and technical specialists in the government and private industry. When I first started working in the government, any meeting on pension issues was referred to as a MEGO meeting, which was "my eyes glaze over." And literally, the wisdom that was frequently passed from one high level official to a successor was "Stay out of pensions" if you didn't want to be bored to death or become ensnared in a technical jungle.

But all that has changed. Pensions have become a very hot and sexy topic; they are now at the center of many economic controversies. Pension funds have been blamed for LBOs; they were also blamed for the stock market crash; and now they're being blamed for lack of capital formation and myopia in corporate America.

Most of this is hogwash, but pensions do play a very important role in our capital markets, as Bodie points out. Pension plans own about a quarter of all corporate equities and about 40 percent of all corporate debt, a substantial ownership share that has increased significantly over the last decade.

Pensions also play another important role. They have a strong influence on our labor force. From 1975 to about 1985, the labor force participation of men over the age of 55 fell a full percentage point a year, which is a dramatic decline. A great deal of this can be explained by changes in pension plans, particularly early retirement provisions. We know, then, that pensions affect our capital markets, and we know they affect our labor markets. Therefore, they must play a role in international competition.

At the beginning of the article, Zvi modestly says that pensions are really not important in international financial markets because they are produced and consumed domestically, but I disagree with that for the reasons that I just cited. In addition, pension funds have driven a great deal of financial innovation and that should give us competitive advantage. One of the few disappointments in this very rich article was that it did not discuss how regulation in the financial services industry affected our ability to capitalize on that natural competitive advantage that arises from innovation. I have been to several conferences recently where people from the financial services industry complained that if we didn't change our regulatory behavior, everyone who worked in finance was going to have to learn Japanese. I would like to find out from the kind of broad overview that Bodie has given whether people in the pension field are also going to have to learn Japanese.

Now, what about the Bodie fallacies? They are probably the most notable aspect of this article, even though Bodie concentrated on the important issue of inflation protection in his comments. The article is extremely thought-provoking, and it's very troubling, because it attacks a great deal of conventional wisdom.

I may not agree with every single point in the article, but as Myron Scholes points out, it's good to have someone ask some very basic questions. Our pension policy is now referred to as a crazy quilt, and justifiably so, because it has been put together without asking any of the basic questions. The Bodie article makes a major contribution by starting that process.

The two most important points in the article, other than the inflation protection issues, are: (1) that funding pensions does not necessarily add to savings, and (2) that bonds are the best investments for most of the assets in pension plans. These are fundamental observations that really go to the heart of much of pension policy.

The conclusion, that pensions do not have to be funded to contribute to savings, is very insightful, and I think for the most part, it's much more right than wrong. Clearly, as is pointed out, the way we measure the contribution of pensions to savings in our national income accounts is wrong. But is there really no relationship between funding and savings?

Recently, the government substantially cut the amount of contributions that could be made to defined benefit pension plans. The basic question when you evaluate this cut is, what happened to funds that were not set aside in pension trusts? Were they invested in the company or were they distributed as dividends? Were any new dividends spent or saved? What we're really looking at here is the analog of the theorem that deficits don't affect our national savings because people make adjustments in their savings according to their perceptions of future tax liabilities.

Bodie's Fallacy 3 is very much like that. Here, too, all the assumptions that are needed to generate it should be examined. Two very important assumptions involve the tax advantages of funding and the Bankruptcy Code. I believe that to get to Bodie's conclusion you need to assume that (1) if firms did not fund pensions, they would be given the same tax advantages for book reserving their pension liabilities and (2) that pension liabilities would be given a high priority in bankruptcy if the firm fails, so that underfunding is really like debt to the firm. Both of those conditions do not hold, so funding may contribute to savings.

Although I think that the debate over Zvi's Fallacy 3 will be very important, it may not be illuminating. People who want to tax pension plans will support the notion that funding doesn't really lead to savings. People who don't want to tax pension plans will support the old belief that funding increases savings. In any event, this issue will be hotly debated over the next few years as pressures mount to reduce the deficit. Pensions are the biggest "tax expenditure" in the federal budget.

What about the investment of pension assest for individuals and for defined benefit plans? I find this the most difficult part of the article, and I am clearly not the only person who chokes on the idea that it is not advantageous to invest in the opportunities that lead to highest expected yields, which are stocks in this case.

I think the basic question comes down to what you care about. Do you care about the variance of potential outcomes, or do you care about the probability that you'll do better over time if you invest in stocks compared to a portfolio of bonds? The probability of doing better increases over the years with stocks, but the variance of possible outcomes also increases.

What is the appropriate measure of risk? The risk that stocks will underperform bonds or the variance in the outcome? This is a technical argument, but it is very important in the development of sound pension policy. This part of the article deserves a good deal of attention.

One problem may be that economists try to rationalize observed behavior, and for years, pension plans have had roughly 50 percent of their assets in bonds and 50 percent of their assets in equities. Bodie thinks that's not the right allocation. His assertion reminds me of the joke about two economists who see $10 laying on the sidewalk and neither of them picks it up. They agree it couldn't be real; otherwise somebody else would have picked it up. Bodie could be right, but I have doubts even though I pick up all $10 bills.

In general, the article was an extremely thought-provoking and challenging. A great deal of work is required to assimilate all his ideas, particularly if you're not a finance expert. I recommend it for anybody who wants to learn about current pension issues, and particularly issues in pension finance.

Journal of Financial Services Research 4:465–469 (1990)
© 1990 Kluwer Academic Publishers

Commentary: *Managing Pension and Retirement Assets: An International Perspective*

MYRON S. SCHOLES
Frank E. Buck Professor of Finance
Graduate School of Business
Stanford University, Palo Alto, CA

Zvi Bodie's article encompasses a lot of material. I like his summary of our past, present, and future pension system. I have a few comments on details and then I will address the future for pension funds and how we should think about them.

Bodie has done an excellent job in pointing out some very common fallacies of pension investing. The proposition that stocks are riskier in the long run is presented nicely. The same can be said for stocks as being a hedge against inflation. The discussion of pension benefits as being part of savings, only if funded, is excellent but, I think, a little incomplete. The discussion of investing in stocks to reduce plan costs is also good.

I was surprised, however, that Bodie restricted his comments so exclusively to pension funds. I think the discussion of pension funding should include all compensation programs. This broadening would produce a better prediction of the future supply of investment funds. For example, to ignore the effects of postretirement health care on the costs to corporations in the 1990s and beyond is to ignore an important aspect of retirement planning and its consequences.

I am less clear than Bodie as to what the economic function is of our retirement system. He claims that its purpose is to replace preretirement employment income or maintain a standard of living. I am not sure that this is its purpose. We have encouraged private savings through the pension system over the years—in part through regulation and in part through tax policy—but the rules have never been set to replace the preretirement standard of living or to protect against inflation.

Bodie argues that requiring each employee to take a life annuity reduces self-selection costs and therefore is beneficial. But it seems to me that this analysis ignores the loss in utility to employees who expect to die sooner, unfortunately, than their cohorts. Moreover, many plans allow for self-selection, in that employees can select guaranteed minimum periods or joint and survivor annuities. The article never addresses the question as to why current defined benefit pension plans are designed to provide a fixed terminal benefit, not indexed to inflation. This is strange if the goal is to provide for cost-of-living or inflation adjustments in retirement.

The article is silent about the effects of inflation on worker mobility, and about whether to use the projected benefit approach or the accrued benefit approach in defining the corporate obligation. Most benefit formulas are tied to final salary and years of service; note the emphasis on final salary and not total compensation. Salary provides one degree of freedom. That allows most corporations to adjust their rate of increase in salary as a function of changes in inflation, and therefore, by ignoring this degree of freedom provides an incomplete description of reality. I predict that, with unanticipated inflation, the increase in salary for employees who have many years of service and who are closer to retirement will be less than for employees who are just starting to work for firms. So salary is a way to adjust for unanticipated inflation.

A major source of the growth of funded pension plans has been tax policy. Tax policy in the past and in the future can dramatically alter the funding policies and the cost of capital to U.S. corporations. At times the tax rules have been quite liberal, encouraging funding and the growth of pension investing as a substitute for private savings. In recent years, the direction has been quite adverse. For example, lower corporate and personal income tax rates now reduce the benefits of funding because of administrative costs of establishing and running pension funds.

Second, we now expect that there will be increases in taxes, either generally or specifically targeted at pension funds, and this reduces workers' demand for pensions.

Third, antidiscrimination rules force down pension growth. Even though it appears to be equitable and beneficial to include lower paid employees on the same terms as more highly paid employees, lower paid employees and those starting in the labor force do not value their pensions as highly as those who are more highly compensated and approaching retirement. These employees with lower pay prefer current salary, with saving deferred to the future. If they are forced to invest in a pension program by accepting a lower salary component of their total compensation, they might need to borrow to meet current consumption. Since our markets are such that borrowing costs exceed investment returns because of asymmetric information problems, these employees then are forced—in present value terms—to take less than a dollar of current compensation for a dollar of incremental pension benefits. That is, they will get less than a dollar's value for every dollar they give up to fund their pensions.

The more highly compensated individuals prefer to save for retirement. The pension program is tax advantageous to them when compared to alternative savings vehicles. But since the system has to be maintained as a whole, these more highly compensated employees, in effect, are forced to subsidize the lower paid employees for the system to be complete. As a result, the antidiscrimination rules intended to foster equity become more onerous, and the demand for defined-benefit-type pensions falls. By similar arguments, any weakening of the integration rules with regard to Social Security also hurts the growth of pension funds. The more we require non-integration with Social Security, the more corporations will want to move away from defined-benefit pension funds.

Placing limits on the maximum benefits that can be earned by any employee also hurts the growth of the defined-benefit pension plan. For example, if tax policy were modified so that the maximum annual amount that the retiree can receive in a pension were reduced to $90,000 or $75,000, then the relative value of the pension program for the more highly compensated individual employee would fall. As a result, there would be movement away from defined-benefit plans to defined-contribution plans or other changes that affect savings.

Revisions in the excess asset rules, such as proposals that Senator Metzenbaum and others have put forward, would also discourage pension funding. Preventing or impairing access by firms to excess pension assets—assets that exceed the liabilities of the plans—reduces the advantage of funding or using defined benefit plans. Demands for "social investing" or for particular uses of our large pool of pension fund assets, some $2 trillion, also reduces the demand for pension assets by reducing prospective returns.

We have recently come to understand that pension funds have large cross-holdings. It has been argued that Japanese firms have large cross-holdings of their securities, but pension plans provide a way for U.S. corporations also to have large cross-holdings of other corporations. If IBM holds General Motors and General Motors holds IBM securities in their portfolio, that is the same thing as Mitsubishi holding Mitsubishi Trust and Mitsubishi Heavy Industries, and so on. These cross-holdings provide the basis for the belief that large passive holdings of pension fund assets mean weaker shareholder control and weaker sanctions against management. This has recently led to a demand by employers for taxation of short-term trading by pension plans, with the objective of fostering a more passive approach toward pension investing. Weaker shareholder control is the real basis for the so-called belief that if we tax pension plan turnover, and if they turn over assets less frequently, then the pension plans will invest for the long term, which is presumably good for America.

I have suggested another extreme form of argument, suggesting that proponents of taxes to reduce turnover would really prefer that the pension plans holding their assets behave as passive investors until their pension obligations come due—that they come back in 50 years and not bother management at all in the meantime. Obviously, if their own pension plans become more active, corporations would prefer that the importance of defined-benefit plans be reduced. I think the concern about short-term investing and turnover in pension plan investment is misdirected.

To answer the turnover question and the concentration of U.S. managers in short-term investments, we should address the question of what our cost of capital is relative to foreign investors. If we have a higher cost of capital, our investment horizons might naturally be relatively short. Turnover of pension fund investments may really have little effect on returns for the corporation's investment, either for the short run or the long run. The emphasis on reducing turnover of pension fund investment may be an excuse to try mainly to keep the pension funds from effectively monitoring actual corporate actions.

Another important issue is raised by the Pension Benefit Guaranty Corporation (PBGC) transfers that occur, when the well-funded pension plans such as IBM have to pay for the defaults of the LTVs. If the PBGC is another disaster that is waiting to happen, just as the FSLIC is a disaster, we need to be concerned about the implications of these federal guarantees.

To understand the future role that pension investing has to play in influencing our cost of capital and affecting American investments, I think we need a much broader study of the role of pension plans. Because it is broad and encompassing, Bodie's article led me to think about the issues. Too little thought has probably been given to pension policy. We have talked about tax policy in the context of taxing turnover, and we talk about tax policy in terms of reducing the demand for pensions, but we have not really looked at fundamental questions about what defined benefits pension plans are supposed to accomplish, what the alternatives are, how we integrate retirement benefits with other interests, and how the cost of capital is affected for corporations in the United States.

In terms of inflation protection, I think the most important element may be postretirement health care. We need to think more seriously about how we should use policies to fund or to foster the payment of health care benefits. Our current system is really not inflation protected at all. It is ill-conceived, in that there is no individual monitoring of policies that encourage corporations to pay for the benefits. The way our tax system is oriented—so that the corporation or employer pays everything—means it is much more cost effective for the beneficiaries after taxes than if we had co-payment or sharing rules, where employees pay some fraction of their own costs. That, at least, would produce some incentives for monitoring.

I like the innovation section in Bodie's article. What I think he does not address, partly because it is much less visible, is our large market of private contracting. The futures market and the auctions markets deal in standardized contracts. Major financial firms, such as Salomon Brothers, with which I am currently associated during my sabbatical, develop contracts that are private contracts. They are of nonstandard variety. We use swaps and auction contracts to help us tailor private contracts specifically to the needs of pension fund investors and corporations around the world. We, in effect, use the futures markets and the auctions markets to hedge the commitments that we make to those who are parties to our private contractual obligations.

We provide a contract which is a CPI-linked asset: for example, a swap contract under which we will provide to any pension fund or corporation the right to receive the CPI plus $2\frac{1}{2}$ percent to 3 percent real. We protect ourselves against the risks inherent in such a commitment by using offsetting contracts in other markets, either using actual securities to hedge or using the futures market. We provide private forward contracts, often through operations in swap markets. The growth of these private contracts has an overwhelmingly international character because we can provide these services at lower transaction costs than they can be provided by direct investments in the various countries involved.

It is very expensive to operate a portfolio in a country, to go through clearing and all the other mechanisms, to know where your securities are, to receive your cash flows, your dividends, and so on. It is more efficient for one organization to specialize in doing this than for everyone to do it. And we, like other investment banking houses, are internationally based. As a result, we could provide these services at much lower costs than individuals could by replicating the arrangements that we develop.

In addition to the ordinary economic costs of providing these services, there are many complicated regulations and rules, including tax rules, around the world. These weird and complicated rules themselves lead to possibilities for developing contracts that tend to reduce their importance and also to bring markets together. So I think that there will be a continued growth in the private contracting market that will specifically tailor arrangements to the demands of pension funds. These pension funds, managed on behalf of corporations in the United States and corporations internationally, are to a large degree the suppliers of funds and also the demanders of funds.

I see continued growth in private contracting, driven by transactions costs and by regulations, and I think we will continue to see further evolution of contracting possibilities and arrangements. Right now it is possible to buy warrants—privately contracted warrants on various international indices. It is possible to swap returns from, say, interest rates indexed to LIBOR. We have had innovations at Salomon Brothers, for example, where we had contracts which are called "spins," which are the short form for S&P-protected investment contracts. Many of these new forms of contracting are born because of the demands for new products by pension funds. The futures market is important to us, but it is not only the futures market that is important—we can tailor more specific contracts to other customers as well, in part by making use of the standardized contracts that futures and securities markets provide.

I enjoyed reviewing Bodie's article because it gave me an opportunity again to think in broad perspective about the role of pension plans in our economy and in financial market developments. It is particularly appropriate to address these issues on a more global basis, as he has done, as opposed to piecemeal attacks on our pension planning system.

Journal of Financial Services Research 471-497 1990
© 1990 Kluwer Academic Publishers

The Corporate Structure of Financial Conglomerates

RICHARD J. HERRING
Professor of Finance
Director of the International Banking Center
The Wharton School
University of Pennsylvania
Philadelphia, PA 19104

ANTHONY M. SANTOMERO
Richard K. Mellon Professor of Finance
The Wharton School
University of Pennsylvania
Philadelphia, PA 19104

1. Introduction

This article considers the public policy issues regarding the appropriate corporate structure of a firm that provides basic banking services along with other financial services. We
refer to such firms as financial conglomerates—a category that includes universal banks,
multiproduct bank holding companies, and other diversified financial firms that perform
basic banking functions. We address the question of how the regulation of the basic
banking business in the United States should be organized in a world economy in which
American banks must compete with financial conglomerates.

As competition in the provision of financial services has intensified, the effect of
regulatory constraints on both the corporate organization and the range of powers of
American banks has become increasingly apparent. Technological improvements in com-
municating and processing information have facilitated financial innovations that have
blurred traditional functional distinctions among financial institutions. This has increased
competitive pressure on banks from other American financial institutions which are often
regulated less stringently. In addition, technological changes have reduced costs of providing financial services across national frontiers, and, consequently, American banks face
heightened global competition from foreign financial institutions that are often suject to
looser regulatory constraints. These trends are especially apparent in international markets where, relatively unconstrained by regulation, American commercial banks compete
with foreign universal banks, merchant banks, investment banks, insurance companies,
and in-house corporate banks.

The authors are grateful to George Benston, Zvi Bodie, William Haraf, Klaus Kohler, Marvin Kosters, Mickey
Levy, Allan Meltzer, and Robert Merton for comments on an earlier draft and to William Gasser, Rinaldo
Pecchioli, and Norbert Walter for data and useful insights into the behavior of conglomerates.

Technology has made it feasible for many bank customers to adopt a global financial perspective and select from an international menu of financial instruments. Transactions costs have fallen to such an extent that sophisticated borrowers may exploit relatively small differences in costs across national and international markets. Similarly, sophisticated depositors can readily compare a bank's deposit rate with returns offered on a broad variety of financial instruments issued in a wide range of national and international financial markets (Santomero, 1989).

In several important financial centers the regulatory authorities have reacted to competitive pressures by relaxing the most burdensome regulations on depository institutions. Indeed, some countries have taken active measures to attract a larger share of international business by improving the infrastructure to support financial services and by virtually eliminating regulatory burdens on international financial transactions (Kane, 1987). In addition, several countries—most notably Canada, France, New Zealand, and the United Kingdom—have relaxed traditional restrictions on the permissible scope of operations of domestic depository institutions to permit them greater flexibility in responding to changing market conditions (Bröker, 1989). Although the leading industrial countries have sought to place some limits on competition among regulators, most notably by negotiating an international agreement to harmonize capital adequacy requirements (BIS, 1988), greater regulatory competition has been the dominant trend.

Regulatory competition has recently intensified with the European Community's bold initiative to enhance the efficiency of financial regulation within the Community (Herring, 1990). From an American perspective, where regulatory reform is typically the result of persistent litigation and creative administrative interpretations, the speed with which the European Community has agreed to a fundamental and thoroughgoing reform of its regulatory framework is remarkable. The Second Banking Directive, approved in December 1989 by the European Parliament, insures that European institutions can choose to become universal banks—banks that comine both commercial and investment banking powers. European banks will be permitted to accept deposits, make long-term loans, issue and underwrite corporate securities, and take equity positions. The Community's approach to harmonization of banking regulation among the member states, which combines the adoption of a single banking license with the principles of mutual recognition and home country control, will create a competitive dynamic, making it likely that the European regulatory system will remain flexible and efficient (Key, 1989).[1]

The freedom of European financial institutions to select from regulatory regimes in any of the 12 member countries for providing financial services throughout the European Community will cause each national regulatory authority to assess carefully the competitive impact of its regulatory structure. The approach deliberately encourages national regulatory authorities to compete (subject to basic safety and soundness constraints) in providing the most efficient regulatory system. As Sir Leon Brittan, Vice-President of the Commission of the European Communities, has observed, the Community "in one bound . . . has moved from twelve fragmented and confusing structures of national (banking) regulation to a single market of a size and simplicity unmatched anywhere else in the world." He emphasized that the motive was not "merely to benefit banks . . . [but] . . . to increase the competitiveness of European industry by giving it access to the cheapest, most efficient, and most innovative financial products in the world" (Brittan, 1990).

Among major industrial countries, only the United States and Japan still insist on a sharp distinction between commercial and investment banking activities in their home markets. And Japan appears to be moving with deliberate speed to dismantle many of the regulations that segment its financial system (Corrigan, 1990). The upshot is that U.S. banks will increasingly face competition from foreign financial conglomerates that can select from a broader menu of corporate structures to provide a wider range of services. This may be expected to intensify competitive pressures on U.S.-based institutions both abroad and at home. Moreover, governments of other major industrial countries are pressing the United States to permit financial conglomerates headquartered in their countries to operate with the same flexibility in the United States which they, in turn, accord U.S. banks operating abroad.

U.S. banks are currently in a weak position to face heightened international competition. A series of shocks during the 1980s—the third world debt crisis, sharp drops in the prices of oil, agricultural commodities, and real estate in some regions—have reduced the quality of bank assets and weakened earnings. This legacy has reduced the relative credit standing of large banks and jeopardized their ability to perform traditional on-balance sheet intermediation profitably. Large banks have attempted to respond by shifting to off-balance sheet, fee-based services which include debt underwriting and securitized lending for their corporate clients plus retail distribution of a broad array of insurance and other investment products. Their ability to pursue this strategy, however, has been constrained by the narrowness of the U.S. bank charter.

In summary, the current weakness of large American banks coupled with technological change, foreign regulatory reforms, and foreign policy pressures to extend broader, reciprocal powers to foreign conglomerates operating in the United States make this an appropriate time to review U.S. policy regarding financial conglomerates. Such a review, however, requires consideration of a number of difficult, interrelated issues, including: Why do financial institutions favor a conglomerate structure? Are conglomerate firms likely to dominate financial markets or are they likely to coexist with specialized firms? What objectives are current American regulations designed to achieve? Finally, can these objectives be attained more efficiently?

In this discussion we take as given that the basic banking business is in some sense "special"[2] and therefore requires some regulatory oversight. Regardless of whether one believes the basic banking business is special, it is undeniably true that throughout the world it is treated as special for regulatory purposes. We regard this as sufficient justification for focusing solely on how that business should be related to other activities within a financial conglomerate.

2. The rationale for financial conglomerates

Financial conglomerates are formed because owners or managers of financial firms believe that they can achieve synergies or economies of scope that will make it more profitable to provide a range of services within an integrated corporate group than to provide each service through a separately managed corporation.[3] These synergies may arise from two distinct sources: the production or consumption of financial services.

Economies of scope in production may be realized whenever the cost of producing a given mix of products jointly is less than the sum of costs of producing each product separately.[4] Economies of scope are likely to be important whenever a significant fixed cost can be shared across products. Several factors would appear to give rise to economies of scope in the provision of financial services. The fixed costs of managing a client relationship (Steinherr and Huveneers, 1989, p. 8)—including human resources, information services, and establishing and maintaining a sound reputation—may be shared across a broad range of financial services. It may also be possible to use distribution channels established for one product to distribute other products at slight marginal cost. In addition, information used to produce one product may be used to produce other products at very little additional cost. More broadly, if the existence or scale of output of one type of product affects the unit cost of another, then an integrated conglomerate firm may produce services at lower marginal cost than an autonomous, single-function firm. Finally, Mayer (1988) has argued that financial conglomerates may also benefit from an enhanced ability to control credit risk to the extent that an equity stake in a borrowing firm improves the conglomerate's capacity to monitor corporate performance and control risk-taking by corporate managers.

Despite the many plausible sources of economies of scope in the provision of financial services, empirical evidence on the existence of significant economies of scope is limited. The traditional literature (Clark, 1988; Gilbert, 1984; and Gilligan, Smirlock, and Marshall, 1984), which focuses exclusively on deposits and loans in a cross-section of small banks, reports some evidence of economies of scale and scope. The relevance of this evidence for large financial conglomerates is doubtful. However, recent literature that expands the specification of the production function to include information technology (Mester, 1990), increases the array of products (Giddy, 1985), and uses large bank data (Shaefer, 1990), finds strong evidence of economies of scope.

Synergies may also exist in the consumption of financial services; users of financial services may value a package of financial services from a single source more highly than the same array of products obtained separately from several different firms. Evidence of such economies of scope in the consumption of financial services, however, is largely impressionistic. The empirical literature has not succeeded in defining and measuring economies of scope in the consumption of financial services.[5] Yet, financial institutions behave as if the potential economies are substantial. Profitability goals are often specified in terms of the overall customer relationship with special emphasis on selling a number of different products to each customer. While customer profitability analysis is not new (Santomero, 1984), it has received greater emphasis (Citicorp, 1989).

In addition to realizing economies of scope in production, the view that cross-selling products to customers increases profitability is based on the assumption that customers will be willing to pay more per product as the number of products obtained from a single institution increases. These economies of scope in consumption may arise from a reduction in search, information, monitoring, and transactions costs which may be realized when several financial products may be purchased from the same firm. The private banking business is explicitly designed to exploit these potential economies of scope in consumption, as are cash management accounts offered by brokerage firms.

The implications for market structure differ if the motive for forming a conglomerate is economies of scope in consumption rather than economies of scope in production. If economies of scope in production are negligible, economies of scope in consumption could be exploited by using the distribution network of one institution to sell packages of financial services that are produced by others. This sort of "agency" conglomerate occurs in the United Kingdom among the building societies and insurance companies (Llewelyn, 1989).[6] The realization of potential gains from cross-selling each other's products appears to be the motivation for several strategic alliances between financial institutions in Europe, Japan, and the United States as well. If consumption economies are essentially static, they may be exploited either by ownership or distribution linkages.

Financial conglomerates, however, may also enjoy a *dynamic* advantage. To the extent that conglomerates have more scope to develop innovative new products and services in response to changing technology and market conditions, they may be better able to respond to customer needs. Integrated conglomerates, within which information flows freely and incentives are harmonized, may have an advantage in meeting the changing needs of customers relative to either specialized firms or autonomous firms whose products are offered in joint distribution. Financial conglomerates may also respond more flexibly and at lower cost to demand shifts across financial products (Steinherr, 1989, p. 8) as client needs require, than other firms that offer only a limited menu of services or financial products. Moreover, the perception of greater flexibility over time may be an advantage for which customers are willing to pay a premium.

Although we have identified several factors that may motivate financial firms to offer an expanded array of financial services, it is by no means obvious that this mode of operation will be either dominant across all financial product lines, or that it will be attractive to *all* financial firms. Specialized financial firms will surely continue to compete effectively by using different production or delivery systems than their mass-market, conglomerate competitors. They may also choose to specialize in activities or products in which economies of scope are less valuable. Just as boutiques continue to thrive alongside department stores, specialized financial firms may be expected to complete effectively with financial conglomerates in some markets under some conditions. This conclusion is given further plausibility by consideration of some of the disadvantages of conglomeration.

Managers of financial firms must weigh the potential *economies* of scope which we have identified against several potential *diseconomies* of scope which may jeopardize the efficiency of multiproduct firms. First, the sheer size of the bureaucracy that usually accompanies a conglomerate structure may be a disadvantage. Bureaucratic procedures may discourage entrepreneurial activity and impede innovative responses to changing market conditions. Ironically, the agency problems in organizing an appropriate response to changing customer needs may inhibit a conglomerate corporation from taking full advantage of its broad capacity to respond.

Second, the complexity of managing several different kinds of business in one integrated structure may also erode some of the potential economies of scope. Deal-oriented investment bankers do not necessarily work easily with relationship-oriented commercial bankers. Disputes over discretion in decision-making and compensation may lead to inefficiencies that offset many of the information gains and product development opportunities.

Third, while some customers may value one-stop financial shopping, other customers may perceive disadvantages in the joint production of financial products. Some customers may be concerned that information that they share with the conglomerate in one transaction could be used to their detriment in other transactions. The costs of reassuring potential customers that they will not be taken advantage of by the conglomerate may undercut some of the economies of joint production. And averting such conflicts of interest between different parts of the conglomerate may lead to a diminished ability to compete with more specialized firms. As a consequence, specialized firms may have a competitive advantage in providing services to customers who are very concerned about conflicts of interest.

The advantages of joint production versus autonomous production may vary from product to product and for a given product over time. While it is possible to identify several potential gains to the formation of financial conglomerates, there are several offsetting disadvantages as well. This may be the reason that no one organizational structure has become dominant. Indeed, in Germany and Switzerland, where all banks may choose to exercise a full range of universal banking powers, only a few of the larger banks actually offer a full range of services. Both multiproduct and specialized firms appear to be viable.

Although it is difficult to forecast how the financial services industry may evolve, it is noteworthy that over the last decade technological change and financial innovations have not necessarily enhanced the competitive position of conglomerate firms. One notable trend, in fact, has favored the competitive position of specialized institutions. The development of techniques to unbundle financial transactions has enabled relatively small, narrowly focused, specialist firms to compete by performing a particular kind of financial service very efficiently.

The important implication for policy is that research on economies of scope indicates that there may be efficiency gains from permitting the formation of financial conglomerates. But the regulatory framework should not attempt to prejudge the question of which structure is the most efficient for providing financial services. Provided that other policy concerns regarding financial conglomerates can be satisfied (see below), entrepreneurs should be given scope to experiment in order to determine which corporate structure best enables them to meet changing customer needs. The stakes are potentially high: realization of economies of scope in the production of financial services may result in higher levels of investment, a larger capital stock, and a higher level of income per capita.

3. Policy concerns regarding financial conglomerates

If private profits could be assumed to be equal to social profits, there would be no public policy reason to regulate or prohibit the formation of financial conglomerates. This is indeed the view that has been taken in several countries, most notably Germany and Switzerland. In fact, many of the most important financial institutions in the United States during the nineteenth and early 20th century were financial conglomerates that combined both commercial and investment banking powers (and often industrial activities as well).[7] However, since the 1930s U.S. policymakers have restricted the formation of financial conglomerates. Regulation since that time has been based on the presumption that the social costs of financial conglomerates outweigh the potential benefits.[8] Concern has focused on six potential costs—three regarding abuses of power and three regarding implications for the stability of the financial system.[9]

3.1. Monopoly power

The concern is that by controlling the full range of substitutes for a financial product, financial conglomerates may be able to acquire and exercise monopoly power to raise prices above marginal costs. This assumes that the financial conglomerate will be able to limit entry and will be able to enforce mandatory joint product sales. Regardless of whether this view may have been plausible in the past, we regard the intensified competition across different kinds of financial institutions and across borders—the trends cited in the introduction—as effectively eliminating this source of concern. All major markets for financial products seem highly contestable under current techno-logical conditions.

3.2. Excessive concentrations of economic and political power

The hypothesis is that financial conglomerates will be so powerful that they will distort economic decision-making and the political process. Among countries that permit finan-cial conglomerates, this concern is most often expressed in Germany where it is frequently asserted that the three large universal banks exercise excessive control over German industry (Protzman, 1989). Equity investments of the ten largest private German banks in nonfinancial companies amounted to only 0.57 percent of the aggregate nominal capitalization of all German corporations in 1989 (Cartellieri, 1990). None-theless, public perceptions are heavily influenced by a few instances in which universal banks have significant ownership position in large firms (for example, Deutsche Bank's 28.24 percent share in Daimler Benz), by their potential control over large numbers of proxy votes, and by their presence on the supervisory boards of many nonfi-nancial corporations.

This particular aspect of the German system is not a fundamental attribute of universal banking. In Switzerland, which also has a universal banking tradition but where banks have traditionally not had extensive involvement in the management of corporations, this concern is seldom expressed. On the other hand, in Japan, where commercial banking has been rigorously separated from investment banking, concerns are frequently voiced about the power of financial *keiretsus* because banks with their affiliates often hold large equity stakes in major customers (American Bankers Association, 1990).

In the United States, populists have long contended that large financial institutions—especially money center banks and Wall Street—exercise excessive economic and political power. The increasingly competitive international marketplace is confronting populists with an unpleasant choice. If American regulatory policy prevents the formation of large

financial conglomerates in the United States, large financial conglomerates headquartered abroad may gain a dominant share in some markets in the United States through
use of on-shore and off-shore affiliates. It is possible to argue that public policy has no
legitimate interest in *who* owns the dominant financial institutions so long as users of
financial services have reliable access to efficient services at minimum cost. This, however,
is not a position that is likely to appeal to those with a predisposition to worry about
concentrations of power.

It is noteworthy that the most egregious and expensive abuse of the political process in
recent years was orchestrated by lobbyists representing the thrift industry—a group of
relatively small, specialized institutions. Political scientists, who emphasize the importance of well-organized minorities with cohesive interests, would not find this a
surprising outcome.

If financial conglomerates do not have monopoly power—and we do not regard monopoly power as a problem in the contemporary competitive environment—then they will
not be able to exert excessive economic power. Moreover, experience has shown that the
political process has at least as much to fear from the activities of small specialized
financial institutions as from large financial institutions. Thus we do not regard this
concern as a significant argument against the formation of financial conglomerates.

3.3. Conflicts of interest

The concern is that financial conglomerates may be subject to severe conflicts regarding
the interests of the conglomerate vis-a-vis the interests of a client or the interests of one
client vis-a-vis those of another[10]. Conflicts of interest are inherent in virtually every
financial transaction, even within the special purpose institutions mandated by current
U.S. regulations.[11] For example, investment bankers eager to generate fees for merger
and acquisition transactions may be tempted to exaggerate their valuation of a target to
increase the probability of the transaction. Likewise, in the course of evaluating a loan, a
bank lending officer may discover information that is of value to the bank's trust department.

Nonetheless, the broader the financial firm's array of products, the greater the likelihood that conflicts will arise. Because conglomerates are involved in a wider range of
transactions, they have a wider range of information. Although this may be an important
source of economies of scope, it may also be the source of abuse if the conglomerate
makes use of the information to exploit the ignorance of counterparties. By integrating
commercial and investment banking activities, a conglomerate could use trust funds to
mask bad underwriting decisions ("stuffing") or generate larger brokerage commissions
by excessive transactions in trust accounts ("churning"). Loans could be converted to
securities of questionable value and access to loans could be limited to underwriting
customers. Current legislation prohibits U.S. banks from engaging in these activities
(Firewalls, 1990). Moreover, as Kelley (1985) notes, these conflicts are likely to present a
very unfavorable opportunity for trading off short-term gains against long-term benefits
for the financial institution. Reputation matters; credibility is essential to long-term

profitability in financial markets. It is in the best interest of the financial institution to resist such short-term gains and to develop a management structure in which such temptations occur infrequently (Diamond, 1989).

Concern over conflicts of interest cannot be dismissed as irrelevant. But since such conflicts are also a problem for specialized institutions, they should not be overemphasized as an argument against the formation of financial conglomerates. Conflicts of interest are not insurmountable in conglomerates, nor are they fully eliminated in specialized institutions.

3.4. Increased systemic risk

This concern has two variations. Financial conglomerates may (1) increase systemic risk—the risk that the default of one or a few large borrowers will endanger the whole financial system—and/or (2) increase the social cost of maintaining the stability of the system when shocks occur. The first variation assumes that the central role of banks as providers of credit and custodian of the payments system merits special prudential protection. Bernanke and Gertler (1988) provide support for the view that banks play a special role in the economy.[12]

If banks require special prudential protection, then it may be argued that they should be prohibited from undertaking activities that increase their risk of failure. The securities industry in the United States has traditionally taken the view that the special role of banks requires that securities activities be kept separate from banking functions.[13] But even if it is accepted that the role of banks requires special prudential protection, the range of powers that should be permitted to banks is an empirical issue to be evaluated in a portfolio context. Several recent studies that have taken a portfolio perspective (Litan, 1987; Brewer, Fortier, and Pavel, 1989; and Saunders, 1985) indicate that the risk of bank failure would not be increased by expanding the permissible range of activities.[14]

Even if the risk of failure of a conglomerate were lower, however, there would be an additional concern that the social cost of coping with the failure might be greater with the collapse of a conglomerate because it would disrupt a wider range of activities. In order to protect the core banking activities, the authorities may be obliged to support a much broader range of functions.[15] While these arguments cannot be dismissed summarily, it is important to recognize that two assumptions are implicit in this view.

First, this view assumes that regulatory standards would be identical for both conglomerate and specialized institutions. Second, this view assumes that what matters is the viability of the firm as a whole rather than its core banking function or some other, separable subset of activities. Neither of these assumptions is necessarily warranted. Regulation of capital could be adjusted to equalize the cost of a systemic shock in both conglomerate and specialized institutions. Moreover, if the policy objective is to protect the core banking business rather than the conglomorate as a whole, the cost of coping with a failure may not be substantially different between conglomerate and specialized institutions. (See section 5 below for further discussion of these issues.)

3.5. More difficult to supervise and regulate

The supervision of the safety and soundness of the financial firm as a whole inevitably consumes resource. Financial conglomerates are more difficult to supervise and regulate effectively because of the inherent complexity of their activities. As financial institutions seek to broaden their product lines, the burden has undoubtedly increased for regulators to evaluate the safety and soundness implications of the conglomerates' activities. Regulatory oversight demands increasingly larger resources to monitor and understand transactions undertaken by the conglomerate. While these costs could be passed on to the firm itself, it may be an inefficient use of scarce resources. In addition, the increased complexity of transactions may threaten to overwhelm the capacity of the supervisory authorities to monitor the firm's activity and control its vulnerability to financial shocks. Such concerns have always arisen when innovations occur; the problem is even greater when innovations take place simultaneously across a wide range of products.

3.6. Cross-subsidy from access to the safety net

This concern stems from the fear that a financial conglomerate may be able to use access to the lender of last resort or the perception of lower risk associated with deposit insurance in order to subsidize other lines of business. This would distort competition with firms that do not have access to similar support.

Bankers are quick to argue that any gains associated with lower costs due to regulation are dissipated by competition. This view has some merit. Cost advantages will be passed on to customers (including nonbank financial institutions) in competitive markets. However, access to funds in times of trouble increases the willingness of banks to take risks relative to their nonbank competitors.

To the extent that the safety net is perceived to protect the conglomerate as a whole in times of crisis, its creditworthiness and access to capital are enhanced. Accordingly, the market will place a lower price on its risky debt relative to that of its competitors that do not have access to the safety net. Recent studies (Avery, Belton, and Hanweck, 1988; Gorton and Santomero, 1990), in fact, show that even the subordinated debt of holding companies that contain an insured bank may be underpriced because of the implicit guarantee associated with the banking charter. This gives rise to a legitimate concern about whether competitors that lack access to the safety net will be able to compete effectively with firms whose riskiness is underpriced in the market.

The policy response to all of these concerns in the United States has been to restrict the powers of depository institutions and to prohibit their participation in some financial activities. As international competitive pressures have increased, however, depository institutions have argued that these regulatory restrictions inhibit their ability to compete effectively. The regulatory response has been to allow some financial firms to broaden their product lines, mainly through holding company affiliations. There are several alternative ways, however, to combine banking and nonbanking activity within a financial conglomerate. In the next section we examine the merits of the major alternative models of conglomerate structure.

4. Alternative models of corporate structure

At the outset it is important to distinguish two different concepts of corporate separateness: legal separateness and operational separateness. *Legal separateness* implies that different products are provided by separate corporate entities, each of which has its own management structure, set of accounts, board of directors, and capital. Its shareholders are legally protected from disastrous outcomes in the separate corporate entity by limited liability. In the absense of additional restrictions, the managers of a conglomerate may coordinate the activities of the separate corporate entities that they control and achieve many of the advantages of an integrated firm.

Operational separateness implies regulatory or self-imposed restrictions—often called firewalls and/or Chinese walls—that inhibit the integrated production of different financial products. These restrictions may prohibit flows of credit and information between different functional units and may require that different products be produced by different people at different locations and be distributed through different channels.[16] Such restrictions inevitably reduce the extent to which a conglomerate and its customers can realize economies of scope in either production or consumption.

If the restrictions are self-imposed, there is a presumption that customers value separateness more than the cost savings or delivery efficiency that would result from more integrated production and distribution of financial products. If the restrictions are imposed by regulators, the rationale may be to prevent abuses of power, the contagious transmission of shocks, cross-subsidies, or an extension of the potential, implicit liability of the lender of last resort or the deposit insuring agency. There is no presumption that the regulatory authorities will have weighed the loss of economies of scope against the social gains of operational separateness;[17] but, increasingly, they face market pressures to do so.

An evaluation of the merits of alternative corporate structures requires an examination of both the public and private gains associated with each approach. Differing combinations of legal and operational separateness give rise to five basic models for organizing a financial conglomerate.

4.1. Model 1: complete integration

Complete integration—what might be termed the German model—permits the managers of a financial conglomerate to conduct all activities within a single corporate entity (see figure 1). Although the conglomerate may choose to erect Chinese walls or to separate particular functions in order to enhance the perceived value of its services to potential customers, it has no regulatory obligation to fragment the production of its services. For this reason, the completely integrated conglomerate should be able to produce any given mix of output at the least cost.

Superior operating efficiency must be offset, however, against concerns about the negative externalities of conglomerates. The concerns reviewed in the previous section are most relevant in this organizational model. The potential for anti-competitive behavior, conflict of interest, and disruptive shocks is greatest in the universal bank form. And potentially there is significant scope to use any implicit subsidies to the core banking

BANK

$$V_{G1} = \sum_j V_i (p_i \mid q_j)$$

where

V_{G1}	=	value of group under model 1
V_i	=	value of business group i
i	=	index of products supplied
p_i	=	price of product i
q_j	=	quantity of product j

Figure 1. Universal Bank

function to support other lines of business. Finally, this structure is more difficult to regulate than a single function institution. Without separation, either operationally or legally, the comingling of the whole range of financial transactions will present the regulator with the challenge of understanding the prudential implications of a large number of different products. The result is likely to be regulations that are both costly and imprecise.

An alternative approach is to attempt to protect certain activities of the bank, but not the institution as a whole. In effect this has occurred when the government guarantees certain lending activities such as mortgages, student loans, or export credits. Another variation of the universal bank model attempts to protect the deposit-taking function with minimal distortion of operating efficiency. This organizational model may be termed complete integration with collateralized deposits (figure 1a). It relies on a mild form of operational separateness—special monitoring of collateral against transactions balances. The recent Brookings Task Force Proposal (1989) and Scott (1989) describe how such an approach could be implemented to retain the efficiency benefits of joint production, distribution, and central funding, while maintaining at least some separation between payments system activity and other banking operations. This approach places special emphasis on protecting deposits and the payments system rather than the institution as a whole.

This relatively unobtrusive form of operational separateness does not allay all concerns regarding the stability implications of financial conglomerates. Regulators and competitors may argue that monitoring of the assets against deposits is not sufficient to prevent implicit subsidies from the deposit-taking function to other functions. This is a direct result of the doubts that remain about whether the regulatory authorities can make a credible commitment to refrain from bailing out other creditors of the conglomerate (Guttentag and Herring, 1987a; Herring, 1990). To the extent that the market perceives even a partial guarantee of the liabilities of the bank, the marginal cost of funds is

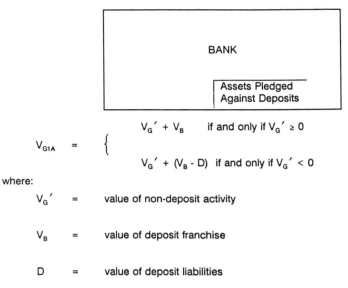

$$V_{G1A} = \begin{cases} V_G' + V_B & \text{if and only if } V_G' \geq 0 \\ \\ V_G' + (V_B - D) & \text{if and only if } V_G' < 0 \end{cases}$$

where:

V_G' = value of non-deposit activity

V_B = value of deposit franchise

D = value of deposit liabilities

Figure 1a. Complete integration with collateralized deposits

underpriced. Experience suggests that the supervisory authorities in every major country are unlikely to permit a large depository institutions to collapse. Because it is probably larger than more specialized institutions that provide the same basic banking services, the universal bank is more likely to be viewed as "too big to fail."

4.2. Model 2: bank parent, nonbank subsidiaries

The second basic structure is one in which the banking function is conducted in the corporate parent and nonbank functions are conducted in separately incorporated subsidiaries of the parent bank. This structure, which might be termed the British model, is shown in schematic form in figure 2.

Legal separateness will entail some efficiency costs, and so the cost of producing a given mix of financial services may be somewhat higher than under model 1. There are two offsetting advantages. First the corporate structure separates nonbanking activity and is more likely to result in functional regulation which would reduce the costs of regulatory oversight. Second, in principle, model 2 protects the bank from disastrous outcomes in other activities undertaken by the conglomerate while permitting it to benefit from all positive returns. As the value functions illustrate at the foot of figure 2, limited liability implies that the nonbank subsidiaries can only increase, but not reduce the value of the bank.

In reality this may be an overly optimistic view. It assumes that the profitability of the bank is unrelated to the performance of its subsidiaries. Two considerations argue against this assumption. First, if operational synergies are important, the profitability of the bank may be adversely affected by the collapse of the subsidiary. Second, the bank's reputation

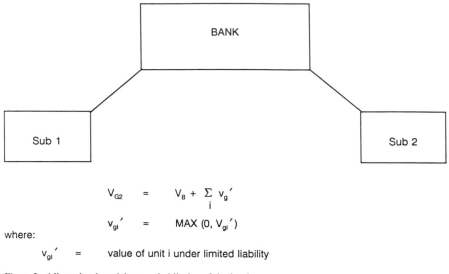

$$V_{G2} = V_B + \sum_i v_g'$$

$$v_{gi}' = \text{MAX}(0, V_{gi}')$$

where:

v_{gi}' = value of unit i under limited liability

Figure 2. All nonbank activity as subsidiaries of the bank

and its cost of funds may be adversely affected by the failure of any of its subsidiaries. Thus the bank parent may have business reasons to support a faltering subsidiary beyond its capital investment. In essence, the advantages of limited liability depicted in figure 2 may be somewhat illusory.

Market confidence that the bank will not exercise the option to walk away from a troubled subsidiary enhances the creditworthiness of the subsidiaries. This is an advantage to the parent bank insofar as it reduces funding costs for the conglomerate, but it may distort competition and prove costly to the regulatory authorities. The parent bank's access to the safety net may be implicitly extended to the subsidiaries. This may weaken market discipline and lower the cost of funding a function organized as a subsidiary of a bank rather than as an autonomous corporation.[18] Furthermore, if trouble occurs, the regulatory authorities may find that it is less costly (in the short run) to validate market expectations by assisting the parent bank in bailing out its subsidiary than to withhold resources from the parent and let the subsidiary fail.

To mitigate this risk, the regulatory authorities may attempt to re-enforce legal separateness with operational separateness by requiring firewalls between the bank parent and its subsidiaries. The cost in loss of operational efficiency is clear, but the benefit in improving market discipline of bank subsidiaries is less certain.

4.3. Model 3: holding company parent, all activities as subsidiaries

This structure might be termed the U.S. model. U.S. banks are currently required to conduct most nonbank activities through a holding company (see the Bank Holding Company Act of 1956, and its 1970 Amendment). In this third approach, a holding company shell is the sole owner of the banking subsidiary and its nonbanking counterparts. As currently implemented, various restrictions concerning cross-affiliate trading are imposed, but the entire entity benefits to some extent from cross-referrals and joint distribution of financial products. Because the legal separateness is more extensive than in model 2, the cost of producing a given mix of financial products is likely to be somewhat more expensive in a model 3 organization. Model 3 captures some of the social benefits of economies of scope in marketing and distribution of financial products, with less risk of the safety-net being used to distort the cost of funds to nonbank subsidiaries; nonetheless, to the extent that firewalls inhibit operational efficiency, some efficiency loss is likely to occur.

From the regulatory perspective, this organizational model has two advantages that are similar to model 2. First, the legal separateness simplifies regulation and supervision of the banking activities of the conglomerate and facilitates functional regulation of its nonbanking activities. Second, the safety and soundness of the bank can be isolated from the performance of the nonbank affiliates and the holding company parent itself. The main advantage of model 3 relative to model 2 is that the bank may have less incentive to bail out a faltering nonbank unit if it is an affiliate rather than a subsidiary. U.S. regulation has attempted to accentuate this separateness on occasion by requiring firewalls such as that an affiliate differ from the bank in name, in employees, in location, and in distribution networks. In part these restrictions are aimed at reducing the potential loss of reputation to the bank if the affiliate should fail. A schematic of this structural form, along with the implied valuation of the bank holding company and the bank, are contained in figure 3.

The Federal Reserve Board has traditionally advanced a "source-of-strength" doctrine that would enhance the position of the bank within the holding company. The source-of-strength doctrine implies that during periods of financial stress or adversity, the regulatory authorities should be permitted to use the resources of the holding company and its subsidiaries to support the bank. This variation is reflected in figure 3a. In this case both the bank holding company *and* the bank have access to the resources of nonbank subsidiaries. In addition, bad outcomes at the bank level are passed on to the holding company level. This is reflected in the modified valuation equations in figure 3a which imply that the remainder of the holding company's assets may be used to satisfy claims on the bank if the value of the bank should fall below zero. In essence, the source-of-strength doctrine would give the regulatory authorities an option on the value of the subsidiaries to prevent the default of the bank.

As Ikeo (1988) has illustrated, debt instruments issued by subsidiaries of bank holding companies would carry a required rate of return that captures the state-contingent payoff structure of such debts.[19] Because the regulatory authorities would have access to the assets of the rest of the holding company if the bank defaults, the required rate of return on debt issued by the nonbank affiliates will be higher than in figure 3. On the other hand, short of perfect correlation between payoff streams across the relevant subsidiaries, default exposure is reduced for bank debt holders and the regulatory authorities. This, of course, is the object of the source-of-strength doctrine. It may be viewed as a way of dissuading financial conglomerates from supporting a troubled subsidiary at the expense of the insured bank subsidiary. The extreme version of the source-of-strength doctrine in which the bank regulatory authorities have a claim on all assets of the holding company has

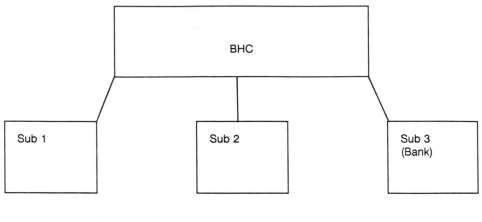

$$V_{G3} = V_{BHC} + \sum_i v_{gi}$$

Figure 3. Bank holding company structure (no preferential bank treatment)

$$V_{G3A} = \begin{cases} V_{BHC} + \sum_i v_{gi} & \text{if and only if } V_B \geq 0 \\ V_{BHC} + \sum_{i \neq B} v_{gi} - V_B & \text{if and only if } V_B < 0 \end{cases}$$

Figure 3a. Bank holding company structure (source of strength doctrine)

recently been rejected by the Federal Appeals Court in New Orleans. The presiding judge, W. Eugene Davis, ruled that obeying the source-of-strength doctrine "would amount to a wasting of the holding company's assets in violation of its duty to its shareholders" (Klinkerman, 1990, p. 9).

The difficulties experienced by the federal regulatory authorities in applying the source-of-strength doctrine in the collapse of MCorp led to inclusion of a more modest version of the doctrine in the Financial Institutions Reform, Recovery and Enforcement Act of 1989 (FIRREA). FIRREA allows the regulatory authorities to use the capital resources of the insured bank subsidiaries of the holding company to support a failing bank. The effect is to treat a multibank holding company as if the subsidiary banks were branches of a single bank. Since most of the assets of bank holding companies are held in insured bank subsidiaries, this legislation sanctions most of the practical impact of the source-of-stength doctrine.

4.4. Model 4: holding company parent, complete operational separateness

Although augmenting complete legal separateness with complete operational separateness may seem to address all of the concerns about financial conglomerates raised in the preceding section, the cost (both social and private) is a complete loss of economies of scope to producers and consumers of financial products. The resultant conglomerate firm is better regarded as an investment company than as an integrated financial corporation. In effect, complete operation separateness resolves concerns about financial conglomerates by eliminating the central rationale for forming a conglomerate. With elimination of all operating synergies, the only remaining benefit from forming a financial conglomerate is diversification of income to the holding company. As any corporate finance textbook will show, this is desirable only if diversification through the holding company is more efficient than portfolio diversification by the investors themselves. It is unlikely that this condition applies to the financial services industry.

5. Corporate structure unconstrained by regulation

Because contemporary U.S. depository institutions are so highly constrained by regulation, it is difficult to infer from their present behavior how they might choose to organize if regulations were relaxed. Some insights may be gained, however, from examining the corporate structure of major German and Swiss universal banks which—although closely supervised—are generally not subject to regulations regarding the separation of banking from other activities.[20] Table 1 sketches the domestic[21] corporate structure (in terms of numbers of subsidiaries and major participations) for the largest German bank (the Deutsche Bank), the largest Swiss bank (the Union Bank of Switzerland [UBS]), and, for contrast, the largest American bank (Citicorp). Note that Citicorp and the UBS are approximately the same size in market value, but Citicorp has 521 domestic subsidiaries and other major participations in comparison to 30 for UBS. Citicorp is smaller than Deutsche Bank as measured by market capitalization, but Deutsche Bank has only 35 domestic subsidiaries.

Although the domestic corporate structure of the two universal banks is much simpler than the corporate structure of the American bank, it is noteworthy that both universal banks have chosen to conduct some domestic business through separately incorporated entities. Thus, a certain degree of corporate separateness may be desired even when it is not required.

Table 1. Domestic corporate structure of largest American, German, and Swiss banks (dollar amounts in billions of U.S. dollars)

	UBS	Deutsche Bank	Citicorp
Total assets (12/31/89)	$114.8	$172.1	$230.6
Market value (4/11/90)	$ 8.8	$ 17.0	$ 9.3
Number of domestic subsidiaries and major participations	35	30	521

Source: Citicorp, Deutsche Bank, and Union Bank of Switzerland.

Other than regulatory compliance, why would a financial conglomerate prefer to operate some business as separately incorporated subsidiaries? Several reasons can be offered. Mian and Smith (1990) argue that corporate separateness (unconsolidated reporting) is associated with independence between activities in terms of operations, financing, and information flows.

Another obvious reason is that limited liability gives the conglomerate the option of limiting losses in the event of a substantial shock to a particular line of business. Not surprisingly, the two universal banks would argue that this is not a relevant motive in any of the cases under consideration because they regard their corporate group as an indivisible entity. The work of Ikeo (1988) implies that separately incorporated subsidiaries can be funded more cheaply if the market can be convinced that the parent does not intend to exercise the option to limit losses by walking away from a failing subsidiary.

Tax laws sometimes encourage the formation of separate subsidiaries in order to capture tax benefits that would be lost in a consolidated reporting of income for tax purposes. In addition, disclosure requirements are less burdensome for some forms of organization.

When a subsidiary is acquired rather than started by the corporate conglomerate, a certain degree of corporate separateness may be maintained in order to make use of the reputational capital of the acquired firm. This appears to have been part of the motive for the separate corporate identity of the several Deutsche Bank and UBS subsidiaries that do not bear the name of the parent bank. A separate corporate identity may also facilitate marketing a service to a particular group of potential consumers.

Corporate separateness, moreover, may facilitate managerial control, particularly if compensation practices for one kind of business are substantially different than for another. Corporate separateness may also be a useful way to deal with differences in business cultures. It may be easier to manage deal-oriented investment bankers separately from relationship-oriented commercial bankers.

Finally, corporate separateness may be a useful way of assuring potential customers that they will be protected from conflicts of interest which might otherwise put them at a disadvantage vis-a-vis other customers of the conglomerate or the conglomerate itself. For example, a bank may find that its investment service is more valuable—that is, its customers are willing to pay for advice—if advice is offered by a separate entity from the broker-dealer and underwriting units. In the case of Deutsche Bank, it seems likely that the management consulting services were established as separate corporate entities in a separate location from the headquarters of the conglomerate parent partly to reassure customers that confidential information acquired in the course of providing consulting services would not be used in lending decisions or to aid other firms in which Deutsche Bank may have an ownership position.

Judging from the corporate structures of the two largest universal banks, it seems plausible that even if all regulatory restrictions on corporate structure were removed, financial conglomerates would not choose to conduct all business through a single corporate entity. But it is unlikely that financial conglomerates would choose a structure as complicated as that which Citicorp employs.

What are the costs of additional, regulatory-imposed corporate separateness? It is difficult to judge the additional costs of Citicorp's highly fragmented corporate structure relative to that of its universal bank competitors, but it seems likely that Citicorp's ability to deliver a competitive package of services to its customers is impeded—if only by the costs of working around the regulatory restrictions in order to coordinate the activities of its 521 domestic subsidiaries. These private costs of circumnavigating regulatory obstacles have no social benefit. In addition, such large differences in regulatory-imposed corporate structures undoubtedly lead to competitive disadvantages.

6. Prudential supervison with conglomerate financial firms

Whatever the choice of corporate structure, financial conglomerates that perform a basic banking function will inevitably be regulated in an attempt to mitigate potential social costs from bank failures. Potential social costs may include the loss of transactions balances, the loss of access to credit by borrowers dependent on that bank, disruption of the payments system, and a contagious loss of confidence in the banking system.[22] Moreover, the perception of investors that the regulatory authorities are likely to attempt to mitigate the impact of an abrupt bank failure undermines market discipline on bank risk-taking. However, the form this regulation should take in a complex and competitive international market is unclear. Just as there are several different models for organizing a financial conglomerate, there are several different approaches to regulating a financial conglomerate or the activities that it conducts. Two basic approaches are predominant in world markets—institutional regulation and functional regulation.

In Continental Europe, any institution that performs some of the functions of a universal bank is likely to be subject to bank regulation. This approach may be termed "institutional regulation." In the United Kingdom, in contrast, the way any particular component of a bank is regulated generally depends on the kind of business it does. This approach may be termed "functional regulation." Since Japan and the United States have not yet officially accepted the universal banking model, most commercial and investment banking functions are performed in separately incorporated entities that are separately regulated. In these countries institutional regulation *has been* broadly congruent with functional regulation; but, as traditional functional distinctions blur, regulatory conflicts emerge.

These contrasting approaches to regulation give rise to a complex international regulatory framework. Within the current international regulatory maze, different institutions are regulated differently even when they undertake the same kind of business. Four regulatory categories may be identified: (1) special-purpose firms that are functionally regulated; (2) universal banks that are institutionally regulated; (3) centrally managed groups of special-purpose institutions that are subject to both institutional and functional regulation; and (4) centrally managed groups of special purpose institutions that are subject to functional regulation with regard to some activities, but have organized many of their activities to be free from regulation. These contrasting regulatory approaches create substantial competitive tensions and give rise to a demand for international harmonization of regulation.

Despite an emerging consensus that harmonization is desirable, there is no agreement regarding how regulation should be harmonized. Both the functional and institutional approaches have their merits. Because functional regulation is more specialized, it is generally viewed as more sensitive to the particular features of a specific kind of business and—especially if systemic risks are not at issue—is likely to pose lower barriers to entry by new firms. Since new entrants are often an important source of innovation, this may contribute to the dynamic efficiency of the financial system. Moreover, if the functions performed by institutions vary substantially over time, functional regulation may adapt more readily to changing market conditions. Functional regulation may provide a more stable regulatory framework than institutional regulation.

When special purpose firms take on multiple functions, however, a trend emphasized in section 1, the functional approach becomes increasingly awkward. In addition, functional supervision of a financial conglomerate tends to fragment prudential supervision and may enable a financial conglomerate to avoid regulation for some activities. If the soundness of the conglomerate as a whole (not just the conduct of particular functions by the conglomerate) is the focus of policy concern, this fragmentation may jeopardize the stability of the system. Moreover, the functional approach risks disagreements among functional supervisors regarding the sharing of supervisory responsibilities and the level of capital adequacy each prefers, and gives rise to the possibility of counterproductive disputes among regulators over enforcement prerogatives and a scramble for assets in the event that the conglomerate experiences financial difficulties. In order to avoid such problems functional supervisory authorities sometimes pressure a financial conglomerate to cordon off the particular functions that they monitor and place them in a separately incorporated subsidiary, perhaps insulated from the rest of the conglomerate by firewalls. In effect, corporate structure tends to be dictated by regulatory convenience but, as noted above, at the social cost of some loss of efficiency.

In principle many of these problems could be mitigated by designing one functional regulator to be a lead regulator charged with responsibility for overseeing the solvency of the financial conglomerate. The lead regulator would facilitate communication among functional regulators and coordinate responses in the event of trouble. The lead regulator, in effect, adopts an institutional view. The United Kingdom has developed this approach to harmonize the efforts of the numerous functional regulatory bodies that have emerged under its Financial Services Act.[23] This approach reduces the gaps and inconsistencies that may occur when functional regulation is applied to a conglomerate institution; however, applying prudential supervision to the institution as a whole may convey an impression to the market that the institution will receive official support in the event of difficulties. This weakens market discipline and may place other specialized institutions at a competitive disadvantage.

Is it essential that the lead regulator supervise the safety and soundness of all activities of the conglomerate? Or, can the lead regulator focus solely on the core banking businesses which have traditionally been regarded as their fundamental charge? Should the conglomerate be subjected to prudential supervision on a consolidated basis even though there is no legal obligation to amalgamate the resources of the separately incorporated entities in the event of trouble? To some extent this depends on a judgment about whether a subsidiary of a financial conglomerate may fail without bringing down the rest of the conglomerate with it.

If the market can be convinced that legal separateness is meaningful—that subsidiaries or affiliates may be permitted to fail without precipitating the collapse of the parent or sister institutions—then prudential supervision may be quite selective, and full consolidation is unnecessary. If, on the other hand, the market views the conglomerate as indissoluble, the insulation provided by operational and legal separateness is illusory, and prudential supervision must take place on a consolidated basis. Indeed, to the extent that firewalls inhibit the transfer of funds within the conglomerate, the lead prudential supervisor of the financial conglomerate may seek to dismantle them because they jeopardize the safety and soundness of the conglomerate.

If the conglomerate is regarded as indissoluble, the lead regulator approach to functional supervision and the institutional approach become substantially the same. In essence the regulator treats the conglomerate firm as if it were a universal bank. This works at cross purposes with the strategy of using legal or operational separateness to insulate the core banking business from activities in the rest of the conglomerate. The result is a financial firm that lacks some of the economies of scale and scope and the risk diversification advantages of a universal bank, but contains some of the disadvantages associated with the universal bank structure.

7. Summary and conclusions

In light of the preceding discussion, what general recommendations can be offered concerning the appropriate corporate structure for a financial conglomerate? The possibility of achieving economies of scope argues, on efficiency grounds, for permitting the formation of financial conglomerates. Although the empirical evidence does not imply that conglomerates will dominate specialized firms, the conglomerate firm may have special advantages for some kinds of services, and it may have a superior capacity to adapt to a changing environment.

Against the potential efficiency gain from the formation of financial conglomerates, however, must be weighed the traditional policy concerns about potential social costs arising from the behavior of financial conglomerates. Some of these concerns strike us as relatively unimportant under current conditions.

1. *Monopoly power.* We do not believe that financial conglomerates would be able to achieve significant monopoly power under current market conditions, but vigilance against anti-competitive practices is a useful precaution nonetheless.

2. *Excessive concentrations of economic and political power.* Since we think it unlikely that financial conglomerates would have significant market power, we are also skeptical that they could deploy significant economic and political power.

3. *Conflicts of interest.* Although the scope for conflicts of interest is undeniably greater in a financial conglomerate than in a specialized firm, the problem is not qualitatively different. Strong disclosure laws, aggressive competition, and rigorously enforced codes of conduct strike us as better remedies to this problem than regulator-imposed corporate separateness.[24]

On the other hand, the traditional concerns regarding the stability of the financial system are less easily dismissed.

4. *Increased systemic risk.* Although we think it plausible that a conglomerate has more scope for diversification and therefore may be less likely to fail than a specialized firm, we do not dismiss the notion. It may be more costly to cope with the failure of a conglomerate if regulators believe that they must protect the creditors of the institution rather than some of the functions that the institution performs.

5. *More difficult to supervise and regulate.* If the safety and soundness of the institution is what matters, then the heterogeneous nature of a conglomerate undoubtedly places greater demands on the supervisory authorities who have not been notably successful in supervising simpler, more specialized institutions. This factor may be offset to some extent if the formation of financial conglomerates were to result in a reduction in the corporate complexity of large financial firms. Even though the domestic activities of the Deutsche Bank may be more heterogenous than the domestic activities of Citicorp, in some respects it is likely to be less burdensome to supervise Deutsche Bank's 35 domestic corporate entities rather Citicorp's 521 domestic corporate entities.

6. *Cross-subsidy from access to the safety net.* We regard this as the most important concern. Large firms in general are more likely to receive official assistance than small firms. And experience in all major countries has shown that if the large firm performs a basic banking function, the authorities will inevitably mobilize assistance.[25] This cross-subsidy from the basic banking function to other activities can be controlled in three ways: (1) financial separateness may be employed to insulate the basic banking function from other activities (Benston et al., 1989); (2) the subsidy may be eliminated by requiring sufficient capital and prompt regulatory intervention (Benston et al., 1989); or (3) the subsidy may be priced—for example, risk-based deposit insurance or risk-based capital requirements—to offset the subsidy (remedies which are discussed in Kane (1985) Kim and Santomero (1988), and have recently been endorsed by the Chairman of the Federal Reserve Board, Alan Greenspan (*American Banker*, 1990)).

In our view the question of appropriate corporate structure is really a question of how best to achieve economies of scope in production and consumption while minimizing any extension of the safety net from the basic banking business to other activities. Among the four models of corporate structure that combine banking activities with other financial services—(1) complete integration, (2) bank parent with nonbank subsidiaries, (3) holding company parent with non-bank affiliates, and (4) holding company parent with complete operational separateness—we reject the fourth as excessively costly to society in terms of the potential loss in efficiency. Complete integration is most likely to facilitate achievement of full economies of scope, however, at the risk of stretching the safety net to include the other activities conducted by the integrated firm. This suggests that models 2 and 3 may also have merit. Yet, 2 and 3 are meaningful only to the extent that the narrow confines of limited liability will be honored in time of crisis. If this is not plausible, then the additional corporate complexity has no compensating gain and some form of model 1 may be preferable.

The question of how best to regulate a model 1 bank, however, remains an issue. Corrigan has argued that expanding the allowable activity of banks requires that the authorities expand their regulatory net to include all activities of universal banks as well as all other institutions engaging in these activities. We do not concur with this view. We are concerned that such a broad assertion of regulatory authority may introduce regulatory inefficiencies in highly competitive international markets. Moreover, in view of the evident difficulties which the authorities have experienced in supervising simpler institutions, it is difficult to be optimistic about their capacity to undertake such an ambitious task. We favor a much more limited role for regulation in the model 1 firm. We believe that concentrating regulatory attention on the basic banking function is likely to be more productive than broadening the focus to include the entire universal bank. We favor regulating functions, not institutions, and confining the safety net to a limited menu of basic banking functions.[26] Model 1A shows how this could be accomplished by pledging assets to secure insured deposits. Guttentag and Herring (1987b) and Litan (1987) have shown that the same objective can be accomplished by establishing the depository institution as a separately monitored subsidiary of the universal bank.[27]

With regard to harmonization of international regulation, it must be expected that different countries will arrive at different conclusions regarding the appropriate corporate structure for financial conglomerates. For historical reasons, the Swiss view on the appropriate corporate structure of a financial conglomerate, for example, is unlikely to converge to the American view. Although institutions are likely to continue to differ, they will, nonetheless, share common functions. Thus harmonization of functional regulation may be more useful and less likely to lead to unwarranted extensions of regulation that would impede the dynamic efficiency of the world financial system.

Notes

1. These benefits are likely to be realized so long as the integration of the European banking market is not disrupted by the reimposition of capital controls that have fragmented European markets during most of the postwar period.
2. The proposition that the basic banking business is special has been defended in a number of ways: (1) to protect vulnerable consumers from being exploited (Jacklin and Bhattacharya, 1988); (2) to protect the payments system (Humphrey, 1987) and the financial system from a contagious collapse; (3) to protect the access to credit of small borrowers who do not have access to financial markets (Bernanke and Gertler, 1989); or (4) because, for political reasons, the basic banking business benefits from implicit public guarantees and must therefore be regulated (Buser, Chen, and Kane, 1981). See Eisenbeis (1989), Benston and Kaufman (1988), and Benston (1983) for a spirited refutation of the proposition that banks are special.
3. The formation of financial conglomerates may also be motivated by the expectation of achieving market power. We consider this possibility in the next section.
4. See Farrell and Shapiro (1990), Panzar and Willig (1981), and Gilligan, Smirlock, and Marshall (1984).
5. Benston has observed in correspondence with the authors that this is part of a broader measurement problem. Given that all banks have the same powers, cross-sectional estimates may capture only accounting mismeasurements of economic values and random errors.
6. A recent American Bankers Association Study (1990) has documented the expansion of interrelationships in Europe between banks and insurance firms via direct ownership, joint ventures, and distribution agreements.
7. State-chartered banks in the United States operated as universal institutions along the lines of the German bank, underwriting and distributing corporate securities. By the turn of the century, big New York state-chartered banks had combined with private banks and trust and insurance companies to create large industrial trusts.

8. Such regulation may also be motivated by the desire to benefit certain competing suppliers of financial services and specific constituents of legislators (Peltzman, 1989).

9. See Benston (1990) for an extensive evaluation of concerns regarding universal banking which concludes that most such concerns are groundless.

10. Bröker (1989, p. 228) notes a conflict of interest situation arises for a bank "dealing with a client if it has a choice between two solutions for a deal, one of which is preferable from its own interest point of view while the other represents a better deal for the client. A conflict of interest situation arises also for a bank...if it carries out activities involving two different groups of customers and if it has to strike a balance between the respective interest of the two customer groups."

11. Saunders (1985) notes that conflicts of interest that confront conglomerates also confront specialized institutions.

12. Several other researchers have argued, however, that even if banks once played a special role, they no longer do (Eisenbeis, 1989; G. Kaufman, 1988; and Saunders, 1985).

13. For the traditional view, see Kaufman (1976). For a revised view that rejects the traditional argument of the securities industry, see Strauss (1990).

14. See Benston (1989) for a review of the literature on how the expansion of permissible bank powers would affect the risk of bank failure.

15. For a discussion of this issue see Black, Miller, and Posner (1978) and Benston (1989).

16. For example, the Federal Reserve Board's recent authorization of Section 20A affiliates requires more than a score of firewalls between the affiliate and the bank.

17. This is especially true if the motivation for regulation is to protect competing suppliers or to distribute favors to political constituents.

18. This advantage is inversely proportional to the conglomerate firm's capital ratio. Proponents of substantial increases in capital argue that the subsidy can be eliminated by sufficiently rigorous capital requirements (Benston et al, 1989).

19. To the extent that the subsidiary becomes riskier, it may be the case that the bank itself is safer and the bank's cost of funds declines. However, if the banking unit is guaranteed by the government, this is not the case.

20. In Germany, mortgage banks, mutual investment fund companies, insurance companies, and building savings banks must be separately incorporated. All other financial activities, however, may be conducted within the parent bank.

21. We focus on the domestic corporate structure because the choice of foreign corporate structure is constrained by regulations in the host country as well as constraints in the source country.

22. For discussion of the rationale for bank regulation see Black, Miller, and Posner (1978); Corrigan (1987); Guttentag and Herring (1987); Kareken and Wallace (1978).

23. The United States faces an additional problem of harmonizing the activities of multiple regulators who supervise the same function.

24. This appears to be the dominant view in most OECD countries (Bröker, 1989, p. 230).

25. The appendix to Corrigan (1990) describes recent rescue operations in Canada, Germany, Japan, and the United Kingdom.

26. Several recent proposals have suggested that the moral hazard problem associated with deposit insurance can be eliminated in such a framework by the use of collaterlization, pledging or limiting permissible investments (Benston et al., 1989; Litan, 1987; Guttentag and Herring, 1987b; Scott, 1989).

27. The choice between the two methods of insulating deposits depends on the cost of monitoring collateral requirements within a universal bank versus the cost of monitoring capital requirements in a separately incorporated ᶜ bsidiary (Benston et al., 1989).

References

American Bankers Association. *International Banking Competitiveness—Why It Matters.* Washington DC: American Bankers Association, 1990.

American Banker, May 12, 1990.

Avery, R., T. M. Belton and M. A. Goldberg. "Market Discipline in Regulating Bank Risk: New Evidence from Capital Markets." *Journal of Money, Credit and Banking* (November 1988).

Bank for International Settlements. "International Convergence of Capital Measurement and Capital Standards." July 1988.

Benston, George. "Federal Regulation of Banking: Analysis and Policy Recommendations." *Journal of Bank Research* (February 1983), 216–244.

Benston, George J. "The Federal "Safety Net" and the Repeal of the Glass-Steagall Act's Separation of Commercial and Investment Banking." *Journal of Financial Services Research* 2 (1989), 287–305.

Benston, George. *The Evidence on the Passage and Continuation of the Glass-Steagall Act Separation of Commercial and Investment Banking: Analysis of a Hoax.* New York: Oxford University Press, 1990.

Benston, George, D. Brumbaugh, J. Guttentag, R. Herring, G. Kaufman, R. Litan, and K. Scott. *Blueprint for Restructuring America's Depository Institutions, Report of a Task Force.* Washington, DC, 1989.

Benston, George and George Kaufman. *Risk and Solvency Regulation of Depository Institutions: Past Policies and Current Options.* Salomon Brothers Center, monograph 1988-1.

Bernanke, Benjamin and Mark Gertler. "Agency Costs, Net Worth and Business Fluctuations." *American Economic Review* 79 (March 1989).

Black, F., M. Miller, and R. Posner. "An Approach to the Regulation of Bank Holding Companies." *Journal of Business* (July 1978), 379–412.

Brewer, Elijah III, Diana Fortier, and Christine Pavel. "Bank Risk from Non-Bank Activities." *The Journal of International Securities Markets* (1989).

Brittan, Sir Leon. "Opening World Banking Markets." Transcript of a speech delivered at the American Enterprise Institute, March 23, 1990.

Bröker, G. *Competition in Banking.* Paris: Organization for Economic Cooperation and Development, 1989.

Buser, Stephen A., Andrew H. Chen, and Edward J. Kane. "Federal Deposit Insurance, Regulatory Policy, and Optimal Bank Capital." *Journal of Finance* (March 1985), 118–132.

Cartellieri, Ulrich. "Statement before the United States Senate Committee on Banking, Housing and Urban Affairs." June 13, 1990.

Citicorp. *1988 Annual Report,* 1988.

Clark, Jeffrey. "Economies of Scale and Scope at Depository Financial Institutions: A Review of the Literature." *Federal Reserve Bank of Kansas City* (September/October 1988), 16–33.

Corrigan, E. Gerald. "Financial Market Structure: A Longer View." *Federal Reserve Bank of New York Annual Report,* 1987.

Corrigan, E. Gerald. "Statement (with appendices) before the United States Senate Committee on Banking, Housing and Urban Affairs." May 3, 1990.

Diamond, Douglas. "Financial Intermediation and Delegated Monitoring." *Review of Economic Studies* 51 (July 1984), 393–414.

Diamond, Douglas and Philip Dybvig. "Bank Runs, Deposit Insurance, and Liquidity." *Journal of Political Economy* 91 (1983), 401–419.

Eisenbeis, Robert. "The Impact of Securitization and Internationalization on Market Imperfections: Implications for Regulatory Reform and the Structure of the Payments System." In *The Future of Financial Systems,* 1989.

Farrell, J. and C. Shapiro. "Horizontal Mergers: An Equilibrium Analysis." *American Economic Review* (March 1990), 107–121.

Gertler, Mark. "Financial Structure and Aggregate Economic Activity: An Overview." *Journal of Money, Credit, and Banking* 20 (August 1988), 559–596.

Giddy, Ian. "Is Equity Underwriting Risky for Commercial Bank Affiliates?" In I. Walter, ed., *Deregulating Wall Street: Commercial Bank Penetration of the Securities Market.* New York: John Wiley & Sons, (1985).

Gilbert, G. "Bank Market Structure and Performance: A Review." *Journal of Money Credit and Banking* (November 1984).

Gilligan, T., M. Smirlock, and W. Marshall. "Scale and Scope Economies in a Multi-product Banking Firm." *Journal of Monetary Economics* (1984), 393–405.

Gorton, Gary and Anthony Santomero. "Market Discipline and Bank Subordinated Debt." *Journal of Money, Credit, and Banking* 22 (February 1990).

Guttentag, Jack M. and Richard J. Herring. "Emergency Liquidity Assistance for International Banks." In R. Portes and A. Swoboda, eds., *Threats to International Financial Stability*. Cambridge: Cambridge University Press, 1987a, pp. 150–186.

Guttentag, Jack M. and Richard J. Herring. "Restructuring Depository Institutions." In *Expanded Competitive Markets and the Thrift Industry*. Proceedings of the Thirteenth Annual Conference of the Federal Home Loan Bank of San Francisco, December 10–11, 1987b, pp. 45–64.

Haraf, William S. "Separating Banking and Securities: The Social Cost of Regulatory 'Firewalls'." Citicorp, January 1990.

Haraf, William S. "The Depository Institution Affiliation Act: A Legislative Proposal for Restructuring Banking and Finance in America." December 1988.

Herring, Richard J. "Comment on European Banking: Prudential and Regulatory Issues." In Jean Dermine, ed., *European Banking After 1992*. Oxford: Basil Blackwell, 1990.

Herring, Richard J. "'92 and After: the International Supervisory Challenge." In Alexander Swoboda, ed., *World Banking and Securities Markets After 1992*. 1990 (forthcoming).

Humphrey, David. "Electronic Payments System Links and Risks." In Elinor H. Solomon, ed., *Electronic Funds Transfers and Payments: The Public Policy Issues*. Boston: Kluwer-Nijhof, 1987.

Ikeo, Kazuhito. "On the Desirability of Different Institutional Arrangements: Should Bank Holding Companies or Banks Themselves Hold Non-Banking Subsidiaries?" unpublished manuscript, 1988.

Jacklin, Charles J. and Sudipto Bhattacharya. "Distinguishing Panics and Information Based Bank Runs: Welfare and Policy Implications." *Journal of Political Economy* (1988), 568–592.

Kane, Edward J. *The Gathering Crisis in Federal Deposit Insurance*. Cambridge, MA: MIT Press, 1985.

Kane, Edward J. "How Market Forces Influence the Structure of Financial Regulation." In W.S. Haraf and R.M. Kushmeider, eds., *Restructuring Banking & Financial Services in America*. Washington, DC: American Enterprise Institute, 1987, pp. 343–382.

Kareken, J. and N. Wallace. "Deposit Insurance and Bank Regulation: A Partial Equilibrium Exposition." *Journal of Business* 51 (July 1978), 413–438.

Kaufman, George. "The Truth About Bank Runs." In C. England and T. Huertas, eds., *The Financial Services Revolution: Policy Directions for the Future*. Boston: Kluwer Academic, 1988.

Kaufman, Henry. "Banks May Be All the Better for a Few Restrictions." *Euromoney* (June 1976), 70–75.

Kelley, Edward J., III. "Conflicts of Interest: A Legal View." In *Deregulating Wall Street: Commercial Bank Penetration of the Securities Market*, New York: John Wiley and Sons, 1985.

Key, Sydney J. "Mutual Recognition: Integration of the Financial Sector in the European Community." *Federal Reserve Bulletin* (September 1989), 591–609.

Kim, D.S. and A. Santomero, "Risk in Banking and Capital Regulation." *Journal of Finance* (December 1988).

Litan, Robert E. *What Should Banks Do?* Washington, DC: The Brookings Institution, 1987.

Llewelyn, David T. "Competition, Diversification and Structural Change in the British Financial System." Working paper, Loughborough University Banking Centre. 1989.

Mayer, Colin. "New Issues in Corporate Finance." *European Economic Review* 32 (1988), 1167–1189.

Mellon Bank, Banc One, et al. "Firewalls," unpublished manuscript 1990.

Mester, Loretta. "Traditional and Non-traditional Banking: An Information Theoretic Approach." Federal Reserve Bank of Philadelphia Working Paper 90-3, 1990.

Mian, Shehzad L. and Clifford W. Smith, Jr. "Incentives for Unconsolidated Financial Reporting." *Journal of Accounting and Economics* 12, North Holland, pp. 141–171.

Panzar, J. C. and R. D. Willig. "Economies of Scope." *American Economic Review* (May 1981), 268–272.

Peltzman, Sam. "The Economic Theory of Regulation after a Decade of Deregulation." *Brookings Papers on Economic Activity, Microeconomics* (1989), 1–60.

Protzman, Ferdinand. "Mighty German Banks Face Curb." *New York Times*, November 7, 1989, pp. D1, D6.

Santomero, Anthony. "Factors Affecting Commercial Loan Pricing." R. Eisenbeis and R. Aspenwall, eds., *Handbook for Banking Strategy*. New York: John Wiley, 1984.

Santomero, Anthony. "The Changing Structure of Financial Institutions." *Journal of Monetary Economics* 24 (September 1989).

Saunders, Anthony. "Bank Safety and Soundness and the Risks of Corporate Securities Activities." In *Deregulating Wall Street: Commercial Bank Penetration of the Securities Market*. New York: John Wiley and Sons, 1985a.

Saunders, Anthony. "Conflicts of Interest: An Economic View." In *Deregulating Wall Street: Commercial Bank Penetration of the Securities Market*. New York: John Wiley and Sons, 1985b.

Scott, Kenneth. "Deposit Insurance and Bank Regulation: The Policy Choices." *Business Lawyer* 44 (1989).

Shaefer, Sherrill. "A Revenue-Restricted Cost Study of 100 Large Banks." Federal Reserve Bank of New York, February 1990.

Steinherr, Alfred and Christian Huveneers. "Universal Banks: The Prototype of Successful Banks in the Integrated European Market." Centre for European Policy Studies 2 (1989).

Strauss, Thomas. "Remarks to the Institute of International Bankers." Transcript of a speech delivered February 12, 1990.

Walter, Ingo. *Deregulating Wall Street: Commercial Bank Penetration of the Corporate Securities Market*. New York: John Wiley and Sons, 1985.

Journal of Financial Services Research 4:499–507 (1990)
© 1990 Kluwer Academic Publishers

Commentary: *The Corporate Structure of Financial Conglomerates*

WILLIAM S. HARAF
Vice President
Policy Analysis
Citicorp/Citibank
1101 Pennsylvania Ave., NW
Washington, DC 20004

There is widespread agreement that the financial structure in the United States is badly out of date and that breaking down barriers to the integration of banking with the rest of financial services would produce a more efficient and competitive system.

The contrast between the United States and Europe is striking. Under the Second Banking Directive, banks can take deposits and make loans throughout the European Community. They can underwrite and distribute any type of security, either directly or through wholly owned subsidiaries. They can own and operate insurance companies. Indeed, banks can affiliate or take substantial equity positions in any type of financial or nonfinancial entity. There are no firewalls restricting the relationships between a bank and its affiliates and subsidiaries, other than ordinary legal lending limits. And there are no holding company capital requirements.

These broad banks and broad banking organizations can offer convenient and cost-effective financial services to their customers. By comparison, the U.S. structure of narrow banks and narrow bank holding companies subject to thick firewalls is cumbersome and inefficient. Moreover, it is a structure that will not permit U.S. banking organizations to be competitive in the highly integrated global marketplace for financial services.

Despite the acknowledged inadequacies of our own financial structure, some people argue that it could be dangerous to allow banking organizations to engage in a broader range of activities because of risks to the safety net. Richard Herring and Anthony Santomero in their article, "Corporate Structure in a World of Financial Conglomerates," generally favor adopting a universal banking structure in the United States, based either on the German or British models, but they express reservations because of such concerns. Rather than dwell on the benefits of universal banking, I would like to focus on their concerns and what to do about them.

1. Two myths about financial structure and the safety net

Two myths endure about the relationship between financial structure and the safety net that are reflected in their article. The first myth is that separating banking from other financial services through firewalls or outright prohibitions on activities can enhance safety and soundness. The second myth is that the safety net provides a subsidy to the banking industry that could be used to cross-subsidize other lines of business and therefore to drive nonbank competitors out of the market.

After briefly discussing both of these myths, I will then turn attention to what I think is the real problem—namely, the "too big to fail" doctrine and associated policies that go along with it.

Of the two myths, the first is easiest to dismiss. Broader banks would be safer banks. A number of studies have clearly shown that the income stream from banking services is not highly correlated with income streams from other financial services. Hence, diversification benefits would be significant. Part of this myth, however, is that the "moral hazard" problem somehow negates diversification benefits. Bankers, it is alleged, have an incentive to take excessive risks because of the safety net. As a result, they would use broader powers to increase risk, not reduce it. This argument simply does not hold up.

The safety net may indeed encourage risk-taking, especially by weak institutions, as many analysts have observed. But activity restrictions and firewalls do not effectively constrain risk-taking. They have not prevented banks from reaching the privately optimal points on their risk/return frontiers, given the incentive distortions that might arise out of the safety net. If bank managers so choose, it is easy enough to bet the bank using currently approved financial instruments and powers. Indeed, the vast majority of bank and savings and loan (S&L) failures in this country take place the old-fashioned way—from excessive credit and interest rate risk, from regional concentration in lending portfolios, and from fraud.

By contrast, the record of broad banks in foreign markets has been strong. The Federal Reserve Bank of New York recently undertook a study of how other countries manage troubled financial institutions. It identified six significant episodes in four countries since 1965: in the United Kingdom a number of smaller "secondary banks" were bailed out in 1973, and there was the Johnson Mathey incident in 1984; in Germany there was the Herstatt failure in 1974, and the private sector bailout of Schroder, Munchmeyer, Hengst & Co, a medium-sized bank, in 1983; in Canada there was a joint public/private effort to provide liquidity to some small Western banks in 1985; and in Japan there was the bailout of Yamaichi Securities in 1965. It is a pretty short list by comparison with our own S&L crisis, the Continental Illinois bailout, the collapse of the Texas and farm banks, and a long litany of other problems.

Many people take the argument about cross-subsidies more seriously, even though it, too, deserves mythic status.

First, it is doubtful that there is a *net* subsidy to the banking industry arising out of the safety net. Any gross subsidy is offset by regulatory burdens such as noninterest-bearing reserve requirements, inefficiently structured capital requirements, CRA provisions, and onerous compliance and reporting costs. The mix of burdens and subsidies will, of course, affect resource allocation in complex ways. The most notorious of these distortions is moral hazard. I will have more to say about that soon. But even with moral hazard, cost-plus pricing for deposit insurance premiums, established under FIRREA, ensures that in the future the industry will pay for its own sins—and the sins of its regulators.

For the sake of argument, however, let's grant that some net subsidy remains. As long as the banking industry is competitive, those subsidies do not accrue to banks; they accrue to bank customers. Just as with any government-provided subsidy, resource allocation is affected, but not the profitability of the subsidized industry.

So, could banks use the safety net to cross-subsidize new activities, if they were granted broader powers?

I conclude that a bank could not increase its profits from a safety-net subsidy by offering additional financial services to its customers any more than a dairy producer could extract additional benefits from dairy-price supports by going into the pizza business. Essentially, there is an opportunity cost involved in funding additional activities through the bank.

If there are no real efficiency gains, or "economies of scope," from combining banking and other financial services, then a bank that uses its access to insured deposits to fund its own financial activities will have to sacrifice lending opportunities to unaffiliated borrowers. The benefit from financing the new activities internally is exactly offset by the cost to the bank of the foregone market rate of interest for loans of equivalent risk to outside customers.

Put differently, the safety-net subsidy may distort banks' lending decisions. But that distortion is there whether borrowers are independent or affiliated. Those who are concerned that broadening the activities of banking organizations would mean "additional financial services activities would be funded with federally insured deposits" should be concerned that these activities are currently being funded with federally insured deposits, and have been since the introduction of deposit insurance. Banks have always played a role in funding the activities of the financial services industry.

An apparent exception to this analysis exists if there are real efficiency gains that could be realized by linkages between banking and other financial services, as I believe is very likely. In that case, a bank could earn a higher risk-adjusted rate of return by offering a combination of banking and other financial services than by making loans to unaffiliated financial services providers.

These efficiency gains, however, would shift the risk/return frontier in the direction of a higher expected return for each level of risk. It is hard to imagine how this would lead the combined organization to accept more rather than less risk. Real efficiency gains could permit organizations offering both banking and other financial services to drive some unaffiliated financial services providers out of the market. Such a result would not be a consequence of access to subsidies, but an efficiency gain that produces a social benefit—a lower marginal cost of financial services to customers.

2. The need for safety-net reform is not a myth

So far I have discussed two myths about the relationship between financial structure and the safety net. The need for deposit insurance reform is not a myth. In present value terms, the FSLIC crisis effectively wasted the equivalent of an entire year's personal savings in the United States on uneconomic projects. This fiasco did not involve big banks. It involved lots of relatively small S&Ls with no one but the regulator looking over their shoulder. Nonetheless, prospects for real reform of the financial structure and the deposit insurance system have been mired down by the debate over what to do about so-called too big to fail (TBTF) banks.

In recent testimony before the Senate Banking Committee, Federal Reserve Board Chairman Alan Greenspan offered a powerful indictment of the effects of the safety net on the economy. In addition to the contingent liability it may represent for federal taxpayers, he recognized the pass-through character of safety-net distortions. Safety-net policies benefit riskier ventures at the expense of sounder ones. Other things being equal, according to Greenspan, they tend to increase real interest rates and to crowd out projects that would be economic at lower real interest rates.

From the narrower perspective of a banker, the deposit insurance system has perpetuated a weak and inefficient banking system—literally thousands of depository institutions could not survive without the deposit insurance sticker on the door. In addition, the deposit insurance system has become very expensive indeed. Deposit insurance premiums are rising rapidly, and as a result of last year's S&L legislation, they can reach .35 percent of domestic deposits—by far the most expensive system in the world. Combined with other regulatory burdens that are indirectly tied to safety-net policies, the operation of the safety net poses a significant competitiveness problem for U.S. banks.

Some believe that the current approach to the safety net is fundamentally sound. All that is needed is better execution. Instead of market discipline, they advocate "market-simulating" regulations such as risk-based deposit insurance premiums and risk-based capital standards. They trust regulators to implement early intervention strategies to minimize the cost of bank failures.

But the spectacular failure of regulation we have experienced over the past decade cannot be remedied with better regulations or better regulators. Edward Kane, among others, has argued that the political/regulatory system may produce systematic incentives to misregulate. This argument must be taken seriously. History shows that government officials have been willing to tolerate extremely high costs to postpone the recognition of problems and to resolve any perceived threat to financial stability.

The problem with the safety net is simple. It is the history of the blank check. The only way the system will be put on a sound footing is by greater reliance on the marketplace. Market discipline is a powerful way to enforce performance—not only by bank managers but by regulators. Regulators cannot permit problems to fester and grow, as they did with the S&Ls and the Texas banks, when the uninsured depositors and other creditors of a troubled institution are on their way out the door. Market discipline also leads to regulatory discipline.

One of the most controversial issues in the debate over the merits of reforms based on market discipline is whether market discipline can really be applied to large institutions. William Seidman, among others, has argued that some institutions must inevitably fall into the too-big-to-fail category. As a result, considerations of fairness have led the FDIC to protect uninsured depositors at banks of all sizes whenever feasible. TBTF has become the political argument for 100 percent deposit guarantees.

Of course, the market does not yet entirely believe in TBTF. Many ex-depositors of the Bank of New England did not believe they would benefit from TBTF, nor did those who left the Continental Illinois Bank. In addition to the discipline provided by large depositors, market discipline has come from other creditors, the debt and equity market, relationship borrowers, and the rating agencies. The influence of these groups on the market has been quite evident in recent months, as we have seen a very substantial tiering in yields on the liabilities of banking organizations in response to ratings changes and to market perceptions of asset quality. Nonetheless, market discipline can and should be improved. Unfortunately, our regulators through their actions and public statements have reinforced the TBTF fallacy.

3. The too-big-to-fail fallacy

There are really three sets of issues in the TBTF debate. One set of issues is depositor-related—concerns about depositor runs on healthy institutions; the treatment of foreign deposits; and administrative problems associated with implementing "haircuts" on numerous depositors at a large financial institution in a timely way.

Another set of issues has to do with other potential adverse spillover effects from the failure of a large financial institution with many diverse financial commitments on and off the balance sheet—concerns about the large dollar electronic payments systems, the clearing and settlement systems for securities and foreign exchange, and the treatment of nondeposit contracts such as SWAP arrangements. These issues have been the primary focus of attention at the Federal Reserve in its capacity as lender of last resort to the financial system.

A third set of issues has to do with the international competitiveness implications of unilaterally breaking away from TBTF policies. How could U.S. banks be competitive with against foreign banks that would continue to operate with the implicit backing of their governments?

Let me discuss each of these in turn.

3.1. Depositor-related issues

One long-standing and frequently debated concern, which I shall just mention briefly, is that the failure of a large bank might lead to contagious runs on healthy banks. Numerous studies have shown that the risk of runs on healthy banks has been exaggerated. In the event that solvent banks do experience a run, they can generally raise funds through asset sales or borrowings from other banks to meet depositor outflows. Moreover, the discount window was established precisely for the purpose of dealing with such situations.

Those who express concern over the disruptive effects of bank runs frequently dismiss the positive effect that the threat of runs can have on the system. If the commitment to depositor discipline were stronger, bankers would have powerful incentives to preserve public confidence in their institutions by maintaining ample capital and liquidity reserves. Rating agencies would devote more resources to assessing bank quality, and market information about banks would improve. Such mechanisms for dealing with the potential for runs would significantly strengthen the stability of the system.

Another issue has to do with the treatment of deposits at foreign branches of U.S. banks. These deposits are *not* officially insured by the FDIC, but many observers have argued that the FDIC would inevitably be forced to protect them. This is not necessarily the case. Foreign branches of U.S. banks are subject to regulation and supervision by local as well as U.S. authorities, and their deposits are often protected by local deposit insurance schemes. Host country regulators generally require branches to maintain reserves with the central bank, to maintain local capital and/or a certain percentage of branch assets locally. Local laws often provide for supervisory actions in the event of serious financial problems affecting the branch and for distribution of branch assets to meet the liabilities owed to local depositors and other creditors.

Thus foreign branch depositors of U.S. banks receive a degree of protection from host country regulators in most instances. Similarly, deposits at U.S. branches of foreign banks can be protected by the FDIC. There is, in effect, a kind of "national treatment" standard in place. If a U.S. bank with foreign branches were to fail, local assets would be available to cover the claims of local depositors. In some cases, foreign branch depositors could receive better treatment than domestic depositors and, in some cases, worse treatment.

There is currently an undesirable ambiguity in these arrangements. Additional clarity would be useful, and this would have to come through a process of negotiations. But it would be a mistake to unilaterally place the FDIC in the position of insuring both the foreign branch deposits of U.S. banks and the U.S. branch deposits of foreign banks simply because the U.S. banks are deemed to be TBTF, since this would substantially increase the exposure of the FDIC fund.

Another depositor-related issue has to do with the FDIC's own concerns about its ability to implement a modified payoff-type transaction on a large institution in a timely fashion. Unfortunately, regulators are not much further along in establishing failure resolution procedures for large banks than they were before the Continental Illinois bailout. For example, the FDIC has not promulgated record-keeping rules to facilitate a modified payoff-type reorganization. With the sophisticated data base systems that are available today, such reorganizations are entirely feasible even for the largest financial institutions in the country, but regulators have made no effort to ensure that they even have the administrative and technical capacity to manage a large reorganization. This in itself has limited market discipline.

3.2. Adverse spillover effects

Another set of concerns has to do with potential adverse spillover effects from the failure of a large financial institution on the large dollar electronic payments systems, the clearing and settlement systems for securities, foreign exchange, and nondeposit contracts.

For years, Gerald Corrigan has warned that the failure of a large securities firm had as much potential to disrupt the financial system as a large bank failure. Now we have some recent evidence of such an occurrence. In many respects, Drexel Burnham Lambert was like a large bank holding company. It had $28 billion in assets—loans, securities, and mortgage instruments—on its books, as well as large off-balance sheet commitments. It engaged in foreign exchange trading and other market-making activities. The main difference between it and a banking organization is that it depended on commercial paper rather than on deposits for its funding. Ultimately, Drexel's downfall was brought about by a "run" by its commercial paper holders.

There were some disruptions associated with Drexel's demise. Firms used extreme caution in their transactions with Drexel, since there were concerns about the quality of Drexel's collateral and its ability to complete trades. As a result, a logjam developed in the exchange of securities, foreign exchange, and cash, which slowed the unwinding of Drexel's positions. But the effects on the market were limited. The shock was easily absorbed. Moreover, the winding down of Drexel took place without the benefit of a bridge bank, a tool that bank regulators could use to facilitate the smooth reorganization of a failing bank.

Nonetheless, the Drexel incident focused attention on some clear weaknesses in the financial system—weaknesses of which both regulators and private sector representatives have been aware and have been attempting to address. For several years now, a number of public and private efforts have been under way to devise focused and relatively efficient mechanisms for reducing individual exposures and systemic risks associated with the failure of a large financial institution. Although these efforts are not complete, progress has been made and more can be expected.

For example, there are significant changes in the operations of the large-dollar electronic payments systems, FedWire and CHIPS, in the works. In recent years, the Federal Reserve has implemented policies to limit its own exposure over FedWire to the failure of a large financial institution. New rules, which take effect in June of next year, will further reduce its exposure, and additional changes are being contemplated. For example, the Fed is considering charging fees for overdrafts and even possibly privatizing many of its funds-transfer operations, according to some reports.

In addition, the private-sector CHIPS system will institute major changes, probably by year-end, that will substantially reduce systemic risk. CHIPS will establish a loss-sharing system such that if a bank fails to settle, the losses will be shared by the remaining participants. Banks will be able to control their own risk through bilateral credit limits and net debit sender caps that can be adjusted daily. Each bank's risk will be related to its own credit judgment about the other banks on the system. Since most of the dollar payments of international banks are routed through CHIPS, the failure of a bank with large overseas operations need not disrupt the overseas dollar market. Loss-sharing agreements would cover the dollar payments.

As for clearing and settlement systems, a number of efforts have gotten under way to design measures to limit risk in the system. A committee of the Group of Thirty, chaired by Citicorp Chairman John Reed, has undertaken an effort to set standards for securities clearing and settlement in the major countries to improve efficiency and reduce risk in the world's financial network. Its recent report includes such recommendations as: establishing institutions such as clearing corporations and central securities depositories to act as intermediaries between trading parties in order to protect participants against counterparty failure; shortening settlement times and requiring payment in "same day" funds on settlement day; encouraging trade netting systems where feasible; and moving to book entry rather than paper-based systems for securities handling.

Financial institutions are already experimenting with many such measures. For example, U.S. and Canadian banks are testing the viability of a clearing house to do multilateral netting for foreign exchange transactions. A similar effort is underway in Europe. U.S. financial institutions and corporations are preparing to test an automated settlement and safekeeping system for the commercial paper market, similar to that used for Treasury securities, which has the potential to reduce significantly daylight overdrafts over Fed-Wire. The Federal Reserve Bank of New York has embarked on a major study of risk in the financial system designed to recommend improvements in network operations and contingency planning for emergencies.

In summary, progress has been made in understanding and controlling risks in the financial system. Although more work needs to be done, the efforts that have been undertaken so far demonstrate that such risks can and should be addressed in ways that are less intrusive to the functioning of private markets than broad-based protections for institutions designated as TBTF by regulators.

3.3. International competitiveness

Finally, there is the international competitiveness issue. The argument is that since foreign governments stand behind their largest banks with TBTF policies, our banks could not be competitive without similar backing from the U.S. government.

International competitiveness is a problem for U.S. banks. A number of recent studies have documented the declining position of U.S. banks in the global marketplace. In addition to macroeconomic forces, these studies blame an inefficient U.S. financial structure and relatively high regulatory burdens imposed on U.S. banks—burdens that are closely associated with safety-net policies.

Contrast the situation in other developed countries. Foreign governments are modernizing their financial structures to adapt to a changing marketplace. The safety-net protections they provide, if anything, go further than might reasonably be expected in the United States, as Federal Reserve Bank President Gerald Corrigan indicated in recent testimony before the Senate Banking Committee. Yet, they have not been plagued with high failure rates among their financial institutions. Put simply, the governments of most developed nations have successfully established financial sector policies to enhance efficiency without jeopardizing their own safety nets. By contrast, in the United States we live with the worst of both worlds. We have an inefficient financial structure with high regulatory burdens and safety-net policies that have been conspicuously unsuccessful.

As a political matter, it is doubtful that the United States would take significant steps toward the universal banking model without eliminating the TBTF doctrine. Yet even so, a legislative package designed to (1) permit some type of universal banking in the United States; (2) enhance market discipline by eliminating TBTF, among other things; and (3) reduce regulatory burdens would enhance the efficiency of the U.S. financial system, but would leave U.S. institutions less well protected by the safety net than their foreign competitors. The net effect on the ability of U.S. institutions to compete in global markets is unclear, but I believe it should still be positive provided that the reforms are sufficiently comprehensive.

Ideally, safety-net policies would be addressed in a multilateral context. Moral hazard, which has apparently not been a significant problem in the major overseas markets to date, may become more of a problem as markets open up and become more competitive. Foreign governments may have to grapple with it in the future. While I do not believe that an international agreement on safety-net policies along the lines of the B.I.S. capital agreement is either feasible or desirable, a joint commitment by governments to adopt market-oriented policies to limit moral hazard would be beneficial. Nonetheless, it would be a mistake to delay reforms in this country until such a commitment could be achieved.

4. Summary

Let me conclude by emphasizing three basic points from my discussion.

1. Safety-net distortions would not be materially affected by permitting integration of banking and other financial services.
2. Nonetheless, safety-net distortions are important. Market discipline is the only effective way to minimize these distortions.
3. Too-big-to-fail need not and should not be accepted policy. The public policy goal should be to establish policies that can facilitate a reorganization of a large financial institution with minimal disruptions to the financial system. That goal is feasible.

Journal of Financial Services Research 4:509–511 (1990)
© 1990 Kluwer Academic Publishers

Commentary: *The Corporate Structure of Financial Conglomerates*

MICHAEL S. HELFER
Partner
Wilmer, Cutler, and Pickering
2445 M St., NW
Washington, DC 20037

After congratulating Richard Herring and Anthony Santomero on a fine article, I will focus my comments mainly on regulatory and legal aspects of the issues they discuss.

The authors point out that if legal separateness is meaningful—defining "meaningful" to mean that subsidiaries or affiliates are permitted to fail without precipitating the collapse of the related institutions—then prudential supervision may be quite selective, and full examination of the consolidated unit is unnecessary. On the other hand, they argue, if the market views the conglomerate as indissoluble, then the insulation provided by legal separateness is illusory, and prudential supervision must take place on a consolidated level. As I thought about that argument, it occurred to me that we have a situation in which the market's view of the effectiveness of legal separation will turn in very large part on regulatory actions, both historical and predicted, concerning whether legal separateness, in fact, will be enforced in times of crisis. If that is right, then regulatory actions, statements, and policies will, in effect, create their own reality in the marketplace in determining what level of supervision is warranted or required.

We have not had a reasoned regulatory view in this country on the issue of legal separation and how it should work, particularly in times of crisis. The Federal Reserve has said in the past, particularly under Chairman Volcker, that holding company supervision—capital requirements and supervisory actions at the holding company level—was necessary, because in times of crisis neither the market nor management would act, or expect the regulators to act, in a way that fully respected corporate separateness. At the same time, the Fed has tried to implement corporate separateness in numerous ways, the best example probably being the firewalls in the Section 20 approvals that permit affiliates of banks to conduct securities activities through a separately incorporated, registered broker-dealer, but subject to a long list of very cumbersome and difficult firewalls. The Fed implemented these firewalls, but at the same time in other contexts, it expressed serious questions about whether legal separation by these firewalls could effectively insulate the bank in times of crisis.

Recent developments seem to me to be moving in a somewhat different direction. The FDIC's "Mandate for Change" certainly indicates that, in its view, holding company separateness can be maintained and that holding company regulation is not essential. Of course, the court in the recent M-Corp decision found that the Fed was without statutory authority to enforce its "source-of-strength" doctrine. This doctrine would have required the downstreaming of funds from the healthy parent firm—or perhaps if not healthy, at least solvent, or at least a company with funds—down into a bank or set of banks when their viability was threatened. But the source of strength doctrine, I think is a reflection of a regulatory regime that is based on consolidation and not on corporate separateness.

We also have some recent examples of corporate separateness being enforced. M-Corp itself, of course, is now in bankruptcy proceedings, but several of its subsidiary banks are alive and doing business; they have not been closed. And here in Washington, within the last month a bank holding company defaulted on commercial paper. It is not in bankruptcy, and its subsidiary bank, at least as reported in the newspapers, appears not to have suffered serious adverse effects and certainly no terminal effects so far. Finally, it has become quite common to have banks rescued, at least rescued in the parlance of the press, while their holding companies go into bankruptcy.

Thus we appear to have some trend toward legal recognition and enforcement of corporate separateness. I think this would lead the market to believe that corporate separateness is meaningful. If so, then, under the logic of the article, selective prudential supervision without full consolidation should be possible. If this characterization of legal trends is correct, it has interesting implications for the holding company model in the United States. The more that legal separateness can be enforced by the Fed (and other regulatory agencies) through the requirements of separate corporations, firewalls, and the like, the less justification there is for capital requirements and supervision at the holding company level.

I should add the obvious point that while legal separateness is important in assessing the kinds of issues that are raised in the article, ultimately it becomes critical only in times of crisis. Legal separateness does not necessarily imply the kinds of separation and the kinds of very unworkable firewalls that the Federal Reserve has imposed under the Section 20 orders, with their restrictions on cross-marketing, restrictions in interlocking personnel, and additional restrictions on funding beyond those ordinarily imposed to protect misuse of a bank by its affiliates. Legal separation need not imply these kinds of restrictions. Indeed, I think a case can be made that a large number of legal entities can be managed functionally; the real problem is not so much the number of legal entities as it is firewall restrictions between them that impair efficiency.

One area where I believe further work would be useful is in defining what we mean by failure. Haraf carefully alluded to closure policies, sometimes called failure control. In order to assess the public policy implications of "too-big-to-fail" and other issues that are implicit in the article, we could use more work on understanding what we mean by failure and what we are trying to accomplish through that process.

We already have in place, or readily could have, systems under which the consequences for senior management and the stockholders of banks could be the same in a closure as in a bankruptcy or in another kind of a takeover by the government authority. So the questions become, What additional market discipline are we going to obtain by imposing similar kinds of results on the creditors and depositors of a bank? And, Are the consequences in terms of additional market discipline worthwhile in terms of reaching public policy goals? These are much broader questions than the article addresses or that I am prepared to discuss.

Some alternative mechanisms may be available to address public policy concerns that would be better than trying to enforce market discipline simply by considering closure of a large bank and making estimates of the effects of a liquidation and the like. Some of those mechanisms may involve early intervention, which I know is a controversial and difficult topic. In principle, at least, it might be possible to have government intervention at a time when the equity holders are wiped out but the creditors and depositors are not.

Important international competitive implications also exist. I was at a lunch at which some of these issues were being discussed, and a senior banker from a large foreign institution sat quietly throughout the lunch and the discussion. While his home country does not have deposit insurance as we know it, there is no question that the depositors of the institution he represented would be protected by the home country government in a time of crisis. There was widespread agreement among the U.S. bankers at the table that too-big-to-fail concept had to go. The banker from the large international bank finally said, "We would be pleased to see the United States announce that none of its banks are too big to fail. We would make sure that our marketing people were told about it right away." It may be that European or Japanese taxpayers would not like the result if they ever need to rescue a large bank. But it could be a long time until they do, and in the interim there could be serious competitive impacts.

Finally, comparing regulatory systems and corporate structures in foreign countries with those in the United States to assess the regulatory impacts of differences is obviously extremely difficult. The number of financial institutions that foreign regulators need to deal with in most foreign countries is much smaller, and the nature of the relationships between those institutions and their regulators is very different. Their relationships are much less adversarial—they do not let the lawyers get in the way as much as we do. Our problem might not be, as some parts of the article seem to suggest, that our regulators have particular difficulty supervising financial institutions. A more serious consideration might be that our regulators are confronted with so many institutions, so many of whom have lawyers, and our regulatory regime and legal system are so adversarial that it is more important to address these kinds of problems than the impact of different corporate structures.